The Web Developer's Guide To Amazon E-Commerce Service

Developing Web Applications Using Amazon Web Services And PHP

The Web Developer's Guide To Amazon E-Commerce Service: Developing Web Applications Using Amazon Web Services And PHP

by Jason Levitt

Printed in the United States of America.

Published by J9T Publications, Inc., PO Box 3866 Austin, TX, 78764.

ISBN: 1-4116-2551-X

For book orders, errata, and source code, see the book web site at *www.awsbook.com*

Cover Design: Amber Moody (amber.moody@gmail.com)

Printing History:

April 2005: Version 1.0

Table of Contents

CHAPTER 2
Developing With Amazon E-Commerce Service

CHAPTER 3
Working With Products: ItemSearch

CHAPTER 5
Customers And Sellers

CHAPTER 6
The Remote Cart

CHAPTER 7
International Amazon E-Commerce Service

CHAPTER 8
Miscellaneous Operations

CHAPTER 9

Amazon Seller Services

Welcome To The Book

This book is the reference and teaching guide to Amazon's Application Programming Interfaces (APIs) that I wanted back in the Fall of 2002. Like many first-time users of Amazon's Web Services, I was excited by the coolness factor of having access to all that Amazon data, but a bit stymied because I didn't know much about Amazon's underlying data model or how to easily get at the data using PHP.

Using Amazon's exposed APIs effectively, I've come to realize, requires that you understand, not only how the APIs work, but also how Amazon categorizes and describes their products. Fortunately, the barriers to entry are low. It's a testament to the abilities of Amazon's internal developers that you don't need to know much about either Amazon's web site, or computer programming, in order to get started with Amazon's offerings. Plus, you might be able to earn a little cash on the side. :-)

Who Should Use This Book

The target audience for this book is intermediate developers who are creating web applications. That might include people making simple sidebar applications for web sites all the way up to more serious storefronts and even backend inventory systems.

Basic understanding of XML and PHP is required, though developers should easily be able to translate the concepts and code samples to other programming languages.

Amazon API Coverage

This book covers these Amazon APIs:

- Amazon E-Commerce Service 4.0
- Amazon Seller Services: AIMS API
- Amazon Seller Services: Merchants@ API

Amazon APIs this book mentions but does not cover:

- Amazon E-Commerce Service 3.0
- Alexa Web Information Service
- Simple Queue Service
- AWS Management Service

Acknowledgements

Many folks contributed their precious time and energy to this book. A -- by no means exhaustive -- list includes:

Laura Grange, Jeff Barr, Gryphon Shafer, Anthony Joseph, Jeremy Hynoski, Elena Dykhno, Clifford Cancelosi, Tiffany Carter-Eldred, Jonathan Marzinke, Julia Leach, Aaron DaMommio, Amber Noxon, Nick Lee, Anil Kalagatla, Steve Saville, Girish Prabhu, Fumiaki Yoshimatsu, and Simon St. Laurent.

About The Ferengi

Each Chapter in this book begins with a quote from the "Ferengi Rules Of Acquisition." The rules are a code of conduct for the Ferengi, an aliens species that have, according to the web site *www.startrek.com*, "a culture which is based entirely upon commerce."

CHAPTER 1

Introducing Amazon Web Services

There are many paths to profit
—Ferengi Rule Of Acquisition #92

Nine years ago it would be hard for anyone to imagine being granted free access to one of the largest online product databases -- let alone displaying that data on their web site in any format desired. Yet today, with Amazon Web Services that's exactly what's going on. And as Amazon expands access to their data, developers are creating more innovative ways of generating sales and sharing in the profits. Where did this idea come from and just what is Amazon offering developers? This chapter explores the answers to those questions.

In The Beginning, There Was Affiliate Marketing

Banner ads are surely one of the banes of online existence. They are obnoxious and annoying, and yet, they generate millions of dollars of revenue for their creators and have continually helped lift the profits of industry players such as Yahoo and Google. Yes, there are people, a lot of people, apparently, who read the ads, click on them, and then are brought to an online destination where they purchase something. Their clicking on the ad, or "click-through" as it's more commonly known, is the central concept behind affiliate marketing.

Affiliate marketing is a simple concept. Web site owners (affiliates) agree to advertise products or services on their web sites. When web site visitors see the advertised products or services and then click-through and purchase those products or services, the advertiser pays the web site owner some small percentage of the sale.

Amazon.com created one of the first, and most successful, affiliate marketing programs in 1996. Called Amazon Associates, the program lets any web site display Amazon products and share in the profits of selling those items for Amazon. When a visitor clicks-through and purchases the product from Amazon, the web site owner automatically gets a small percentage of the sale (usually 5%) desposited into their Amazon.com account. Like most affiliate marketing programs, Amazon Associates is a free service. Amazon gains exposure, volume sales, and general Internet community goodwill from the affiliate sales. The third-party web sites get to display product images and information that may relate to their web site theme and they may also make some money in the process. It's a cooperative commerce agreement that seems to work well for everyone involved.

Enter Amazon Web Services

Legend has it that Amazon CEO Jeff Bezos was prompted to develop the Amazon Web Services platform on the suggestion of O'Reilly and Associates' CEO Tim O'Reilly. The reality, according to Tim's blog, *http://www.oreillynet.com/pub/wlg/1707*, was that a "skunkworks" team at Amazon.com had already started building a web services platform but that Tim's suggestion (explained Bezos) gave it more viability.

The first version of Amazon Web Services rolled out quite informally in the Spring of 2002. But things didn't get interesting for developers until version 2 which went into beta in July of 2002 and was released in October, 2002. It included a software development kit with application samples and some developer support infrastructure. Version 2 of Amazon Web Services included 23 different operations that developers could use to search for various types of product information on Amazon.com, even things like Wish Lists created by Amazon customers.

> Amazon uses the term "operation" to describe a discrete function in their Web Services API. Most XML jockeys, or programmers familiar with object-oriented techniques, would call it a "method".

Amazon included both REST (REpresentational State Transfer) and SOAP (Simple Object Access Protocol) interfaces, and an XSLT (eXtensible Stylesheet Language Transformation) service (I'll discuss REST, SOAP, and XSLT further in Chapter Two).

Amazon's Web Services gave Amazon Associates members the chance to build very content-rich web applications utilizing data obtained directly from Amazon's own product database. Instead of using static links, site developers could dynamically search for and fetch product data directly from Amazon to enhance their own customers' experience. Amazon Web Services also made it practical to use Amazon product information, not just on third party web sites, but inside of desktop applications. And still, of course, when a customer purchases a product from within the application, the application owner gets a percentage of the sale.

Version 3 of Amazon Web Services, with an expanded set of accessible Amazon data, launched in July, 2003. With version 3, it was now possible to recreate in an application almost any kind of product search that one could do using a web browser on

Amazon.com. Additionally, developers could create more sophisticated searches that aren't possible using the search forms on Amazon.com. Version 3 also returned a fairly comprehensive set of data about most products on Amazon, including things like product descriptions, user reviews, and detailed music and video product information.

With version 3, it was also becoming clear to the Amazon Web Services team within Amazon that, in order to continue adding new features to the API, they would need to completely redesign the API for Amazon Web Services. Indeed, versions 1 through 3 of Amazon Web Services were very much like a "skunkworks" project. The XML data model was not chosen very carefully and there was no structured way of adding future enhancements to the data model.

The completely redesigned version 4, renamed Amazon E-Commerce Service (ECS), has seven fewer operations than version 3, but more functionality since many redundant operations in version 3 were folded into single operation interfaces in version 4.

The XML request and response structures were also optimized and restructured into a modular format that will more easily accommodate future enhancements. Along with these optimizations is a much greater number of available product data points which is reflected in the size of the WSDL file.

A WSDL (Web Services Description Language) file describes all of the operations and elements in the Amazon Web Services API. We'll talk more about WSDL files in Chapter Two.

AWS Version	Introduced	Number of Operations	WSDL File Size
1	Spring 2002	11	23Kbytes
2	Fall 2002	23	52Kbytes
3	Fall 2003	26	64Kbytes
4	Spring 2004	18	94Kbytes

Table 1-1 Amazon Web Services Releases

Amazon Web Services has brought a lot more people, mostly content creators and software developers, into the Amazon Associates program. As a result, independent developers have found many creative and innovative ways to harness Amazon Web Services for both web sites and standalone applications.

A list of ways to make money using various Amazon.com features, including Web Services, is available at http://www.amazon.com/makemoney

International Amazon Web Services

During the Amazon version 2 and version 3 rollouts, Amazon also extended Web Services to some of their international sites. Amazon runs six other sites besides the

The Naming Game

There's nothing like a bit of success to get the marketing and branding folks involved. For the rest of us, it's just a bit of confusion. Here's how Amazon is naming their Web Services. Since the launch of Amazon Web Services 1.0 in 2002, through version 3.0, there was only one API and it was called simply "Amazon Web Services". Today, there are several different Amazon Web Services APIs. The primary one, which would have been Amazon Web Services 4.0, is now called Amazon E-Commerce Service 4.0. Similarly, Amazon Web Services 3.0 is now called Amazon E-Commerce Service 3.0. The term "Amazon Web Services" now refers to the entire family of various Amazon Web Service APIs.

US site, amazon.com, and five of them have their own localized version of Amazon Web Services. There are Amazon web sites for Japan (www.amazon.co.jp), France (www.amazon.fr), Germany (www.amazon.de), Canada (www.amazon.ca), England (www.amazon.co.uk), and China (www.joyo.com).

> There are a few other Amazon sites, such as www.amazon.at and www.amazon.ch, but these sites just redirect you to one of the six amazon sites.

As of January, 2005, all Amazon web sites except the Chinese site, www.joya.com, are enabled for Web Services.

> Amazon purchased joyo.com, a Chinese retail site, in August, 2004. As this book goes to press, the site has not yet been converted to the technology used on the other Amazon sites. Ultimately, it will become Amazon.cn.

Country	Amazon web site	Web Services enabled?
Canada	`www.amazon.ca`	yes
China	`www.joyo.com`	no
England	`www.amazon.co.uk`	yes
France	`www.amazon.fr`	yes
Germany	`www.amazon.de`	yes
Japan	`www.amazon.co.jp`	yes
United States	`www.amazon.com`	yes

Table 1-2 Amazon's web sites

Amazon maintains separate databases for each of the seven Amazon sites, and the contents of each database are in the native language and reflect the local culture. For example, the French amazon site, Amazon.fr, has customer reviews and product information in French, and features products that you would normally find for sale in France, and priced in the local currency, Euros.

> The six international Amazon sites also sell some U.S. products that are displayed in English usually because localized versions of the products are not available.

Fortunately, we'll be able to use much of the same code and techniques across all the web services-enabled Amazon sites. I cover international use of Amazon Web Services in Chapter Seven.

Other Amazon Web Services Offerings

Amazon's E-Commerce Service is just one of several Web Services that Amazon offers, or plans to offer in the future. Ultimately, Amazon hopes to become a development "platform" that gives developers the tools to handle a whole spectrum of e-commerce tasks, from storefront management to payment processing and fullfilment. Almost anything you can currently do with a web browser on Amazon.com today may eventually become a Web Service that can be accessed from other web sites and applications. Though currently, Amazon offers only part of this spectrum to developers.

In addition to Amazon E-Commerce Service, Amazon now has a number of other Web Services APIs that are of interest (and they've probably released some new ones since this book went to press!). The techniques I discuss in this book are applicable to these Web Services APIs, but I don't cover these APIs.

Amazon Alexa Web Information Service

Alexa (*www.alexa.com*) is a web statistics company founded in 1996. Their primary asset is a massive database of statistics about web sites, and web site usage, that they license and sell to other companies. They were acquired by Amazon in 1999.

In October 2004, along with the release of Amazon E-Commerce Services 4.0, the first beta of Alexa Web Information Service 1.0 (AWIS) was released. The service lets developers access Alexa's database of web statistics using REST and SOAP interfaces.

Amazon Simple Queue Service

Originally developed to serve the needs of Amazon's own internal development projects, Amazon Simple Queue Service is a distributed message queue service that developers can use to add distributed messaging to their own applications.

The first beta of Amazon Simple Queue Service 1.0 was released in November, 2004. The API lets developers create message queues, and send messages to and from those queues.

AWS Management Service

The AWS Management Service lets you track usage of your Amazon Web Services Subscription ID. Since every request to Amazon E-Commerce Service requires a valid Subscription ID, you can track your usage of Amazon E-Commerce Service. The service can report storage and access statistics for a subscription ID on a per operation, per service or overall basis.

The first beta of Amazon Management Service 1.0 was released in November, 2004. The API lets developers retrieve statistics for a given Subscription ID.

Amazon Seller Services

Amazon's Seller Services is not considered part of Amazon Web Services even though it offers a Web Service. That's because Amazon Seller Services and Amazon Web Services are handled by two different divisions within Amazon.

Beginning in September 2000, individuals and businesses have been able to sell products on Amazon.com. And since that time, Amazon has provided an API for developers. Although not the primary topic of this book, Amazon's Seller Services is a useful API for anyone interested in selling goods on Amazon.com. The API is focused on inventory management for sellers, so it's of limited use to developers who are trying to use Amazon content for web sites and applications.

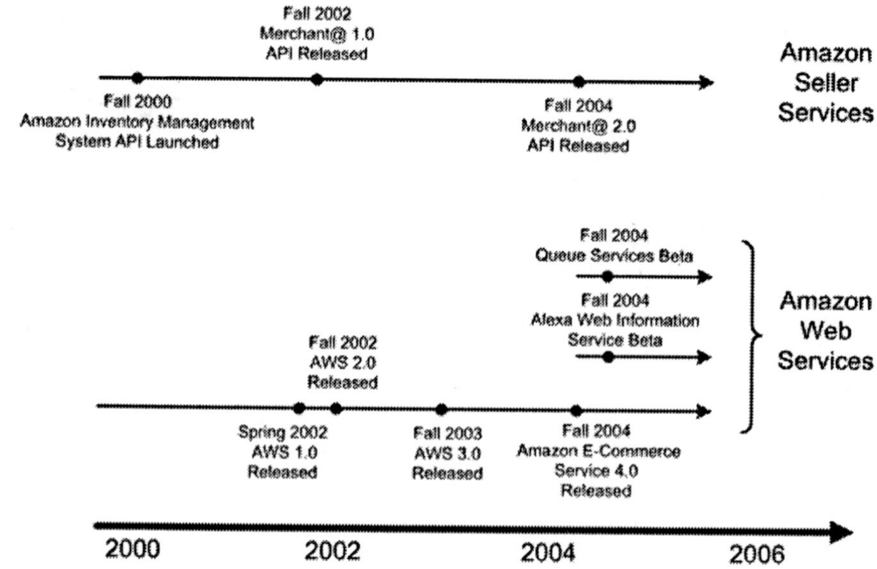

Figure 1-1 Timeline of various Amazon API Releases

The Seller Services API is designed mainly to facilitate uploading of inventory spreadsheets and the downloading of sales reports. Amazon has offered various versions of their APIs for these tasks since 2000. Amazon released a full SOAP version of their API in September, 2004. I cover Amazon Seller Services in Chapter Nine.

Where Amazon Products Come From

To make effective use of the Amazon E-Commerce Service API, it's helpful to first understand who is selling on Amazon and where they're doing their selling on the Amazon.com web site. Amazon.com has different classes of merchants and different areas on the Amazon.com web site where they sell their products. The various operations and elements of the E-Commerce Service API refer to these types merchants and the areas on Amazon where they sell.

Who's Selling And Where Are They Selling?

Amazon has three basic classes of third party sellers: Individuals, Pro Merchants, and Merchants@Amazon Sellers (usually abbreviated as simply Merchants@). The Pro Merchants category is further sub-divided into two types of sellers, Marketplace Pro Merchants and Merchants@ Pro Merchants. The main seller on Amazon.com is

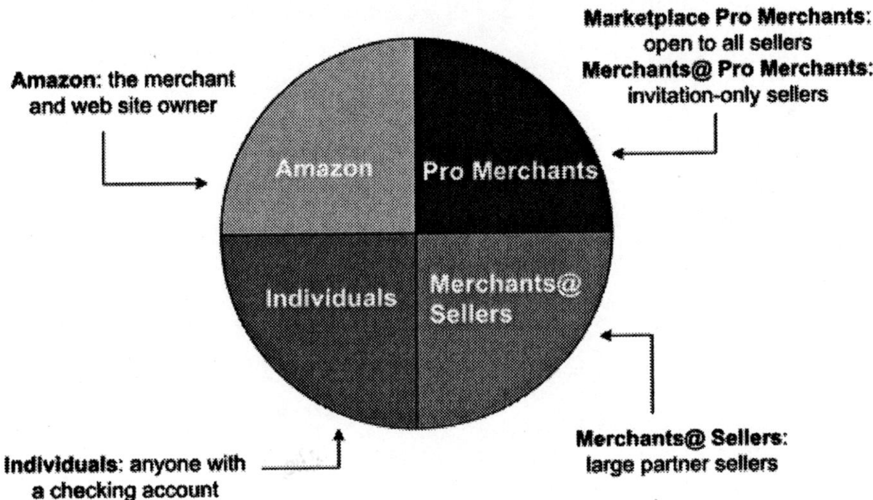

Figure 1-2 Who's selling on Amazon.com

Amazon itself. Though Amazon runs Amazon.com, they are also competing to some degree with their third party sellers. Each type of seller has a certain kind of business relationship with Amazon, and their inventory listings may only appear in certain places on the Amazon.com web site. The four basic areas on the Amazon web site where seller listings appear are the Amazon Marketplace, the Amazon Auctions, the Amazon Stores, and the Amazon zShops.

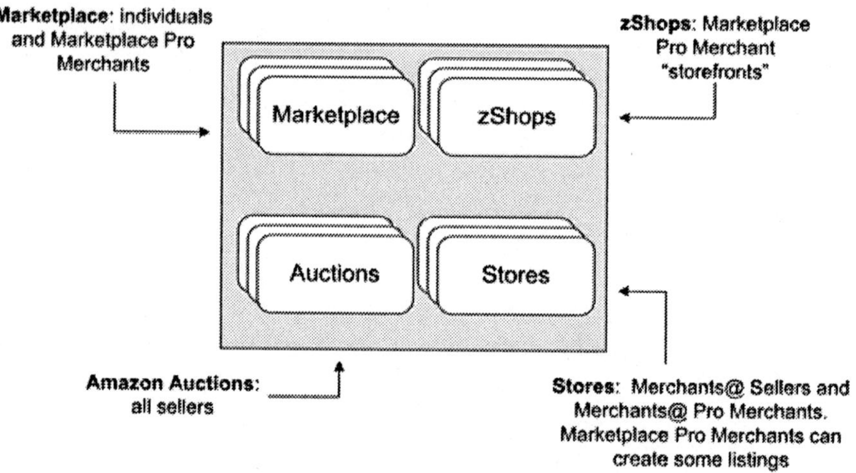

Figure 1-3 Where sellers are selling on Amazon.com

Individual Sellers

Any individual is allowed to sell certain types of new and used products on Amazon. com. It costs no up front money for individuals to list items for sale, but they are

Figure 1-4 Marketplace listings appear when you click on the "used & new" link on a product page

limited to selling only certain product categories and may only sell Items that Amazon also sells. Their products are listed in what Amazon calls the "Amazon Marketplace" or simply, the "Marketplace". The easiest way to view Marketplace listings is to click on the "used & new" link on an Amazon product detail page (Figure 1-4). Individuals may also place items up for bid in Amazon Auctions.

Pro Merchants

Amazon Pro Merchants pay a fee for the right to sell products on Amazon.com. There are two different types of Pro Merchants: Marketplace Pro Merchants, and Merchant@ Pro Merchants. The primary difference between the two is how they become sellers and where they are allowed to sell on the Amazon web site.

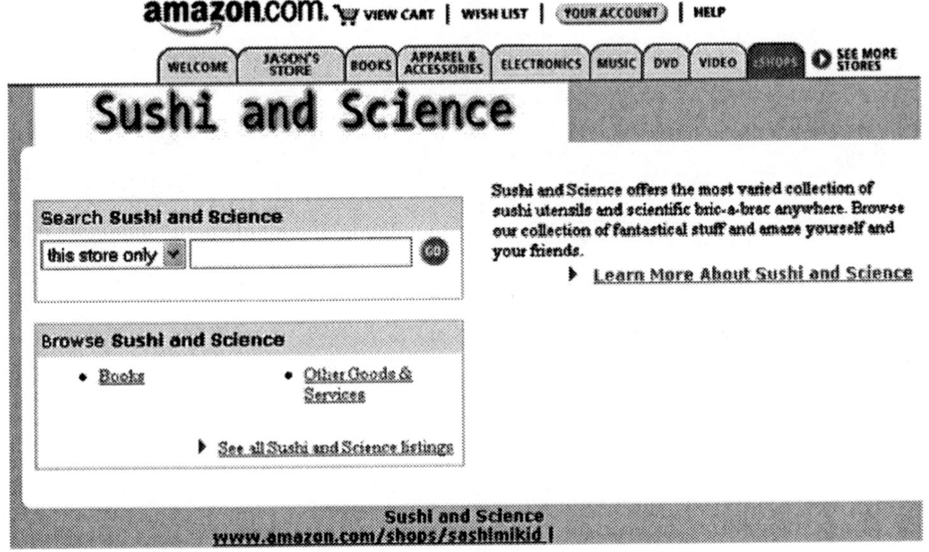

Figure 1-5 The "Sushi and Science" store is my Marketplace Pro Merchant zShop

Any individual or business can become a Marketplace Pro Merchant simply by signing up on Amazon.com. Marketplace Pro Merchants have four places they may list products for sale on Amazon. They can choose to create a virtual "storefront" by creating a series of web pages called a "zShop" (you can view the plethora of zShops by going to *zshops.amazon.com*). They can also place products in the Amazon Marketplace or in Amazon Auctions. Finally, they are allowed to sell items by creating, or adding to, custom product pages in most (but not all) of the various Amazon stores.

In contrast, Merchants@ Pro Merchants must be invited by Amazon to become sellers. Typically, Amazon recruits these sellers in order to fill out particular product categories on Amazon.com. Merchants@ Pro Merchants may sell in the Marketplace and in any Amazon Store by creating, or adding to, custom product pages. They are also allowed to sell in Amazon Auctions. Merchants@ Pro Merchants have storefront pages that are typically within a specific Amazon product category. For example, the Toddy Cafe storefront is inside of the Amazon Home & Garden category (Figure 1-6).

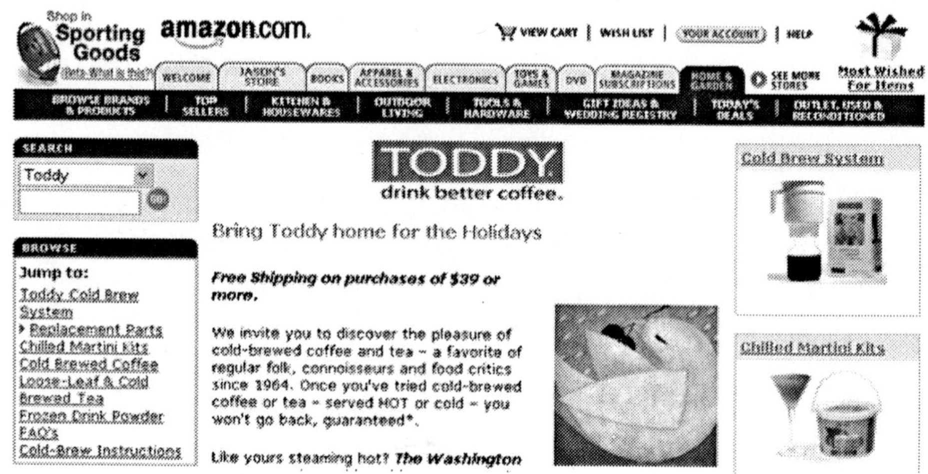

Figure 1-6 The Toddy Cafe storefront

Merchants@ Sellers

Merchants@Amazon.com (usually referred to as just "Merchants@" and pronounced "Merchants at") sellers are larger, high-volume sellers who have a special contractual relationship with Amazon. Increasingly, Amazon has partnered with these sellers, which include high-profile merchants such as Peet's Coffee and

Figure 1-7 Amazon's Jewelry and Watch store home page

Nordstrom, to add richness to the overall Amazon catalog. Merchants@ listings appear within various top-level Amazon product categories, such as Jewelry, Apparel, or Gourmet Foods.

Compared to Merchants@ Pro Merchants, Merchant@ sellers, such as Office Depot (Figure 1-8), often have more sophisticated storefronts with large tabs, extensive search capabilities, and access to more inventory tools. The extra features depends on the type of contract the Merchants@ seller has with Amazon. Note that only the U.S. site, Amazon.com, has Merchants@ sellers.

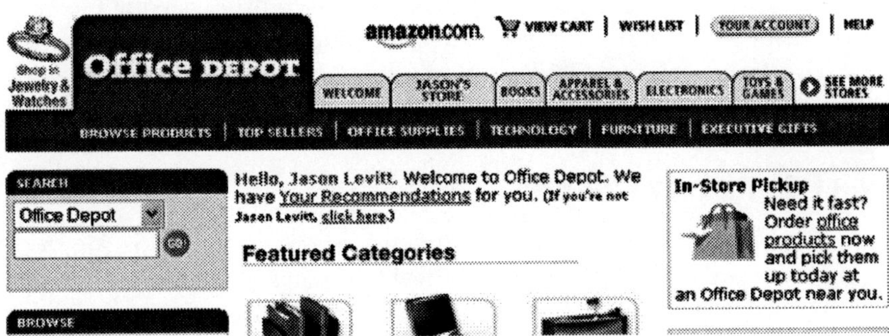

Figure 1-8 The Office Depot storefront on Amazon.com

Amazon, the merchant.

Though not a "class" of seller, per se, Amazon is still the primary seller of inventory on Amazon.com. In fact, throughout this book, I will frequently refer to Amazon as a separate merchant.

Amazon.com Features And Interfaces

Developers have access to a broad range of data via Amazon Web Services. If you have used Amazon a lot, and are familiar with some of its more esoteric features, then you will quickly recognize how many of the Amazon E-Commerce Service and Amazon Seller Services operations map to the Amazon.com web site. That's because most of the operations in the various Amazon Web Services APIs are based on functionality that merchants and customers can already access interactively via web pages on Amazon.

Amazon.com's web site offers four basic types of functionality: buying, selling, community, and fulfillment. Buying features help users search and select products. Selling features let sellers manage their Amazon listings. Community features give Amazon users the ability to promote themselves, influence purchasing decisions, and connect with friends. Fulfillment features enable the final steps of buying products on Amazon.com such as managing shopping carts, credit card processing, and shipping.

As developers, we're interested in accessing the Amazon services for which there are APIs. Many of the buying and community features are accessible in Amazon E-Commerce Service 4.0. The selling side of Amazon is not quite as evolved but we'll spend some time looking at those features in Chapter Nine.

Many Amazon site features that aren't accessible via Amazon's Web Services can usually be accessed via the time-honored operation of "screen-scraping." Screen scraping is the quite manual technique of fetching a web page, parsing the HTML in it, and then using the data on your web site or in your application. It's a popular way to access data from web sites that is otherwise inaccessible by other operations. I don't cover any screen-scraping techniques in this book.

Amazon Community Features

The community aspects of the Amazon.com site are rich fodder for Amazon Web Services, but currently very little of it is accessible via an API. Only some of the user-created lists can be accessed. Hopefully, Amazon will be improving access in this area over time.

Community Feature	Description	Developer Interface	Developer Access
WishList, Listmania, Wedding Registry, Baby Registry, So You'd Like To, Purchase Sharing	Various lists that users can create.	Amazon E-Commerce Service	Read only (no support for 'So You'd Like To' or 'Purchase Sharing'). Limited support for Wedding and Baby Registries.
Purchase Circles	Amazon maintains statistical breakdown of items people are purchasing by city and region	None	-
Amazon Friends	User-maintained lists of friends	None	-
Share The Love	Recommend products to friends.	none	-
Share Your Images	Upload pictures of people using Amazon products	none	-
Amazon Chat	Online chat rooms	none	-
Discussion Boards	Online bulletin board system	none	-
Customer Reviews	Product reviews written by Amazon customers	Amazon E-Commerce Service	Read-Only

Community Feature	Description	Developer Interface	Developer Access
E-cards	Send electronic greeting cards	none	-

Table 1-3 Amazon.com Community features

If you are an Amazon.com user, you can find out about some of your contributions to the Amazon "community" by going to this URL:

```
http://www.amazon.com/exec/obidos/subst/community/community-home.html
```

Look at the "Your Participation" box on the right side of the page to get a summary of your participation. I discuss Amazon customers in more detail in Chapter Five.

Amazon Buying and Selling Features

On the Internet, the buying process is all about search. Amazon E-Commerce Services lets you search for products, sellers, and customers using a wide range of search criteria. Similar, Amazon Seller Services supports the listing and maintenance of seller inventory via the Seller Services API.

Buying and Selling Features	Description	Developer Interface	Developer Access
product search	Various ways to find products and product data	Amazon E-Commerce Service	Read only
seller search	Searches for information about businesses selling products on Amazon.com	Amazon E-Commerce Service	Read only
manage inventory	List and manage your own products for sale on Amazon.com, including Amazon Auctions	Amazon Seller Services	Read/Write
customer search	Searches for information about customers who have bought products on Amazon.	Amazon E-Commerce Service	Read only

Table 1-4 Amazon.com buying and selling features

Amazon Fulfillment Features

Fulfillment is the checkout process -- the billing, payment, and shipping of goods. Though Amazon has not fully exposed their payment services, they do offer shopping cart access and the ability to track sales.

Fulfillment Features	Description	Developer Interface	Developer Access
shopping cart	The online "container" that stores your current product selections	Amazon E-Commerce Service	Read/Write
payment	Amazon's credit-card based payment system, including order changes, additions, and cancellation	Amazon E-Commerce Service, Amazon Seller Services	Read only
shipping	Amazon's shipping fulfillment system, including changes and tracking	Amazon Seller Services	Read only

Table 1-5 Amazon fulfillment features

An Overview Of Amazon's APIs

Now that you have an idea of who's selling on Amazon.com, where they're selling on Amazon.com, and what kinds of features the Amazon.com site offers, the various E-Commerce and Seller Services operations may make more sense.

Amazon E-Commerce Service Operations

Amazon E-Commerce Service 4.0 provides developers with a set of operations that they can use to search for products, manage remote shopping carts, and access community features such as wishlists. There is also the Help operation, a self-referential operation that returns information about how to format requests for various operations, and a TransactionLookup operation which provides customer transaction information to sellers on specific transactions.

Operation	Purpose
BrowseNodeLookup	Find Parent and Child Browse Nodes of a given Browse Node Id
CartAdd	Add items to an existing remote shopping cart
CartClear	Lets you remove the contents of a remote shopping cart.
CartCreate	Creates a new remote shopping cart
CartGet	Lets you retrieve the contents of a remote shopping cart.
CartModify	Lets you modify the quantity of items in a remote shopping cart as well as move items from the active area of a cart to the 'save for later' area.
CustomerContentLookup	Lookup all publicly information on an Amazon customer. Lookup is by Amazon Customer ID.

Operation	Purpose
CustomerContentSearch	Search for Amazon customers who have opted to make their customer information public. Search is by name or email address.
Help	Retrieves documentation about Amazon E-Commerce Service operations and response groups. Useful for IDEs and self-documenting systems.
ItemLookup	Lookup product information by ASIN, UPC, EAN, or SKU.
ItemSearch	Search for products using a wide variety of criteria.
ListLookup	Lookup specific Amazon Listmania and Wishlist lists.
ListSearch	Search for Wishlists, Baby registries, and Wedding registries
SellerListingLookup	Returns information about Marketplace and Zshops product listings. Lookups are by Listing ID or Exchange ID
SellerListingSearch	Search for Marketplace and zShops listings by keyword.
SellerLookup	Returns information about specific Amazon Sellers.
SimilarityLookup	Search for items that are similar to one or more specific items.
TransactionLookup	Sellers use this operation to retrieve information about their customer transactions. Lookups are by transaction ID.

Table 1-6 Amazon E-Commerce Service Operations

Amazon Seller Services Operations

Amazon Seller Services provides two very different APIs for sellers who wish to maintain their inventory on Amazon.com. The Merchants@ API is usable only by Merchants@ Pro Merchants and Merchants@ sellers. The Amazon Inventory.

Operation	Purpose
getAllPendingDocumentInfo	Requests a list of all available order or payment settlement reports
getDocument	Requests a specific document using the document ID
getDocumentInfoInterfaceConformance	Used to test retrieval of lists of available documents
getDocumentInterfaceConformance	Used to test download of a given document
getDocumentProcessingStatus	Requests the status of document that have been posted to Amazon
getLastNDocumentInfo	Requests a list of the specified number of documents
getLastNDocumentProcessingStatuses	Request a list of the status of the last N documents that the Seller has posted to Amazon
getLastNPendingDocumentInfo	Requests a list of the latest N order or payment settlement reports
postDocument	Uploads various types of documents
postDocumentDownloadAck	Used by Seller to notify Amazon that a particular orders or payment report has been received.
postDocumentInterfaceConformance	Used to test posting of documents to Amazon

Table 1-7 Merchants@ operations

Management System (AIMS) API is usable only by Marketplace Pro Merchants. Amazon Seller Services will be discussed in more detail in Chapter Nine

Operation	Purpose
add-modify-delete	Add, modify, or delete inventory
batch-refund	Issue refunds
errorlog	Download an error log of inventory upload errors
generate-report-now	Generate open listings reports
get-batches	Check the status of inventory upload requests
get-pending-uploads-count	Get number of uploads awaiting processing
get-report-status	Retrieve list of refund reports
modify-only	Simpler Add, modify, or delete of inventory
purge-replace	Purge and replace all inventory listings
quickfix	Download specific error log of inventory upload errors
report	Download specific order or refund reports

Table 1-8 Amazon Inventory Management System API Operations

Amazon Identifiers

Like most dynamic, database-driven web sites, Amazon.com has certain key data elements that identify most of the things displayed on the web site. These identifiers point to some things that are easy to find and see, such as product descriptions, and some things that aren't so easy to find, such as third-party seller information and specific seller transaction information. These identifiers, which are stored in Amazon's database, are not always readily accessible from Amazon's web site, but they are used extensively when working with Amazon E-Commerce Service.

Amazon Product Identifiers

Amazon has four main identifiers that identify product data or instances of products for sale. The Amazon Standard Item Number (ASIN) is the primary product identifier used by Amazon. A second, less-commonly used identifier, the Listing ID, is only used in the zShops, and only for certain products which do not have an ASIN.

All product information on Amazon.com can be looked up using either an ASIN or a Listing ID although the Listing ID identifies only a small fraction of items compared to the ASIN. Thus, the Listing ID is rarely used for looking up products.

While you use ASINs and Listing Ids to retrieve product details, Exchange IDs and Offer Listing IDs identify the instances of those products available for sale on Amazon. An instance of a product for sale is known as an "offer listing," or simply an "offer."

Identifier	Description
ASIN (Amazon Standard Item Number)	Amazon Standard Item Number. The general-purpose product identifier assigned by Amazon to identify products. In the future, it will be possible for any third-party seller to assign their own ASINs to items for which Amazon does not have an ASIN.
Listing ID	Identifies instances of products for sale by Marketplace Pro Merchants in the Amazon zShops area. These products are ones for which there is no existing ASIN. This identifier is called "zShops Id" on the Amazon web site.
Exchange ID	Identifies instances of products for sale by third-party sellers in the Amazon Marketplace and zShops.
Offer Listing ID	Identifies an instance of a product for sale.

Table 1-9 The primary Amazon product identifiers

The All-Powerful ASIN

Understanding the Amazon Standard Item Number (ASIN) is crucial. ASINs are used by many Amazon E-Commerce Service operations and come in several flavors. The ASIN is the all-powerful 10 character identifier that uniquely identifies nearly every product offered on Amazon.com. Not surprisingly, ASINs are also the primary way of identifying products when developing with Amazon E-Commerce Service. ASIN's are assigned to products by Amazon's staff. The one exception is books. For books, the 10 character ASIN is the same as the 10 character ISBN (International Standard Book Number) of the book.

> The only products sold on Amazon that don't have an ASIN are certain items in the zShops. They don't have ASINs because they're products sold by third-party sellers and Amazon has never assigned an ASIN to the product. Typical examples are collectibles and antiques which are often one-of-a-kind items. Though Amazon has recently added the capability for sellers to create their own ASINs, there are still many zShops items without ASINs.

Some products that Amazon sells may also have -- in addition to an ASIN -- a Universal Product Code (UPC), European Article Number (EAN), or Stock Keeping Unit (SKU) identifier stored in their Amazon product record, but, from an Amazon point of view, those are second class identifiers and are not always a part of a product's record in the Amazon database.

> Amazon also uses the Japanese Article Number (JAN) which has the same format as the EAN. EANs and JANs are only used on Amazon's European and Japanese sites.

For more detailed information on how UPCs are handled, visit the Uniform Code Council's web site: *www.uc-council.org*. For more information on EANs, visit EAN

International's site at: *www.ean-int.org*. For ISBN information, check out: *www.isbn.org*.

Exchange And Offer Listing IDs

A listing of a product for sale is known as an "offer". Thus, a product has only one ASIN or Listing ID, but may have multiple unique Offer Listing IDs and Exchange IDs associated with it. If one seller is selling a used copy of the Beatle's Abbey Road CD, and a different seller is also selling a used copy of the same CD, there will be a different Offer Listing ID for each of those product listings.

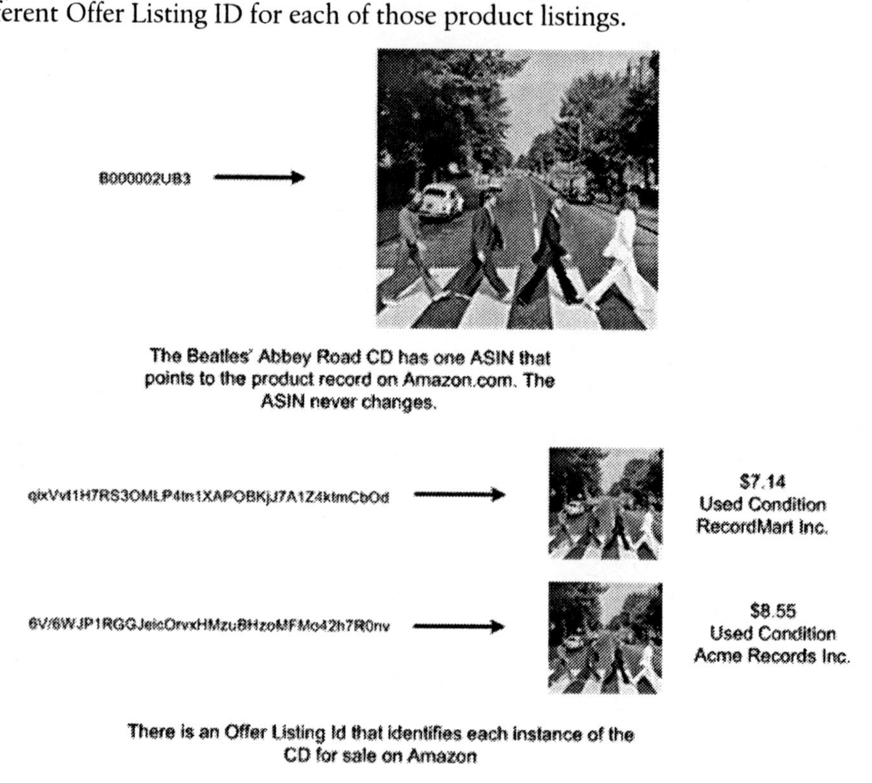

Figure 1-9 The difference between ASINs and Offer Listing Ids

However, regardless of how many different merchants are selling copies of the Abbey Road CD on Amazon, the CD will always have the same ASIN, which happens to be "B000002UB3".

Offer Listing IDs and Exchange IDs both identify instances of products for sale. Every instance of an item for sale on Amazon has an Offer Listing ID and you should always use the Offer Listing ID if it's available. The Exchange ID is less common as it is only used to identify offers in the zShops and Marketplace. All offers that have an Exchange ID also have a corresponding Offer Listing ID.

Exchange IDs are assigned automatically to products that Marketplace Pro Merchants sell in their zShops. Offer Listing IDs are dynamically generated for all products sold on Amazon.

> Amazon expects to eventually phase out the Exchange ID and Listing Id. All items will be identified by ASINs, and all offers by Offer Listing ID.

Parent And Child ASINs

Figure 1-10 The difference between regular ASINs and Parent ASINs

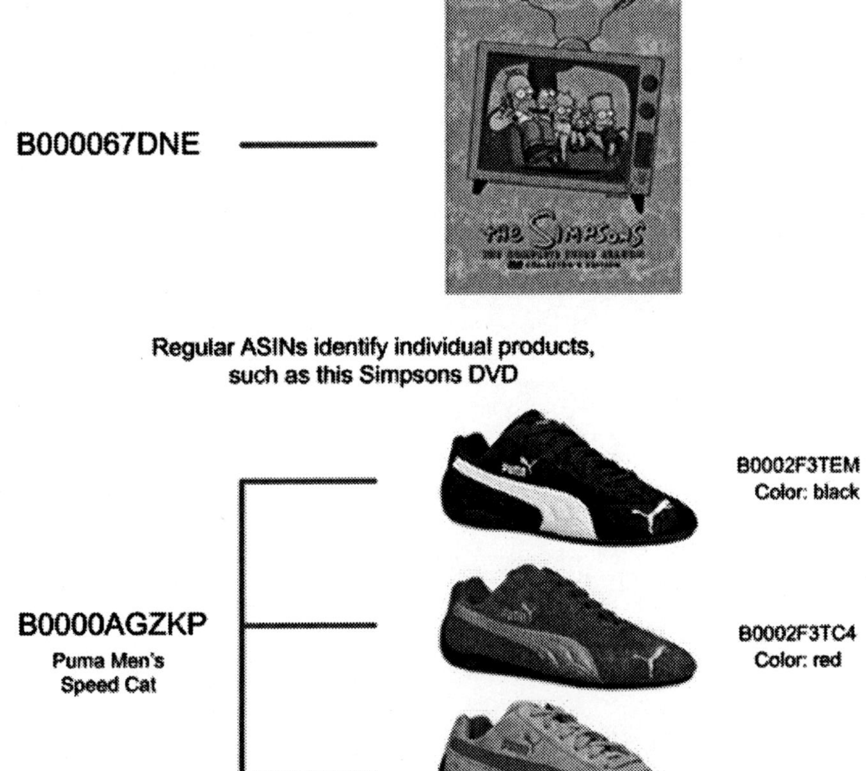

B000067DNE
Regular ASINs identify individual products, such as this Simpsons DVD
B0000AGZKP
Puma Men's Speed Cat
B0002F3TEM
Color: black
B0002F3TC4
Color: red
B0002U7LIM
Color: white
Parent ASINs identify a generic product that has one or more Child ASINs, such as this Puma athletic shoe

Certain classes of products have what are called Parent and Child ASINs. The Parent ASIN identifies the product, and the Child ASIN(s) identify buyable variations of the same product. Typical examples of such products are jewelry and apparel items which typically come in several sizes and colors.

The Parent ASIN for a shoe, such as the Puma shoe in Figure 1-10, identifies the generic item, B0000AGZKP, while various Child ASINs identify each instance of the shoe -- the black shoe that is size 6, the red shoe that is size 11, the white shoe that is size 12, and so on.

Parent ASINs are like generic placeholders for a product. Parent ASINs never have offers associated with them which makes sense since you have to have the size and/or color selected before you know how much it costs. Child ASINs are like regular ASINs in that they identify a specific product and thus they may have offers associated with them. Product data associated with Parent and Child ASINs are called "Variations"

Amazon Seller And Customer Identifiers

Identifier	Description
Merchant ID	`Identifies Amazon partner sellers known as Merchants@ (pronounced Merchants At). These are typically big-name, high-volume sellers such as Target and Nordstrom. This id is expected to be deprecated in favor of the Seller Id.`
Seller ID	`Currently identifies individual sellers, Marketplace Pro Merchants, Merchants@ Pro Merchants, and most (but not all) Merchants@ sellers. It will eventually identify all sellers on Amazon.com`
Customer ID	`Identifies individual Amazon users (anyone with an Amazon account)`

Table 1-10 Amazon customer and seller identifiers

Every seller on Amazon has a Seller ID. The Seller ID is the primary identifier of sellers on Amazon. Merchant IDs are another, less common, type of seller identifier. Merchant IDs were originally intended to specifically identify only Amazon's larger Merchants@ sellers.

All Amazon customers have a Customer ID (whether they know it or not).

Amazon Purchasing Identifiers

Identifier	Description
Remote Cart ID	`Identifies temporary remote shopping carts`

Identifier	Description
Transaction ID	`Identifiers customer purchase transactions. For privacy purposes, this ID is only available to third-party sellers who are looking up information on their own customer transactions.`

Table 1-11 Amazon purchasing identifiers

Amazon lets developers create remote shopping carts whose content information is maintained via Amazon E-Commerce Service. The Cart ID, which is determined by Amazon when you create a remote cart via Amazon E-Commerce Service, is used to manage the remote shopping cart.

Transaction IDs have limited use for developers since a Transaction ID is only returned to sellers whose customers have purchased something from them. For privacy purposes, this id is only going to be available to third-party sellers who are looking up information on their own customer transactions.

Amazon Community Identifiers

Identifier	Description
Listmania ID	`Identifies customer-created Listmania list`
Wishlist ID	`Identifies customer-created Wishlist list`
Wedding Registry List ID	`Identifies customer-created Wedding Registry list`
Baby Registry List ID	`Identifies customer-created Baby Registry list`

Table 1-12 Amazon list identifiers

Amazon customers are able to create several different kinds of lists to promote themselves or their interests. Each time a customer creates a list, Amazon stores a list identifier in the Amazon database that uniquely identifies that list. List identifiers are available for Listmania lists, Wishlists, Wedding Registry lists, and Baby Registry lists.

Amazon Search Architecture

Amazon's web site is driven primarily by the Mason web templating system, *www.masonhq.com*, which is written in the Perl programming language. The site architecture details are proprietary, yet still, you can see the dynamically generated URLs created by the underlying Perl code as you browse around Amazon.com. Some architectural details are revealed by examining these URLs and the HTML source of the generated pages. In particular, two types of identifiers, root categories and Browse Node IDs, appear frequently all over the Amazon sites. Browse Node IDs are quite useful for product searching.

Root Categories And Search Indexes

All products displayed on Amazon.com are organized in a many-to-one tree structure where a single product can appear in more than one product category. Every product in the Amazon database is descended from at least one root category. A list of most root, or top-level, product categories can be found by going to any Amazon home page (amazon.com, amazon.de, amazon.co.uk, amazon.co jp, amazon.fr, amazon.ca) and viewing the page source code. (Use View > Source on Internet Explorer and View > View Source on Safari). In The HTML source for the home page, search for the first occurrence of the word "select" to find the first HTML select tag. The list of root categories with their display names are listed. For Amazon.com, a partial list of the select tag looks like this:

```
<select name=url>
<option value="index=blended" selected>All Products
<option value="index=stripbooks">Books
<option value="index=music">Popular Music
<option value="index=music-dd">Music Downloads
<option value="index=classical">Classical Music
<option value="index=dvd">DVD
<option value="index=vhs">VHS
<option value="index=apparel-index&dispatch=search&results-process=bin">Apparel
<option value="index=restaurants">Restaurants
<option value="index=theatrical">Movie Showtimes
<option value="index=toys">Toys
.......
```

The root categories in the select tag are blended, stripbooks, music, music-dd, etc.... For the German Amazon site, www.amazon.de, the select tag looks like this:

```
<select name="url">
  <option value="index=blended" selected>Alle Produkte
  <option value="index=books-de">B&uuml;cher
  <option value="index=books-de-intl-us">Englische B&uuml;cher
  <option value="index=magazines-de">Zeitschriften
  <option value="index=pop-music-de">Pop Musik
  <option value="index=classical-de">Klassik
  <option value="index=dvd-de">DVD
  <option value="index=vhs-de">Video VHS
 ......
```

Here, the root categories are blended, books-de, books-de-intl-us, etc...

Each Amazon web site has its own set of root category identifiers. To make it easier to use root categories with Amazon E-Commerce Service, the Amazon E-Commerce Service team provides a generic category identifier called a Search Index.

The Search Index maps to the same root category for each Amazon site. For example, the Search Index called "DVD" maps to the root category "dvd-de" if you are accessing Amazon.de, and "dvd" if you are accessing Amazon.com. A table of Search Indexes is listed in Appendix H.

> Most, but not all, of Amazon's root categories are available via Amazon E-Commerce Service.

Browse Nodes

The entire product catalog, as well as Amazon help pages, Movie Showtimes, and other services available on Amazon, is categorized using an identifier that Amazon calls a Browse Node ID. Browse Node IDs are positive integers that Amazon assigns to product categories. For example, Browse Node ID 145663 is the product category "Canon camera accessories" (the category name is called the Browse Node Name). Browse Node ID 1239 has the Browse Node Name "Music by composed Johann Sebastian Bach". Browse Nodes are similar in spirit to the Dewey Decimal System that libraries use to assign book categories. The main difference is that, while most of the Dewey Decimal System categories have remained the same for decades, Amazon Browse Node IDs change frequently, may sometimes point to empty or inaccessible categories, and aren't assigned to categories in any sensible way.

> The assignment strategy for Browse Nodes is proprietary, so, if there is some rhyme or reason to the assignment, no one but the Amazon employees understand it.

It's impossible to determine from the number alone what category a particular Browse Node ID, say, 5000, is assigned to without first browsing to it. If you want to see what category (if any) a Browse Node ID has been assigned, pick a random positive integer and put it in one of the following urls:

- http://www.amazon.com/exec/obidos/tg/browse/-/**[your number here]**
- http://www.amazon.co.uk/exec/obidos/tg/browse/-/**[your number here]**
- http://www.amazon.de/exec/obidos/tg/browse/-/**[your number here]**
- http://www.amazon.co.jp/exec/obidos/tg/browse/-/**[your number here]**
- http://www.amazon.ca/exec/obidos/tg/browse/-/**[your number here]**
- http://www.amazon.fr/exec/obidos/tg/browse/-/**[your number here]**

> Browse Node Id assignments are almost always different on each Amazon site. For example. Browse Node Id 10 on Amazon,.com is Health-related books. However, Browse Node Id 10 doesn't exist on either Amazon.co.uk or Amazon.ca.

The reason that Browse Nodes are so dynamic is that different Amazon departments are constantly adding products to their Browse Nodes, as well as re-arranging them to make them (we hope) more coherent. This is quite annoying for developers, but we can still use them effectively.

Amazon does not release any statistics or details on their Browse Node architecture, but by using simple crawling techniques, I crawled four of the Amazon sites, testing each browse node in order, from one to one million (two million on amazon.com). The table below summarizes the results.

Country Site	lowest accessible browse node	highest accessible browse node	total number of accessible browse nodes in the first million browse nodes (two million for Amazon.com)
amazon.com	1	1205294	122158
amazon.co.uk	51	988944	21903
amazon.de	1	977674	29825
amazon.co.jp	1	977648	25885

Table 1-13 Accessible Browse Nodes (August, 2004)

There are currently few, if any, Browse Node IDs higher than one million on the international Amazon sites.

Browse Node Structure

Products in the Amazon.com database can appear in more than one product category and therefore, in more than one Browse Node as well. For example, on Amazon.com, the DVD "Harry Potter and the Sorcerer's Stone (Widescreen Edition)" appears in all of the following Amazon Browse Node categories (this is not a complete list, by any means):

```
Top Sellers > DVD > Genres > Kids & Family
DVD > Used DVDs > Kids & Family
DVD > Genres > Kids & Family > Characters & Series > Harry Potter
DVD > Genres > Science Fiction & Fantasy > Fantasy > Fantasy Adventures
DVD > Titles > ( H )
DVD > Actors & Actresses > ( S ) > Somerville, Geraldine
```

This left-to-right category notation when displayed on a web page is called a “breadcrumb” because it’s like a trail of breadcrumbs that a user can follow to navigate a hierarchy of web pages.

I found these categories by constructing the appropriate Amazon E-Commerce Service request string and placing it in my browser.

The ins and outs of such requests will be explained in later sections, but for now, you can look at the XML generated by placing the request in your browser:

```
http://webservices.amazon.com/onca/xml?Service=AWSECommerceService&
SubscriptionId=1A7XKHR5BYD0WPJVQEG2&AssociateTag=ws&Operation=ItemLookup&
ItemId=B00003CXI1&IdType=ASIN&ResponseGroup=BrowseNodes&Version=2005-02-23
```

In general, Amazon's categorizations are quite dynamic, with products being re-categorized every few minutes in categories that change frequently, such as Top Sellers, and other categories changing much less frequently. If this DVD starts to sell poorly, it will no longer appear under the "Top Sellers" category, and if third party sellers aren't offering any used DVDs, it would drop out of the 'Used DVDs' category. The dynamic quality of Amazon's categorizations means that we must be careful about storing and re-using Browse Nodes.

In Figure 1-10, notice that I can find the Browse Node Id (1048166) by looking in the address field of the browser. I can also see the Browse Node Name by looking either at the breadcrumbs or at the title bar of the browser. Each category has a corresponding Browse Node.

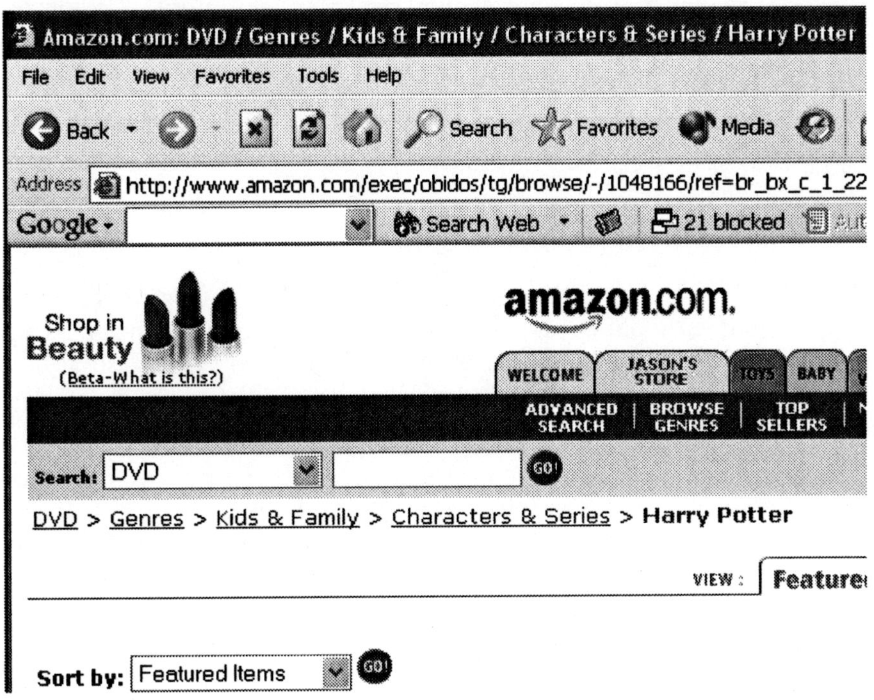

Figure 1-11 The breadcrumb trail for Harry Potter DVDs on Amazon.com.

So we can also identify the categories by their Browse Nodes and realize a hierarchy of Browse Nodes. The Browse Nodes corresponding to our categories from the previous listing are as follows:

```
Top Sellers > DVD > Genres > Kids & Family
286723 > 130 > 404276 >  286742

DVD > Used DVDs > Kids & Family
130 > 864690 > 865622

DVD > Genres > Kids & Family > Characters & Series > Harry Potter
130 > 404276 > 163414 > 292345 > 1048166

DVD > Genres > Science Fiction & Fantasy > Fantasy > Fantasy Adventures
130 > 404276 > 163431 > 163440 > 735772

DVD > Titles > ( H )
130 > 579510 > 579526

DVD > Actors & Actresses > ( S ) > Somerville, Geraldine
130 > 404278 > 444858 > 447398
```

Note that services, such as Movie Showtimes, and even help information for Amazon.com, is also similarly categorized. For example, help information on how to logout of amazon.com is under this category:

```
Help > Using Your Account > Signing Out
```

Which has browse nodes:

```
508510 > 468536 > 515722
```

Ephemeral Nature Of Browse Nodes

As mentioned before, Browse Nodes are constantly being reorganized, added to, deleted, and shuffled about by various product teams within Amazon.com. You may have already tried to browse to some of the Browse Nodes I previously mentioned and found that they don't return what I claimed. Or, you may even get a "page not found" error indicating that the page no longer exists.

Some Browse Nodes are temporary in nature and therefore are not available through Amazon E-Commerce Service. Typical examples are Browse Nodes associated with holidays, such as a "Christmas" gifts category or categories that list best sellers or daily specials. Such Browse Nodes may be accessible via Amazon E-Commerce Service for days or weeks, but could disappear at any time.

Also some Merchants@ Sellers don't want their products available via Amazon E-Commerce Service and so the corresponding Browse Nodes to their stores are not accessible via Amazon E-Commerce Service.

Yet, despite their somewhat ephemeral nature, Browse Nodes are quite useful in Amazon E-Commerce Service. They are used to narrow down searches to specific product categories and to provide browseable product hierarchies for end-users.

An Overview Of The Amazon E-Commerce Service Operations

Amazon E-Commerce Service 4.0 has 18 operations (see Table 1-6) available for developers. Other than the Remote Cart operations and the Help operation, all the rest of the operations either perform searches on Amazon's databases (operations with the word "search" in the operation name) or lookup individual pieces of information (operations with the word "lookup" in the operation name). Not surprisingly, the variety of information available to developers is quite similar to the information displayed on Amazon when you browse the site with a web browser. A quick overview of the various operations will help you understand what types of information each operation deals with and which ones you should use to find the information you want.

Help

Help is sort an oddball operation. It's used almost exclusively by IDE developers to provide contextual help information for people programming using Amazon E-Commerce Service. Help takes as its main parameter either the name of an Amazon E-Commerce Service operation or the name of an Amazon E-Commerce Service Response Group. If it's a operation, then Help returns the list of possible parameters for that operation. If it's a Response Group, then Help returns the list of operations that can use that Response Group and the list of XML values returned by the Response Group.

CustomerContentLookup and CustomerContentSearch

These two operations let you look up information about Amazon customers. CustomerContentSearch lets you search customers using email addresses and names. Searches only succeed if the Amazon customer has opted to make their personal information public on Amazon.com. By default, such information is not publicly available, but some of it can become automatically available if you create a publicly accessible list such as an Amazon Wedding Registry list or Listmania list. Returned information never includes street addresses or buying history.

CustomerContentLookup lets you look up Amazon customer information when you know the customer's Customer Id. Customer Ids are only returned by CustomerContentLookup and CustomerContentSearch requests.

ItemLookup and ItemSearch

ItemLookup and ItemSearch are the bread and butter operations of Amazon E-Commerce Service. ItemLookup lets you lookup individual items using either the Amazon ASIN, or an EAN, UPC, or SKU identifier. A broad range of results are possible depending on the Response Groups requested. ItemLookup is typically used to retrieve offers and Browse Nodes for a particular item.

ItemSearch essentially duplicates the search box on the Amazon home page. You can search using many different parameters and have results returned in many different forms depending on the Response Group requested. ItemSearch, as you might expect, is typically used to search for specific types of items that are then displayed or otherwise offered to users.

BrowseNodeLookup

This operation takes a Browse Node Id as an argument, and then returns the parent and child Browse Nodes of that Browse Node Id. It's useful for creating dynamic search hierarchies since you can use it to find related product categories.

SimilarityLookup

SimilarityLookup lets you duplicate the "You may also like...." product recommendations found on Amazon. SimilarityLookup takes one or more Amazon ASINs as parameters and returns items that are similar based on subject area, matching descriptive text, and other criteria.

ListLookup and ListSearch

ListLookup and ListSearch perform searches and lookups on various Amazon lists. ListLookup takes as its parameter the List Id of an Amazon WishList or Listmania list, and returns all the items and list details (support for other types of Amazon lists, such as Baby Registries, will be added in future versions).

ListSearch lets you search for various lists. It takes as parameters the list owners' name, email, or city/state they live in. Currently, you can search for Amazon Wish Lists, Baby Registries, or Wedding Registries. (support for other types of Amazon lists, such as So You'd Like To..., will be added in future versions).

CartAdd, CartClear, CartCreate, CartGet, and CartModify

The Remote Cart operation let you create, retrieve, and modify, and delete remote shopping carts. When you create a Remote Cart using CartCreate a CartId is returned that is a pointer into a temporary storage area in the Amazon database. The various Remote Cart operations let you manage the Remote Cart until it is ultimately passed to Amazon so that the customer can purchase the items.

SellerLookup

SellerLookup lets you lookup specific Amazon sellers. It takes as its parameter an Amazon Seller Id and returns background information on Amazon sellers, including customer reviews, if any. CustomerIds are included in the customer reviews. It does not return any item listings, however. SellerIds are usually obtained in item listings returned by operations such as ItemSearch. SellerLookup can be used to lookup general information about any Amazon seller, including Merchants@ sellers.

SellerListingLookup and SellerListingSearch

SellerListingLookup and SellerListingSearch let you return item listings from third-party sellers (individuals and Marketplace Pro Merchants) who sell in the Amazon Marketplace and Zshops sellers. These operations are necessary because zShops items are not returned by other operations. SellerListingLookup lets you lookup specific items in the zShops and Marketplace by Offer Listing Id or Exchange Id.

Seller Listing Search lets you search for zShops and Marketplace items using keywords and other parameters. You can filter by Seller Id, for example (the ItemSearch operation lets you filter by Merchant Id).

TransactionLookup

The TransactionLookup operation is only of use to Amazon sellers who wish to retrieve details of existing transactions. A Transaction Id parameter is required to use this operation. The Transaction Id is available via Amazon's Seller Services (see Chapter Eight).

As this book goes to press, the functionality of the Transaction-Lookup operation is limited. Amazon only grants special partners access to many of the fields returned by this operation.

Exercises For The Reader

Write a program that creates a map of all of the Browse Node IDs from any (or all!) of the Amazon sites. Organize your map so that programs can quickly find related Browse Nodes IDs and Browse Node Names. Flag each Browse Node so that programs can tell whether they have products in them, and create links between Browse Node entries so that developers can build their own product hierarchies.

CHAPTER 2

Developing With Amazon E-Commerce Service

There's always a catch
—Ferengi Rule Of Acquisition #116

Amazon offers developers an embarrassment of riches when it comes to accessing E-Commerce Service 4.0. Developers can choose from either SOAP or REST-like interfaces, and Amazon also provides an XSLT transformation service as an extension to the REST-like interface. But developing applications that access Amazon's E-Commerce Service may be a bit different than what you're used to. Your application is essentially accessing a 3rd-party database over the Internet. Since you have no control over the data source, your applications have to be able to recover from a range of potential problems, from total denial of service to errors in Amazon's database records. Developing Amazon E-Commerce Service applications is a challenge, but the results are worth it.

If you've never attempted an Amazon E-Commerce Service application, one of the first things you'll want to do is decide whether to develop applications using Amazon's SOAP or REST interface.

> Sure, you can mix and match interfaces, but maintenance can be tricky when you're trying to maintain two different request interfaces.

Each has it's pluses and minuses, but which ever one you choose, I suggest learning two things:

- **If you choose SOAP, learn how to create and use REST-like requests.** Not only do many of the examples in this book use the REST format, but it's much easier to test and prototype applications using REST. You'll save development time by testing out requests using REST before deploying them with SOAP.
- **If you choose REST, learn how to read the Amazon WSDL (Web Services Description Language) file.** Amazon's WSDL file, which is consumed by SOAP clients, sums up the entire functionality of Amazon E-Commerce Service in one

file. It's the fastest and most direct way to see exactly what data elements are returned by Amazon E-Commerce Service requests.

The SOAP Model For Accessing Amazon E-commerce Service

SOAP, Simple Object Access Protocol, is a standardized way of making programmatic requests over a network. The standard is maintained by the World Wide Web Consortium (*http://www.w3.org/TR/soap*) and is currently at version 1.2.

Accessing Amazon E-commerce Service using SOAP is just a matter of properly using a SOAP client to access Amazon's SOAP server. The SOAP client is a software component, separate from your application, that is responsible for serializing and packaging SOAP messages to and from the server (figure 2-1). The format of the parameters for each request is described in a Web Services Description Language (WSDL) file provided by Amazon.

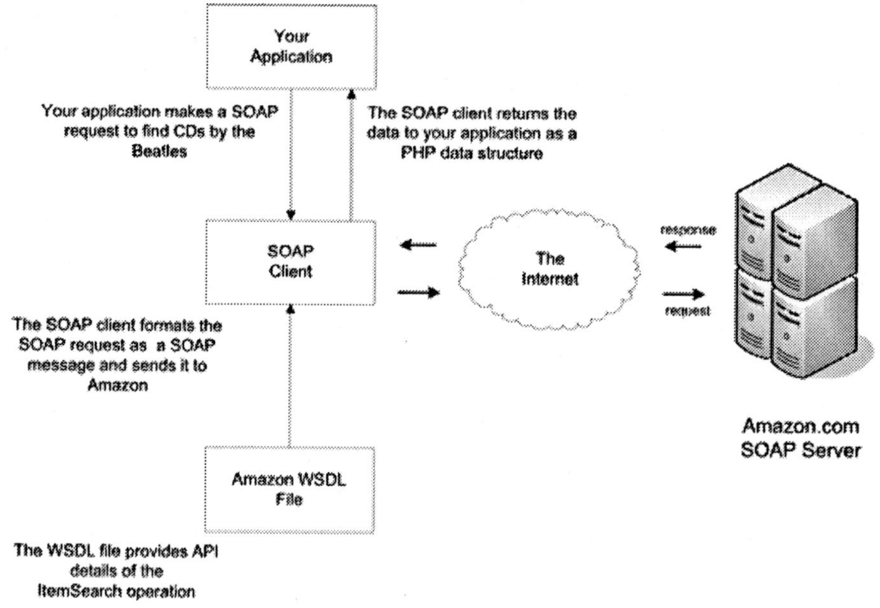

Figure 2-1 The SOAP model for accessing Amazon E-Commerce Service

Responses from the Amazon SOAP server are valid XML. The SOAP client parses the XML and returns it to your PHP application as a PHP data structure.

REST Model For Accessing Amazon E-commerce Service

REST stands for "REpresentational State Transfer", a name coined by Roy Fielding in his Ph.D thesis (*http://www.ics.uci.edu/~fielding/pubs/dissertation/top.htm*). REST is a design philosophy for software architecture that is particularly well-suited to Amazon E-Commerce Service.

The REST model for accessing network-based resources over the Internet utilizes the fundamental operations that are specified in the HTTP standard: POST, GET, PUT, and DELETE. Much to the dismay of REST purists, Amazon has chosen to only use HTTP GET requests with Amazon E-Commerce Service.

> Serious discussions about REST take place frequently on the rest-discuss mailing list. You can join the Yahoo Group at http://groups.yahoo.com/group/rest-discuss

In Amazon's implementation, a request is a single URL that uses HTTP GET encoding -- all input parameters are appended to the request URL with ampersands. A developer creates the URL and simply sends it to Amazon programmatically by using an "open" call. Amazon responds by returning the XML-encoded response directly (figure 2-2).

The elegance of Amazon's take on the REST model is that all requests are simply URLs and can be demonstrated by cutting and pasting the request URL into a web browser.

A request to search for information about an Amazon customer with the email address jeff@amazon.com looks like this:

```
http://webservices.amazon.com/onca/xml?Service=AWSECommerceService&
SubscriptionId=1A7XKHR5BYDOWPJVQEG2&AssociateTag=ws&Version=2005-02-23&
Operation=CustomerContentSearch&Email=jeff%40amazon.com
```

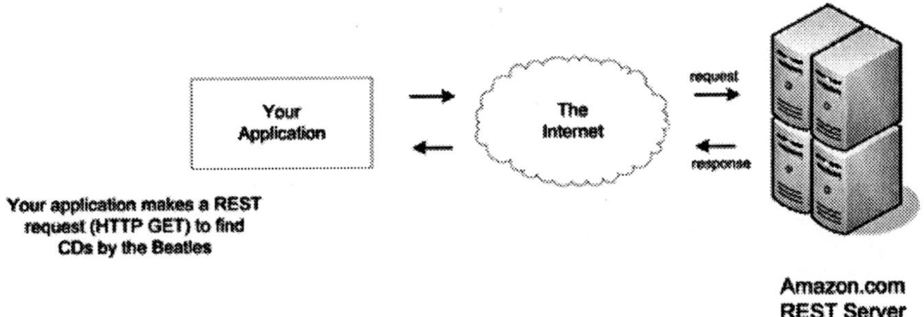

Figure 2-2 Using REST to access Amazon E-Commerce Service

The Amazon XSLT Service

Amazon maintains an XSLT server that can be used with the REST style request to transform your requests into other data formats. XSLT, which stands for eXtensible Stylesheet Language Transformations (*http://www.w3.org/TR/xslt*), is a language for describing how to transform XML data into another data format. In the case of Amazon E-commerce Service, this usually means transforming XML data into HTML for display in our web pages. Developers place their XSLT stylesheet on a publicly accessibly web site and include the URL to the stylesheet in their REST request. The Amazon server uses the stylesheet to transform the XML result into HTML or whatever format the stylesheet specifies (figure 2-3).

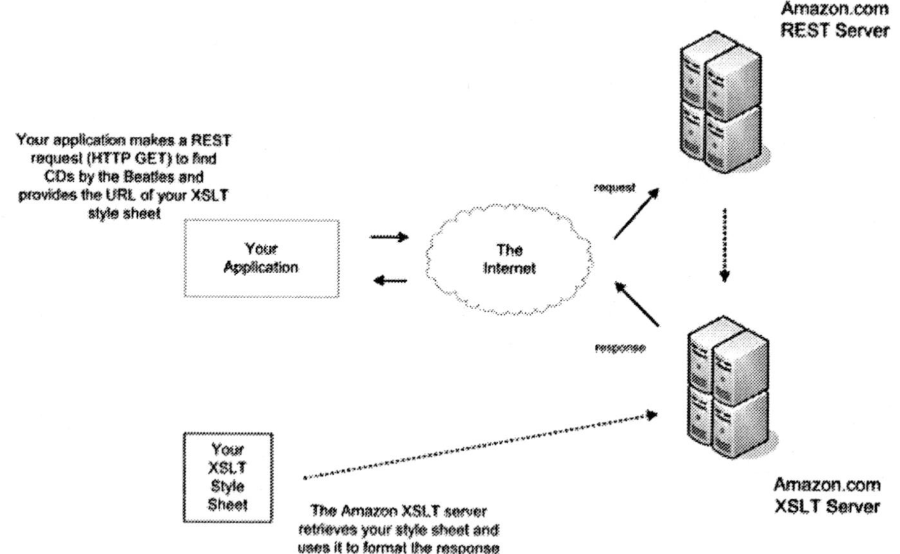

Figure 2-3 Using XSLT to access Amazon E-Commerce Service

SOAP Or REST? Making The Choice

SOAP or REST? Developers may use both if they choose, but from a design and maintenance standpoint, it's easier to go with one method or the other. The majority of developers used the REST API with Amazon Web Services version 3, and there is little reason to expect that will change in Amazon E-Commerce Service 4. The main reason is that the REST API is more intuitive. It requires nothing other than a web browser to demonstrate and is easier to understand than SOAP. SOAP's primary advantage is its support in various programmer toolkits and libraries. Thus, despite the fact that SOAP is more complex than REST, it can be easier to deploy for professional developers.

> If Amazon E-Commerce Service required secure authentication or attachments, there would be fewer advantages to using REST over SOAP. SOAP has standards for deploying secure authentication and attachments while REST developers must use ad hoc approaches.

Ultimately, choosing which one to use depends on your priorities. If you're adding Amazon E-commerce Service to an existing application, and raw speed isn't an absolute priority, then SOAP may be the easiest path. If you want to design the leanest and fasted possible application from scratch that depends on Amazon E-commerce Service, REST is the best choice. Non-programmers who want quick results, or people on a very tight budget, will find that using Amazon's XSLT service via the REST interface is the way to go.

	REST		SOAP	
Performance	✓	Encoded URLs are simple and fast		Verbose XML protocol slows transactions
Programming Ease	✓	The HTTP GET model is simple for even non-programmers to understand		SOAP requires that the programmer deal with a more complex XML request structure
Toolkit Support		The HTTP GET model lacks the standardized formats available for SOAP	✓	Most toolkits have SOAP objects that are easy to manipulate.
Learning Curve	✓	See Programming Ease above.		SOAP's platform and transport-independent architecture is harder to understand

Table 2-1 REST versus SOAP: which one should you use with Amazon E-Commerce Service?

The Case for REST

REST has raw speed, a simpler programming model and the ability to make XSLT transforms going for it. In my own benchmarks, I found that REST requests, including parsing using PHP's expat library, were generally about twice as fast as a SOAP client written in PHP. We're still talking only hundreds of milliseconds here, but with enough users hitting your site, the difference may begin to be noticeable. REST is easier to grasp than SOAP because it can be demonstrated using just URLs that even non-programmers are familiar with. In contrast, SOAP uses a more traditional function call interface, usually wrapped in an object-oriented class structure, which, although fairly easy to demonstrate, is not as straightforward as REST. Using the REST interface also offers the option of letting the Amazon E-commerce Service server do XSLT transformations for you (the XSLT transformation service is not accessible via SOAP). This can be quite a boon for non-programmers as it offers the potential of doing most, or even all, of your interactions using XSL style sheets. Though XSL is, after all, a scripting language as well, it's considerably easier to deploy since it requires no programming language support on your server.

The Case for SOAP

SOAP has good toolkit support from many vendors. If you're a professional programmer, you'll appreciate that many vendors offer plug-n-play tools for SOAP interfaces. Microsoft's Visual Studio.NET and IBM's Eclipse, for example, both make it easy to add SOAP interfaces to your applications. Most SOAP clients also have built-in XML parsers, so they return Amazon's XML-encoded data to you as a data structure in your native language. With REST, you have to develop your own parser or interface with an existing parser library which usually requires more effort.

Because they are written in PHP, the overhead of using the two most popular PHP SOAP clients, NuSOAP and PEAR SOAP, is about twice as much as using REST. Still, for many applications, the extra milliseconds of difference may not be significant. If you can use PHP5, you'll gain another 50% more performance (PHP5's built-in SOAP library is compiled C code).

Getting Started With Amazon E-commerce Service

The rest of this chapter will show you how to get up and running with Amazon E-Commerce Services.

> The techniques and technologies described in this chapter are also applicable to other Amazon Web Services, such as Amazon's Simple Queue Service or Alexa Web Information Service.

In order to do anything with Amazon E-commerce Service, you need to obtain a Subscription ID, and, optionally, an Associates ID (also called an Associates Tag). You'll also want to download Amazon's developer documentation.

Obtaining An Amazon Subscription ID

All Amazon E-commerce Service developers must get their 20 character, alphanumeric, Subscription ID from the same place:

```
http://www.amazon.com/gp/aws/registration/registration-form.html
```

Your Subscription ID lets you make a web services request to any of the Amazon web services-enabled sites: amazon.ca, amazon.com, amazon.de, amazon.fr, amazon.co.uk, and amazon.co.jp. Your Subscription ID also acts as the primary form of user identification (the other is the originating IP address of your application). Amazon uses your Subscription ID to keep track of requests made by applications you've written. If you distribute the applications you've written, you should make sure that requests generated by your application use your Subscription ID so that Amazon can generate statistics on your application usage.

Since you can create as many Subscription IDs as you want by merely signing up using a different email address, it makes sense to use one Subscription ID for development purposes and another to distribute with your application. In general, you should keep your development Subscription ID private.

Currently, if an application breaches the terms of the Amazon Web Services licensing agreement, it's possible that the originating IP address of the application will be blacklisted (I discuss the terms of the Amazon Web Services Licensing Agreement later in this chapter). In the future, it's possible that Amazon might blacklist offending Subscription IDs as well.

When Amazon starts charging for access to some premium services, such as Amazon Simple Queue Services, your Subscription ID will be used to charge you for access to those services (should you choose to subscribe to them). That's yet another reason to keep your Subscription ID private.

As I mentioned, you can sign-up for several Subscription IDs by simply providing different email addresses. I recommend doing so, just in case you need to distribute some working code, or test your applications in a non-secure environment.

Obtaining An Associates ID

Although the Subscription ID is the only required piece of developer identification that you need to use Amazon E-commerce Service, it's worthwhile to also obtain an Associates ID as that's the only way to make money when people click-through from your applications and purchase products from Amazon.

You get an Associates ID when you join the Amazon Associates program. Unlike the Subscription Id, the Associates ID is country-dependent. You must have an Associates ID from each country whose web services you are using if you want to make money on sales from that Amazon country site (see Chapter Seven for details on signing up for the Associates program for Amazon's international web sites).

You can sign-up for an Associates ID for the United States here:

```
http://associates.amazon.com/exec/panama/associates/apply
```

> If you don't feel like signing up for an Associates ID yet, you can use the generic Associates Id, "ws". Though the Associates ID is an optional parameter, it's useful to get in the habit of including it in your requests. You will not receive credit for click-through purchases when using the Associates ID, "ws".

Download The Developer Kit

Although this book largely supplants the need to use the documentation pages provided by Amazon, their pages may contain updated information that could provide insight into why things aren't quite working as expected. You can download the

Amazon E-Commerce Service 4.0 documentation at Browse Node ID 3487571, *http://www.amazon.com/exec/obidos/tg/browse/-/3487571*

> If this link doesn't work for some reason, you can go to the main Amazon E-Commerce Service site at http://webservices.amazon.com

The Amazon Licensing Agreement

The applications you develop using Amazon E-Commerce Service should adhere to the Amazon Web Services licensing agreement. The licensing restrictions keep users from abusing the service which could affect performance or access for other users. Unfortunately, as we'll see, the licensing terms also require more work for developers. The agreement can be found at *http://www.amazon.com/aws-licensing-agreement*

> As we go to press, the title of the document is "Web Services Licensing Agreement".

The licensing agreement puts several restrictions on your use of Amazon E-commerce Service that will affect how you can access and use the data. Failure to adhere to the licensing agreement may result in the blacklisting of your Subscription ID or originating IP address.

The One Request Per Second Rule

The licensing agreement states:

You may make calls... to Amazon Web Services 24hrs a day, 7 days a week, provided you: (i) do not exceed 1 call per second....If you build and release and application, the 1 call per second limitation applies to each installed copy of the Application.

The one call per second rule was arrived at arbitrarily -- someone at Amazon decided that "it sounded about right." The reality is that Amazon's Web Service lets you make slightly more than one call (request) per second.

> As we'll see later in this chapter, it's possible to make batch or multi-operation requests that bundle up to four requests in a single request to Amazon's servers. A batch or multi-operation request counts as "one call". It's also possible to execute multiple REST requests from within an XSLT style sheet using the XSLT document() function. This is also considered "one call".

When your average request time stays at more than one call per second for a brief period of time, Amazon's servers will start returning errors and no results. Specifically, when your call fails because you're making requests too quickly, you may get an HTTP error code of 503 (service unavailable) or 500 (internal server error) returned. Or, you may get an error code returned within your response, typically an AWS.InternalError code. Amazon may return these codes several times before resuming successful responses to your requests. For application developers, this means that caching of queries is essential for high volume Amazon applications -- for lower-volume applications, you may be able to get by with just pausing and re-trying the request multiple times.

The phrase "each installed copy" refers to each unique IP address from which the application originates. So, if your application is installed on a web server, and ten people use it simultaneously, Amazon still sees that as one installed copy and those ten users must make, together, only one call per second to Amazon's servers (that's a slow application!). As I mentioned before, caching, or re-trying requests, is essential.

The 40k File Size Rule

The licensing agreement states:

You may make calls... to Amazon E-commerce Service 24hrs a day, 7 days a week, provided you: (i) do not...send files greater than 40K.

This rule only applies to Amazon's XSLT server since that's the only time a file that you provide is uploaded to Amazon's servers. The 40 kilobyte file size refers to the maximum size of a single XSL stylesheet. Practically speaking, this limitation will keep developers from overloading Amazon's XSLT server with huge stylesheets.

Storing Amazon Data

Data you extract from Amazon via Amazon E-commerce Service must be refreshed frequently to ensure its accuracy. The reason for this is that most of the data describes products, and that product data, especially prices, tends to change frequently. On the other hand, some product data, such as the singer on a particular CD, never changes. Thus, Amazon's licensing agreement varies on the lengths of time you may store data before the information must be refreshed.

> I use the term "store" loosely. Storage could be a set of static web pages that contain data extracted via Amazon E-commerce Service or it could be an Oracle or MySQL database. Amazon's licensing agreement refers to "storage" and also to "caching". In a pure legal sense, if the data you extract from Amazon resides anywhere, it must adhere to these database guidelines.

For Amazon E-commerce Service 4.0, the following are the storage guidelines. When the data points are refreshed in the database, they must also be refreshed on any public-facing web sites:

- The following XML data elements can be stored for up to 3 months: URL, ASIN, Title, Artist, Author, Director, Manufacturer, Release Date, Publisher, Num Media, UPC, Reading Level, Theatrical Release Date, Platform, ESRBAgeRating, Encoding
- Pricing and availability information must be refreshed every week.

- All other data retrieved from Amazon E-commerce Service must be refreshed every 24 hours.

> As this book goes to press, Amazon has still not updated the list of data elements for E-Commerce Service 4.0. The list of elements above is from E-Commerce Service 3.0 (though most are in ECS 4 as well), but there are many more data elements to consider in ECS 4.

Handling Price and Availability Data

Prices and availability data retrieved from Amazon requires special handling since those data points are among the most volatile, and also the most likely to get you into trouble. If you display the Amazon price of a camcorder as $500, but Amazon had raised the price to $600 the day before, you are likely to have some irate customers. To minimize the chances of such situations occurring, Amazon's licensing agreement spells out how pricing and availability data should be handled.

If you decide to display prices, the last refresh time, as well as a linked or displayed disclaimer, should be included when you display pricing or availability data. If you refresh your data less than once a day, you would need to include the date, otherwise, the time is sufficient.

An example of displaying prices when refreshing the price less than once a day:

```
Amazon.com Price: $32.77 (as of 01/07/2004) more info
```

An example of displaying prices when refreshing the price at least once a day:

```
Amazon.com Price: $32.77 (as of 2pm PST) more info
```

The "more info" link should lead to a popup or other box that reads: "Price is accurate as of the date/time indicated. Prices and product availability are subject to change. Any price displayed on the Amazon website at the time of purchase will govern the sale of this product."

You can link to the disclaimer (as above) or just display it on your web page.

If you're just displaying availability, it would need to look something like this:

```
Item usually ships in 1-2 business days   more info
```

Using Amazon Graphics

It's generally ok to download or link to graphics used by Amazon, such as their star ratings stars or shopping cart icon, provided that you are using them in conjunction with data retrieved via Amazon E-commerce Service. The licensing agreement states:

As long as you are in compliance with the terms of this Agreement, we grant you a non-exclusive, revocable, royalty-free license to use any graphic images and text described in Section 4...solely for the purpose of indicating that a material, product or process that you created is used or based on Amazon E-Commerce Service.

Section 4 further states that:

We will make available to you certain small graphic images that you may use in conjunction with the display of the Amazon Properties. For instance, if you display Listmania(r) information on or within your Application, you may... display the Listmania logo.

The phrase "will make available" suggests that there is a package of graphics that you can download, but no such set of graphics has ever been offered by Amazon. You simply scrape the images that you need off of the Amazon web site.

> If you have questions about the licensing agreement, send email to webservices@amazon.com

Licensing Agreement Enforcement

If you look at existing Amazon-based applications, you may notice that some are totally in compliance with the Amazon licensing agreement while others are not. In particular, I see a lot of applications based on Amazon E-Commerce Service that don't display the price and availability disclaimers, and they probably aren't refreshing their data from Amazon as much as they should. Amazon has no specific enforcement policy, other than the 1 second rule which is automatically enforced when Amazon's servers throttle your access, and the 40Kbyte maximum XSLT style sheet size which is similarly handled. With thousands of live applications using Amazon E-Commerce Service, you may never be censured for breaking some aspects of the licensing agreement, but if any customers complain about your application, you may get noticed. Is it worth taking a chance? I won't say either way.

Conditions Of Use Agreement

At the very bottom of every page on the Amazon.com web site, you'll see a link for "Conditions Of Use." This link spells out, in rather draconian terms, all of the basic legalese necessary to protect Amazon's trademarks, patents, copyrights, and other intellectual property.

> The Conditions of Use agreement can be found here: http://www.amazon.com/exec/obidos/subst/misc/policy/conditions-of-use.html

The agreement, at first glance, seems to conflict with the Web Services Licensing agreement. There are statements like this one:

This site or any portion of this site may not be reproduced, duplicated, copied, sold, resold, visited, or otherwise exploited for any commercial purpose without express written consent of Amazon.com.

Of course, these are exactly the things that Amazon E-Commerce Service allows developers to do. You should first look to the Web Services Licensing agreement to determine what you are allowed to do with Amazon E-Commerce Service and related

Amazon properties, and then look at the Conditions Of Use agreement for other possible restrictions.

Configuring PHP For Use With Amazon E-Commerce Service

In order to run the various code samples in this book, you'll need to make sure your PHP installation is configured properly.

PHP4

If you're using PHP4, I assume you're using PHP 4.3 or newer. Many examples in the book will run on PHP version 4.1 or greater, but for both stability and security reasons, you should run version 4.3 or newer.

- The fopen url wrappers should be on so that you can open URLs with file_get_contents(). Make sure the line "allow_url_fopen = On" is in your php.ini file.

For the advanced XSLT examples, Seller Services, and International Amazon examples, you should have the Mbstring, Sablotron, and Curl with OpenSSL extensions loaded.

- The Curl with OpenSSL extension should be loaded so that you can connect via HTTPS to Amazon Seller Service. For Windows servers, uncomment the line "extension=php_curl.dll" in your php.ini file. For Unix servers, uncomment the line extension=curl.so.
- The Mbstring extension should be loaded so that you can handle character encoding translations for the International Amazon examples. For Windows servers, uncomment the line "extension=php_mbstring.dll" in your php.ini file. For Unix servers, uncomment the line extension=mbstring.so. Instead of mbstring, you may use the iconv library -- see *www.php.net/iconv*

PHP5

PHP5 hasn't been around that long, but running the latest version available is a good idea. All of the examples in this book have been tested on version 5.03. Most of the examples in the book will work with vanilla PHP5 installations provided fopen wrappers are turned on.

- The fopen url wrappers should be on so that you can open URLs with file_get_contents(). Make sure the line "allow_url_fopen = On" is in your php.ini file.

If you are developing with SOAP then you'll want PHP5's bundled SOAP extension loaded:

- The libxml2 SOAP extension should be loaded so that you can run the SOAP examples. For Windows servers, uncomment the line "extension=php_soap.dll" in your php.ini file. For Unix servers, uncomment the line extension=soap.so.

For the Seller Services and International Amazon examples, you should have the Iconv, Sablotron, Curl, and OpenSSL extensions loaded:

- The Curl and OpenSSL extensions should be loaded so that you can connect via HTTPS to Amazon Seller Service. For Windows servers, uncomment the line "extension=php_curl.dll" in your php.ini file. For Unix servers, uncomment the line extension=curl.so.
- The Iconv extension should be loaded so that you can do character encoding translations for the International Amazon examples. For Windows servers, uncomment the line "extension=php_iconv.dll" in your php.ini file. For Unix servers, uncomment the line "extension=iconv.so".

Checking For PHP Compatibility

You can easily determine what PHP features are enabled or disabled on your server by running this one line PHP script and examining the output.

```
<?php
echo phpinfo();
?>
```

Tools for Developing with Amazon E-commerce Service

There are a plethora of available development tools for developing with PHP and XML, both free and commercial. While it's perfectly ok to use just a text editor and your web browser to develop applications using Amazon E-commerce Service (and some people do), a good-quality XML-savvy editor and PHP development environment can help immensely. I used Zend's Zend Studio and Altova's XMLspy to validate and create the examples in this book.

IDE	Cost	Mac	Win	Linux	Notes
Zend Studio	$249	Y	Y	Y	From the creators of PHP, Zend Studio is feature-packed and cross-platform. www.zend.com
NuSphere PHPed	$299	N	Y	Y**	A somewhat more mature IDE than Zend Studio with better database integration. www.nusphere.com
PHP Coder	free	N	Y	N	A basic IDE for Windows. www.phpide.com
IDE.PHP	free	Y	Y	Y	Not an IDE, but an innovative browser-based PHP development tool. Very simplistic but quite useful for rapid prototyping. www.ekenberg.se/php/ide
PHP Designer 2005	free	N	Y	N	An impressive PHP design tool that has a full-featured editing environment though it lacks a debugger. http://www.mpsoftware.dk/

** Red Hat Linux only

Table 2-2 Selected PHP development tools

A good XML editor can tidy-up your XML tags, validate XML and XSLT, display WSDL details, and let you build SOAP requests. They are quite useful for debugging and managing your XML usage, but they are not absolutely essential.

XML tools	cost	Mac	Win	Linux	Notes
Altova XMLspy Professional	$499	N	Y	N	www.altova.com. Pricey but feature-packed. This product is used by Amazon.com's own developers.
Tibco Turbo XML	$269	Y	Y	Y**	www.tibco.com. A more Enterprise-focused product line with deep cross-platform support.
Oxygen	$69	Y	Y	Y**	www.oxygenxml.com. Lots of features, including extensive document generation capabilities make Oxygen worth checking out. Also has a plugin for the Java Eclipse IDE.

** Also runs on many Unix variants

Table 2-3 Selected XML development tools

Amazon WSDL Files

Web Service Description Language (WSDL) is an XML language used to describe a Web Services API.

The WSDL standard is available at http://www.w3.org/TR/wsdl

Amazon's WSDL file completely describes the Amazon E-Commerce Service API. Both request elements and response elements are listed. Though the WSDL file is used only when making SOAP requests, I'll be referring to it throughout the book.

File Type	Location
Amazon WSDL File	http://webservices.amazon.com/AWSECommerceService/US/AWSECommerceService.wsdl
Amazon Schema File	http://webservices.amazon.com/AWSECommerceService/US/AWSECommerceService.xsd

Table 2-4 The Amazon.com WSDL and Schema files

Amazon also has XML Schema files which are another format for describing a web services API.

The XML Schema standard is available at http://www.w3.org/TR/xmlschema-0

Developing With REST And PHP

REST eschews the overhead of SOAP messaging and instead uses the standard protocols of the web to request data. This turns out to be a great solution for Amazon since Amazon E-commerce Service requests tend to be small and simple. The main advantage of using REST over SOAP is raw speed, but REST with PHP4 also requires more work to use. The extra work required is the need to write (or find) a suitable XML parser to turn the XML data returned by amazon into a PHP data structure that we can work with (With PHP5, we can use the built-in SimpleXML parser).

Making A REST Request

Creating REST requests requires that you string together a series of parameters separated by ampersands. To illustrate, we'll create an ItemLookup request. ItemLookup looks up an item from the Amazon product database. In this case, we'll request the item whose ASIN is equal to B0001BKAEY. This turns out to be the DVD "Matrix Revolutions".

The first part of all REST requests to Amazon E-Commerce Service is always the same. It's the domain name and path to the entry point for Amazon E-Commerce Service:

```
http://webservices.amazon.com/onca/xml?
```

Next are a series of parameter/value combinations in the form:

```
parameter=value & parameter=value & parameter=value ...
```

The complete request, which you can type into your web browser to run, looks like this:

```
http://webservices.amazon.com/onca/xml?Service=AWSECommerceService&
SubscriptionId=1A7XKHR5BYD0WPJVQEG2&AssociateTag=ws&Version=2005-02-23&
Operation=ItemLookup&ItemId=B0001BKAEY&IdType=ASIN&ResponseGroup=Request,Small
```

A breakdown of the parameters in our request is in Table 2-5.

parameter	value	purpose
Service	AWSECommerceService	Directs the request to Amazon E-Commerce Service
SubscriptionId	1A7XKHR5BYD0WPJVQEG2	A Subscription Id
AssociateTag	ws	Identifies our Amazon Associates account
Version	2005-02-23	The version of Amazon E-commerce Service we are using
Operation	ItemLookup	The method we wish to invoke
ItemId	B0001BKAEY	The ID of the product we're looking for

parameter	value	purpose
IdType	`ASIN`	`The type of product ID we're looking up. In this case, an ASIN`
ResponseGroup	`Request,Small`	`The types of data we want returned in the response from Amazon.com`

Table 2-5 Elements of the sample REST request

A couple of important things to note about our request:

- The order of parameters does not matter.
- Case does matter. All Amazon requests are case-sensitive.

The request URL may look long and daunting at first, but when you realize that the first four parameters will almost always be the same for every request, it's much easier to digest. The Service, SubscriptionId, and AssociateTag, will probably never change for any request you make. The Version will eventually change (we'll talk more about versions of Amazon E-Commerce Service later) but rarely more than once a month. So, you can safely begin all of your REST requests with the following string (use your Subscription ID in place of this one, of course!):

```
http://webservices.amazon.com/onca/xml?Service=AWSECommerceService&
SubscriptionId=1A7XKHR5BYD0WPJVQEG2&AssociateTag=ws&Version=2005-02-23
```

A REST Request Using PHP

I'll use PHP's file_get_contents() function which reads the data from a file (or URL in this case) to make a REST request and return the response in a string. In order to make the output look good in our web browser, we have to run it through the PHP htmlspecialchars function. We do that because most web browsers will attempt to interpret anything enclosed in angle brackets '<'...'>' (such as our XML output). The htmlspecialchars function turns the XML angle bracket characters into HTML entities. The web browser will interpret the encoded characters and display their decoded values instead of evaluating them as if they were some kind of HTML tag.

> The allow_url_fopen option must be set on your server's PHP installation in order to allow fopen or file_get_contents to open a URL.

Example 2-1 Making a simple REST request

```
<?php

// Our REST request
$request='http://webservices.amazon.com/onca/xml?Service=AWSECommerceService
&SubscriptionId=1A7XKHR5BYD0WPJVQEG2&AssociateTag=ws&Operation=ItemLookup&
ItemId=B0001BKAEY&IdType=ASIN&ResponseGroup=Request,Small&Version=2005-02-23';

// Fetch the URL into a string
```

```
$response=file_get_contents($request);

// Echo the string, encoding any angle brackets and other special characters
echo htmlspecialchars($response, ENT_QUOTES);
?>
```

The output of this program is:


```
<?xml version="1.0" encoding="UTF-8"?>
<ItemLookupResponse xmlns="http://webservices.amazon.com/AWSECommerceService/2005-02-
23">
  <OperationRequest>
    <HTTPHeaders>
      <Header Name="UserAgent"/>
    </HTTPHeaders>
    <RequestId>1F7NAZQ8K28B1KPAW9DB</RequestId>
    <Arguments>
      <Argument Name="Service" Value="AWSECommerceService"/>
      <Argument Name="AssociateTag" Value="ws"/>
      <Argument Name="SubscriptionId" Value="1A7XKHR5BYDOWPJVQEG2"/>
      <Argument Name="Version" Value="2005-02-23"/>
      <Argument Name="ItemId" Value="B0001BKAEY"/>
      <Argument Name="IdType" Value="ASIN"/>
      <Argument Name="ResponseGroup" Value="Request,Small"/>
      <Argument Name="Operation" Value="ItemLookup"/>
    </Arguments>
    <RequestProcessingTime>0.0113139152526855</RequestProcessingTime>
  </OperationRequest>
  <Items>
    <Request>
      <IsValid>True</IsValid>
      <ItemLookupRequest>
        <IdType>ASIN</IdType>
        <ItemId>B0001BKAEY</ItemId>
        <ResponseGroup>Request</ResponseGroup>
        <ResponseGroup>Small</ResponseGroup>
      </ItemLookupRequest>
    </Request>
    <Item>
      <ASIN>B0001BKAEY</ASIN>
      <DetailPageURL>http://www.amazon.com/gp/redirect.html?tag=ws&amp;location=/
exec/obidos/ASIN/B0001BKAEY%3FSubscriptionId=1A7XKHR5BYDOWPJVQEG2</DetailPageURL>
      <ItemAttributes>
        <Actor>Laurence Fishburne</Actor>
        <Director>Larry Wachowski</Director>
        <Director>Andy Wachowski</Director>
        <ProductGroup>DVD</ProductGroup>
        <Title>The Matrix Revolutions (Widescreen Edition)</Title>
      </ItemAttributes>
    </Item>
  </Items>
</ItemLookupResponse>
```

Your output may not look as nice as this (I used XMLSpy to format the tag output). In fact, your output may even have somewhat different data. Such is the dynamic nature of Amazon's product database.

Structure Of An Amazon Response

Amazon's XML responses always contain certain sections. The general structure of all Amazon E-Commerce Service responses looks like this:

```
<?xml version="1.0" encoding="UTF-8">
<[Your Operation Name+"Response"] xmlns="http://webservices.amazon.com/
AWSECommerceService/2005-02-23">
  <OperationRequest>
      <HTTPHeaders>
            [Some HTTP Headers sent in your request are listed here]
      </HTTPHeaders>
      <RequestId>[A unique ID generated by Amazon's server]</RequestId>
      <Arguments>
            [Your request arguments are echoed here]
      </Arguments>
      <RequestProcessingTime>[Request processing time]</RequestProcessingTime>
  </OperationRequest>
  <[Operation-dependent container tag here]>
             ...
            [Amazon's response]
             ...
  </[Operation-dependent container tag here]>
</[Your Operation Name+"Response"]>
```

The response always begins with the standard XML header:

```
<?xml version="1.0" encoding="UTF-8"?>
```

Since we did an ItemLookup request, the [Your Method Name+"Response"] is ItemLookupResponse. The Amazon namespace identifier is always included.

```
<ItemLookupResponse xmlns="http://webservices.amazon.com/AWSECommerceService/2005-02-
23">
```

Inside the HTTPHeaders container tag, Amazon echoes your UserAgent HTTP header which usually identifies the type of program or web browser that makes the request. There is none here since a PHP program initiated the request.

```
<Header Name="UserAgent"/>
```

Amazon also generates a unique RequestId for every request that is placed in the RequestId tag. If there's a problem with your request, you can contact Amazon and give them the RequestId and UserAgent information so that they can try to isolate the problem.

```
<RequestId>1A7XKHR5BYDOWPJVQEG2</RequestId>
```

The arguments that you sent in your request are echoed back inside the <Arguments> tag. This is useful when you're debugging and want to make sure that Amazon is receiving your request parameters correctly. It's also quite useful for passing parameters to your XSLT applications (See the "XSLT Version Of ProductSense" in Chapter Three).

```
<Arguments>
     <Argument Name="Service" Value="AWSECommerceService"/>
     <Argument Name="AssociateTag" Value="ws"/>
     <Argument Name="SubscriptionId" Value="1A7XKHR5BYD0WPJVQEG2"/>
     <Argument Name="Ver sion" Value="2005-02-23"/>
     <Argument Name="ItemId" Value="B0001BKAEY"/>
     <Argument Name="IdType" Value="ASIN"/>
     <Argument Name="ResponseGroup" Value="Request,Small"/>
     <Argument Name="Operation" Value="ItemLookup"/>
  </Arguments>
```

Strangely enough, when Internet Explorer, Netscape Communicator, and some other browsers display XML, they automatically shorten empty tags into terminated tags. So, in this example, the Argument tags are actually returned like this: <Argument Name="Service" Value="AWSECommerceService"></Argument>But when displayed in your browser, the browser alters them to look like this: <Argument Name="Service" Value="AWSECommerceService"/>

Amazon also returns the amount of time it took to process your request in seconds.

```
<RequestProcessingTime>0.0113139152526855</RequestProcessingTime>
```

The actual response data from Amazon is inside a method-dependent container tag. For most of the methods, that tag is <Items>, which indicates that product information follows.

The contents of the response data from Amazon depends on the Response Groups that you indicate in your request. Here, we used ResponseGroup=Small,Request, which asks for the Request and Small Response Groups.

Small and Request are also the default Response Groups for the ItemLookup method, so we could have omitted them from the request entirely.

The <Request> section is always returned first if the Request Response Group is returned (the Request Response Group is always returned by default unless you specify otherwise).

Inside the <Request> section is the tag <IsValid> which tells us whether Amazon thinks your request is valid or not. If the word False is contained there, then our request is invalid and Amazon includes an error message section explaining why the request is invalid. If the word True is there, then our request is valid (though there may still be a request execution error, such as the inability to find a requested item).

The rest of the <Request> section lists the parameters to our request, wrapped in <Method Name + "Request"> tags. In this case, <ItemLookupRequest>.

```
<Items>
 <Request>
   <IsValid>True</IsValid>
   <ItemLookupRequest>
     <IdType>ASIN</IdType>
     <ItemId>B0001BKAEY</ItemId>
     <ResponseGroup>Request</ResponseGroup>
     <ResponseGroup>Small</ResponseGroup>
   </ItemLookupRequest>
 </Request>
```

Finally, we get to the actual data returned, which is contained in the <Item> tag. Typically, this is a list of products. In our case, we got back just one item. The ASIN is returned, as well as the Detail Page URL, which is the URL we'll use in our applications to bring users to Amazon to purchase the product. Note that our Developer's Token and Associate's ID are embedded in the DetailPageURL.

```
 <Item>
     <ASIN>B0001BKAEY</ASIN>
     <DetailPageURL>http://www.amazon.com/gp/redirect.html?tag=ws&amp;location=/exec/
obidos/ASIN/B0001BKAEY%3FSubscriptionId=1A7XKHR5BYD0WPJVQEG2</DetailPageURL>
     <ItemAttributes>
       <Actor>Laurence Fishburne</Actor>
       <Director>Larry Wachowski</Director>
       <Director>Andy Wachowski</Director>
       <ProductGroup>DVD</ProductGroup>
       <Title>The Matrix Revolutions (Widescreen Edition)</Title>
     </ItemAttributes>
   </Item>
```

E-Commerce Service Error Handling

Amazon's E-Commerce Service server tries to identify two types of errors -- errors in the syntax or logic of your request, and errors in the execution of your request.

Errors in the syntax or logic of your request

If there is an error in the syntax or logic of your request, then the request is not processed by Amazon. The <IsValid> tag is set to "False" and an error section is returned in the XML response explaining the error.

Suppose our request in Example 2-1 was:

```
http://webservices.amazon.com/onca/xml?Service=AWSECommerceService&
SubscriptionId=1A7XKHR5BYD0WPJVQEG2&AssociateTag=ws&Operation=ItemLookup&
ItemId=B0001BKAEY&IdType=asin&ResponseGroup=Request,Small&Version=2005-02-23
```

I've changed IdType=ASIN to IdType=asin. Since requests are case-sensitive, this request is invalid. Placing this request in my web browser, the output I get is:

```
<?xml version="1.0" encoding="UTF-8"?>
```

```
<ItemLookupResponse xmlns="http://xml.amazon.com/AWSECommerceService/2005-02-23">
    <OperationRequest>
        <HTTPHeaders>
            <Header Name="UserAgent" Value="Mozilla/4.0 (compatible; MSIE 6.0;
Windows NT 5.1)"/>
        </HTTPHeaders>
        <RequestId>15K1EKN26YDMWKJHA7XY</RequestId>
        <Arguments>
            <Argument Name="Service" Value="AWSECommerceService"/>
            <Argument Name="AssociateTag" Value="ws"/>
            <Argument Name="SubscriptionId" Value="1A7XKHR5BYDOWPJVQEG2"/>
            <Argument Name="ItemId" Value="B0001BKAEY"/>
            <Argument Name="IdType" Value="asin"/>
            <Argument Name="ResponseGroup" Value="Request,Small"/>
            <Argument Name="Operation" Value="ItemLookup"/>
        </Arguments>
    </OperationRequest>
    <Items>
        <Request>
            <IsValid>False</IsValid>
            <ItemLookupRequest>
                <IdType>asin</IdType>
                <ItemId>B0001BKAEY</ItemId>
                <ResponseGroup>Request</ResponseGroup>
                <ResponseGroup>Small</ResponseGroup>
            </ItemLookupRequest>
            <Errors>
                <Error>
                    <Code>AWS.InvalidEnumeratedParameter</Code>
                    <Message>The value you specified for IdType is invalid. Valid
values include UPC, SKU, EAN, ASIN.</Message>
                </Error>
            </Errors>
        </Request>
    </Items>
</ItemLookupResponse>
```

Note that <IsValid> is set to “False” and that the <Errors> section is where the Amazon response would normally be. Each Error has a <Code> element and a <Message> element. The list of error Codes is in Appendix D.

Errors in the execution of your request

If the request is valid, the <IsValid> tag is set to “True” and your request is executed by Amazon’s servers. If there are any execution errors in your request, an error section is returned in the response.

Suppose our request in Example 2-1 was:

```
http://webservices.amazon.com/onca/xml?Service=AWSECommerceService&
SubscriptionId=1A7XKHR5BYDOWPJVQEG2&AssociateTag=ws&Operation=ItemLookup&
ItemId=20001ZZZZZ&IdType=ASIN&ResponseGroup=Request,Small&Version=2005-02-23
```

This is a valid request, but I've changed the ASIN from B0001BKAEY to 20001ZZZZZ, and 20001ZZZZZ is not a valid ASIN value. Again, placing this request in my web browser, the output is:

```
<?xml version="1.0" encoding="UTF-8"?>
<ItemLookupResponse xmlns="http://xml.amazon.com/AWSECommerceService/2005-02-23">
    <OperationRequest>
        <HTTPHeaders>
            <Header Name="UserAgent" Value="Mozilla/4.0 (compatible; MSIE 6.0;
Windows NT 5.1)"/>
        </HTTPHeaders>
        <RequestId>1GDEWNAZ87JQK762K1WD</RequestId>
        <Arguments>
            <Argument Name="Service" Value="AWSECommerceService"/>
            <Argument Name="AssociateTag" Value="ws"/>
            <Argument Name="SubscriptionId" Value="1A7XKHR5BYDOWPJVQEG2"/>
            <Argument Name="ItemId" Value="20001ZZZZZ"/>
            <Argument Name="IdType" Value="ASIN"/>
            <Argument Name="ResponseGroup" Value="Request,Small"/>
            <Argument Name="Operation" Value="ItemLookup"/>
        </Arguments>
    </OperationRequest>
    <Items>
        <Request>
            <IsValid>True</IsValid>
            <ItemLookupRequest>
                <IdType>ASIN</IdType>
                <ItemId>20001ZZZZZ</ItemId>
                <ResponseGroup>Small</ResponseGroup>
                <ResponseGroup>Request</ResponseGroup>
            </ItemLookupRequest>
            <Errors>
                <Error>
                    <Code>AWS.InvalidParameterValue</Code>
                    <Message>20001ZZZZZ is not a valid value for ItemId. Please
change this value and retry your request.</Message>
                </Error>
            </Errors>
        </Request>
    </Items>
</ItemLookupResponse>
```

Note that <IsValid> is set to "True" because the request is valid. However, since the ASIN doesn't exist, Amazon returns an execution error.

Errors Returned With Good Data

In the case where <IsValid> is True but there are errors, it's possible that Amazon will return both good data **and** error messages in the same XML response.

Suppose our request in Example 2-1 was:

```
http://webservices.amazon.com/onca/xml?Service=AWSECommerceService&
SubscriptionId=1A7XKHR5BYDOWPJVQEG2&AssociateTag=ws&Operation=ItemLookup&
ItemId=B0001BKAEY,20001ZZZZZ&IdType=ASIN&ResponseGroup=Request,Small&
Version=2005-02-23
```

In this request, I've taken advantage of the fact that the ItemLookup operation can take a comma-separated list of up to ten ASINs to lookup in each request. The first ASIN is valid and the second ASIN is not.


```
<?xml version="1.0" encoding="UTF-8"?>
<ItemLookupResponse xmlns="http://webservices.amazon.com/AWSECommerceService/2004-11-
10">
  <OperationRequest>
    <HTTPHeaders>
      <Header Name="UserAgent" Value="Mozilla/4.0 (compatible; MSIE 6.0; Windows NT
5.1)"/>
    </HTTPHeaders>
    <RequestId>08QF7QY5Y9WWD2Q50FYP</RequestId>
    <Arguments>
      <Argument Name="Service" Value="AWSECommerceService"/>
      <Argument Name="AssociateTag" Value="ws"/>
      <Argument Name="SubscriptionId" Value="1A7XKHR5BYDOWPJVQEG2"/>
      <Argument Name="Version" Value="2005-02-23"/>
      <Argument Name="IdType" Value="ASIN"/>
      <Argument Name="ItemId" Value="B0001BKAEY,20001ZZZZZ"/>
      <Argument Name="ResponseGroup" Value="Request,Small"/>
      <Argument Name="Operation" Value="ItemLookup"/>
    </Arguments>
    <RequestProcessingTime>0.0123190879821777</RequestProcessingTime>
  </OperationRequest>
  <Items>
    <Request>
      <IsValid>True</IsValid>
      <ItemLookupRequest>
        <IdType>ASIN</IdType>
        <ItemId>20001ZZZZZ</ItemId>
        <ItemId>B0001BKAEY</ItemId>
        <ResponseGroup>Request</ResponseGroup>
        <ResponseGroup>Small</ResponseGroup>
      </ItemLookupRequest>
      <Errors>
        <Error>
          <Code>AWS.InvalidParameterValue</Code>
          <Message>20001ZZZZZ is not a valid value for ItemId. Please change this
value and retry your request.</Message>
        </Error>
      </Errors>
    </Request>
    <Item>
      <ASIN>B0001BKAEY</ASIN>
      <DetailPageURL>http://www.amazon.com/gp/redirect.html?tag=ws&amp;location=/
exec/obidos/ASIN/B0001BKAEY%3FSubscriptionId=1A7XKHR5BYDOWPJVQEG2</DetailPageURL>
      <ItemAttributes>
        <Actor>Laurence Fishburne</Actor>
```

```
        <Director>Larry Wachowski</Director>
        <Director>Andy Wachowski</Director>
        <ProductGroup>DVD</ProductGroup>
        <Title>The Matrix Revolutions (Widescreen Edition)</Title>
      </ItemAttributes>
    </Item>
  </Items>
</ItemLookupResponse>
```

Here, the error response is included along with the successful lookup of the other ASIN.

Amazon E-commerce Service Versioning For REST

All requests to Amazon E-Commerce Service can optionally include a version number which indicates which version of Amazon E-Commerce Service should be invoked to process the request. In the previous examples, the version parameter was "Version=2005-02-23". As Amazon makes incremental improvements to their service, the version will be changed. Note that the version is actually just a date, in this case, February 23rd, 2005.

> YYYY-MM-DD is an international standard calendar date format, according to the ISO 8601 standard. You have to pay for a copy of the standard, but many good discussions to it are linked from this page: http://dmoz.org/Science/Reference/Standards/Individual_Standards/ISO_8601

As Amazon E-commerce Service is updated, the calendar date on which the update occurs will be the new Version value.

> Amazon sometimes makes minor updates to E-Commerce Service without changing the version. These improvements should not cause problems for existing applications.

The Version parameter is optional. If you don't specify it, the latest version of Amazon E-commerce Service will always process your request by default. Because changes to Amazon E-commerce Service may break your application, it's a good idea to **always** specify the Version in your REST requests. Older versions of Amazon E-commerce Service should continue to be available for a long time as new versions are rolled out.

> Announcements about new versions of Amazon E-commerce Service are posted to the Amazon E-commerce Service forums at http://forums.prospero.com/n/mb/listsf.asp?webtag=am-assocdevxml, but the fastest way to find out about new versions is to simply check the default SOAP WSDL URL for changes: http://webservices.amazon.com/AWSECommerceService/US/AWSECommerceService.wsdl

To see how to adjust the version for SOAP applications, see "Amazon E-Commerce Versioning For SOAP". For XSLT applications, see "Amazon E-Commerce Versioning For XSLT".

> The very first released version of Amazon E-Commerce Service 4.0 was version "2004-08-01". As this book goes to press, the version is "2005-02-23"

A Better Read Routine

Although file_get_contents(), fopen(), and file(), are simple and convenient ways to send and receive data from PHP programs, they also offer less control and are typically twice as slow as the lower-level fsockopen call. Using fsockopen, our reads will be faster than fopen, and we will be able to capture HTTP responses from the Amazon server that wouldn't be available to us using other methods. Using fsockopen requires more coding than these other methods. We have to pretend our application is a web browser and send HTTP headers to mimick the call and response of an actual web browser (this call and response is handled automatically with calls like fopen()).

Our new replacement for file_get_contents() will be a function call named GetData that lets us specify the length of time we'll wait for data in case our network connection has problems or Amazon is slow. It returns false if an error occurs, or the Amazon data otherwise. GetData() can be used under either PHP4 or PHP5. GetData does for us exactly what file_get_contents() did, but also lets us set a timeout to wait for Amazon to respond, and also gives us access to the HTTP return code (if any) returned by Amazon.

With the addition of our new GetData routine, our simple example becomes:

Example 2-2 GetData, a better fopen routine for Amazon E-Commerce Service

```
function GetData($url, $timeout) {

    // Parse the URL into parameters for fsockopen
    $UrlArr = parse_url($url);
    $host = $UrlArr['host'];
    $port = (isset($UrlArr['port'])) ? $UrlArr['port'] : 80;
    $path = $UrlArr['path'] . '?' . $UrlArr['query'];

    // Zero out the error variables
    $errno = null;
    $errstr = '';

    // Open the connection to Amazon
    $fp = @fsockopen($host, $port, $errno, $errstr, $timeout);

    // Failed to open the URL
    if (!is_resource($fp)) {
```

```
        // fsockopen failed
        return false;
    }

    // Send an HTTP GET header and Host header
    if (!(fwrite($fp, 'GET '. $path .' HTTP/1.0' . "\r\n". 'Host: ' . $host . "\r\n\
r\n"))) {
        fclose($fp);
        // Could not write HTTP requests
        return false;
    }

    // Block on the socket port, waiting for response from Amazon
    if (function_exists('socket_set_timeout')) {
        @socket_set_timeout($fp, $timeout);
        socket_set_blocking($fp, true);
    }

    // Get the HTTP response code from Amazon
    $line = fgets($fp , 1024);

    if ($line == false){
        fclose($fp);
        // Amazon didn't respond
        return false;
    }

    // HTTP return code of 200 means success
    if (!(strstr($line, '200'))) {
        fclose($fp);
        // Didn't get the proper HTTP response code -- log this, if desired
        return false;
    }
    // Find blank line between header and data
    do {
        $line = fgets($fp , 1024);
        if ($line == false) {
            fclose($fp);
            // Didn't get data back from Amazon
            return false;
        }
        if (strlen($line) < 3) {
            break;
        }
    } while (true);

    $xml='';
    // Fetch the data from Amazon
    while ($line = fread($fp, 8192))
    {
        if ($line == false) {
            fclose($fp);
            // Couldn't read any data from Amazon
            return false;
```

```
        }
        $xml .= $line;
    }

    fclose($fp);
    return $xml;
}
?>
```

What GetData() does is build an HTTP GET call to Amazon using the request URL provided. You can add code to log the HTTP response, where indicated. The HTTP response code can be quite useful for determining the nature of connection problems when Amazon's service decides to temporarily flake out.

```
The unusual combination of the "GET" and "Host" HTTP headers in a single statement,
e.g.  fwrite($fp, 'GET '. $path .' HTTP/1.0' . "\n\n". 'Host: ' . $host . "\n\n") is
necessary because of a bug in Amazon's server.  The bug causes "GET" requests to
foreign Amazon web sites to redirect back to Amazon.com. The bug does not occur if
you use file_get_content() or fopen() instead of fsockopen().
```

Parsing XML

Unless we are using Amazon's XSLT engine (discussed later in this chapter), all REST requests sent to Amazon return XML. Even when there are logic errors in our requests, Amazon will return the error messages encoded as XML. In order to make sense of the response, we have to parse the XML into something that is usable by our application.

For the majority of applications based on Amazon E-Commerce Service, the goal is to take the XML returned by Amazon and parse it as quickly as we can into a PHP data structure. This means that we don't spend time validating the XML before parsing it, so a parsing error means that we dump the XML (and possibly log the error). Amazon is supposed to always return valid XML and we don't want to spend precious processing cycles dealing with cases when it doesn't.

Writing an XML parser that can handle all of the possible tag constructs in the XML 1.0 specification could be rather complex. Fortunately, Amazon doesn't return CDATA or more esoteric XML constructs, so we can focus on just parsing the types of XML data Amazon does return.

Parsing With PHP4

PHP4 does not come bundled with a ready-to-use XML parser, so we have to write our own. We want an event-driven parser, which means that we parse the XML stream as we receive it, quickly dumping the data into a PHP data structure.

PHP4 also comes with a DOM (Document Object Model) type of tree-based parsing library which is bundled as an extension to PHP4 (http://www.php.net/domxml).

There are a couple of approaches we can take to parsing data in PHP4 depending on how much information we're dealing with. For large amounts of XML, PHP4 includes a convenient XML parsing library, called expat, that we can use to help us write a parser. Expat is based on James Clark's expat parser, an event-driven parser, and it is included by default in PHP 4 distributions. Since it is written in C instead of PHP, it is quite fast.

> If you use a shared hosting provider who doesn't include expat, you can use the freely available expat clone, saxy, from Engage Interactive, that is written in PHP. (www.engageinteractive.com).

If you're just looking to extract a few data points, regular expressions may be both faster and simpler than using expat. XSLT is also a good choice for XML parsing, and it handles both parsing and layout at the same time.

Parsing Using Regular Expressions

It's surely possible to do all of your XML parsing using regular expressions, but it's only convenient when you need to extract a handful of data points from a large XML response. It's difficult to express all possible types of Amazon XML responses using regular expressions However, we can extract certain values fairly easily, and this may save you time when you're building your applications.

<table>
<tr><th>regular expression</th><th>purpose</th></tr>
<tr><td>/<(tagname)>(.*?)<\/tagname>/</td><td>Retrieve data for specified tag name</td></tr>
<tr><td>/<Argument Name="(.*?)" Value="(.*?)">/</td><td>Retrieve Name and Value attribute values from Amazon Argument tags</td></tr>
<tr><td>/<(tag1|tag2|tag3|tag4)*>(.*?)<\/\1>/</td><td>Retrieve all simple tags named tagN and their values</td></tr>
</table>

Table 2-6 Some useful regular expressions for parsing Amazon E-Commerce Service responses

We'll use PHP's preg_match_all function to illustrate returning selected tag values using the 3rd regular expression in Table 2-6. The regular expression returns the IsValid, ItemId, DetailPageURL, Title, and ProductGroup tags and their values using the regular expression

```
/<(IsValid|ItemId|DetailPageURL|Title|ProductGroup)*>(.*?)<\/\1>/
```

Out program uses the same data as in the previous section.

Example 2-3 XML parsing using regular expressions

```
<?php
// Our request string
$request='http://webservices.amazon.com/onca/
xml?Service=AWSECommerceService&SubscriptionId=1A7XKHR5BYDOWPJVQEG2&AssociateTag=ws&
Operation=ItemLookup&ItemId=B0001BKAEY&IdType=ASIN&ResponseGroup=Request,Small&
Version=2005-02-23';
```

```
// Fetch the URL into a string
$response=file_get_contents($request);

// Get listed tag values
$p='/<(IsValid|ItemId|Title|ProductGroup)*>(.*?)<\/\1>/';

// initialize array
$matches=array();

// fill matches array with tags and values
$num = preg_match_all ($p, $response, $matches);

// put array output into a string for easy display
$s=print_r($matches,true);

// print arrays to screen, escaping special characters
echo '<pre>'.htmlspecialchars($s, ENT_QUOTES).'</pre>';
?>
```

The preg_match_all function returns three arrays in this case. The first array contains the fully matched pattern. The second array contains the first matched pattern contained in '(...)', and the third array contains the second matched pattern contained in '(...)'.

```
Array
(
    [0] => Array
        (
            [0] => <IsValid>True</IsValid>
            [1] => <ItemId>B0001BKAEY</ItemId>
            [2] => <ProductGroup>DVD</ProductGroup>
            [3] => <Title>The Matrix Revolutions (Widescreen Edition)</Title>
        )
    [1] => Array
        (
            [0] => IsValid
            [1] => ItemId
            [2] => ProductGroup
            [3] => Title
        )
    [2] => Array
        (
            [0] => True
            [1] => B0001BKAEY
            [2] => DVD
            [3] => The Matrix Revolutions (Widescreen Edition)
        )
)
```

We can access the parsed values by using the array_search function.

```
// See if the string "ItemId" is in the $matches[1] array
$v=array_search('ItemId',$matches[1]);
// If ItemId is in $matches[1] array, then the corresponding value is
```

```
// in the $matches[2] array
if ($v !== false) {
$value=$matches[2][$v];
echo "Value of ItemId is: ".$value;
}
```

Regular expressions are fast and simple for retrieving specific tags, but become unwieldy when we try to parse and return repeated XML elements. Often, a better approach is to just parse the entire Amazon response into a PHP array.

The No Schema Problem

Before I get into parsing techniques, I want to mention a parsing problem that I call "The No Schema Problem," for lack of a better name. The No Schema Problem arises because we're parsing XML without the benefit of an XML Schema. An XML Schema tells us about the structure of the XML and the data types for each XML element.

> Amazon's schema is defined in their WSDL and XSD files. See the "Amazon WSDL Files" section later in this Chapter for details.

The specific problem we encounter when parsing XML without a schema occurs when we have to parse repeated XML data elements. It's not always clear how to handle them.

For example, in the XML outputs from Example 2-1, there was one such case with the Director tag. Two Director tags were returned in the response:

```
<Director>Larry Wachowski</Director>
<Director>Andy Wachowski</Director>
```

Since an XML parser has no understanding of what type of data structure is used for the Director element, it treats two adjacent Director tags as an array and returns a PHP array structure like this:

```
Director => array(  [0] => 'Larry Wachowski'
                    [1] => 'Andy Wachowski' )
```

But what if only one Director element was returned (most movies have only one director)? Our parser would assume that was a scalar quantity and return an associative array element like this:

```
['Director'] => 'Ingmar Bergman'
```

We can let the XML parser make these assumptions, but then we'll have to write extra code to check whether a scalar or array quantity is returned for any XML element that is defined as an array in the Amazon schema. When array elements get nested, the programming effort is greater.

The solution to the No Schema Problem is that, in order to do consistent parsing of the Amazon response, we have to include some knowledge of Amazon's schema in our parser.

All At Once Parsing Using Expat

PHP is interpreted code, so it's slow at parsing -- the more we can use compiled C code, the better. I like to use expat's parse_into_struct() function to quickly put all the XML elements into an array and then parse the array. The advantages of this approach is that parse_into_struct() is compiled C and is quite fast, we get some XML validation (if the call to parse_into_struct() fails, we know there's a problem with our XML), and we get a convenient structure that contains all the information we need to create a PHP data structure.

Our strategy will be to first use parse_into_struct() on the returned XML, and then go through the array recursively, building a PHP data structure as we go.

> The XML parser in Example 2-4 was originally written by Torsten Köster. I modified it for use with Amazon E-Commerce Service.

To solve the No Schema Problem mentioned in the last section, any array type elements returned by E-Commerce Service 4.0 are listing in array called $xml_list_elements. This will save programming time for us as we'll always be able to consistently treat these elements as arrays when they appear in Amazon responses. I've taken the liberty of going through the Amazon E-commerce Service 4.0 WSDL (Web Service Description Language) file and defining those tags for you.

Example 2-4 An all-at-once parser using expat

```
<?php

// List elements from the 2005-02-23 Amazon WSDL
$xml_list_elements = array(
"Accessory","Actor","Argument","Artist","ASIN","AudioFormat","Author","BrowseNode",
"BrowseNodes","CameraManualFeatures","CartItem","ChildTransactionItems","Creator",
"Customer","CustomerReviews","Customers","Director","Disc","EditorialReview",
"Element","Error","Feature","Feedback","Format","Header", "Information","Item",
"Items","Language","List","ListmaniaList","ListItem","Lists","Offer","OfferListing","
Operation", "OperationInformation","Package","Parameter","PhotoFlashType",
"PictureFormat","Platform","ResponseGroup","ResponseGroupInformation","Review",
"SavedForLaterItem","SearchIndex","Seller","SellerListing","SellerListings",
"Sellers","Shipment","SimilarProduct","SpecialFeatures","SupportedImageType","Track",
"Transaction","TransactionItem","TransactionItemId","Transactions"
);

// Global error string for XmlParser
$parser_error='';

// returns associative array or false on error. If there's an error,
// the global $parser_error will contain the error details
```

```
function XmlParser($string)
{
    global $parser_error;

    $parser_error='';
    $values=array();

    // Create parser
    $p = xml_parser_create("UTF-8");
    xml_parser_set_option($p,XML_OPTION_CASE_FOLDING,false);
    xml_parser_set_option($p,XML_OPTION_SKIP_WHITE,true);

    // Parse into array structure
    $rc = xml_parse_into_struct($p,$string,$values);

    /* Check for Parsing Error */
    if (!$rc)
    {
        $errorcode = xml_get_error_code($p);
        $errstring = xml_error_string($errorcode);
        $byte= xml_get_current_byte_index($p);
        $parser_error = "XML PARSER ERROR: Error Code= $errorcode, Explanation=
$errstring, Byte Number= $byte";
        xml_parser_free($p);
        return false;
    }

    xml_parser_free($p);

    // We store our path here
    $hash_stack = array();

    // This is our target
    $ret = array();

    foreach ($values as $val) {

        switch ($val['type']) {
            case 'open': // Start array structure
            array_push($hash_stack, $val['tag']);
            $valarg= (isset($val['attributes'])) ? $val['attributes'] : null;
            $ret = composeArray($ret, $hash_stack, $valarg);
            break;

            case 'close': // All done with this element
            array_pop($hash_stack);
            break;

            case 'complete':
            array_push($hash_stack, $val['tag']);
            $valarg=(isset($val['value']))? $val['value'] : null;
            // handle all attributes except those in 'open' container tags
            if (isset($val['attributes'])) {
                $temparr=array($val['tag'] => $valarg);
```

```
                $valarg=array_merge($val['attributes'], $temparr);
            };
            $ret = composeArray($ret, $hash_stack, $valarg);
            array_pop($hash_stack);
            break;

            default:
            // Ignoring CDATA type
        }
    }

    return $ret;
}

function &composeArray($array, $elements, $value)
{
    global $xml_list_elements;

    // Get current element
    $element = array_shift($elements);

    // Does the current element refer to a list?
    if (in_array($element,$xml_list_elements))
    {
        // Are there more elements?
        if(sizeof($elements) > 0)
        {
            $array[$element][sizeof($array[$element])-1] =
&composeArray($array[$element][sizeof($array[$element])-1], $elements, $value);
        }
        else // It's an array
        {
            $size = (isset($array[$element]))?  sizeof($array[$element]) : 0;
            $array[$element][$size] = $value;
        }
    }
    else
    {
        // Are there more elements?
        if(sizeof($elements) > 0)
        {
            $array[$element] = &composeArray($array[$element], $elements, $value);
        }
        else
        {
            $array[$element] = $value;
        }
    }

    return $array;
}
```

Parsing the Amazon request from example 2-1 using XmlParser() yields this PHP structure:

```
Array
(
    [ItemLookupResponse] => Array
        (
            [xmlns] => http://xml.amazon.com/AWSECommerceService/2005-02-23
            [OperationRequest] => Array
                (
                    [HTTPHeaders] => Array
                        (
                            [Header] => Array
                                (
                                    [0] => Array
                                        (
                                            [Name] => UserAgent
                                            [Header] =>
                                        )

                                )

                        )

                    [RequestId] => 1MXSNP36YYAQMEDJF4F6
                    [Arguments] => Array
                        (
                            [Argument] => Array
                                (
                                    [0] => Array
                                        (
                                            [Name] => Service
                                            [Value] => AWSECommerceService
                                            [Argument] =>
                                        )

                                    [1] => Array
                                        (
                                            [Name] => AssociateTag
                                            [Value] => ws
                                            [Argument] =>
                                        )

                                    [2] => Array
                                        (
                                            [Name] => SubscriptionId
                                            [Value] => 1A7XKHR5BYD0WPJVQEG2
                                            [Argument] =>
                                        )

                                    [3] => Array
                                        (
                                            [Name] => Version
                                            [Value] => 2005-02-23
                                            [Argument] =>
                                        )
```

```
                                    [4] => Array
                                        (
                                            [Name] => IdType
                                            [Value] => ASIN
                                            [Argument] =>
                                        )

                                    [5] => Array
                                        (
                                            [Name] => ItemId
                                            [Value] => B0001BKAEY
                                            [Argument] =>
                                        )

                                    [6] => Array
                                        (
                                            [Name] => ResponseGroup
                                            [Value] => Request,Small
                                            [Argument] =>
                                        )

                                    [7] => Array
                                        (
                                            [Name] => Operation
                                            [Value] => ItemLookup
                                            [Argument] =>
                                        )

                                )

                        )

                )

            [Items] => Array
                (
                    [0] => Array
                        (
                            [Request] => Array
                                (
                                    [IsValid] => True
                                    [ItemLookupRequest] => Array
                                        (
                                            [IdType] => ASIN
                                            [ItemId] => B0001BKAEY
                                            [ResponseGroup] => Array
                                                (
                                                    [0] => Request
                                                    [1] => Small
                                                )

                                        )

                                )
```

```
                              [Item] => Array
                                  (
                                      [0] => Array
                                          (
                                              [ASIN] => Array
                                                  (
                                                      [0] => B0001BKAEY
                                                  )

                                              [DetailPageURL] => http://www.amazon.com/
gp/redirect.html?location=/exec/obidos/ASIN/B0001BKAEY/
ws%3FSubscriptionId=1A7XKHR5BYD0WPJVQEG2%26camp=2025%26link_code=xm2
                                              [ItemAttributes] => Array
                                                  (
                                                      [Actor] => Array
                                                          (
                                                              [0] => Laurence Fishburne
                                                          )

                                                      [Director] => Array
                                                          (
                                                              [0] => Larry Wachowski
                                                              [1] => Andy Wachowski
                                                          )

                                                      [ProductGroup] => DVD
                                                      [Title] => The Matrix Revolutions
(Widescreen Edition)
                                                  )

                                          )

                                  )

                          )

                  )

          )

  )
```

XML attributes and nested structures are handled consistently, reducing the amount of code needed to go through the PHP array structure.

You may notice that the ASIN element is treated as an array even though it is defined in the Schema as a scalar value in this response. The reason for this is that the Amazon developers have another element named ASIN in the Amazon schema and it is an array. Since our parser doesn't know the difference between various ASIN elements, we have to treat all ASIN elements as arrays.

Parsing With PHP5

If you are using PHP5, you can use PHP5's built-in SimpleXML parser to parse the XML using just one line of PHP code. SimpleXML is quite fast and returns a nice PHP5 object structure you can use in your applications. It returns the boolean false if there's an error during parsing.

```
$parsed_xml = simplexml_load_string($response);
```

Since SimpleXML has no knowledge of Amazon's XML Schema (or any XML Schema, for that matter) it falls victim to the No Schema Problem, so it returns an array structure for two or more repeated XML elements:

```
[Director] => Array
        (
                [0] => Larry Wachowski
                [1] => Andy Wachowski
        )
```

It returns a scalar value if only one element appears:

```
[Director] => Ingmar Bergman
```

You will need to adjust your PHP code to deal with this situation for all array type elements that you want to handle.

> PHP5 also has a new XML DOM extension that replaces the one in PHP4. You can find out more details for it at http://www.php.net/dom.

There's really no reason to consider other parsing methods under PHP5 since SimpleXML is both fast and convenient. However, the PHP4 parsing techniques I mentioned in previous sections will also run under PHP5, so you can use those if cross-PHP compatibility is an issue.

Developing With SOAP And PHP

The beauty of developing application using a SOAP client is that the SOAP client does a lot of the heavy lifting for us. The cost we pay is in performance and a bit more complexity creating requests. The three most popular SOAP client packages for PHP are NuSOAP, PEAR SOAP, and PHP5's bundled SOAP extension.

NuSOAP and PEAR SOAP are freely available and were derived from SOAPx4, a package developed by Dietrich Ayala and distributed by NuSphere Corporation. NuSOAP is licensed under the Gnu Lesser Public License and PEAR SOAP under the PHP license. Both licenses allow free use of the code for both commercial and non-commercial applications.

PHP5 has a bundled SOAP extension written by Shane Caraveo and Brad LaFountain with contributions from Dmitri Stogov. PHP5's SOAP is still considered "experimental" quality in PHP 5.03. However, in practice, I found PHP5 SOAP to be quite stable and, understandably, quite a bit faster than either PEAR SOAP or NuSOAP. That's because PHP5 is written in C (it's code is taken from the excellent Gnome XML library -- *http://www.xmlsoft.org*) while NuSOAP and PEAR SOAP are written in PHP.

Which package should you use? As this book goes to press, the PHP5 SOAP extension works quite well with Amazon E-Commerce Service 4.0, as does NuSOAP. PEAR SOAP cannot correctly parse the Amazon WSDL at this time, and it also has problems parsing XML attributes returned by Amazon. These problems will no doubt be resolved by mid-2005, if not earlier.

As this book goes to press, PEAR SOAP is not usable with Amazon E-Commerce 4.0. However, I'll use it to demonstrate the Merchants@ API in Chapter 9.

SOAP Client	Runs under	Amazon E-Commerce Issues	Home page
NuSOAP 1.86	PHP4	none	http://dietrich.ganx4.com/nusoap/index.php
PEAR SOAP 0.81	PHP4, PHP5	WSDL and parsing problems	http://pear.php.net/package/SOAP
PHP5 SOAP extension	PHP5	none	http://www.php.net/soap

Table 2-7 PHP SOAP clients and their issues

I'll use PHP5's SOAP extension to illustrate SOAP usage in this chapter. For details on using NuSOAP and PEAR SOAP, see Appendix C.

Installing the PHP5 SOAP Extension

PHP5 comes bundled with a SOAP extension. If you're compiling PHP5 from scratch, make sure you use the "--enable-soap" flag. Once you've installed PHP5, you must uncomment one line in your php.ini file: extension=php_soap.dll (for Windows servers) or extension=soap.o (for Unix servers), and restart your web server.

Making A SOAP Request

Amazon E-commerce Service uses Document/Literal, also called doc-lit, format for requests. The term Document/Literal is from the SOAP standard and refers to the way parameters are serialized onto the SOAP message stream. For Amazon E-Commerce Service, it means that we need to encode our SOAP requests as a PHP associative array structure that matches the Amazon E-Commerce Service request structure.

Later in this chapter, I'll go into more detail in how to analyze the WSDL (Web Service Description Language) file to determine the structure of a SOAP request for each method, but just to get things started, below is our REST request parameters from example 2-1, contrasted with the corresponding SOAP request parameters.

```
REST Request Parameters:

SubscriptionId=1A7XKHR5BYDOWPJVQEG2&AssociateTag=ws&Operation=ItemLookup&
ItemId=B0001BKAEY&IdType=ASIN&ResponseGroup=Request,Small&Version=2005-02-23

SOAP Request Parameters:

array(
    'SubscriptionId' => '1A7XKHR5BYDOWPJVQEG2',
    'AssociateTag' => 'ws',
    'Request' => array (
                          array(
                               'ItemId' => array('B0001BKAEY'),
                               'IdType' => 'ASIN',
                             'ResponseGroup' => array('Request', 'Small')
                               )
                      )
    )
```

Note that neither the Version nor the Operation parameters are in the SOAP request format. The Operation parameter is used in the SOAP function call and the Version parameter is specified by the WSDL file.

Amazon E-commerce Service Versioning For SOAP

In Amazon E-commerce Service, the version of Amazon E-commerce Service that you are using is determined by the WSDL file that you reference. If you want to reference a specific version of Amazon E-commerce Service, encode the version in the WSDL URL as shown in Table 2-7 below. If you always want the latest version of Amazon E-commerce Service, choose the URL without a date in the URL

.

Version	WSDL File
2004-11-10	http://webservices.amazon.com/AWSECommerceService/2004-11-10/US/AWSECommerceService.wsdl
Latest version	http://webservices.amazon.com/AWSECommerceService/US/AWSECommerceService.wsdl

Table 2-8 SOAP versioning for Amazon E-Commerce Service

As Amazon makes incremental improvements to their service, new WSDL files, with different URLs will be made available. Note that the version is actually just the date when the version was rolled out, in this case, November 10th, 2004.

> YYYY-MM-DD is an international standard calendar date format, according to the ISO 8601 standard.

As Amazon E-commerce Service is updated, the date of the update will create a new Version value.

> Amazon sometimes makes minor releases without changing the version. These improvements should not cause problems for existing applications.

Because changes to Amazon E-commerce Service may break your application, it's a good idea to *always* use the WSDL with the date in your SOAP requests. Older versions of Amazon E-commerce Service should continue to be available for a long time as new versions are rolled out.

> Announcements about new versions of Amazon E-commerce Service are posted to the Amazon Blog at http://aws.typepad.com. The blog has an RSS feed you can subscribe to.

Making SOAP Requests

PHP5's bundled SOAP extension is particularly fast and easy to use, so I'm going to use it demonstrate making SOAP requests to Amazon E-Commerce Service. For details on using NuSOAP with Amazon E-Commerce Service, see Appendix C.

The series of steps for making E-Commerce Service requests using a PHP SOAP client is:

- Build the Document/Literal parameter array
- Parse the WSDL to retrieve the operations (methods)
- Make the request using the desired operation

The PHP5 program (Example 2-5 demonstrates these steps).

Example 2-5 Making a SOAP request using the PHP5 SOAP client

```
<?php

// URL of the Amazon WSDL file which includes the version namespace
$wsdl='http://webservices.amazon.com/AWSECommerceService/2005-02-23/US/
AWSECommerceService.wsdl';

// The Document/Literal parameter array
$request = array (
                array(
                      'ItemId' => array('B0001BKAEY'),
                      'IdType' => 'ASIN',
                      'ResponseGroup' => array('Request', 'Small')
                    )
                );

$params=array(
              'SubscriptionId' => '1A7XKHR5BYD0WPJVQEG2',
              'AssociateTag' => 'ws',
```

```
                'Request' => $request
                );

// Parse the WSDL to get the client methods
$client = new SoapClient($wsdl);

// The method we're using
$method='ItemLookup';

// Make the request using the ItemLookup operation
$Result = $client->$method($params);

// Output the results
echo '<pre>';
print_r($Result);
echo '</pre>';
?>
```

PHP5's SOAP extension makes full use of PHP5's object data structures and formats the SOAP responses as a tree-structured hierarchy of objects.

```
stdClass Object
(
    [OperationRequest] => stdClass Object
        (
            [HTTPHeaders] => stdClass Object
                (
                    [Header] => stdClass Object
                        (
                            [Name] => UserAgent
                            [Value] => PHP SOAP 0.1
                        )
                )
            [RequestId] => 07G39CC65MJ2T0XGQFCD
            [Arguments] => stdClass Object
                (
                    [Argument] => stdClass Object
                        (
                            [Name] => Service
                            [Value] => AWSECommerceService
                        )
                )
        )
    [Items] => stdClass Object
        (
            [Request] => stdClass Object
                (
                    [IsValid] => True
                    [ItemLookupRequest] => stdClass Object
                        (
                            [IdType] => ASIN
                            [ItemId] => B0001BKAEY
                            [ResponseGroup] => Array
                                (
```

```
                                    [0] => Request
                                    [1] => Small
                                )
                        )
                )
            [Item] => stdClass Object
                (
                    [ASIN] => B0001BKAEY
                    [DetailPageURL] => http://www.amazon.com/gp/redirect.
html?location=/exec/obidos/ASIN/B0001BKAEY/
ws%3FSubscriptionId=1A7XKHR5BYD0WPJVQEG2%26camp=2025%26link_code=sp1
                    [ItemAttributes] => stdClass Object
                        (
                            [Actor] => Laurence Fishburne
                            [Director] => Array
                                (
                                    [0] => Larry Wachowski
                                    [1] => Andy Wachowski
                                )
                            [ProductGroup] => DVD
                            [Title] => The Matrix Revolutions (Widescreen Edition)
                        )
                )
        )
)
```

Error Checking With PHP5 SOAP

By default, PHP5 SOAP will throw an exception if an error occurs. PHP5's exception handling gives us a lot more control over the error response, but for typical web applications involving Amazon E-commerce Service, that level of error feedback isn't necessary. Fortunately, we can revert to the traditional way of error handling -- immediately returning an error code -- by passing an option, called exceptions, and setting it to false.

```
$client = new SoapClient($wsdl, array('exceptions' => false));
$Result = $client->$method($params);
(is_soap_fault($Result)) {
    echo 'SOAP Fault: faultcode: '. $Result->faultcode .' faultstring: '. $Result->
faultstring .' faultactor: '. $Result->faultactor . '<br />';
}
```

The code above also demonstrates retrieving a SOAP fault. A SOAP "fault" is the fancy name that the SOAP standard gives to an error condition that arises during the execution of a SOAP request on either the SOAP client or server. The PHP5 is_soap_fault() function checks to see if a SOAP fault occurs, and returns the details as three strings: faultcode, faultstring, and faultactor.

Outputting PHP5 SOAP Debug Information

PHP5 has two internal methods, __getLastRequest(), and __getLastResponse(), that we can use to see the raw SOAP request and response. To enable it, you must set two options, one which will turn on program tracing, and another that will turn off SOAP exceptions.

```
$client = new SoapClient($wsdl, array('exceptions' => false, 'trace' => true));
$Result = $client->$method($params);
echo '<h2>Request</h2>';
echo "<pre>".htmlspecialchars($client->__getLastRequest(), ENT_QUOTES)."</pre>";
echo '<h2>Response</h2>';
echo "<pre>".htmlspecialchars($client->__getLastResponse(), ENT_QUOTES)."</pre>";
```

As mentioned earlier in this Chapter, the htmlspecialchars() function, wrapped in HTML <pre> tags, ensures that our web browser displays a nice output format and doesn't try to interpret the XML tags.

PHP5 WSDL Caching

In the previous SOAP examples, the WSDL file is fetched from the Amazon server and parsed every time the program is executed. To avoid that overhead, you can use WSDL caching. A WSDL cache stores a pre-parsed WSDL file locally for some specified amount of time. When the time limit is reached, the WSDL cache downloads the WSDL file again, parses it, and stores the result locally, replacing the old local version.

PHP5's SOAP extension has three parameters that control its WSDL cache. They are specified in the php.ini file:

```
soap.wsdl_cache_enabled = "1"  // Set to '1' if the WSDL cache is enabled, "0" if not
soap.wsdl_cache_dir = "/tmp"   // The directory where WSDL cache files are placed
soap.wsdl_cache_ttl = "86400"  // Number of seconds before the cache becomes stale
```

You can change these parameters in your PHP5 applications by using the ini_set() function. If it succeeds, the previous value of the parameter will be returned:

```
$rc = ini_set("soap.wsdl_cache_ttl", "0");  // Set the cache time to live to zero
```

The soap.wsdl_cache_dir must exist and be accessible to the SOAP client or else no WSDL caching occurs. The SOAP extension is silent about WSDL cache failure, so it's up to you to check and see if it's working. If it's working, you'll see files appear with the prefix "wsdl-" in the cache directory. The default WSDL cache directory is "/tmp", which is usually "C:\tmp" if you're running PHP under Windows. The soap.wsdl_cache_ttl should be set to "0" if you want the cache to never get stale.

The only caveat when using WSDL caching with Amazon E-Commerce Service 4.0 is that we need to make sure that we specify the version in the WSDL URL. New WSDL versions may break your applications, so when Amazon updates the WSDL, you should test the new version offline and decide whether to move to the new version. PHP5 will automatically update your WSDL cache when you change the version string in the WSDL URL.

Developing With XSLT

Amazon provides an online XSLT server that application developers can use to create dynamic XSLT applications. XSLT (eXtensible Stylesheet Language Transformations) provides a way to translate your Amazon response into HTML, plain text, a different XML encoding, or some other format. XSLT requests are made by using the "Style" parameter in your REST requests and specifying an XSLT stylesheet to use.

Additionally, you should use the special XSLT server domain name, xml-us.amznxslt.com, instead of the usual REST request domain name, webservices.amazon.com.

> As this book goes to press, XSLT requests that use the REST domain are automatically redirected to the XSLT domain, but Amazon may not keep doing that.

For a quick example, I'll use an XSLT stylesheet that displays the title of the DVD and links it to the Amazon purchase page using the DetailPageURL link provided by Amazon. I'll call this stylesheet, example.xsl.

Example 2-6 The example.xsl stylesheet

```
<xsl:stylesheet version="1.0" xmlns:xsl="http://www.w3.org/1999/XSL/Transform" xmlns:
aws="http://webservices.amazon.com/AWSECommerceService/2005-02-23" exclude-result-
prefixes="aws">
    <xsl:output method="html" />
    <xsl:template match="aws:ItemLookupResponse">
        <html>
            <body>
                <table cellpadding="2" cellspacing="0">
                    <tr>
                        <td>
                            <a href="{aws:Items/aws:Item/aws:DetailPageURL}"
target="_blank">
                                <xsl:value-of select="aws:Items/aws:Item/aws:Ite
mAttributes/aws:Title"/>
                            </a>
                        </td>
                    </tr>
                </table>
            </body>
        </html>
    </xsl:template>
</xsl:stylesheet>
```

You must specify a namespace prefix in your stylesheet. Here, the namespace prefix is defined as "aws".

```
xmlns:aws="http://webservices.amazon.com/AWSECommerceService/2005-02-23"
```

But we could define our own namespace string, such as "nsx".

```
xmlns:nsx="http://webservices.amazon.com/AWSECommerceService/2005-02-23"
```

> The namespace identifier contains the version of AWS that we're using, in this case, "2005-02-23". This version must match the Version parameter in your REST request or else the request will fail. You should **always** use the Version parameter in your REST requests when stylesheets are involved to ensure that the version matches the version in the namespace identifier.

The directive:

```
exclude-result-prefixes="aws"
```

tells the Amazon XSLT server not to embed "aws" (or "nsx", if that's the namespace identifier) namespace identifiers in the HTML returned. Without this directive, the first tag returned in the Amazon response will contain the namespace identifier:

```
<html xmlns:aws="http://webservices.amazon.com/AWSECommerceService/2005-02-23">
```

This is still valid HTML, of course, so you don't have to include this directive.

Finally, we have to use the XSL output tag in order to tell the Amazon XSLT server that we want HTML output:

```
<xsl:output method="html" />
```

If we don't use this output tag, the Amazon XSLT server will assume that it's returning XML and will prefix the response with the standard XML header:

```
<?xml version="1.0" encoding="UTF-8"?>
```

Now we need to place example.xsl onto a publicly accessible web server so that the Amazon service can reference it. If we place it on the web server, www.myserver.com, then it will be referenced as http://www.myserver.com/example.xsl. Using the REST request from example 2-1, we have:

```
http://xml-us.amznxslt.com/onca/xml?Service=AWSECommerceService&
SubscriptionId=1A7XKHR5BYD0WPJVQEG2&AssociateTag=ws&Operation=ItemLookup&
ItemId=B0001BKAEY&IdType=ASIN&Version=2005-02-23&ContentType=text%2Fhtml&
Style=http://www.myserver.info/junk.xsl
```

You must use the ContentType parameter to specify the MIME type you want Amazon to use when sending the response back to you. Here, I use MIME type "text/html", which is URL-encoded because of the slash character, so that it's "text%2Fhtml".

Putting this into a web browser, you should see the clickable link for the Matrix DVD:

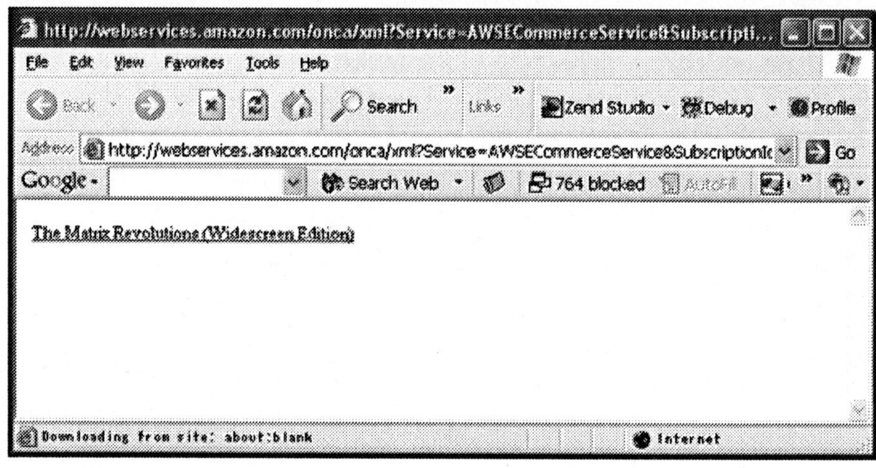

Figure 2-4 Sample XSLT request output

XSLT Caching

The Amazon E-Commerce Service XSLT engine will cache your XSL file when you first make a request with it. There is no direct way to control the caching. The only downside to the caching is that, during development, you may make changes to your XSL stylesheet but then find that when you run your request again, you get the same result you got before. Typically, you will have to make the request several times before the cache gets stale and grabs your new style sheet instead of using the old one.

One way to be certain that the new stylesheet is being used, is to add a bit of extra HTML to your stylesheet whenever you modify it -- perhaps by incrementing a number at the bottom of the stylesheet. When the style sheet is used, you'll see the number in the output.

Developing Stylesheets With A Web Browser

Constantly uploading XSLT files to a web server in order to test them is tedious. It's much easier to have an XSLT engine on your computer so that you can quickly test changes to your stylesheets. If you have the money for a product such as Altova's XMLspy or Tibco's TurboXML, they can be very helpful for validating your Stylesheets and helping you apply them to Amazon data. However, it's possible to develop stylesheets using nothing more than your web browser by using the built-in XSLT engine in your browser.

Currently, Internet Explorer 6.0 and newer (Windows only), and Netscape Navigator 7.0 and newer (all Netscape platforms) have built-in XSLT engines that are XSLT

1.0 compliant. As this book goes to press, IE 6 or newer is the best choice for XSLT development because Microsoft offers an add-on that lets you look at the output raw source of your transformation (see the next section for details). Firefox 1.0, and similar vintage Mozilla-based browsers work fine but they do not do serialization, so you can't use the disable-output-escaping function, nor can your view the raw source of your transformation (until someone writes an extension to do that).

Configuring Internet Explorer 6 for XSLT development

If you are running IE 6, then you can develop stylesheets using just a text editor and your web browser.

> IE 5.x browsers have a pre-XSLT 1.0 engine. Although they can be upgraded to XSLT 1.0 compliance, I don't think it's worth the hassle.

You should also install one Microsoft add-in for your browser called "Internet Explorer Tools for Validating XML and Viewing XSLT Output". This browser add-in will let you view the HTML source created by the XSLT transformation and it will also let you validate your XSL and XML. Without this add-in, you can see the transform in your web browser, but doing a "view source" only shows you the original XML, not the generated HTML.

The add-in can be found by going to *http://www.microsoft.com/downloads* and searching using the keyword "XSLT" in the “Search for a Download” box. The download contains two .inf files which you right-click on to install.

Configuring Firefox 1.0 for XSLT development

You shouldn't have to do any special configuration to use Firefox 1.0 (or similar Mozilla-based browsers) for XSLT development. However, it would be nice if there was an extension that let developers look at the source of their transformation like the one for IE mentioned in the last section.

Creating Sample data to work with

In order to test our style sheet, we need to create an XML file filled with some typical Amazon data. The easiest way to do this is to put an Amazon REST URL into our IE browser and then do “Save As” and select “XML Files *.xml”.

```
http://webservices.amazon.com/onca/xml?Service=AWSECommerceService&
SubscriptionId=1A7XKHR5BYDOWPJVQEG2&AssociateTag=ws&Operation=ItemLookup&
ItemId=B0001BKAEY&IdType=ASIN&ResponseGroup=Request,Small&Version=2005-02-23
```

We'll call the file test.xml. Now edit the file test.xml with your favorite text editor and add this line as the second tag in the file (immediately after the opening xml tag):

```
<?xml-stylesheet href="example.xsl" type="text/xsl" encoding="UTF-8"?>
```

So now the first two tags in the file are:

```
<?xml version="1.0" encoding="UTF-8"?>
```

```
<?xml-stylesheet href="example.xsl" type="text/xsl" encoding="UTF-8"?>
```

This line will instruct our web browser to apply the style sheet named "example.xsl" to the XML data in the file and then display the output in the web browser window. We could also use a fully qualified URL instead of just the file name:

```
<?xml version="1.0" encoding="UTF-8"?>
<?xml-stylesheet href="http://www.myserver.com/example.xsl" type="text/xsl"
encoding="UTF-8"?>
```

If we use a fully-qualified URL, we must make sure we set the following security setting in IE:

```
Options->Security->Custom Level
```

And enable:

```
access data sources across domains
```

Firefox 1.0, and other Mozilla browsers, won't allow a fully-qualified URL here.

Using our stylesheet, example.xsl, we simply make sure that the files test.xml and example.xsl are in the same directory. Then, in order to view the output of our style sheet in Internet Explorer 6.0 or Firefox 1.0, all we have to do is open or drag test.xml to the browser window and we should see Figure 2-4. Since we installed "Internet Explorer Tools for Validating XML and Viewing XSLT Output", we can right-click on the browser window and select either "validate XML" or "view XSL output".

Structure Of Amazon E-commerce Service Requests

Before getting in the details of programming actual applications using Amazon E-Commerce Service, I need to talk further about the structure of E-Commerce Service requests.

Amazon E-commerce Service 4.0 lets developers make three types of requests: simple, batch, and multioperation. The difference between each type of request is the number and type of operations (methods) contained in the request.

- **Simple requests** are the type of requests we've used so far in the book. Simple requests contain one operation and one set of parameters.
- **Batch requests** contain more than one simple request using the same operation, such as two ItemLookup requests.
- **Multioperation requests** contain any combination of batch and simple requests where each request uses a different operation. An example of a MultiOperation

request would be a batch request containing two ItemLookup requests, and a simple CustomerContentLookup request.

> Batch and Multioperation requests are currently limited to two requests in a single call to Amazon, but that may change in future versions of Amazon Web Service.

The purpose of Batch and Multioperation requests is to be able to receive more data in a single call to Amazon.com.

Although REST and SOAP use the same methods and have most of the same parameters, their request structure looks very different.

> The few minor differences in parameters for SOAP and REST requests are because the Amazon XSLT engine can be accessed via REST but not via SOAP.

Common REST Parameters

A REST request, whether Simple, Batch, or Multioperation, is simply a long URL. While each operation has its own parameters, there are a number of parameters that are common to all requests. The following elements of the REST request URL are common to all operations.

- URL Prefix. This is required and indicates what Amazon country is being targeted: amazon.com for the United States, amazon.de for Germany, and so on. (required)

  ```
  http://webservices.amazon.com/onca/xml?
  ```

- Service. It tells Amazon that you're using Amazon E-commerce Service 4.0. instead of another Amazon Web Service such Amazon Simple Queue Services or Alexa Web Information Service.

  ```
  Service=AWSCommerceService
  ```

- SubscriptionId. This is your Amazon Subscription Id. Your request will fail if it's not valid. (required)

  ```
  SubscriptionId=9K7XBXAABYDOWJ3BBEG2
  ```

- AssociateTag. This is your Amazon Associates Tag. It's not required, but you will not receive money for click-through payments unless this tag is in the URLs you use on your web site. You can construct those URLs in your applications, of course, but it's much easier to let Amazon do it for you by including it here. If you don't care about the click-throughs, you can use the generic tag which has a value of "ws". (optional)

  ```
  AssociateTag=ws
  ```

- Operation. It's a comma-separated list of one or more operations (methods) that you're using in your request. In Simple and Batch requests, there is only one operation. In Multioperation requests, there are two operations. (required)

```
Operation=ItemLookup
```

- Style. This parameter is used for requests to the Amazon XSLT engine (see the previous section on XSLT development). For all other requests, the default value of "XML" is assumed. (optional)

  ```
  Style=XML
  ```

- ContentType. This parameter lets developers specify what MIME type Amazon should use to identify responses. The default is "text/xml". (optional)

  ```
  ContentType=text%2Fxml   The '/' character must be urlencoded, hence the %2F
  ```

- Validate. This parameter tells Amazon that you want your request validated but not executed. If Validate is set to "true", You'll receive either receive the "IsValid" XML tag set to true in your response, or "IsValid" set to false and a list of errors. (optional)

  ```
  IsValid=true
  ```

- Version. This parameter indicates the version of Amazon E-Commerce Service that you are using. If it isn't specified, Amazon's servers will always assume you're using the latest version. Since new versions can sometimes break your applications, it's a good idea to always include the Version in every request.

  ```
  Version=2004-11-10
  ```

- Besides the parameters listed above, everything else in the URL is a parameter for the requested operation(s).

  ```
  ItemId=B0001BKAEY&IdType=ASIN&ResponseGroup=Request,Small
  ```

Here's what the request from Example 2-1 looks like with all the default parameters included:

```
http://webservices.amazon.com/onca/xml?Service=AWSECommerceService&
SubscriptionId=1A7XKHR5BYD0WPJVQEG2&AssociateTag=ws&Operation=ItemLookup&
ItemId=B0001BKAEY&IdType=ASIN&ResponseGroup=Request,Small&
Version=2005-02-23&Style=XML&Validate=false&ContentType=text%2Fxml
```

The reference manual in Appendix B lists all the operations, their parameters, and default values (if any).

REST Batch Requests

Batch Requests let developers use more than one set of parameters in the same request. In order to specify parameters for Batch requests, we use the operation name followed by the request number and then the parameter:

```
ItemLookup.1.ItemId=B0001BKAEY
```

Amazon currently has a limit of two sets of parameters per Batch request. However that may change in future versions.

We can also specify that parameters be shared between the requests. For shared parameters, we replace the request number above with the word "Shared".

`ItemLookup.Shared.IdType=ASIN`
: Any parameter may be shared between requests except for Operation, AssociateTag, SubscriptionId, Service, and Style.

Using this Batch notation, we can construct a batch version of the request that adds a second ItemLookup parameter and shares the IdType and ResponseGroup parameters across both requests.

```
http://webservices.amazon.com/onca/xml?Service=AWSECommerceService&
SubscriptionId=1A7XKHR5BYD0WPJVQEG2&AssociateTag=ws&Operation=ItemLookup&
ItemLookup.1.ItemId=B0001BKAEY&ItemLookup.2.ItemId=B000088KH1&
ItemLookup.Shared.IdType=ASIN&ItemLookup.Shared.ResponseGroup=Request,Small&
Itemlookup.Shared.Version=2005-02-23
```

Our new Batch request now consists of two Simple requests. The first request returns the information for the DVD "Matrix Revolutions" (`ItemId=B0001BKAEY`) as before, and the second request returns the product information for the Playstation2 Video Game, "Enter the Matrix" (`ItemId=B000088KH1`). The IdType, ResponseGroup, and Version parameters are shared between the two ItemLookup requests. The XML response from Amazon contains the responses to both requests.

```
<?xml version="1.0" encoding="UTF-8"?>
<ItemLookupResponse xmlns="http://xml.amazon.com/AWSECommerceService/2005-02-23">
    <OperationRequest>
        <HTTPHeaders>
            <Header Name="UserAgent" Value="XML Spy"/>
        </HTTPHeaders>
        <RequestId>13ABJZK3V73VVVN5WVFX</RequestId>
        <Arguments>
            <Argument Name="Itemlookup.Shared.Version" Value="2005-02-23"/>
            <Argument Name="Service" Value="AWSECommerceService"/>
            <Argument Name="AssociateTag" Value="ws"/>
            <Argument Name="ItemLookup.Shared.IdType" Value="ASIN"/>
            <Argument Name="ItemLookup.1.ItemId" Value="B0001BKAEY"/>
            <Argument Name="ItemLookup.Shared.ResponseGroup" Value="Request,Small"/>
            <Argument Name="SubscriptionId" Value="1A7XKHR5BYD0WPJVQEG2"/>
            <Argument Name="ItemLookup.2.ItemId" Value="B000088KH1"/>
            <Argument Name="Operation" Value="ItemLookup"/>
        </Arguments>
    </OperationRequest>
    <Items>
        <Request>
            <IsValid>True</IsValid>
            <ItemLookupRequest>
                <IdType>ASIN</IdType>
                <ItemId>B0001BKAEY</ItemId>
                <ResponseGroup>Request</ResponseGroup>
                <ResponseGroup>Small</ResponseGroup>
            </ItemLookupRequest>
```

```
            </Request>
            <Item>
                <ASIN>B0001BKAEY</ASIN>
                <DetailPageURL>http://www.amazon.com/gp/redirect.html?location=/exec/
obidos/ASIN/B0001BKAEY/ws%3FSubscriptionId=1A7XKHR5BYD0WPJVQEG2%26camp=2025%26link_
code=xm2</DetailPageURL>
                <ItemAttributes>
                    <Actor>Laurence Fishburne</Actor>
                    <Director>Larry Wachowski</Director>
                    <Director>Andy Wachowski</Director>
                    <ProductGroup>DVD</ProductGroup>
                    <Title>The Matrix Revolutions (Widescreen Edition)</Title>
                </ItemAttributes>
            </Item>
        </Items>
        <Items>
            <Request>
                <IsValid>True</IsValid>
                <ItemLookupRequest>
                    <IdType>ASIN</IdType>
                    <ItemId>B000088KH1</ItemId>
                    <ResponseGroup>Request</ResponseGroup>
                    <ResponseGroup>Small</ResponseGroup>
                </ItemLookupRequest>
            </Request>
            <Item>
                <ASIN>B000088KH1</ASIN>
                <DetailPageURL>http://www.amazon.com/gp/redirect.html?location=/exec/
obidos/ASIN/B000088KH1/ws%3FSubscriptionId=1A7XKHR5BYD0WPJVQEG2%26camp=2025%26link_
code=xm2</DetailPageURL>
                <ItemAttributes>
                    <ProductGroup>Video Games</ProductGroup>
                    <Title>Enter the Matrix</Title>
                </ItemAttributes>
            </Item>
        </Items>
</ItemLookupResponse>
```

REST Multioperation Requests

Multioperation requests let you combine any number of Batch and Simple requests, using different Operations, into a single request.

> Amazon currents limits Multioperation requests to two operations per request. However that may change in future versions.

The syntax for Multioperation requests is the same as Batch requests except that the Operation parameter is now a comma-separated list of Operations. We'll create a Multioperation request by adding a SellerListingSearch to our ItemLookup Batch request.

```
http://webservices.amazon.com/onca/xml?Service=AWSECommerceService&
SubscriptionId=1A7XKHR5BYDOWPJVQEG2&AssociateTag=ws&
Operation=ItemLookup,SellerListingSearch&ItemLookup.1.ItemId=B0001BKAEY&
ItemLookup.2.ItemId=B00008KH1&ItemLookup.Shared.IdType=ASIN&
ItemLookup.Shared.ResponseGroup=Request,Small&
ItemLookup.Shared.Version=2005-02-23&
SellerListingSearch.1.SearchIndex=Marketplace&
SellerListingSearch.1.Title=Matrix&SellerListingSearch.1.Version=2005-02-23
```

In addition to the two ItemLookup requests, we'll also receive the results of a SellerListingSearch request. The parameters SellerListingSearch.1.SearchIndex=Marketplace and SellerListingSearch.1.Title=Matrix will search the Amazon Marketplace for products with the word "Matrix" in the title.

SOAP Request Structure

For developers using PHP, parameters for SOAP requests are constructed using associative arrays that match the XML structure of the requests. The format of the associative arrays is determined by the WSDL (Web Service Description Language) file provided by Amazon.

```
http://webservices.amazon.com/AWSECommerceService/2005-02-23/US/AWSECommerceService.
wsdl
```

The location and use of WSDL files for non-US Amazon sites is discussed in Chapter Seven

The parameters for all Amazon E-commerce Service SOAP requests have the same basic PHP associative array format.

```
$params = array( 'SubscriptionId' => 'YourSubscription Id',
                 'AssociateTag' => 'YourAssociatesTag',
                 'Validate' => 'True or False',
                'Shared' => array ( operation dependent structure ),
                 'Request' => array (
                                    array( operation dependent structure ),
                                    array( operation dependent structure ),
                                     ......
                                   )
                );
```

The top-level array entries are either parameters or pointers to parameters.

- SubscriptionId. This is your Amazon Subscription Id. Your request will fail if it's not valid. (required)
- AssociateTag. This is your Amazon Associates Tag. It's not required, but you will not receive money for click-through payments unless this tag is in the URLs you use on your web site. You can construct those URLs in your applications, of course, but it's much easier to let Amazon do it for you by including it here. If

you don't care about the click-throughs, you can use the generic tag which has a value of "ws". (optional)

- Validate. This parameter tells Amazon that you want your request validated but not executed. If Validate is set to "true", You'll receive either the "IsValid" XML tag set to true in your response, or "IsValid" set to false and a list of errors. (optional)
- Shared. This is the top-level array identifier for any parameters that are shared across Batch requests. (optional)
- Request. This is the top-level array identifier for operation's parameters. It points to an array of arrays. Each array is a set of parameters for a Simple or Batch request.

The array structure above is the same for every SOAP request (Multioperation requests are slightly different -- see the Multioperation section below), but the format of the parameters that we can use in the Request and Shared arrays will be somewhat different depending on which operation we're using. We must manually examine the WSDL file to determine what the format of those parameter arrays will look like.

Fortunately, there are some general rules we can use to translate the WSDL entries into corresponding PHP array structures.

Here are the rules:

- Rule 1. If the element tag starts with <xs:element name="NAME" type="xs:SIMPLETYPE"... /> where SIMPLETYPE is a scalar type such as string or int, then:

  If the element uses minOccurs="0" then NAME is a single associative array entry.

  If the element uses maxOccurs="unbounded" then NAME is the start of a numerically indexed array of NAME.

  If the element uses neither minOccurs="0" nor maxOccurs="unbounded" then NAME is a single associative array entry

- Rule 2. If the element tag starts with <xs:element name="NAME" type="tns:IDENTIFIER"... /> then NAME is the name of an associative array element that points to a set of arguments. To find the arguments, search for <xs:complexType name="IDENTIFIER" in the WSDL.

  If the element uses minOccurs="0" then NAME is a single associative array entry that points to the arguments.

  If the element uses maxOccurs="unbounded" then NAME is the start of a numerically indexed array of NAME.

- Rule 3. If the element tag starts with <xs:element ref="tns:IDENTIFIER"... /> then IDENTIFIER is the name of an associative array element that points to a set of arguments. To find the arguments, you must search the WSDL for <xs:element name="IDENTIFIER".

If the element uses minOccurs="0" then IDENTIFIER is a single associative array entry that points to the arguments.

If the element uses maxOccurs="unbounded" then IDENTIFIER is the start of a numerically indexed array of IDENTIFIER.

- Rule 4. If the element tag is <xs:element name="NAME"/> then NAME is either an associative array element that points to a set of arguments, or just an associative array element.

If there is an enumeration directly below it, such as:

```
<xs:simpleType>
<xs:restriction base="xs:string">
<xs:enumeration value="val1" />
<xs:enumeration value="val2" />
<xs:enumeration value="valn" />
</xs:restriction>
</xs:simpleType>
```

then NAME is just an associative array element. Otherwise, NAME points to a set of arguments defined below it.

- Rule 5. If the element tag is <xs:element name="NAME" minOccurs="0"/> then NAME is just an associative array element.
- Rule 6. If the element tag is <xs:element name="NAME" maxOccurs="unbounded"/> then NAME is an associative array element that points to an array of arguments defined below it.

To figure out what the PHP array structure is for a particular method, we open the WSDL and search for the method with the word "Request" appended in a complex-Type tag. For the CustomerContentSearch method, that would be:

```
<xs:complexType name="CustomerContentSearchRequest">
```

Underneath this tag in the WSDL file are the request parameters for the Customer-ContentSearch method.

```
    <xs:complexType name="CustomerContentSearchRequest">
      <xs:sequence>
        <xs:element name="CustomerPage" type="xs:positiveInteger" minOccurs="0" />
        <xs:element name="Email" type="xs:string" minOccurs="0" />
        <xs:element name="Name" type="xs:string" minOccurs="0" />
        <xs:element name="ResponseGroup" type="xs:string" minOccurs="0"
maxOccurs="unbounded" />
      </xs:sequence>
    </xs:complexType>
```

From the Reference Manual in Appendix B, we know that the Email and Name parameters can not be used together, so we'll do a search for Customers using just the Name parameter. Using Rule #1 above, the "Name" parameter is just an associative array entry, "ResponseGroup" is a simple array:

```
'Name' => 'Jeff Bezos'
'ResponseGroup' => array('CustomerInfo', 'Request')
```

Thus, our request is generated by formatting the input parameters in a PHP associative array like this:

```
$params = array( 'SubscriptionId' => '9K7XBXAABYDOWJ3BBEG2',
                 'AssociateTag' => 'ws',
                 'Request' => array (
                              array( 'Name' => 'Jeff Bezos',
                                     'ResponseGroup' => array ('CustomerInfo',
'Request')
                                   )
                                   )
               );
```

Note that the optional Validate parameter defaults to a value of 'false' and that the Shared array pointer isn't needed since it's only used for Batch requests.

We can look at the resulting SOAP request message generated by the NuSOAP SOAP client using this bit of code:

Example 2-7 A simple SOAP request

```
<?php
require_once("nusoap.php");
$wsdl='http://webservices.amazon.com/AWSECommerceService/2005-02-23/US/
AWSECommerceService.wsdl';

$params = array( 'SubscriptionId' => '9K7XBXAABYDOWJ3BBEG2',
                 'AssociateTag' => 'ws',
                 'Request' => array (
                              array( 'Name' => 'Jeff Bezos',
                                'ResponseGroup' => array ('CustomerInfo', 'Request'
)
                                   )
                                   )
             );

$client = new soapclient($wsdl, true);
$client->soap_defencoding = 'UTF-8';
$Result = $client->call('CustomerContentSearch', array('body' => $params));
echo '<pre>' . htmlspecialchars($client->request, ENT_QUOTES) . '</pre>';
?>
```

Note that the operation, CustomerContentSearch, is specified in the call() function and not in the parameter array. It outputs just the SOAP message request generated by NuSOAP:


```
<?xml version="1.0" encoding="UTF-8"?>
<SOAP-ENV:Envelope xmlns:SOAP-ENV="http://schemas.xmlsoap.org/soap/envelope/" xmlns:
xsd="http://www.w3.org/2001/XMLSchema" xmlns:xsi="http://www.w3.org/2001/XMLSchema-
instance" xmlns:SOAP-ENC="http://schemas.xmlsoap.org/soap/encoding/" xmlns:si="http:/
/soapinterop.org/xsd" xmlns:ns3646="http://tempuri.org">
    <SOAP-ENV:Body>
```

```
        <CustomerContentSearch xmlns="http://xml.amazon.com/AWSECommerceService/
2005-02-23">
            <SubscriptionId>9K7XBXAABYDOWJ3BBEG2</SubscriptionId>
            <AssociateTag>ws</AssociateTag>
            <Request>
                <Name>Jeff Bezos</Name>
                <ResponseGroup>CustomerInfo</ResponseGroup>
                <ResponseGroup>Request</ResponseGroup>
            </Request>
        </CustomerContentSearch>
    </SOAP-ENV:Body>
</SOAP-ENV:Envelope>
```

SOAP Batch Requests

Batch Requests let developers use more than one set of parameters in the same request. In order to specify parameters for Batch requests, we add more arrays to our "Request" pointer. In our previous CustomerContentSearch example, we can add a second search that searches using the Email parameter. Looking at the entry for the Email parameter in the WSDL, we can apply Rule #1 and see that it's just a simple associative array entry.

```
'Email' => 'jeffb@amazon.com'
```

Adding that parameter to the "Request" array yields our new Batch request.

```
$params = array( 'SubscriptionId' => '9K7XBXAABYDOWJ3BBEG2',
                 'AssociateTag' => 'ws',
                'Shared' => array(
                              'ResponseGroup' => array ('CustomerInfo', 'Request')
                                ),
                'Request' => array (
                            array( 'Name' => 'Jeff Bezos'),
                            array( 'Email' => 'jeffb@amazon.com')
                                )
        );
```

Each array element in the Request array is effectively a separate request to the CustomerContentSearch operation, but we can see that the ResponseGroup parameter is redundant, so we can add it to the Shared array so that it is shared by each request. Sharing parameters is never required but it reduces the size of the request and puts less load on the Amazon server.

```
$params = array( 'SubscriptionId' => '9K7XBXAABYDOWJ3BBEG2',
                 'AssociateTag' => 'ws',
                'Shared' => array(
                              'ResponseGroup' => array ('CustomerInfo', 'Request')
                                ),
                'Request' => array (
                            array( 'Name' => 'Jeff Bezos'),
                            array( 'Email' => 'jeffb@amazon.com')
                                )
```

```
        );
```

Substituting this array into the code fragment from the previous section, we can see the Batch request in all its glory.

```
<?xml version="1.0" encoding="UTF-8"?>
<SOAP-ENV:Envelope xmlns:SOAP-ENV="http://schemas.xmlsoap.org/soap/envelope/" xmlns:
xsd="http://www.w3.org/2001/XMLSchema" xmlns:xsi="http://www.w3.org/2001/XMLSchema-
instance" xmlns:SOAP-ENC="http://schemas.xmlsoap.org/soap/encoding/" xmlns:si="http:/
/soapinterop.org/xsd" xmlns:ns2632="http://tempuri.org">
    <SOAP-ENV:Body>
        <CustomerContentSearch xmlns="http://xml.amazon.com/AWSECommerceService/
2005-02-23">
            <SubscriptionId>9K7XBXAABYDOWJ3BBEG2</SubscriptionId>
            <AssociateTag>ws</AssociateTag>
            <Shared>
                <ResponseGroup>CustomerInfo</ResponseGroup>
                <ResponseGroup>Request</ResponseGroup>
            </Shared>
            <Request>
                <Name>Jeff Bezos</Name>
            </Request>
            <Request>
                <Email>jeffb@amazon.com</Email>
            </Request>
        </CustomerContentSearch>
    </SOAP-ENV:Body>
</SOAP-ENV:Envelope>
```

Multioperation Requests

Multioperation requests let developers make combinations of Simple and Batch requests using different operations. The associative array format is slightly different for Multioperation requests. For each Operation, we make the operation name point at the request and bundle the entire thing into an array.

```
$params = array('Operation1' => array( 'SubscriptionId' => 'YourSubscriptionId',
                    'AssociateTag' => 'YourAssociatesTag',
                    'Validate' => 'True or False',
                  'Shared' => array ( operation dependent structure ),
                  'Request' => array (
                                     array( operation dependent structure ),
                                     array( operation dependent structure ),
                                      ......
                                  )
                                ),
                 'Operation2' => array( 'SubscriptionId' => 'YourSubscriptionId';
                    'AssociateTag' => 'YourAssociatesTag',
                    'Validate' => 'True or False',
                  'Shared' => array ( operation dependent structure ),
                    'Request' => array (
                                     array( operation dependent structure ),
```

```
                                    array( operation dependent structure ),
                                     ......
                                  )
                                 ),
                'OperationN' => array( ......
          )
```

To illustrate, we'll use PHP5 SOAP and combine our ItemLookup request from with out CustomerContentSearch Batch request to create a Multioperation request

Example 2-8 SOAP multioperation request

```
$params =  array(
              'CustomerContentSearch' => array( 'SubscriptionId' =>
'9K7XBXAABYDOWJ3BBEG2',
                   'AssociateTag' => 'ws',
                  'Shared' => array(
                             'ResponseGroup' => array ('CustomerInfo', 'Request')
                               ),
                   'Request' => array (
                           array( 'Name' => 'Jeff Bezos'),
                           array( 'Email' => 'jeffb@amazon.com')
                               )
                      ),
                  'ItemLookup' => array(
                    'SubscriptionId' => '9K7XBXAABYDOWJ3BBEG2',
                    'AssociateTag' => 'ws',
                     'Request' => array (
                             array(
                             'ItemId' => array('B0001BKAEY'),
                             'IdType' => 'ASIN',
                            'ResponseGroup' => array('Request', 'Small')
                             )
                    )
               )
     );
```

The PHP5 script to generate the request is as follows:

Example 2-9 A SOAP multioperation request

```
<?php

// URL of the Amazon WSDL file
$wsdl='http://webservices.amazon.com/AWSECommerceService/2005-02-23/US/
AWSECommerceService.wsdl';

// The Document/Literal format request parameters
$params =  array(
                   'CustomerContentSearch' => array(
                          'SubscriptionId' => '1A7XKHR5BYDOWPJVQEG2',
                          'AssociateTag' => 'ws',
                    'Shared' => array(
                             'ResponseGroup' => array ('CustomerInfo', 'Request')
```

```
                        ),
            'Request' => array (
                    array( 'Name' => 'Jeff Bezos'),
                    array( 'Email' => 'jeffb@amazon.com')
                        )
            ),
            'ItemLookup' => array(
                'SubscriptionId' => '1A7XKHR5BYDOWPJVQEG2',
                'AssociateTag' => 'ws',
            'Request' => array (
                    array(  'ItemId' => array('B0001BKAEY'),
                            'IdType' => 'ASIN',
                        'ResponseGroup' => array('Request', 'Small')
                    )
            )
        )
    );

// Parse the WSDL to get the client methods
$client = new SoapClient($wsdl, array('exceptions' => false, 'soap_version' => SOAP_
1_1, 'trace' => true));

// The method we're using
$method='MultiOperation';

// Send the SOAP request to Amazon
$Result = $client->$method($params);

// Output just the request
echo "<pre>".htmlspecialchars($client->__getLastRequest(), ENT_QUOTES)."</pre>";
?>
```

Note the use of the special "MultiOperation" method which indicates that the Amazon request methods will be specified inside the parameter array. The array entries 'ItemLookup' and 'CustomerContentSearch' simply point to their respective Simple or Batch requests. Substituting this array into the code fragment yields the SOAP message:

```
<?xml version="1.0" encoding="UTF-8"?>
<SOAP-ENV:Envelope xmlns:SOAP-ENV="http://schemas.xmlsoap.org/soap/envelope/" xmlns:
ns1="http://xml.amazon.com/AWSECommerceService/2005-02-23">
    <SOAP-ENV:Body>
        <ns1:MultiOperation>
            <ns1:ItemLookup>
                <ns1:SubscriptionId>1A7XKHR5BYDOWPJVQEG2</ns1:SubscriptionId>
                <ns1:AssociateTag>ws</ns1:AssociateTag>
                <ns1:Request>
                    <ns1:IdType>ASIN</ns1:IdType>
                    <ns1:ItemId>B0001BKAEY</ns1:ItemId>
                    <ns1:ResponseGroup>Request</ns1:ResponseGroup>
                    <ns1:ResponseGroup>Small</ns1:ResponseGroup>
                </ns1:Request>
```

```
            </ns1:ItemLookup>
            <ns1:CustomerContentSearch>
                <ns1:SubscriptionId>1A7XKHR5BYD0WPJVQEG2</ns1:SubscriptionId>
                <ns1:AssociateTag>ws</ns1:AssociateTag>
                <ns1:Shared>
                    <ns1:ResponseGroup>CustomerInfo</ns1:ResponseGroup>
                    <ns1:ResponseGroup>Request</ns1:ResponseGroup>
                </ns1:Shared>
                <ns1:Request>
                    <ns1:Name>Jeff Bezos</ns1:Name>
                </ns1:Request>
                <ns1:Request>
                    <ns1:Email>jeffb@amazon.com</ns1:Email>
                </ns1:Request>
            </ns1:CustomerContentSearch>
        </ns1:MultiOperation>
    </SOAP-ENV:Body>
</SOAP-ENV:Envelope>
```

Response Groups

The ResponseGroup parameter lets developers tell the Amazon E-commerce Service server what kinds of data they want returned in the response to their Amazon E-commerce Service request. Amazon E-commerce Service 4.0 has 35 different Response Groups each offering different types, or granularities, of data. Many Response Groups only work with specific methods. Refer to Appendix F for a description of each Response Group and to find out which operations each Response Group works with.

Default Response Groups

Developers can specify more than one Response Group for most operations, and all operations have default Response Groups which are used when none are specified in the request. Recall that our request for the DVD "Matrix Revolutions" used the Request and Small Response Groups.

```
http://webservices.amazon.com/onca/xml?Service=AWSECommerceService&
SubscriptionId=1A7XKHR5BYD0WPJVQEG2&AssociateTag=ws&Operation=ItemLookup&
ItemId=B0001BKAEY&IdType=ASIN&ResponseGroup=Request,Small&Version=2005-02-23
```

However, we can see in Appendix B that the default Response Groups for the method ItemLookup are Request and Small, so we could have written this request without them and still received the same results.

```
http://webservices.amazon.com/onca/xml?Service=AWSECommerceService&
SubscriptionId=1A7XKHR5BYD0WPJVQEG2&AssociateTag=ws&Operation=ItemLookup&
ItemId=B0001BKAEY&IdType=ASIN&Version=2005-02-23
```

Parent And Child Response Groups

When developing Amazon E-commerce Service applications, we want to choose the Response Groups that will provide us with the information we need and no more. Fortunately, Response Groups come in a variety of granularities that suit most common request needs.

Some Response Groups are made up of several smaller Response Groups. These are called "parent" response groups. For example, as noted in Appendix F, the ListFull Response Group is made up of two child Response Groups, ListInfo and ListItems. So, you'll get the same response from Amazon whether you choose to use ListFull as your Response Group or choosing both ListInfo and ListItems as your Response Groups. In other words, these two requests are functionally equivalent:

```
http://webservices.amazon.com/onca/xml?Service=AWSECommerceService&
AssociateTag=ws&SubscriptionId=1A7XKHR5BYD0WPJVQEG2&Operation=ListLookup&
ListType=WishList&ListId=1PQ2HOS7401DU&ResponseGroup=ListFull&Version=2005-02-23

http://webservices.amazon.com/onca/xml?Service=AWSECommerceService&
AssociateTag=ws&SubscriptionId=1A7XKHR5BYD0WPJVQEG2&Operation=ListLookup&
ListType=WishList&ListId=1PQ2HOS7401DU&ResponseGroup=ListInfo,ListItems&
Version=2005-02-23
?>
```

E-Commerce Service makes no judgements about which Response Groups you choose. You can specify many redundant Response Groups in the same request and all the data will be returned.

The easiest way to find out what elements a specific Response Group will return is to use the Help operation (See Chapter 8, "Getting Help With The Help Operation"). The Help operation can return the list of elements returned by a specific Response Group. Then lookup the element in the WSDL file to find out its specific data type.

Throughout the book, we'll make use of various Response Groups to retrieve different types of data.

Some Common Amazon Units

In ECS 4.0, Amazon has settled on a few encodings for some of the data points that they use frequently. Amazon also has a few special numbers they use. It's worth pointing them out here since you'll encounter them frequently when developing with Amazon ECS.

Amazon Sales Rank

The Amazon Sales Rank is a positive integer greater than zero that indicates an item's sales rank on Amazon relative to other items in the same Search Index. Thus, the highest selling item in the Toys Search Index has an Amazon Sales Rank of 1, and the highest selling item in the Books Search Index also has an Amazon Sales Rank of 1. Items that have sold at low volumes may have very large Sales Rank numbers, possibly greater than 100,000. You can explicitly request E-Commerce Service to return the Sales Rank for an item by using the SalesRank Response Group in your request for certain operations (See Appendix F to determine which Response Groups can be used with the various operations).

Amazon StarRatings

Amazon's site is full of ratings. There are customer ratings of sellers, there are customer ratings of products, and there are probably some ratings that haven't even been revealed yet. When things are rated on Amazon, they use a simple star rating system where one star is the worst and five stars is the best rating. Internally, the "stars" are simply represented by positive integers (one star = the number one). Amazon users may only enter a whole number rating, from one to five. For some operations, ECS returns an "average rating," which is a simple average, and is therefore typically a fraction, such as 4.3.

Amazon Prices

Whenever a price element appears in a response, it looks like this:

```
<Price>
  <Amount>1000</Amount>
  <CurrencyCode>USD</CurrencyCode>
  <FormattedPrice>$10.00</FormattedPrice>
</Price>
```

The Amount element is in terms of the currency's smallest unit. For the United States, that would be the number of pennies in the price. So, if the FormattedPrice is $10.00, the Amount is (10 x 100 pennies) 1000. The CurrencyCode "USD" is the ISO standard currency code for the United States. In Chapter 7 we'll look at the foreign Amazon sites which use different currencies.

> The currency codes are from ISO Standard 4217 available at http://www.iso.org/iso/en/prods-services/popstds/currencycodes.html

Amazon Date Format

There are several places where Amazon returns a <Date> element in ECS. The format for this element is always in a particular ISO 8601 standard format for date and time that fits together neatly as a single string:

YYYY-MM-DDTHH:MM+hhmm (or -hhmm)

The breakdown of this string is as follows:

- **YYYY** is the year, as in 2004
- **MM** is the numerical month with a leading zero if it's a single digit. April would be 04
- **DD** is the day of the month with a leading zero if it's a single digit.
- **T** the letter T merely indicates that the time string comes next.
- **HH** is the hour on the 24 hour clock with a leading zero if it's a single digit. 16 would be 4pm.
- **MM** is the number of minutes with a leading zero if it's a single digit.
- **+hhmm** (or **-hhmm**) is the time zone offset from UTC (Coordinated Universal Time). Eastern Standard Time is five hours behind UTC, so it would be -0500. Tokyo is 9 hours ahead of UTC, and thus it would be +0900.

Example: May 22nd, 2004 at 3:45 AM in Honolulu, Hawaii (10 hours behind UTC) would be represented as: 2004-05-22T03:45-1000

> Amazon's Seller Services adds an extra semicolon to the time zone information. So, the time format would look like 2004-05-22T03:45-10:00

You can use PHP's strtotime function to translate Amazon's date format to something more human readable. Under PHP5, you can translate the date string with no problems:

```
<?php
// Turn the Amazon time string into "Unix" time (seconds since January 1st, 1970)
$time = strtotime('2004-05-22T03:45-1000');
// Translate "Unix" time into desired date/time format
$strt = date('l, F j, Y, g:ia T', $time);
echo $strt;
?>
```

The output is:

```
Saturday, May 22, 2004, 8:45am Central Daylight Time
```

Since I live in the Central Daylight Time time zone, PHP translated from Hawaii's time zone to mine. The strings used for time zones vary from system to system so you may not see "Central Daylight Time" when you run it, you might see "CDT", or "Mexico City/America".

> The output can be massaged into any date/time format you could possibly want by changing the 'l, F j, Y, g:ia T' string according to the formatting strings found at http://www.php.net/date

Under PHP4, the strtotime() function doesn't understand the "T" that's in the date string so we have to remove it before running strtotime().

```
<?php
// Remove "T"
```

```
$date=str_replace('T', ' ', '2004-05-22T03:45-1000');
// Turn the Amazon time string into "Unix" time (seconds since January 1st, 1970)
$time = strtotime($date);
// Translate "Unix" time into desired date/time format
$strt = date('l, F j, Y, g:ia T', $time);
echo $strt;
?>
```

Amazon's Merchants@ API (see Chapter Nine) uses an extra semicolon in the timezone e.g. 2004-05-22T03:45-10:00. PHP4's strtotime() function won't work with that semicolon.. You can remove it with:

```
$date=substr_replace ($date, '', -3,1);
```

Exercises For The Reader

Create PHP functions that use regular expressions to retrieve interesting E-Commerce Service results.

CHAPTER 3

Working With Products: ItemSearch

More is good... all is better
—Ferengi Rule Of Acquisition #242

As the success of companies like Google and Yahoo has made clear, search is big business. One might even claim that a good portion of Amazon's business is due to the safe product searching environment they provide their customers. Not surprisingly, most of the operations in Amazon E-Commerce Service have to do with search to some degree or another.

The cool thing about searching with E-Commerce Service is that you can customize the search with a higher granularity, and with more focus, than you could ever do when searching directly on the Amazon.com web site. In search engine parlance, the precision, the degree to which products match your query, and the relevance, how well the products returned from a search match your personal goal for the search, can be guided by developers using the E-Commerce Service operations.

Still, finding the types of products you want can be challenging, and once you find a way to focus in on those products, you also have to decide which product attributes are important for your application. A myriad of product details are available via Amazon E-Commerce Service 4.0, but typically, you'll only fetch and display some subset of all the possible details for any given product. You might choose to display an image of the product, some new or used pricing information, the name of the product, or perhaps the manufacturer or publisher. In this chapter, I'll discuss some ways to use the ItemSearch operation to find products, and also look at how Amazon E-commerce Service handles product pricing, condition, and availability.

Searching With ItemSearch

The ItemSearch method is the Swiss Army Knife of Amazon E-commerce Service methods. It mimics much of the search capabilities of Amazon's site, providing 28 different search parameters (see Appendix B for a list of all parameters).

While 28 parameters may seem like a lot, in practice, only a handful of parameters are typically used. In fact, many of the 28 search parameters can only be used to search for certain types of products. For example, the Cuisine parameter can only be used when searching in the Search Index of Restaurants. Table 3-1 shows which ItemSearch parameters can be used to search which Search Indexes.

The SearchIndex parameter is the only required parameter for an ItemSearch request. The Search Index, as you may recall from Chapter one, is the name of a top-level product category on Amazon (the Search Indexes are listed in Appendix H).

After choosing an appropriate Search Index, you further focus your search by choosing from among ItemSearch's optional search parameters that are valid for that Search Index. The search parameters near the top of Table 3-1 work with most Search Indexes.

The most powerful and general-purpose search parameters are the BrowseNode, Keywords, and Title parameters, since these provide the broadest search capabilities and can be used with almost all of the Search Indexes.

The Keywords parameter does string matching of words you specify against various parts of the product description, title, and other product attributes, looking for matches. The Title parameter does string matching of words you specify against words in the product's <Title> tag, which is the name of the product. The BrowseNode parameter lets you specify a Browse Node ID which further limits the search to a specific sub-category under the specified Search Index.

ItemSearch Parameter(s)	Valid When Searching These Search Indexes
Keywords	`All`
BrowseNode	`All but Blended`
Condition **MaximumPrice** **MerchantId** **MinimumPrice** **Title**	`All but Blended and Merchants`
DeliveryMethod	`All but Blended, Restaurants, and Merchants`
Brand **Manufacturer**	`Apparel, Baby, Beauty, Electronics, HealthPersonalCare,Kitchen, Merchants, Miscellaneous, MusicalInstruments, OfficeProducts, OutdoorLiving, PCHardware, Photo, Software, SportingGoods, Tools, VideoGames`

ItemSearch Parameter(s)	Valid When Searching These Search Indexes
TextStream	Apparel, Books, Classical, DigitalMusic, DVD, Electronics, GourmetFood, Jewelry, Merchants, Music, Photo, Toys, Video, VideoGames
Publisher	Books, DigitalMusic,DVD, Magazines, Merchants, VHS, Video
Actor Director	Video, VHS, DVD, DigitalMusic, Merchants
Artist MusicLabel	Music, Classical, Merchants
City Cuisine Neighborhood	Restaurants, Merchants
Composer Conductor Orchestra	Classical, Merchants
Author Power	Books, Merchants

Table 3-1 ItemSearch parameters and the Search Indexes they work with

Using ItemSearch With Browse Nodes

Browse Node searches are very powerful because they let you refine your search to a specific product category beneath a Search Index. For example, if you are only interested in books about the Holocaust, you would likely want to search in Browse Node Id 4994 (Books > Subjects > History > Jewish > Holocaust) in the Search Index of Books.

A common search strategy is to use the BrowseNode parameter to narrow searches down to a specific Browse Node then add the Keywords and Title parameters to further focus the search. The goal is to try to get Amazon to return item listings that closely match what we're looking for.

To see what Amazon returns for a search within Browse Node ID 4994, you can put this request in your web browser:

```
http://webservices.amazon.com/onca/xml?Service=AWSECommerceService&
AssociateTag=ws&SubscriptionId=1A7XKHR5BYD0WPJVQEG2&Operation=ItemSearch&
BrowseNode=4994&SearchIndex=Books&Version=2005-02-23
```

This search will return books from the Holocaust Browse Node using the default Sort order of bestselling and the default Response Groups of Small and Request.

If you wanted to narrow down the search to books that mention Auschwitz in various product fields, such as the product title and description, you can add the Keywords parameter and set it to the word "Auschwitz".

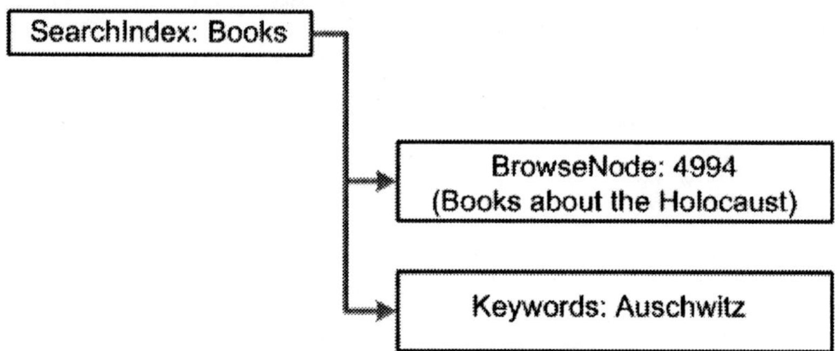

Figure 3-1 The BrowseNode and Keywords parameters narrow down your search

You can look at the results of this request by putting this URL in your browser:

```
http://webservices.amazon.com/onca/xml?Service=AWSECommerceService&
AssociateTag=ws&SubscriptionId=1A7XKHR5BYDOWPJVQEG2&
Operation=ItemSearch&BrowseNode=4994&SearchIndex=Books&
Keywords=Auschwitz&Version=2005-02-23
```

This search will return only books from Browse Node 4994 that have the word Auschwitz in the product title or description. If there was a Browse Node for Holocaust books about Auschwitz, you could use that, but there isn't one.

> Such a book would likely be in the category:
> Books > Subjects > History > Jewish > Holocaust > Auschwitz

Finding Usable Browse Nodes

The question that may come to mind right now is: how do I find the Holocaust Browse Node ID? Amazon's E-Commerce Service has two helpful mechanisms for finding BrowseNodes:

- **The BrowseNodeLookup operation** returns a list of Child Browse Nodes for a given Browse Node Id.
- **The BrowseNode Response Group** can be used with the ItemSearch operation to return a list of Browse Nodes for each item in the response.

The BrowseNodeLookup operation is very useful for creating search trees that you can use to help users browse Amazon's product categories (see the BrowseNodeLookup section in Chapter Eight for an example), but it doesn't directly help us find usable Browse Node IDs.

> Amazon maintains a list of popular Browse Nodes in their software development kit here: http://www.amazon.com/gp/aws/sdk/main.html?s=AWSEcommerceService&v=2005-02-23&p=ApiReference/BrowseNodeValuesArticle

The BrowseNode Response Group, however, will return a list of Browse Node IDs that match each item returned in ItemSearch and ItemLookup requests. So, to find usable Browse Nodes for a certain class of product, we can use the ItemLookup operation with the BrowseNodes Response Group and analyze the Browse Node IDs returned in the response.

First, we go to Amazon.com and find some ASINs that are typical of the products we want. We can then write a simple PHP script that runs an ItemLookup on the items and lists the Browse Nodes they appear under. Taking the intersection of those Browse Nodes is a good basis for searching.

In this example, we're looking for sushi preparation knives. I found two of them on Amazon by searching for "sushi knives". I can use their ASINs to find what Browse Nodes they're listed under.

Example 3-1 A program to list product Browse Nodes

```
<?php
require_once('tools.inc.php');

// List of ASINs (up to 10) to find browse nodes for
$asins='B000288KD4,B0000CE0IA';

// Our Amazon request. Note use of BrowseNodes Response Group
$request='http://webservices.amazon.com/onca/
xml?Service=AWSECommerceService&AssociateTag=ws&SubscriptionId=1A7XKHR5BYD0WPJVQEG2&O
peration=ItemLookup&MerchantId=All&ItemId='.$asins.
'&ResponseGroup=BrowseNodes&Version=2005-02-23';

//  Fetch and process the request
$xml = GetData($request, 10);
$Result = xmlparser($xml);

// Go through each item listing
foreach ($Result['ItemLookupResponse']['Items'][0]['Item'] as $item) {

    // The ASINs should always be returned, but you check anyway
    $asin= (isset($item['ASIN'][0])) ? $item['ASIN'][0] : ' No ASIN!??';

    echo '<br />ASIN = '.$asin.'<br />';

    // Loop through the browsenodes of each item
    foreach ($item['BrowseNodes'][0]['BrowseNode'] as $bnode) {

        // Check for browse node name
        $name=(isset($bnode['Name']))?$bnode['Name']:'No browse node name';

        echo 'Browse Node = '.$bnode['BrowseNodeId'].'<br />';
        echo 'Browse Name = '.$name .'<br />';
        echo '<br />';
    }
}
```

```
?>
```

The ItemLookup method can accept a comma-separated list of up to 10 ASINs. So, you could look at the Browse Nodes for up to ten products in a single request.

```
ASIN = B000288KD4
Browse Node = 289852
Browse Name = Asian Knives

Browse Node = 289854
Browse Name = Boning & Fillet Knives

Browse Node = 1063512
Browse Name = Great Gadgets

Browse Node = 3000591
Browse Name = Under $25

Browse Node = 3375131
Browse Name = Travel

Browse Node = 3737371
Browse Name = All Knives

Browse Node = 13466181
Browse Name = Komachi

Browse Node = 13875901
Browse Name = All Specialty Knives

Browse Node = 13875931
Browse Name = Seafood Knives

ASIN = B0000CE0IA
Browse Node = 289852
Browse Name = Asian Knives

Browse Node = 712216
Browse Name = Bunmei

Browse Node = 3737371
Browse Name = All Knives
```

The first knife appears in nine Browse Nodes, while the second one appears in three Browse Nodes. The two Browse Nodes they share in common, 3737371 and 289852 are the likely the best ones to use for searching for sushi preparation knifes. The Asian Knives Browse Node seems like a more specific choice than the All Knives Browse Node, but only testing them in actual Item Searches will prove which one works better.

If we added more ASINs to our example, manually determining the Browse Nodes they have in common would be tedious. Fortunately, we can change our PHP code around a bit to return only the Browse Nodes that both products appear under.

Example 3-2 A program to find the intersection of product Browse Nodes among several products

```
<?php
require_once('tools.inc.php');

// List of ASINs (up to 10) to find browse nodes for
$asins='B000288KD4,B0000CE0IA';

// Our Amazon request. Note use of BrowseNodes Response Group
$request='http://webservices.amazon.com/onca/
xml?Service=AWSECommerceService&AssociateTag=ws&SubscriptionId=1A7XKHR5BYD0WPJVQEG2&O
peration=ItemLookup&MerchantId=All&ItemId='.$asins.
'&ResponseGroup=BrowseNodes&Version=2005-02-23';

//  Fetch and preocess the request
$xml = GetData($request, 10);
$Result = xmlparser($xml);

// Index to keep track of number of items
$i=0;

// Array of browse nodes in each item
$allnodes=array();

// Loop through items
foreach ($Result['ItemLookupResponse']['Items'][0]['Item'] as $item) {

    // Loop through browse nodes for each item
    foreach ($item['BrowseNodes'][0]['BrowseNode'] as $bnode) {

        // Store browse nodes for each item in the allnodes array
        $allnodes[$i][]=trim($bnode['BrowseNodeId']);

    }
    // Increment index for the next item
    $i++;
}

// Find intersection of browse nodes for all items
$i=0;
$arr1=$allnodes[$i];
$arr2=$allnodes[$i+1];

// Use array_intersect on each set of browse nodes
While (true) {
    $arr2=array_intersect($arr1, $arr2);
    $i++;
    if (!isset($allnodes[$i+1])) break;
    $arr1=$allnodes[$i+1];
}
```

```
echo 'Intersection of browse nodes: ';
print_r($arr2);
?>
```

Running it yields:

```
Intersection of browse nodes: Array ( [0] => 289852 [1] => 3737371 )
```

You can examine these Browse Nodes further by inserting them into the Browse Node template links provided in Chapter One and opening them the URL in a web browser:

```
http://www.amazon.com/exec/obidos/tg/browse/-/289582
```

We can test how well the Browse Nodes work using the ItemSearch operation. The ItemSearch operation only lets us search in one Browse Node at a time, but you can do a batch search to do two Item Searches at once. This batch request returns products in the two Browse Nodes, 289852 and 3737371.

```
http://webservices.amazon.com/onca/xml?Service=AWSECommerceService&
SubscriptionId=1A7XKHR5BYD0WPJVQEG2&AssociateTag=ws&Operation=ItemSearch&
ItemSearch.1.BrowseNode=289852&ItemSearch.2.BrowseNode=3737371&
ItemSearch.Shared.ResponseGroup=Medium&ItemSearch.Shared.SearchIndex=Kitchen&
Version=2005-02-23
```

We can do four ItemSearch operations at once by combining two batch searches in a Multi-Operation request. This Multi Operation specifies two ItemSearch operations. The Item Search operations just return products from the four Browse Nodes: 289852, 3737371, 289854, and 289862.

```
http://webservices.amazon.com/onca/xml?Service=AWSECommerceService&
SubscriptionId=1A7XKHR5BYD0WPJVQEG2&AssociateTag=ws&
Version=2005-02-23&Operation=ItemSearch,ItemSearch&
ItemSearch.1.BrowseNode=289852&ItemSearch.2.BrowseNode=3737371&
ItemSearch.3.BrowseNode=289854&ItemSearch.4.BrowseNode=289862&
ItemSearch.Shared.ResponseGroup=Medium&ItemSearch.Shared.SearchIndex=Kitchen
```

Since the “All Knives”, “Specialty Knives”, and “Boning and Filet Knives” categories are rather broad, we'll narrow them down by adding a Keywords parameter to each of those categories. Here, I added the search keyword “sushi” to those request parameters.

```
http://webservices.amazon.com/onca/xml?Service=AWSECommerceService&
SubscriptionId=1A7XKHR5BYD0WPJVQEG2&AssociateTag=ws&
Operation=ItemSearch,ItemSearch&ItemSearch.1.BrowseNode=289852&
ItemSearch.2.BrowseNode=3737371&ItemSearch.3.BrowseNode=289854&
ItemSearch.4.BrowseNode=289862&ItemSearch.Shared.ResponseGroup=Medium&
ItemSearch.Shared.SearchIndex=Kitchen&ItemSearch.2.Keywords=sushi&
ItemSearch.3.Keywords=sushi&ItemSearch.4.Keywords=sushi&Version=2005-02-23
```

As a general rule of thumb, if the Browse Node is exactly the type of product you want, you can just use it as is, but if the Browse Nodes category is too broad or not specific, you can add the Keywords parameter to focus the search.

Using ItemSearch With Keywords And Title

Browse Nodes are the best way to search and retrieve specific product categories, but what do you do when you can't find a Browse Node that even comes close to matching the products we're looking for? The next best thing is to just use a Keywords or Title search and choose your words carefully. The Keywords parameter takes a search string and searches across various product fields including the product title and description fields. A Keywords search tries to return products that match the entire string you provide.

Here, I search for the key words "sushi knives" using the SearchIndex "Kitchen".

```
http://webservices.amazon.com/onca/xml?Service=AWSECommerceService&
Version=2005-02-23&AssociateTag=ws&SubscriptionId=001VHHVC74XFD88KCY82&
Operation=ItemSearch&SearchIndex=Kitchen&Keywords=sushi%20knives
```

> Note that you must URL encode the search string to ensure that the URL is valid, so the space between the words "sushi and "knives" is set to "%20", the hex representation for a space character.

Amazon returns the results containing the entire string "sushi knives" first, and then returns results that contain both the words "sushi" and "knives". Amazon will only search using words it recognizes as real words or words that are close enough to real words. If you had used "sushi zjdhs" as our search string, Amazon would just use the word it recognized and we'd only get results for "sushi". But it ignores "zjdhs" because it doesn't even recognize it as a word. If you used "sushi nives" (using "nives" instead of "knives"), Amazon's search engine figures out the misspelling and correctly searches for "sushi knives". If you search on "sushi Beatles", you get no results because there are no products in the Kitchen Search Index that have both the words sushi and Beatles in their listing (nor are there any results in the Music Search Index either, by the way). Amazon ignores conjunctions and simple words such as "the", "or", and "and".

The Title parameter searches only within the Title tag, which contains the name of the product. It should only be used when you have a very specific word or phrase you want to match in a product name. Any words in the Title parameter must match the same words or words exactly (case insensitive), and in the same order. Thus, "sushi knives" yields no results because there is no product title that has the exact phrase in its title. However, "sushi knife" has many matches.

Product Pricing, Condition, And Availability

Even if your Amazon E-commerce Service applications have beautiful product layout displays and fantastic usability features, you'll have unhappy users if they can't easily buy the products you're displaying. Just like in any other kind of store, some products may be out of stock, may take weeks for delivery, or may be discontinued. In many applications, it's important to convey this information to your customers. Understanding how product pricing, condition, and availability is handled by Amazon E-commerce Service is crucial for designing applications that provide users with accurate product information.

The majority of Amazon E-commerce Service applications will use the ItemSearch method to find and retrieve product data, so you will focus on how to use it to obtain desired results.

Using The ItemSearch Method To Find Products

As we've seen, the Keywords, Title, and BrowseNode search parameters afford us the most flexibility when searching with ItemSearch However, the three parameters that determine what kinds of offer listings and availability information you get in our responses are MerchantId, Condition, and ResponseGroup. These three parameters are the keys to making sure you can find products in the pricing, condition, and with the availability, that you want.

There are several key things to keep in mind when using the Item Search request:

- Every Item listing returned always has an ASIN

All Item listings returned in ItemSearch responses will have an ASIN. In fact, the ASIN is the only piece of product data that you know will be returned.

> This is only true because we're using the ItemSearch method which never returns products from Amazon zShops, where some products don't have ASINs. SellerListingLookup and SellerListingSearch can return zShops item that may not have ASINs.

- The ASIN will either be a regular ASIN or a Parent ASIN

Child ASINs are never returned as the result of an ItemSearch response. Child ASINs may appear in the Variations section underneath a Parent ASIN in the response, but they never appear as the result of the actual search. You may recall from Chapter 1 that product data associated with Parent and Child ASINs are known as "Variations". Parent ASINs identify the product, say, Converse tennis shoes, while the corresponding Child ASINs identify the "variations" of the shoe -- the different sizes and colors. So, one Child ASIN might be for the Converse tennis shoe, size: 13, color: white.

- The default MerchantId is Amazon's Merchant Id

If you don't specify a MerchantId, you only get offers from Amazon (the merchant) returned in the response. So, not specifying a MerchantID is the same as "MerchantId=ATVPDKIKX0DER" since that is Amazon's Merchant Id. With MerchantId = All, you get Amazon as well as all other sellers of an item. you can also get just one seller, MerchantId = [specific merchant id], which gives you only the listings for that specific Merchant Id. Finally, Merchant Id = Featured gives you the one merchant that Amazon "features" for the returned products.

> The "featured" merchant is usually the one that Amazon displays as the primary seller on the page where you can add the product to your Amazon shopping cart. The method Amazon uses to determine "featured" status is proprietary.

- The default Condition is New and Amazon only sells items in New condition

With no Condition parameter specified, only products in New condition are returned. Many merchants sell both used and new items, but Amazon only sells items in New condition. The possible values for the Condition parameter are All, New, Used, Refurbished, and Collectible.

- The default Response Groups are Small,Request

The default response groups for ItemSearch are Small and Request which doesn't return much data. You will always have to specify other Response Groups in order to get availability and pricing data.

- Items listed for sale only in zShops never show up in ItemSearch responses

zShops are showing their age in the Amazon catalog and fewer merchants are using them. Amazon, in fact, is encouraging sellers to move their listings to custom product pages and Marketplace listings. Because of the unusual categorizations and structure of the zShops, items only listed in zShops never get returned by ItemSearch requests (to search zShops, use the SellerListingSearch() operation).

Table 3-2 shows how you can combine various MerchantId, Condition, and ResponseGroup parameters to get desired item listings returned by your requests. The word "default" in the table means that you don't use the parameter in your request which is the same thing as specifying its default value.

An ItemSearch request to search the DVD Search Index for used items matching the keyword "ring" and returning offers from all merchants, would look like this:

```
http://webservices.amazon.com/onca/xml?Service=AWSECommerceService&
SubscriptionId=1A7XKHR5BYD0WPJVQEG2&Version=2005-02-23&
AssociateTag=ws&Operation=ItemSearch&SearchIndex=DVD&Keywords=ring&
ResponseGroup=Medium&MerchantId=All&Condition=Used
```

Table 3-2 Finding products from specific sellers

What Kind Of Products I Want Returned	MerchantId value	Condition value
Only New Products Offered by Amazon	`default`	`default`
Only New Products Offered by all sellers including Amazon	`All`	`default`
Only New Products Offered by Target[a]	`A1VC38T7YXB528`	`default`
Only Used Products Offered by all sellers	`All`	`Used`
All product conditions offered by all sellers	`All`	`All`

[a] You may wonder where I found Target's MerchantId. See Appendix A for techniques for manually finding various Amazon IDs.

Determining Product Availability

There are two measures of product availability. On Amazon, if a product can be purchased, then it is available. However, a secondary measure of product availability has to do with things like inventory and fulfillment time -- can the product be shipped today or in 2-4 weeks? Is it back-ordered? Is it a new DVD that hasn't been released yet? It is a special order item? Such products may still be considered "available" because they can be purchased, but they may not be ready to ship in the quantities, or in the desired time frame, for some customers.

A product is available for sale if it has offers. This is the base-level definition of availability on Amazon. An offer, or more specifically, an Offer Listing ID, identifies a specific instance of an inventory item for sale on Amazon.

For regular ASINs, you can examine the OfferSummary element to determine if a regular ASIN has any offers. For Parent ASINs, you can examine the Child ASINs in order to determine product availability.

> Parent ASINs never have offers because they are not items for sale. Only the Child ASINs of a Parent ASIN can have offers.

Recognizing Parent ASINs

Before you can determine whether an ASIN is available, you first you need to know if the ASIN returned in a response is a regular ASIN or a Parent ASIN.

You can tell if an ASIN is a Parent ASIN by making sure you use one of the Variations Response Groups -- either Variations or VariationSummary -- and test for the appearance of the VariationSummary tag in the response. If the VariationSummary tag appears in the response, then the ASIN is a Parent ASIN. If there is no VariationSummary tag, then it's a Regular ASIN.

> Amazon returns an OfferSummary tag along with the VariationSummary tag when you specify both the Variations and Medium Response Groups. You can ignore the OfferSummary tag (it will have all zeroes in it) if the VariationSummary tag is present.

There is no way to accurately tell if an ASIN is a Regular ASIN, but if it's not a Parent ASIN, then it must be a Regular ASIN.

Some Search Indexes, such as Books, Music, Video, and DVD, have no Variations. Other Search Indexes, such as Apparel, Jewelry, and Sporting Goods, have many Variations, but they also have some Regular ASINs as well.

Availability For Regular ASINs

Consider this request:

```
http://webservices.amazon.com/onca/xml?Service=AWSECommerceService&
SubscriptionId=001VHHVC74XFD88KCY82&AssociateTag=ws&Operation=ItemSearch&
SearchIndex=Music&Keywords=Beatles&ResponseGroup=Medium&Version=2005-02-23
```

This request searches the SearchIndex "Music" with the keyword "Beatles". The Response Group Medium returns the OfferSummary element which you can use to determine if products returned are available or not.

> The Medium, Large, Offers, OfferFull, and OfferSummary Response Groups all return the OfferSummary element if the ASIN is a Regular ASIN.

OfferSummary summarizes all offers available on an item regardless of what you specify for the MerchantId and Condition parameters. For example, you may specify Condition=Used in your request, but you'll still get back an OfferSummary showing the number of offers in New, Refurbished, and Collectible condition as well.

One of the items returned in this request is the CD "Magical Mystery Tour," which has ASIN B000002UDB. The OfferSummary for "Magical Mystery Tour" looks like this:

```
<OfferSummary>
    <LowestNewPrice>
        <Amount>885</Amount>
        <CurrencyCode>USD</CurrencyCode>
        <FormattedPrice>$8.85</FormattedPrice>
    </LowestNewPrice>
    <LowestUsedPrice>
        <Amount>779</Amount>
        <CurrencyCode>USD</CurrencyCode>
        <FormattedPrice>$7.79</FormattedPrice>
    </LowestUsedPrice>
    <LowestCollectiblePrice>
        <Amount>899</Amount>
        <CurrencyCode>USD</CurrencyCode>
        <FormattedPrice>$8.99</FormattedPrice>
    </LowestCollectiblePrice>
    <TotalNew>19</TotalNew>
    <TotalUsed>15</TotalUsed>
    <TotalCollectible>9</TotalCollectible>
    <TotalRefurbished>0</TotalRefurbished>
```

```
</OfferSummary>
```

You can just look at the TotalNew, TotalUsed, TotalCollectible, and TotalRefurbished data points to determine availability. If they're non-zero, there's at least one seller on Amazon selling it in that condition. Or, you can check the LowestNewPrice, LowestUsedPrice, LowestCollectiblePrice, and LowestRefurbishedPrice. If they exist, then there's an offer for it at the stated price.

OfferSummary will always appear in the response for each item even if there are no offers on the item. If no one on Amazon was selling the CD in any condition, the OfferSummary would look like this:

```
<OfferSummary>
     <TotalNew>0</TotalNew>
     <TotalUsed>0</TotalUsed>
     <TotalCollectible>0</TotalCollectible>
     <TotalRefurbished>0</TotalRefurbished>
</OfferSummary>
```

If you want more detailed information about product availability, you need to retrieve some actual offers as well. Adding the "Offers" Response Group to the request retrieves detailed offer information.

```
http://webservices.amazon.com/onca/xml?Service=AWSECommerceService&
SubscriptionId=001VHHVC74XFD88KCY82&AssociateTag=ws&Operation=ItemSearch&
SearchIndex=Music&Keywords=Beatles&ResponseGroup=Medium,Offers&Version=2005-02-23
```

Since I have not specified any MerchantId or Condition parameters, I'll only get back offers from Amazon, if they exist, and only items in "New" condition. For "Magical Mystery Tour", Amazon's offer looks like this:

```
<Offers>
  <TotalOffers>1</TotalOffers>
  <TotalOfferPages>1</TotalOfferPages>
  <Offer>
    <Merchant>
      <MerchantId>ATVPDKIKXODER</MerchantId>
      <GlancePage>http://www.amazon.com/gp/help/seller/home.
html?seller=ATVPDKIKXODER</GlancePage>
    </Merchant>
    <OfferAttributes>
      <Condition>New</Condition>
    </OfferAttributes>
    <OfferListing>
      <OfferListingId>QG%2BFR%2BMrPq9U01LFH5jEtcd2ByBiZ5SIhBgSbon7sObUucVXMR45059/
J5Ee4zHxmsQKn5BZBig%3D</OfferListingId>
      <Price>
        <Amount>1299</Amount>
        <CurrencyCode>USD</CurrencyCode>
        <FormattedPrice>$12.99</FormattedPrice>
```

```
      </Price>
      <Availability>Usually ships in 24 hours</Availability>
    </OfferListing>
  </Offer>
</Offers>
```

The <OfferListingId> element indicates an actual purchaseable item -- sort of like a price tag on a CD. Overall, the offer matches what you see on Amazon.com for the same listing, including the <Availability> string.

Magical Mystery Tour
The Beatles

Share your own customer images

List Price: ~~$18.98~~
Price: **$12.99** & eligible for **FREE Super Saver Shipping** on orders over **$25**. See details.
You Save: $5.99 (32%)

Availability: Usually ships within 24 hours

Want it delivered Tomorrow? Order it in the next 2 hours and 41 minutes, and choose **One-Day Shipping** at checkout. See details.

93 used & new from $8.97

Figure 3-2 The Amazon.com detail page for the Beatle's Magical Mystery Tour CD

Availability Strings

In Figure 3-2, the "Availability" element tells us that Amazon "Usually ships within 24 hours".

> The Availability strings returned by Amazon E-Commerce Service 4.0 are often shorter than the same strings you see on Amazon.com. E-Commerce Services uses shortened versions of the same strings to save space. In this particular case, the strings match.

The Availability element is the approximate answer to how quickly the item can be obtained once purchased. If you look at the list of Availability strings in Appendix E, you'll also see that many of the Availability strings indicate why an item is not available.

> Appendix E only lists Availability strings returned for Amazon (the merchant) products. There is no exhaustive list available (yet) of strings used by third party sellers.

Availability strings are useful for notifying your customers about detailed product availability, however, they aren't a reliable way of determining whether or not a product can be purchased. Always use the OfferSummary tag, or the OfferListingId to determine base-level product availability.

Availability For Parent ASINs

Consider this request which searches the Apparel Search Index using the keyword "blouse":

```
http://webservices.amazon.com/onca/xml?Service=AWSECommerceService&
SubscriptionId=1A7XKHR5BYD0WPJVQEG2&AssociateTag=ws&Operation=ItemSearch&
SearchIndex=Apparel&Keywords=blouse&MerchantId=All&ResponseGroup=Medium,Variations&
Version=2005-02-23
```

> Note that, if you want to return Variations information, you should include the MerchantId parameter since Amazon (the merchant) sells few, if any, items with variations.

Apparel and Jewelry are SearchIndexes that contain a lot of variations and thus return a lot of Parent ASINs. If you want to tell whether a Parent ASIN has any available offers on its Child ASINs, then you must use the Variations Response Group.

Using the Variations Response Group, you get the first ten Child ASINs and their Offers (if any) returned for each Parent ASIN in the response.

> A little trick is to use both the Variations and the Medium Response Groups. If the ASIN is a regular ASIN, you'll get the OfferSummary element, and if the ASIN is a Parent ASIN, you'll get back Child ASINs.

One of the ASINs returned by this search is a Liz Claiborne silk shirt that comes in various sizes and colors. It's a parent ASIN with a value of B0002I9HNQ.

The VariationSummary for this Parent ASIN looks like this:

```
<VariationSummary>
 <LowestPrice>
  <Amount>4900</Amount>
  <CurrencyCode>USD</CurrencyCode>
  <FormattedPrice>$49.00</FormattedPrice>
  </LowestPrice>
 <HighestPrice>
  <Amount>4900</Amount>
  <CurrencyCode>USD</CurrencyCode>
  <FormattedPrice>$49.00</FormattedPrice>
  </HighestPrice>
 <LowestSalePrice>
  <Amount>1715</Amount>
  <CurrencyCode>USD</CurrencyCode>
  <FormattedPrice>$17.15</FormattedPrice>
  </LowestSalePrice>
 <HighestSalePrice>
  <Amount>1715</Amount>
  <CurrencyCode>USD</CurrencyCode>
  <FormattedPrice>$17.15</FormattedPrice>
  </HighestSalePrice>
```

```
<SingleMerchantId>A3DEAPFTG94WC6</SingleMerchantId>
</VariationSummary>
```

The VariationSummary tells us the highest and lowest pricing, and the highest and lowest sale pricing, from among all Child ASINs of this Parent ASIN. If only one seller offers this set of Child ASINs, then their MerchantId is listed in the element SingleMerchantId. If more than one seller offers them, then there will be no SingleMerchantId listed.

However, unlike the OfferSummary for Regular ASINs, the <VariationSummary> section of the response does not tell us anything about availability of the actual Child ASINs. To find out if a particular Child ASIN is available, you must look further in the <Variations> section for the Child ASINs and their Offers (if any). If there are any Offers for Child ASINs in the <Variations> section, then you know that at least one Child ASIN (e.g. one size and color) of the Parent ASIN can be purchased.

Below, is the first Child ASIN returned and the Offer for it.

```
<Variations>
   <TotalVariations>9</TotalVariations>
   <TotalVariationPages>1</TotalVariationPages>
   <Item>
        <ASIN>B0002I9H0O</ASIN>
        <ItemAttributes>
             ...
              ...
             <ProductGroup>Apparel</ProductGroup>
             <Title>3/4-SLEEVE SILK SHIRT SILK IVORY Large</Title>
        </ItemAttributes>
        <Offers>
             <Offer>
                  <Merchant>
                       <MerchantId>A3DEAPFTG94WC6</MerchantId>
                       <Name>Liz Claiborne</Name>
                  </Merchant>
                  <OfferAttributes>
                       <Condition>New</Condition>
                       <SubCondition>new</SubCondition>
                  </OfferAttributes>
                  <OfferListing>
                       <OfferListingId>
z%2BZkiSfdpSeJHpdzA8P37pXUsHzYdTsnAM3ckB6Uspz7pOpWeKjIfCMfVqnM3Ysb6Fp2NU1CcyEpAfH%2BF
bF5JH6iMe7SrVAoJEja5djaak3LhdTD4zaTRg%3D%3D</OfferListingId>
                       <ExchangeId>Y11M5380553M5472821</ExchangeId>
                       <Price>
                            <Amount>4900</Amount>
                            <CurrencyCode>USD</CurrencyCode>
                            <FormattedPrice>$49.00</FormattedPrice>
                       </Price>
                       <SalePrice>
                            <Amount>1715</Amount>
                            <CurrencyCode>USD</CurrencyCode>
                            <FormattedPrice>$17.15</FormattedPrice>
```

```
                    </SalePrice>
                    <Availability>Usually ships in 1-2 business days</Availability>
                </OfferListing>
            </Offer>
        </Offers>
    ...
    ...
```

Here, a Child ASIN is listed. Because there is an Offer element for it, you know it is available. There is also an Availability string (see the previous "Availability Strings" section).

Pricing

The material we've just covered on availability is also applicable to finding pricing, since pricing is contained in the various offer listings. By picking the right Response

Information We're Looking For	Simplest Response Group Choice	Key Data Points Returned
List price for regular, Parent, and Child ASINs	`ItemAttributes`	`<ListPrice>`

Lowest available price for regular ASINs	`OfferSummary`	`<LowestNewPrice>`
		`<LowestUsedPrice>`
		`<LowestCollectiblePrice>`
		`<LowestRefurbishedPrice>`

Lowest and highest pricings for variations (the Child ASINs of a given Parent ASIN)	`VariationSummary`	`<LowestPrice>`
		`<HighestPrice>`
		`<LowestSalePrice>`
		`<HighestSalePrice>`

Specific seller prices for regular ASINs	`Offers`	`Look at the <Price> arrays in the <Offers> element`
Specific seller prices for variations (Child ASINs)	`Variations`	`Look at the <Price> arrays in the <Variations> element`

Table 3-3 How to find pricing for products using various Response Groups

Groups, you can get the prices for the various products returned.

In the previous two sections, you can see the various pricing structures in the listed responses. The <ListPrice> is an element that is regular, Parent, and Child ASINs, but it's not guaranteed to appear. Sometimes, the list price is simply missing.

Product Images

One of the huge benefits of Amazon E-Commerce Services is free access to Amazon's image server. As any web site owner will tell you, serving up images is a huge bandwidth hog, and the fact that you can let Amazon's site provide the image data for your applications is a real plus.

Links to product images are returned by the operations ItemSearch, ItemLookup, and SimilarityLookup when you use the Images, Medium, or Large Response Groups. A request to retrieve just the images of a product using ItemLookup might look like this:

```
http://webservices.amazon.com/onca/xml?Service=AWSECommerceService&
SubscriptionId=1A7XKHR5BYDOWPJVQEG2&AssociateTag=ws&Operation=ItemLookup&
ItemId=B0001BKAEY&IdType=ASIN&ResponseGroup=Images&Version=2005-02-23
```

which returns:

```
....
 <Item>
  <ASIN>B0001BKAEY</ASIN>
   <SmallImage>
      <URL>http://images.amazon.com/images/P/B0001BKAEY.01._SCTHUMBZZZ_.jpg</URL>
      <Height>60</Height>
      <Width>47</Width>
  </SmallImage>
  <MediumImage>
       <URL>http://images.amazon.com/images/P/B0001BKAEY.01._SCMZZZZZZZ_.jpg</URL>
       <Height>140</Height>
       <Width>111</Width>
  </MediumImage>
  <LargeImage>
       <URL>http://images.amazon.com/images/P/B0001BKAEY.01._SCLZZZZZZZ_.jpg</URL>
       <Height>500</Height>
       <Width>396</Width>
  </LargeImage>
  </Item>
 ....
```

For any item, Amazon returns three sizes, <SmallImage>, <MediumImage>, and <LargeImage>. If the image doesn't exist in one of those sizes, then that size is not returned. For example, if the <MediumImage> size didn't exist, then only the <SmallImage> and <LargeImage> elements would be returned. Although there is no way to know whether a particular image size (or any image at all) exists for a given product without requesting it, in general, the <LargeImage> size is least likely to be available of the three sizes.

For each image, the pixel dimensions are also returned which is useful if you need to do exact image placement in your application. Images are 96dpi (dots per inch) and 24 bit color (I've never seen any other resolutions, but they might exist).

Unfortunately, there is no hard and fast rule on the dimensions of the small, medium, and large images returned by Amazon. For particular product types e.g. CD and DVD images, dimensions tend to stay relatively constant for each image size, but for other product types, the image sizes can vary by as much as a 100 pixels in each dimension. Overall, the image size range I've found are listed in Table 3-4.

Table 3-4 Typical image sizes for Amazon product images

Image size	Height range	Width range
small	50-80 pixels	40-80 pixels
medium	100-160 pixels	100-160 pixels
large	220-500 pixels	220-500 pixels

Decoding Image URLs

Amazon's image server offers some image manipulation options not yet available through Amazon's E-Commerce Service, but you have to manually construct the image URLs to get at them. Consider the medium size "Matrix Revolutions" DVD from the previous section.

```
http://images.amazon.com/images/P/B0001BKAEY.01._SCMZZZZZZZ_.jpg
```

To add a 40% off circle, you add "__PE40" to the URL:

```
http://images.amazon.com/images/P/B0001BKAEY.01.__PE40_SCMZZZZZZZ_.jpg
```

The resulting image now looks like this:

To add a "Look Inside" arrow, add "PIm.arrow,TopLeft,20,-19" to the URL:

```
http://images.amazon.com/images/P/B0001BKAEY.01.__PE40_PIm.arrow,TopLeft,20,-19_
SCMZZZZZZZ_.jpg
```

Breaking down this URL yields details on how to construct similar URLs:

- **http://images.amazon.com/images/P/B0001BKAEY.01.** The prefix includes the ASIN of the item, B0001BKAEY, the domain name of the image server, images. amazon.com, and Amazon's own "country code" for the United States, 01. (for details on constructing images for use on Amazon's International sites, see Chapter 7). The capital P means that it's part of Amazon's main product catalog (as opposed to Auctions and zShops, which is "A", or "L" for scanned catalog images -- Amazon.com now sells items via scanned catalog pages, in case you didn't know).
- **__PE40_** This is the percentage off circle. Change 40 to whatever percent off you want the circle to say, between 1 and 99 inclusive.
- **PIm.arrow,TopLeft,20,-19** This adds a Look Inside or Search Inside arrow at x,y coordinates, 20, -19. "TopLeft" refers to the origin of the x,y coordinates. Other choices are "TopRight," "BottomLeft," and "BottomRight". m.arrow says to create an arrow for medium size images. The small letter "m" adjusts the size of the arrow where "t" is for small images (e.g. thumbnail size), and "m" is for medium size. If that letter is proceeded by an "s", e.g. sm.arrow, then a Search Inside arrow is presented instead of a Look Inside arrow. An additional choice is to add Amazon's little Schmoo character, by replacing m.arrow with "dp-schmooS".
- **_SCMZZZZZZZ_.jpg** Here, the letter "M" refers to the medium size image. Use "L" for the large image, and _SCTHUMBZZZ_.jpg for the small image. Most images also have an alternative size represented by _TZZZZZZZ_.jpg that Amazon uses to advertise products on their web site. It's about halfway between the size of the small and medium size images returned by Amazon E-Commerce Service.

Variations And Other Images

Variations items, e.g. Parent and Child ASINs, have a slightly different image URL format than regular ASINs. For example, the image URL for the medium size image of a particular Converse tennis shoe is:

```
http://images.amazon.com/images/P/B0001Y9114.01-AP74B9DWTEE7F._SCMZZZZZZZ_.jpg
```

It's identical to the image URL discussed in the previous section but with the addition of "-AP74B9DWTEE7F." The AP74B9DWTEE7F string is the Seller Id of the Merchant that's selling this particular shoe.

Variations items may also have alternative images for a product, such as a rear view of a shoe or a specialized sizing chart. Alternative views have the string "PTnn" inserted after the Seller Id, where "nn" are the alternative views numbered starting from "01" to "99". An example of such a URL is this glove sizing chart:

```
http://images.amazon.com/images/P/B0000AV5LG.01-A2ITH13LFQ00L5.PT02._SCLZZZZZZZ_.gif
```

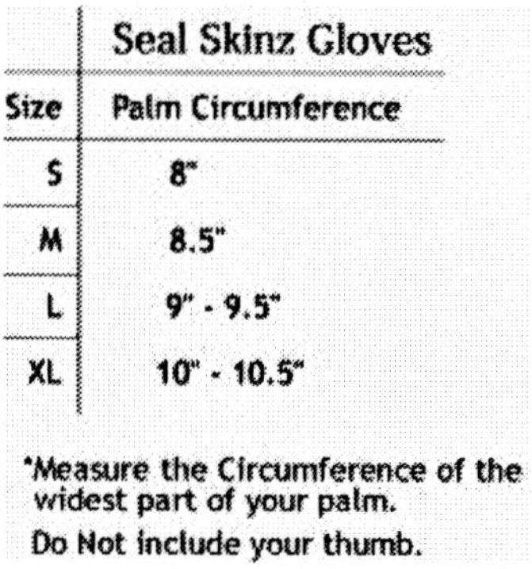

Size	Seal Skinz Gloves Palm Circumference
S	8"
M	8.5"
L	9" - 9.5"
XL	10" - 10.5"

*Measure the Circumference of the widest part of your palm.
Do Not include your thumb.

Items listed in zShops will often have an Exchange Id in the image URL:

```
http://images.amazon.com/images/A/Y04X0558760X1409306.0001.04.THUMBZZZ.jpg
```

or a redirection to a personal web site or 3rd party image server:

```
http://images.amazon.com/images/A/tiny-/images.tfaw.com/covers/sm/b/bonelunchbox.jpg
```

Empty Images

Amazon's image server never returns an error if you give it a syntactically valid image URL, instead it returns an (almost) empty image. Actually, it returns a transparent 1x1 pixel GIF image. For example, if we take one of the image URLs from the previous section and change the ASIN to something bogus:

```
http://images.amazon.com/images/P/00000BKAEY.01._SCMZZZZZZZ_.jpg
```

We have a syntactically valid Amazon image URL, but the image does not exist, so a 1x1 pixel GIF image is returned. This information will come in handy in Chapter Four when we work with variations and manually construct image URLs for Child ASINs.

Code Example: Amazon ProductSense

As Google's context-sensitive ad engine, AdSense, has proven, people are much less likely to be annoyed by advertisements on a web page if the ads are somehow associated with the content of the page they are viewing. If you are viewing a web page that reviews cell phone handsets, for example, you are less likely to be annoyed by accompanying ads that are selling cell phone accessories.

Our first application is a spin on AdSense, but using products from Amazon instead of advertisements (I'll call it ProductSense as a little play on words).

Google's AdSense works so well because Google has already indexed all of your web pages and therefore can easily find good contextual ad choices for your web pages. I take a much lighter weight approach and predefine the types of product searches I do based on an existing web site.

Like Google's AdSense, I'm going to display a box on a web page. Inside the box will be a list of Amazon products that (hopefully) have some relevance to the content on the rest of the page. Visitors to my web pages will be hopelessly spellbound by the product listings, click on them, and purchase them from Amazon. In turn, I'll receive 5% or so of the proceeds from each sale.

My fictional target site for deployment will be www.sushinewswire.com, a site that provides sushi bars and sushi lovers with the latest news and tips about sushi.

Displaying A Box On A Web Page Using PHP

There are several approaches you can use to programmatically create a box on a web page using PHP. You can:

1. Embed a PHP script directly in the HTML code
2. Target an HTML Iframe or frame with a PHP script
3. Use the HTML Script tag and reference a PHP script using Javascript.

Each approach has advantages and disadvantages. The advantages of using Iframes is that it doesn't require that the user have Javascript, however, it also forces you to hardcode the size of the frame (the product box) in advance. Using Javascript and the Script tag dynamically generates the box nicely, but the user must have Javascript enabled. The only disadvantage of embedding PHP is that it requires PHP generation of the web pages which can be problematic for sites that aren't using PHP to generate their web pages.

> You could also use DHTML and PHP, but that seems a bit redundant here.

Although I'm using Javascript sparingly in this book, I like the Javascript approach in this particular case. It lets sites without PHP take advantage of the script (by querying a remote server), and it only requires adding one line of code to an existing web page.

The HTML Page

You can embed ProductSense on a web page by adding a single <script> tag to each web page. When the web page is viewed, the script tag will load the PHP program which in turn outputs our product list from Amazon. The output of the PHP script must be Javascript, however, so I wrap the output in a Javascript document.write() call.

> Although any URL or file can be specified in the "src" attribute of the Script tag, most web browsers will only allow Javascript or VBscript to be output by the target script.

I call the PHP script, productsense.php, and it will require only one argument, i. The argument i is the index into the hardcoded array of product categories that I'll set up.

Below, when this web page is loaded, the PHP script is sent the argument i which has the value '2', and the output of the PHP script replaces the Script tag on the web page.

```
<HTML>
<HEAD>
</HEAD>
<BODY>
...
...
<SCRIPT type="text/javascript" language="javascript" src="http://www.mydomain.com/
productsense.php?i=2">
</SCRIPT>
...
</BODY>
</HTML>
```

I'll call this page sample1.html

Choosing Search Parameters

We'll use the ItemSearch method with either the Keywords or BrowseNodes parameter to search for relevant products. We'll also have to choose the appropriate SearchIndex, a required parameter. The Search Index is the top-level category we're searching in (valid Search Indexes are listed in Appendix H). We'll also take advantage of the Sort parameter so that you can have the products returned in a pre-sorted order, and the ResponseGroups parameter so that you can get back the level of product detail information that you need to construct our product box. The only other parameters you'll need are your Associates ID and Developer's Token which you should already have. We'll hardcode the Sort parameter, as well as the Associates ID and Subscription Id. The Keywords, BrowseNodes, and SearchIndex will be selected from a pre-defined array according to the $i parameter passed in from the previous section. We'll use the Response Groups Medium and VariationSummary so that you can get the list price (when available) as well as the pricing for any Parent ASINs you receive. Thus, our request url can be constructed like this for requests using Keywords:

```
$url='http://webservices.amazon.com/onca/xml?Service=AWSECommerceService&
AssociateTag='.ASSOCIATES_ID.'&SubscriptionId='.TOKEN.'&Operation=ItemSearch&
Keywords='.$searchterms[$i][1].'&SearchIndex='.$searchterms[$i][0].'&
Sort='.SORT.'&MerchantId=All&ResponseGroup=Medium,VariationSummary&Version='.VERSION;
```

For searching via BrowseNodes, you simply replace the word "Keywords" in the above request with the word "BrowseNode". In order to give ourselves more data to work with, we'll do a batch request that could get us as many as 20 items returned. The batch request uses the ItemPage parameter to request the first and second results pages for the search. All other parameters for each request stay the same -- they are "Shared" by the two requests.

```
url='http://webservices.amazon.com/onca/xml?Service=AWSECommerceService&
AssociateTag='.ASSOCIATES_ID.'&SubscriptionId='.TOKEN.'&Operation=ItemSearch&
ItemSearch.Shared.Keywords='.$searchterms[$i][1].'&
ItemSearch.Shared.SearchIndex='.$searchterms[$i][0].'&
ItemSearch.Shared.Sort='.SORT.'&ItemSearch.Shared.MerchantId=All&
ItemSearch.Shared.ResponseGroup=Medium,VariationSummary&
ItemSearch.1.ItemPage=1&ItemSearch.2.ItemPage-2&Version='.VERSION;
```

The maximum items that will be displayed by ProductSense is settable by the MAXITEMS_TO_DISPLAY define. you simply count how many items we've added to the display and exit when you reach MAXITEMS_TO_DISPLAY.

We'll include the MerchantId parameter and set it to All so that you can determine pricing and availability for any Parent ASINs you encounter. Pricing and availability for the regular ASINs will be returned by the Medium Response Group. you won't use the Condition parameter as you are only interested in products in "New" condition.

To keep things simple, we'll create an array, $searchterms, and fill it with pairs of Search Indexes and strings. The string will either be a string for a Keywords search, or a number for a BrowseNode search. The way we'll figure out what to put in the arrays will be a combination of looking at the contents of our fictional web site and testing various search parameters at the Amazon.com web site.

Our fictional web site, www.sushinewswire.com, a news and information site for sushi lovers, has several sections: a book reviews page, a video reviews page, a rice information page, a how-to cooking page, and a page with the latest news. Using the Search Index possibilities listed in Appendix H, I'll use techniques discussed previously for finding a relevant BrowseNode for product categories, or use a Keywords search otherwise.

```
$searchterms = array(
array('Books', '4269'),      // Book reviews page
array('Kitchen', '289939'),  // Rice information page, display rice cookers
array('Video',  'sushi'),     // Video reviews
array('GourmetFood', '3580501'),  // Cooking page
array('Apparel', 'sushi'),  // News page 1
array('Jewelry' , 'sushi') // News page 2
);
```

The $searchterms array consists of pairs of values. The first value is the Search Index, such as "Books", and the second value is either a Keyword or Browse Node. to search with.

Building The Display Loop

The bulk of the ProductSense application is just one big loop that goes through the PHP array returned by XmlParser(), picks out the data points you need, formats them in HTML, and stores them in a big string. The kind of HTML you use to display each product (table tags or div tags or whatever), as well as which pieces of product data you choose to display, is definitely a matter of taste. We'll use a very straightforward display, formatting our ProductSense box as an HTML table using the <table> tag with <div> tags inside to create separate lines within each table cell. We'll display a long box, from top to bottom, targeting a 160-pixel width (a standard width from the Internet Advertising Bureau, *www.iab.net*)

For each product, we'll display the small image, the name of the product, the list price, and the lowest new price. We'll loop through the parsed XML in order to list the products. We'll accumulate the output in a string that we'll output in a Javascript document.write() method.

```
// Fetch the request URL
$xml = GetData($url, 5);

// Parse the XML returned by Amazon
$Result = xmlparser($xml);

// Create table to output
$data='<table bgcolor="ECF8FF"><tr><div style="text-align:center">Product Sense</div>
</tr>';

// Loop through the list of items
foreach ($Result['ItemSearchResponse']['Items'][0]['Item'] as $item) {
      .
      .
      . [process the product details here]
      .
      .
// Add a product to our output table
    $data .= '<tr><td><img src="'.$image.'" alt="'.$realtitle.'" /></td><td><a
href="'.$detailpage.'" title="'.$realtitle.'" target="_blank">'. $title .'</a><div>
List Price: '. $listprice.'</div><div>Your Price: '.$yourprice.'<br /></div></td></
tr>';

}

// Close the output table
$data .= '</table>';
```

```
// Output our data as a one line Javascript script.
echo 'document.write(\''.$data.'\');';
```

Not all Amazon product records are complete or accurate, so it's always a good idea to test for the presence of data before you use it (this will also help keep PHP from spewing out warning messages about trying to use a non-existent array member).

> You should NEVER assume that any Amazon product record contains complete or accurate information -- or even valid XML. Minimally, you should always check each product data point to make sure it exists.

The data points we're using are the small product image, the list price, the lowest price in new condition, the link to the Amazon product page, and the name of the product. you can handle product pricing and availability at the same time. First you figure out if it's a Parent ASIN or a regular ASIN by testing to see if the "VariationSummary" structure is returned. If it is, you look for the price in either the VariationSummary or OfferSummary structure, as appropriate.

```
    if (isset($item['VariationSummary'])) {
$yourprice=(isset($item["VariationSummary"]["LowestPrice"]["FormattedPrice"]))?
$item["VariationSummary"]["LowestPrice"]["FormattedPrice"] : '';
    } else {
$yourprice=(isset($item["OfferSummary"]["LowestNewPrice"]["FormattedPrice"]))?
$item["OfferSummary"]["LowestNewPrice"]["FormattedPrice"] : '';
    }
```

If you don't find either of those prices, then you know the product is not available for purchase in new condition, so you skip that product and go on to the next one.

```
    if ($yourprice == '') continue;
```

The list price is found in the ItemAttributes section.

```
$listprice=(isset($item["ItemAttributes"]["ListPrice"]["FormattedPrice"]))?
$item["ItemAttributes"]["ListPrice"]["FormattedPrice"] : 'N/A';
```

The name of the product is in the <Title> tag. It should be *very* rare (but not impossible) to not find the <Title> element returned in the response. you then need to shorten the length of the title text to make sure it doesn't push the borders of our table out too far.

```
// Shorten the length of the title, if necessary, to prevent expanding the table cell
$realtitle=$item['ItemAttributes']['Title'];
$title = (strlen($realtitle) > MAXTITLELEN) ? substr($realtitle,0, MAXTITLELEN).'...'
: $realtitle;
```

Most items on Amazon.com have thumbnail images you can use. If there isn't an image available, none will be returned. Fortunately, Amazon has pre-made "no image available" images for each product category that you can use. I created the array $emptyimage to store those special images. If there's no thumbnail image available, we'll index into the emptyimage array using the Search Index.

```
 $image = (isset($item["SmallImage"]["URL"])) ? $item["SmallImage"]["URL"] :
$emptyimage[$searchterms[$i][0]];
```

We must check to make sure that the Detail Page URL is available. The Detail Page URL is the link to the product listing on the Amazon site. The link contains your Amazon Associates Id so that you are credited with any sales that are made by click-throughs.

```
$detailpage = (isset($item["DetailPageURL"])) ? $item["DetailPageURL"] : '';
```

Before encapsulating our output in a Javascript document.write() function, you must make one last pass through the output and make sure there are no newlines or unencoded single quotes. Either one will break the Javascript document.write() function. Our output is enclosed in single quotes, so you must encode any single quotes in our output with the HTML entity for single quotes, '. Newlines will cause the document.write() function to expect either a closing single quote or a line continuation character, so you simply remove any newlines (they'd server no purpose in browser output anyway).

```
$data=str_replace("'", "&#039;", $data);
$data=str_replace("\n", "", $data);
```

Caching For ProductSense

Our ProductSense application is likely to run into big trouble when it's put on a live web site. Once the code gets executed repeatedly by people accessing the web site, it will almost certainly violate the Amazon E-Commerce License Agreement which, as you may recall (see "The Amazon Licensing Agreement" in Chapter Two), says that a single Subscriber ID and IP address may not exceed more than one request per second. In order to come into compliance with the agreement you need to add caching.

There are many ways to cache, but for ProductSense, a simple flat-file file swap cache technique (courtesy of George Schlossnagle's "Advanced PHP Programming" book, *www.developers-library.com*) should work fine. This cache technique relies on the fact that a file can be removed from a filesystem via the unlink() system call, but any processes that are currently reading the file can continue to do so. The file is formally removed when the last process finishes reading from it. This side-effect lets us remove a stale cache file, and create a new cache file, at the same time without causing read or write errors.

We could choose to cache either the XML or the HTML. Caching the HTML seems like the way to go as you aren't doing anything with the XML except formatting it in HTML and displaying it.

Our initial cache code, which executes before you make a request from Amazon, checks to see whether you have any cached HTML and whether or not it is stale yet.

```
define('CACHE_PATH','/cache/');
define('CACHE_FILEPREFIX', 'psense_');
define('CACHE_REFRESH', '1'); // Hours before cache becomes stale

// Get the token passed in the URL
$i=isset($_GET['i']) ? $_GET['i'] : DEFAULT_SEARCH ;

// Check cache
$cachefile=getcwd().CACHE_PATH.CACHE_FILEPREFIX.$i.'.txt';
if (file_exists($cachefile)) {
    $modtime=filemtime($cachefile);
    if ((time() - $modtime) < CACHE_REFRESH*60*60) {
        $data=file_get_contents($cachefile);
        echo 'document.write(\''.$data.'\');';
        exit;
    }
    unlink($cachefile);
}
```

We first create the cache file name $cachefile and check to see if it exists. If it exists, you check the last modification time on the file. If the file doesn't exist, you make a new request from Amazon and create a new file. If the cache is stale, you delete the cache file and then you go and make a new request from Amazon. If the cache exists and isn't stale, you use it and exit.

Note that you must refresh the cache at least once an hour because you are displaying product prices. According to the License Agreement, if you refreshed the prices more than once an hour, we'd have to also display a disclaimer (as explained in Chapter Two, "The Amazon Licensing Agreement").

At the end of our script, you create a new cache file, since the old one either doesn't exist or is stale.

```
// Create new cache file
$cachefile_tmp=$cachefile.getmypid();
$fp=fopen($cachefile_tmp, 'w');
fwrite($fp, $data);
fclose($fp);
@rename($cachefile_tmp, $cachefile);
```

We first create a temporary file name, which is the cache file name with the process id tagged onto the end of it, and you write the data to the temporary file. Then you do a rename call, which actually does an unlink() under the hood, to move the temporary file to the cache file name. Any instances of ProductSense that are reading the cache file when this occurs will continue to read the old cache file until they finish. Any new instances of ProductSense will read the new cache file.

Error Handling

Finally, you need to add some simple error handling to deal with cases when either Amazon, our network connection, or some issue, keeps us from returning results.

```
if (!$Result or
(isset($Result['ItemSearchResponse']['Items'][0]['Request']['Errors']['Error'][0]['Co
de']))) {
    $data='Amazon is unavailable right now.<br /> Try again later.';
    echo 'document.write(\''.$data.'\');';
    return;
}
```

If our GetData call returns false because of a connection or Amazon issue, then the xmlparser() routine will immediately return false. If GetData returns invalid XML, then xmlparser() will also return false. If Amazon processes our request, but there's an error of some sort, I try to detect that by looking for the first Amazon error code string. you don't have time to process this here, so it's best to just exit.

> In a live production environment, you may wish to log the errors returned by XmlParser() and productsense as well as any HTTP return code or error that occurs in GetData().

Running ProductSense

Placing the xmlparser() and GetData() routines from Chapter Two into the file tools.inc.php, you now have a complete Product Sense application.

Example 3-3 Product Sense application for PHP4

```
<?php

error_reporting(E_ALL);
require_once("tools.inc.php");

define('VERSION','2005-02-23');
define('DEFAULT_SEARCH', 5);
define('SUBID', '1A7XKHR5BYDOWPJVQEG2');
define('ASSOCIATES_ID','ws');
define('MAXTITLELEN', 20);
define('MAXITEMS_TO_DISPLAY', 10);
define('CACHE_PATH','/cache/');
define('CACHE_FILEPREFIX', 'psense_');
define('CACHE_REFRESH', '1'); // Hours before cache becomes stale

// Get the token passed in the URL
$i=isset($_GET['i']) ? $_GET['i'] : DEFAULT_SEARCH ;

// Check cache
$cachefile=getcwd().CACHE_PATH.CACHE_FILEPREFIX.$i.'.txt';
if (file_exists($cachefile)) {
    $modtime=filemtime($cachefile);
    if ((time() - $modtime) < CACHE_REFRESH*60*60) {
        $data=file_get_contents($cachefile);
```

```
        echo 'document.write(\''.$data.'\');';
        exit;
    }
    unlink($cachefile);
}

// Array of Amazon 'image not found' images
$emptyimage = array(
'Video' => 'http://g-images.amazon.com/images/G/01/video/icons/video-no-image.gif',
'Books' => 'http://g-images.amazon.com/images/G/01/books/icons/books-no-image.gif',
'Kitchen' => 'http://g-images.amazon.com/images/G/01/kitchen/placeholder-icon.gif',
'Jewelry' => 'http://g-images.amazon.com/images/G/01/jewelry/nav/jewelry-icon-no-
image-avail.gif',
'Apparel' => 'http://g-images.amazon.com/images/G/01/apparel/general/apparel-no-
image.gif',
'GourmetFood' => 'http://g-images.amazon.com/images/G/01/gourmet/gourmet-no-image.
gif'
);

// Search Indexes and either relevant browse node or keyword search string
$searchterms = array(
array('Books', '4269'),      // Book reviews page
array('Kitchen', '289939'),  // Rice information page, display rice cookers
array('Video',  'sushi'),     // Video reviews
array('GourmetFood', 'sushi'),  // Cooking page
array('Apparel', 'sushi'),  // News page 1
array('Jewelry' , 'sushi') // News page 2
);

// Do a BrowseNode search if it's a number, a Keywords search otherwise
if (is_numeric($searchterms[$i][1])) {
    $search='ItemSearch.Shared.BrowseNode';
} else {
    $search='ItemSearch.Shared.Keywords';
}

// The search request string
$url='http://aws-beta.amazon.com/onca/xml?Service=AWSProductData&AssociateTag='.
ASSOCIATES_ID.'&SubscriptionId='.SUBID.'&Operation=ItemSearch&'.$search.'='.
$searchterms[$i][1].'&ItemSearch.Shared.MerchantId=All&ItemSearch.Shared.
SearchIndex='.$searchterms[$i][0].'&ItemSearch.Shared.
ResponseGroup=Medium,VariationSummary&ItemSearch.1.ItemPage=1&ItemSearch.2.
ItemPage=2&Version='.VERSION;

// Open the search request and get the response from Amazon
$xml = GetData($url, 5);
// Parse the XML returned by Amazon
$Result = xmlparser($xml);

// Check for Amazon error or no data returned
if (!$Result or
(isset($Result['ItemSearchResponse']['Items'][0]['Request']['Errors']['Error'][0]['Co
de']))) {
    $data='Amazon is unavailable right now.<br /> Try again later.';
```

```
    echo 'document.write(\''.$data.'\');';
    exit;
}

// Create the outside of the output table
$data='<table bgcolor="ECF8FF"><tr><div style="text-align:center">Product Sense</div>
</tr>';

$items_processed=1;
// Loop through the list of products returned by Amazon
foreach ($Result['ItemSearchResponse']['Items'] as $Items) {

    // Stop processing if second batch request has not items
    if (!isset($Items['Item'])) {
        break;
    }
    foreach ($Items['Item'] as $item) {

        // Check each data point to make sure it was returned by Amazon
        if (isset($item['VariationSummary'])) {

$yourprice=(isset($item["VariationSummary"]["LowestPrice"]["FormattedPrice"]))?
$item["VariationSummary"]["LowestPrice"]["FormattedPrice"] : '';
        } else {

$yourprice=(isset($item["OfferSummary"]["LowestNewPrice"]["FormattedPrice"]))?
$item["OfferSummary"]["LowestNewPrice"]["FormattedPrice"] : '';
        }

        // Item is not available for sale in New condition
        if ($yourprice == '') continue;

        $listprice=(isset($item["ItemAttributes"]["ListPrice"]["FormattedPrice"]))?
$item["ItemAttributes"]["ListPrice"]["FormattedPrice"] : 'N/A';

        $image = (isset($item["SmallImage"]["URL"])) ? $item["SmallImage"]["URL"] :
$emptyimage[$searchterms[$i][0]];

        // Shorten the length of the title, if necessary, to prevent expanding the
table cell
        $realtitle=$item['ItemAttributes']['Title'];
        $title = (strlen($realtitle) > MAXTITLELEN) ? substr($realtitle,0,
MAXTITLELEN).'...' : $realtitle;

        $detailpage = (isset($item["DetailPageURL"])) ? $item["DetailPageURL"] : '';

        // Add a product to our output table
        $data .= '<tr><td><img src="'.$image.'" alt="'.$realtitle.'" /></td><td><a
href="'.$detailpage.'" title="'.$realtitle.'" target="_blank">'. $title .'</a><div>
List Price: '. $listprice.'</div><div>Your Price: '.$yourprice.'<br /></div></td></
tr>';

        // Number of displayed items controlled by MAXITEMS_TO_DISPLAY
        if ($items_processed++ >= MAXITEMS_TO_DISPLAY) {
```

```
                break 2;
            }
        }
    }

    // Close the table
    $data .= '</table>';

    // Encode single quotes and remove newlines so Javascript does not break
    $data=str_replace("'", "&#039;", $data);
    $data=str_replace("\n", "", $data);

    // Create new cache file
    $cachefile_tmp=$cachefile.getmypid();
    $fp=fopen($cachefile_tmp, 'w');
    fwrite($fp, $data);
    fclose($fp);
    @rename($cachefile_tmp, $cachefile);

    // Output everything in Javascript format
    echo 'document.write(\''.$data.'\');';

    ?>
```

To launch productsense.php, you use our sample HTML page, sample1.html, and choose an index that will use the appropriate Search Index for the page. In this case, we'll use i=4, which will search for the word 'sushi' in the Search Index 'Apparel'. You will need to set the Javascript "src" parameter to point at the location of your productsense.php script.

```
<script type="text/javascript" language="javascript" src="http://www.yourdomain.com/
productsense.php?i=4">
</script>
```

Your output should look something like figure 3-3 below.

> Of course, any keyword search on Amazon is unlikely to return exactly the same results from day to day. Your output may vary.

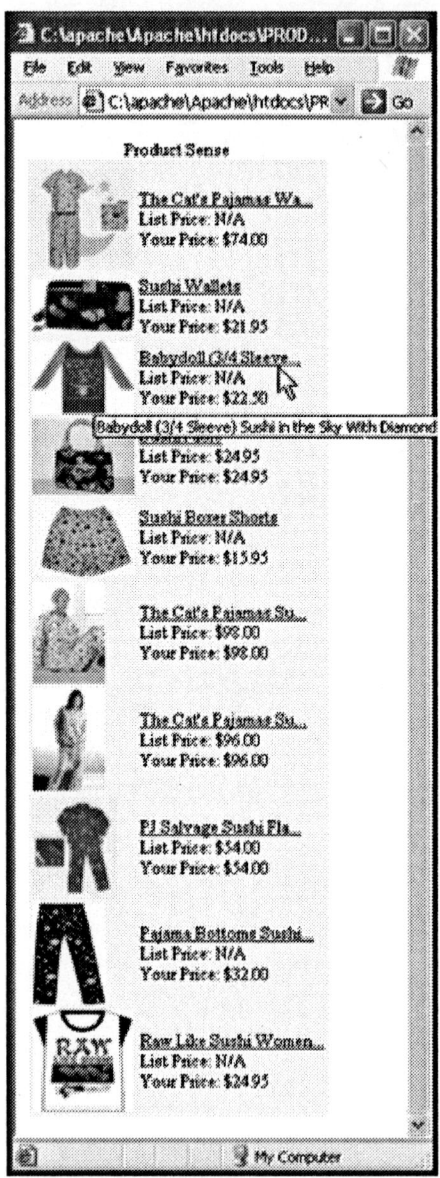

Figure 3-3 Output of the ProductSense application

The full product name is displayed via rollovers -- tooltips are displayed when the mouse cursor rolls over the abbreviated product name.

> Tooltips are a de facto standard for displaying helpful text when the cursor rolls over a link. It's generated by using the "title" attribute in the <a> anchor tag

ProductSense Using NuSOAP

The built-in XML parser in NuSOAP returns a data structure that is very similar to the one returned by the XmlParser() function, so very little has to be changed in order to get things to run. The VERSION define now depends on the WSDL file. We also need to add WSDL caching so that we aren't parsing the WSDL file on every call (for details on WSDL caching, see Appendix C).

For SOAP calls, the version of E-Commerce Service that we use depends on the WSDL file:

```
define('VERSION','2005-02-23');
define('WSDL', 'http://webservices.amazon.com/AWSECommerceService/'.VERSION.'/US/
AWSECommerceService.wsdl');
```

To cache the WSDL file, I use the code from Appendix C to grab the cached WSDL file, or cache it if it isn't already cached.

```
// Create a new instance of the caching class
$cache = new wsdlcache(WSDL_CACHE_DIR, WSDL_CACHE_TIME);

// Get the cached WSDL, if it exists
$wsdl = $cache->get(WSDL);

// If WSDL is not cached, cache it
if (is_null($wsdl)) {
    $wsdl = new wsdl(WSDL);
    $cache->put($wsdl);
}
```

Finally, we replace the XmlParser() and GetData() calls from the REST version with the equivalent SOAP calls.

```
// The Document/Literal input parameters
$Params = array( 'Request' => array( array( 'ItemPage' => '1' ), array( 'ItemPage' =>
'2' )), 'Shared' => array ( 'MerchantId' => 'All', $search => $searchterms[$i][1],
'SearchIndex' => $searchterms[$i][0], 'ResponseGroup' => array ( 'VariationSummary',
'Medium' )), 'SubscriptionId' => SUBID, 'AssociateTag' => 'ws' );

// Parse the WSDL to get Amazon methods
$Client = new soapclient(WSDL, true);

// Make sure encoding is UTF-8 -- nusoap has no constructor for this
$Client->soap_defencoding = 'UTF-8';

// Make the request
```

```
$Result = $Client->call('ItemSearch', array('body'=>$Params));
```

A PHP5 Version Of ProductSense

Our initial version of ProductSense is done using PHP4 and suffers from PHP4's lack of a good XML parser. You can significantly reduce the code size by making use of PHP5's SimpleXML extension. We can replace our GetData() and XmlParser() routines with one built-in call.

```
// Parse the XML returned by Amazon
$Result = simplexml_load_file($url);
```

> Because you are not using the GetData() function, there is no direct way to either set a timeout nor obtain the HTTP error code from the request (if any). An alternative is to use GetData() and then load the resulting string using the simplexml_load_string() function. The entire PHP4 version of ProductSense runs fine under PHP5.

SimpleXML returns PHP object structures instead of arrays, so you have to turn our array references into pointers. you now loop over a pointer to our items.

```
foreach ($Result->Items as $Items) {
    foreach ($Items->Item as $item) {
```

Only code that references the object returned by simplexml needs to be changed. The new code is below.

```
// Parse the XML returned by Amazon
$Result = simplexml_load_file($url);

// Check for Amazon error or no data returned
if ((!isset($Result->OperationRequest)) or (isset($Result->Items->Request->Errors->
Error->Code))) {
    $data='Amazon is unavailable right now.<br /> Try again later.';
    echo 'document.write(\''.$data.'\');';
    return;
}

// Create the outside of the output table
$data='<table bgcolor="ECF8FF"><tr><div style="text-align:center">Product Sense</div>
</tr>';

$items_processed=1;
// Loop through the list of products returned by Amazon
foreach ($Result->Items as $Items) {
    foreach ($Items->Item as $item) {

        // Check each data point to make sure it was returned by Amazon
        if (isset($item->VariationSummary)) {
            $yourprice=(isset($item->VariationSummary->LowestPrice->FormattedPrice))?
$item->VariationSummary->LowestPrice->FormattedPrice : '';
        } else {
```

```
            $yourprice=(isset($item->OfferSummary->LowestNewPrice->FormattedPrice))?
$item->OfferSummary->LowestNewPrice->FormattedPrice : '';
        }

        if ($yourprice == '') continue;

        $listprice=(isset($item->ItemAttributes->ListPrice->FormattedPrice))? $item->
ItemAttributes->ListPrice->FormattedPrice : 'N/A';

        $image = (isset($item->SmallImage->URL)) ? $item->SmallImage->URL :
$emptyimage[$searchterms[$i][0]];

        // Shorten the length of the title, if necessary, to prevent expanding the
table cell
        $realtitle=$item->ItemAttributes->Title;
        $title = (strlen($realtitle) > MAXTITLELEN) ? substr($item->ItemAttributes->
Title,0, MAXTITLELEN).'...' : $realtitle;
        $detailpage = (isset($item->DetailPageURL)) ? $item->DetailPageURL : '';
...
...
...
    }
...
}
```

ProductSense Using The PHP5 SOAP Extension

PHP 5.0, released in July of 2004, comes with a fast SOAP library. With only minor changes to our PHP5 REST version in the last section, you can be up and running with SOAP. PHP5's SOAP client, like PHP5's Simplexml extension, returns objects instead of arrays. They don't return exactly the same object structures, but they are close enough that, for ProductSense, you won't have to change any of the display code. In fact, you simply replace the call to SimpleXML with a WSDL instantiation and a method call, and you're up and running.

For SOAP calls, the version of E-Commerce Service that we use depends on the WSDL file:

```
define('VERSION','2005-02-23');
define('WSDL', 'http://webservices.amazon.com/AWSECommerceService/'.VERSION.'/US/
AWSECommerceService.wsdl');
```

PHP5 SOAP's WSDL caching happens behind the scenes. The configuration parameters are in your php.ini file. For configuration details, see "PHP5 WSDL Caching" in Chapter Two.

Replace the call to SimpleXML in the previous example with this PHP5 SOAP code.

```
// The Amazon method we're using
$method='ItemSearch';
```

```
// Our Document/Literal parameter array
$Params = array( 'Request' => array( array( 'ItemPage' => '1' ), array( 'ItemPage' =>
'2' )), 'Shared' => array ( 'MerchantId' => 'All', $search => $searchterms[$i][1],
'SearchIndex' => $searchterms[$i][0], 'ResponseGroup' => array ( 'VariationSummary',
'Medium' )), 'SubscriptionId' => SUBID, 'AssociateTag' => 'ws' );

// Parse the WSDL to get Amazon methods
$Client = new SoapClient(WSDL, array('exceptions' => false, 'soap_version' => SOAP_1_
1, 'trace' => true));

// Make the call to Amazon
$Result = $Client->$method($Params);
```

An XSLT Version Of ProductSense

We can take advantage of Amazon's XSLT server to generate our HTML output automatically. All you have to do is provide the proper XSL stylesheet. The style sheet replaces all the output logic that was in our PHP script.

The PHP code that skips unavailable items:

```
if (isset($item['VariationSummary'])) {
$yourprice=(isset($item["Variations"]["Item"][0]["Offers"]["Offer"][0]["OfferListing"
][0]["Price"]["FormattedPrice"]))?
$item["Variations"]["Item"][0]["Offers"]["Offer"][0]["OfferListing"][0]["Price"]["For
mattedPrice"] : '';
        } else {
$yourprice=(isset($item["OfferSummary"]["LowestNewPrice"]["FormattedPrice"]))?
$item["OfferSummary"]["LowestNewPrice"]["FormattedPrice"] : '';
        }
 // Item is not available for sale in New condition
 if ($yourprice == '') continue;
```

is handled by a single line of XSLT that skips any XML item nodes that lack both of those prices:

```
<xsl:variable name="productdata" select="/aws:ItemSearchResponse/aws:Items/aws:
Item[count(aws:Variations/aws:Item/aws:Offers/aws:Offer/aws:OfferListing/aws:Price/
aws:FormattedPrice) != 0 or count(aws:OfferSummary/aws:LowestNewPrice/aws:
FormattedPrice) != 0]"/>
```

Since we've already removed the items that aren't available and stored the remaining items in the variable productdata, you can then select as many nodes as you want by noting our position while you move through the items stored in productdata:

```
<xsl:for-each select="$productdata[position() &lt; $maxitems+1]">
```

We can simulate the selection of the "no image" image via our PHP $emptyimage array by grabbing the SearchIndex from the XML Arguments returned by Amazon, and selecting the appropriate URL based on the value:

```
      <xsl:variable name="searchindex" select="/aws:*/aws:OperationRequest/aws:
Arguments/aws:Argument[@Name='SearchIndex']/@Value"/>
     <xsl:variable name="no-image-url">
          <xsl:choose>
               <xsl:when test="($searchindex)='Video' ">http://g-images.amazon.com/
images/G/01/video/icons/video-no-image.gif</xsl:when>
               <xsl:when test="($searchindex)='Books' ">http://g-images.amazon.com/
images/G/01/books/icons/books-no-image.gif</xsl:when>
               <xsl:when test="($searchindex)='Kitchen' ">http://g-images.amazon.com/
images/G/01/kitchen/placeholder-icon.gif</xsl:when>
               <xsl:when test="($searchindex)='Jewelry' ">http://g-images.amazon.com/
images/G/01/jewelry/nav/jewelry-icon-no-image-avail.gif</xsl:when>
               <xsl:when test="($searchindex)='Apparel' ">http://g-images.amazon.com/
images/G/01/apparel/general/apparel-no-image.gif</xsl:when>
               <xsl:when test="($searchindex)='GourmetFood' ">http://g-images.amazon.
com/images/G/01/gourmet/gourmet-no-image.gif</xsl:when>
               <xsl:otherwise>http://g-images.amazon.com/images/G/01/v9/icons/no-
picture-icon.gif</xsl:otherwise>
          </xsl:choose>
     </xsl:variable>
```

Recall from Chapter Two that REST requests with style sheets use the special domain *xml-us.amznxslt.com* instead of *webservices.amazon.com*. The full style sheet is relatively small.

```
<?xml version="1.0" encoding="UTF-8"?>
<xsl:stylesheet version="1.0" xmlns:xsl="http://www.w3.org/1999/XSL/Transform" xmlns:
aws="http://webservices.amazon.com/AWSECommerceService/2005-02-23" exclude-result-
prefixes="aws">
 <xsl:output method="html" />
<!-- the variable productdata holds the entire product node minus -->
<!-- the items which do not have any pricing information         -->
          <xsl:variable name="productdata" select="/aws:ItemSearchResponse/aws:Items/
aws:Item[count(aws:VariationSummary/aws:LowestPrice/aws:FormattedPrice) != 0 or
count(aws:OfferSummary/aws:LowestNewPrice/aws:FormattedPrice) != 0]"/>
     <xsl:variable name="maxitems" select="/aws:*/aws:OperationRequest/aws:Arguments/
aws:Argument[@Name='maxitems']/@Value"/>
     <xsl:variable name="maxtitlelen" select="/aws:*/aws:OperationRequest/aws:
Arguments/aws:Argument[@Name='maxtitlelen']/@Value"/>
     <xsl:variable name="searchindex" select="/aws:*/aws:OperationRequest/aws:
Arguments/aws:Argument[@Name='SearchIndex']/@Value"/>
     <xsl:variable name="no-image-url">
          <xsl:choose>
               <xsl:when test="($searchindex)='Video' ">http://g-images.amazon.com/
images/G/01/video/icons/video-no-image.gif</xsl:when>
               <xsl:when test="($searchindex)='Books' ">http://g-images.amazon.com/
images/G/01/books/icons/books-no-image.gif</xsl:when>
               <xsl:when test="($searchindex)='Kitchen' ">http://g-images.amazon.com/
images/G/01/kitchen/placeholder-icon.gif</xsl:when>
```

```
                <xsl:when test="($searchindex)='Jewelry' ">http://g-images.amazon.com/
images/G/01/jewelry/nav/jewelry-icon-no-image-avail.gif</xsl:when>
                <xsl:when test="($searchindex)='Apparel' ">http://g-images.amazon.com/
images/G/01/apparel/general/apparel-no-image.gif</xsl:when>
                <xsl:when test="($searchindex)='GourmetFood' ">http://g-images.amazon.
com/images/G/01/gourmet/gourmet-no-image.gif</xsl:when>
                <xsl:otherwise>http://g-images.amazon.com/images/G/01/v9/icons/no-
picture-icon.gif</xsl:otherwise>
            </xsl:choose>
        </xsl:variable>
        <xsl:template match="/">
            <table bgcolor="ECF8FF">
                <tr>
                    <div style="text-align:center">Product Sense</div>
                </tr>
                <xsl:for-each select="$productdata[position() &lt; $maxitems+1]">
                    <tr>
                        <td>
                            <xsl:choose>
                                <xsl:when test="count(aws:SmallImage/aws:URL) != 0">
                                    <img src="{aws:SmallImage/aws:URL}" alt="{aws:
ItemAttributes/aws:Title}"/>
                                </xsl:when>
                                <xsl:otherwise>
                                    <img src="{$no-image-url}" alt="{aws:
ItemAttributes/aws:Title}"/>
                                </xsl:otherwise>
                            </xsl:choose>
                        </td>
                        <td>
                            <a href="{aws:DetailPageURL}" title="{aws:ItemAttributes/
aws:Title}" target="_blank">
                                <xsl:choose>
                                    <xsl:when test="string-length(aws:ItemAttributes/
aws:Title) &gt;  $maxtitlelen">
                                        <xsl:value-of select="concat(substring(aws:
ItemAttributes/aws:Title, 1, $maxtitlelen),'...')"/>
                                    </xsl:when>
                                    <xsl:otherwise>
                                        <xsl:value-of select="aws:ItemAttributes/aws:
Title"/>
                                    </xsl:otherwise>
                                </xsl:choose>
                            </a>
                            <div>
List Price:
<xsl:choose>
                                    <xsl:when test="count(aws:ItemAttributes/aws:
ListPrice/aws:FormattedPrice) != 0">
                                        <xsl:value-of select="aws:ItemAttributes/aws:
ListPrice/aws:FormattedPrice"/>
                                    </xsl:when>
                                    <xsl:otherwise>
                                        N/A
```

```
                                    </xsl:otherwise>
                                </xsl:choose>
                            </div>
                            <div>
Your Price:
<xsl:choose>
                                    <xsl:when test="count(aws:VariationSummary/aws:
LowestPrice/aws:FormattedPrice) != 0">
                                        <xsl:value-of select="aws:VariationSummary/
aws:LowestPrice/aws:FormattedPrice"/>
                                    </xsl:when>
                                    <xsl:when test="count(aws:OfferSummary/aws:
LowestNewPrice/aws:FormattedPrice) != 0">
                                        <xsl:value-of select="aws:OfferSummary/aws:
LowestNewPrice/aws:FormattedPrice"/>
                                    </xsl:when>
                                    <xsl:otherwise>
                                        N/A
                                    </xsl:otherwise>
                                </xsl:choose>
                                <br/>
                            </div>
                        </td>
                    </tr>
                </xsl:for-each>
            </table>
        </xsl:template>
</xsl:stylesheet>
```

Although it possible to put all the program logic into a single style sheet, it's a better idea in this instance to keep the basic program logic intact. Our PHP is now minimal.

```
<?php

error_reporting(E_ALL);

// you just need the GetData() function
require_once("tools.inc.php");

define('VERSION','2005-02-23');
define('DEFAULT_SEARCH', 5);
define('SUBID', '1A7XKHR5BYDOWPJVQEG2');
define('ASSOCIATES_ID','ws');
define('MAXTITLELEN', 20);
define('MAXITEMS_TO_DISPLAY', 9);
define('CACHE_PATH','/cache/');
define('CACHE_FILEPREFIX', 'psense_');
define('CACHE_REFRESH', '1'); // Hours before cache becomes stale

// Get the token passed in the URL
$i=isset($_GET['i']) ? $_GET['i'] : DEFAULT_SEARCH ;

// Check cache
$cachefile=getcwd().CACHE_PATH.CACHE_FILEPREFIX.$i.'.txt';
```

```
if (file_exists($cachefile)) {
    $modtime=filemtime($cachefile);
    if ((time() - $modtime) < CACHE_REFRESH*60*60) {
        $data=file_get_contents($cachefile);
        echo 'document.write(\''.$data.'\');';
        exit;
    }
    unlink($cachefile);
}

// Search Indexes and either relevant browse node or keyword search string
$searchterms = array(
array('Books', '4269'),      // Book reviews page
array('Kitchen', '289939'),  // Rice information page, display rice cookers
array('Video',  'sushi'),      // Video reviews
array('GourmetFood', 'sushi'),  // Cooking page
array('Apparel', 'sushi'),  // News page 1
array('Jewelry' , 'sushi') // News page 2
);

// Do a BrowseNode search if it's a number, a Keywords search otherwise
if (is_numeric($searchterms[$i][1])) {
    $search='BrowseNode';
} else {
    $search='Keywords';
}

$stylesheet='http://www.myserver.com/example.xsl';

// The search request string
$url='http://xml-us.amznxslt.com/onca/xml?Service=AWSECommerceService&
AssociateTag='.ASSOCIATES_ID.'&SubscriptionId='.SUBID.'&Operation=ItemSearch&
'.$search.'='.$searchterms[$i][1].'&ItemSearch.Shared.MerchantId=All&
ItemSearch.Shared.SearchIndex='.$searchterms[$i][0].'&
ItemSearch.Shared.ResponseGroup=Medium,VariationSummary&
ItemSearch.Shared.Style='.$stylesheet.'&maxtitlelen='.MAXTITLELEN.'&
maxitems='.MAXITEMS_TO_DISPLAY.'&ItemSearch.Shared.ContentType=text%2Fhtml&
ItemSearch.1.ItemPage=1&ItemSearch.2.ItemPage=2&Version='.VERSION;

// Open the search request and get the response from Amazon
$Result = GetData($url, 5);

// Single quotes break Javascript
// Newlines break document.write
$data=str_replace("'", "&#039;", $Result);
$data=str_replace("\n", "", $data);

// Check for no data returned or Amazon ignores stylesheet and returns XML
if (!$data or (substr($data, 0, 5) == '<?xml')){
    $data='Amazon is unavailable right now.<br /> Try again later.';
    echo 'document.write(\''.$data.'\');';
    return;
}
```

```
// Create new cache file
$cachefile_tmp=$cachefile.getmypid();
$fp=fopen($cachefile_tmp, 'w');
fwrite($fp, $data);
fclose($fp);
@rename($cachefile_tmp, $cachefile);

// Output everything in Javascript format
echo 'document.write(\''.$data.'\');';

?>
```

Exercises For The Reader

Modify ProductSense to use Iframes instead of a Javascript tag.

Instead of using an array of search terms, modify ProductSense so that it accepts input from a user's search of a web site or from another source.

Modify the XSLT version of ProductSense so that it uses no PHP. The entire application will reside in one stylesheet.

Modify the PHP5 version of ProductSense so that it uses PHP's output buffering (e.g. the ob_start() function) to generate the cache file output. (hint: this method is used in Schlossanagle's book).

Add the Sort parameter to ProductSense to see if you can get different results.

Modify ProductSense to use CSS and the image dimensions to give it a fresh look. Allow the CSS to be customized (color, borders, fonts, etc) from parameters that come from Javascript or PHP.

CHAPTER 4

Pagination, Sorting, Product Details, And Variations

Faith moves mountains... (of inventory)
—Ferengi Rule Of Acquisition #104

There are gazillions of product records stored in Amazon's databases and E-Commmerce Service gives you access to much of that data. To deal with the possibility that your E-Commerce search request will retrieve 10,000 items requires a bit of finesse and a few tools.

Pagination, expressing data as a series of document pages, is a way to reveal the existence of data without having to actually retrieve the data. Sorting lets you (or your users) change the order in which those quantities of data are displayed.

In this Chapter, I show techniques for managing large quantities of data by applying pagination and sorting to your E-Commerce Service requests. Finally, I delve deeper into product data records and retrieve some of the fine product details E-Commerce Service makes available to developers as well as show an example of dealing with Amazon's Variations.

Pagination

When you go to Amazon.com and search for something popular, you'll likely get hundreds (maybe thousands) of results. Searching Amazon's music section for the artist "Beatles" got me 232 results (Figure 4-1).

If I make this same search request using Amazon E-Commerce Service, I'll only get the first ten items returned in my request.

> In a future version of Amazon E-Commerce Service, Amazon may allow developers to specify the number of results returned, up to some reasonable maximum.

The rest of the results, if there are any, are available by making subsequent requests and using a paging parameter. The paging parameter is different depending on the type of request being made. In the case of the ItemSearch request, you can retrieve subsequent sets of results by incrementing the ItemPage parameter for each request.

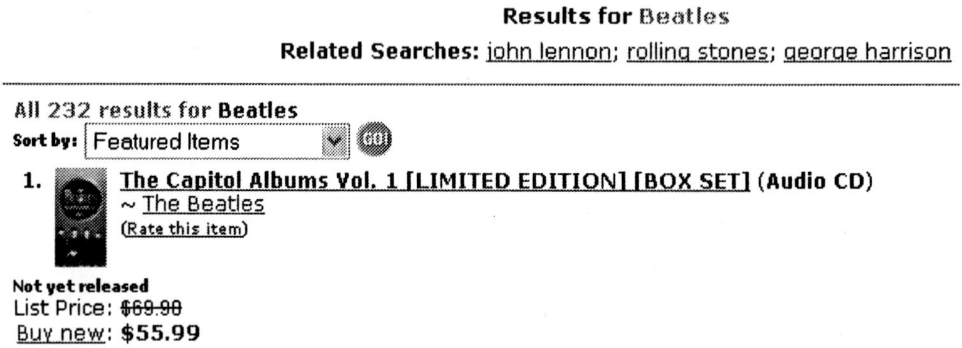

Results for Beatles
Related Searches: john lennon; rolling stones; george harrison

All 232 results for **Beatles**
Sort by: Featured Items GO!

1. **The Capitol Albums Vol. 1 [LIMITED EDITION] [BOX SET] (Audio CD)**
~ The Beatles
(Rate this item)

Not yet released
List Price: ~~$69.98~~
Buy new: **$55.99**

Figure 4-1 Searching for the keyword "Beatles" in Amazon.com's Music store

To aid developers in paginating results, Amazon E-Commerce Service always returns the total number of items found by our search request, and the total pages, in each response. The two elements in each response, <TotalResults> and <TotalPages>, contain those numbers.

TotalResults is the total number of items that were found by the search. TotalPages is the number of pages (ten items per page) that were found by the search.

For example, the ItemSearch request that corresponds to the Amazon.com request I used to get the result in Figure 4-1 looks like this:

```
http://webservices.amazon.com/onca/xml?Service=AWSECommerceService&
AssociateTag=ws&SubscriptionId=1A7XKHR5BYD0WPJVQEG2&
Operation=ItemSearch&Artist=Beatles&SearchIndex=Music&Version=2005-01-19
```

In the results for this request, it tells us there are 232 results and thus 24 total pages.

```
<TotalResults>232</TotalResults>
<TotalPages>24</TotalPages>
```

By default, Amazon only returns the first page (the first 10 items) of the results. To get more of the 23 pages of results, we must make subsequent requests using the ItemPage parameter. Setting ItemPage=2 will return page 2 of the results.

```
http://webservices.amazon.com/onca/xml?Service=AWSECommerceService&
AssociateTag=ws&SubscriptionId=1A7XKHR5BYD0WPJVQEG2&
Operation=ItemSearch&Artist=Beatles&SearchIndex=Music&Version=2005-01-19&ItemPage=2
```

> If you try to retrieve a page that is beyond the number of pages of results, in this case, ItemPage=30, you will receive an AWS.ECommerceService.NoExactMatches error.

There are many more things besides items that are returned en masse by Amazon. Seller Feedback, Customer Reviews, and Offers are a few of the objects that have paging parameters. Table 4-1 summarizes all of the paginated objects returned by Amazon E-Commerce Service.

Table 4-1 Paginated objects returned by Amazon E-Commerce Service

Data you are looking for	operation	Pagination parameter	Count nodes returned by Amazon	Per[a]	Total[b]
All items returned for a search	ItemSearch	ItemPage	<TotalResults> <TotalPages>	10	5000
All items returned for a zShops and MarketPlace search	SellerListingSearch	ListingPage	<TotalResults> <TotalPages>	10	5000
All Child ASINs for a given Parent ASIN (e.g. all Variations)	ItemLookup	VariationPage	<TotalVariations> <TotalVariationPage s>	10	1500
All reviews for an item	ItemLookup	ReviewPage	<TotalReviews> <TotalReviewPages>	5	100
All offers for an item	ItemLookup	OfferPage	<TotalOffers> <TotalOfferPages>	10	1000
All customers who match a name or email address search	CustomerContent Search	CustomerPage	<TotalResults> <TotalPages>	20	400
All items in a list	ListLookup	ProductPage	<TotalItems> <TotalPages>	10	300
All lists that match search criteria	ListSearch	ListPage	<TotalItems> <TotalPages>	10	200
All customer reviews from a specific customer	CustomerContentL ookup	ReviewPage	<TotalReviews> <TotalReviewPages>	10	100
All feedback for a specific seller	SellerLookup	FeedbackPage	<TotalFeedback> <TotalFeedbackPages >	5	50

[a]Maximum number of objects returned for each Amazon request
[b]Maximum number of objects Amazon exposes for a given request

Note that Amazon, in some cases, severely limits the number of results we have access to. We can only retrieve a maximum of 100 reviews from the CustomerContentLookup operation, for example. Limiting ItemSearch responses to the first 5000 items is also quite a limitation when one considers that search requests on the Amazon web site can easily return 10000 or more matches.

The order in which items are returned is determined by the Sort parameter. For other objects, the sort order is fixed. I'll discuss sorting in more detail later in this chapter.

Pagination Example

In this pagination example, we'll search for every CD from the saxophonist Lou Donaldson and let the user page through all the results. We'll use an ItemSearch with the "Artist" parameter which, since Lou's name is pretty distinctive, should work ok.

> It's possible, of course, for artists to have the same name and thus an ItemSearch by Artist search will return CDs by everyone with that name.

```
$request='http://webservices.amazon.com/onca/xml?Service=AWSECommerceService&
AssociateTag='.ASSOCIATES_ID.'&SubscriptionId='.SUBID.'&Operation=ItemSearch&
SearchIndex=Music&Artist=Lou%20Donaldson&ItemPage='.$page.'&
ResponseGroup=Small,Images&Version='.VERSION;
```

A common way to handle pagination in web applications is to pass paging parameters in a URL using HTTP GET calls. Since we know the total number of pages from the <TotalPage> parameters, we can build the subsequent retrieval strings in our display.

```
for ($i=1; $i <= $Result['ItemSearchResponse']['Items'][0]['TotalPages']; $i++)
        {
            $p = ($i == $page) ? $page : '<a href="lou.php?page='.$i.'">'.$i.'</a>';
            echo $p.' ';
        }
```

If we're looking at the page we want, then we just print the number, but if it's a page that the user can request, then we build an HTTP GET request that will display a clickable page number e.g.

```
<a href="lou.php?page=3">3</a>
```

This will display a clickable number 3 that will launch our script (named lou.php) with page=3 as a parameter.

Example 4-1 is a simple script that demonstrates these concepts.

Example 4-1 Pagination program example

```
<?php

require_once("tools.inc.php");

define('SEARCH', 'Lou Donaldson');              // The artist
define('SUBID', '1A7XKHR5BYDOWPJVQEG2');        // Your subscription id
define('ASSOCIATES_ID','ws');                   // Your Associates id
define('VERSION','2005-02-23');                 // The version of AES

// A 'no image' image to use
define ('NOIMAGE', 'http://g-images.amazon.com/images/G/01/x-site/icons/no-img-lg.
gif');
// If we don't have a page parameter, this is the default page
define('DEFAULT_PAGE', '1');
```

```
// Get the page parameter from the GET request
$page=(isset($_GET['page'])) ? $_GET['page'] : DEFAULT_PAGE;

// Make the request for more CDs
$request='http://webservices.amazon.com/onca/
xml?Service=AWSECommerceService&AssociateTag='.ASSOCIATES_ID.'&SubscriptionId='.
SUBID.'&Operation=ItemSearch&SearchIndex=Music&Artist=Lou%20Donaldson&ItemPage='.
$page.'&ResponseGroup=Small,Images&Version='.VERSION;

// Get the response from Amazon
$xml = file_get_contents($request);
// Parse the results
$Result = xmlparser($xml);

// The main display routine
function theContent() {
    global $Result;

    echo '<table cellspacing="2" cellpadding="2"><tr>';
    $rowcount=0;
    // Display two rows of CDs
    foreach ($Result['ItemSearchResponse']['Items'][0]['Item'] as $item) {
        // Show the CD image, else the no image image
        if (isset($item['MediumImage']['URL'])) {
            $image='<img src="'.$item["MediumImage"]["URL"].'" />';
        } else {
            $image='<img src="'.NOIMAGE.'" />';
        }
        // Get the CD title
        $title = '<a href="'.$item["DetailPageURL"].'" target="_blank">'.
$item["ItemAttributes"]["Title"].'</a>';
        // After displaying five CDs, move to the next line
        if (is_int($rowcount/5)) echo '</tr><tr>';
        echo '<td><div style="text-align: center;">'.$title.'</div><div style="text-
align: center;">'.$image.'</div></td>';
        $rowcount++;
    }
    echo '</tr></table';
    return;
}

// Display the pagination footer
 function thePagination() {
    global $Result;
    global $page;

    echo '<div style="text-align: left;"><b>More results.......</div><div>';
    // Display a clickable page number
    for ($i=1; $i <= $Result['ItemSearchResponse']['Items'][0]['TotalPages']; $i++)
    {
        $p = ($i == $page) ? $page : '<a href="lou.php?page='.$i.'">'.$i.'</a>';
        echo $p.' ';
    }
```

```
        echo '</b></div>';
        return;
    }

    ?>
    <html>
    <head>
    <title>Lou Donaldson CDs</title>
    </head>
    <body>
    <table width="100%" border="1" cellpadding="2" cellspacing="2">
       <tr>
         <td width="100%" height="250"><?php theContent(); ?> </td>
      </tr>
       <tr>
         <td colspan="2">
      <table width="100%">
         <tr>
          <td width="100%"> <?php thePagination(); ?></td>
         </tr>
      </table>
    </td>
    </tr>
    </table>
    </body>
    </html>
```

Using this ItemSearch, and examining the XML output, we find that Lou has <TotalResults>70</TotalResults> and <TotalPages>7</TotalPages>.

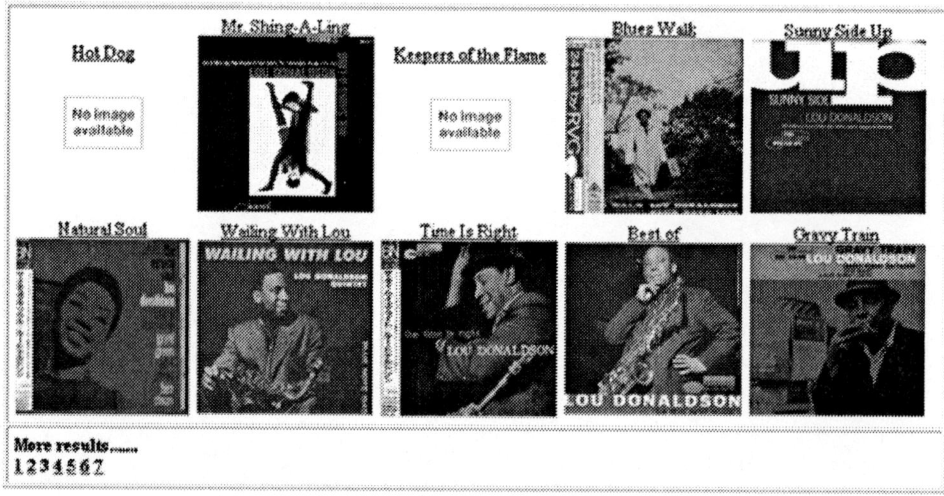

Figure 4-2 Displaying 10 CDs at a time using pagination

Running the script and clicking on the number three causes the third set of ten results to display.

Fetching Two Pages At A Time

There's one simple modification to the Lou Donaldson example that will let us fetch and display two pages of results at a time. We simply use a Batch request (for details on REST Batch request formats, see the "REST Batch Requests" section in Chapter Two). Developers can make up to two requests at once using Batch requests, so that means we can get twenty results (two pages).

In this batch request, all parameters are shared between the two requests except for the ItemPage parameter. When we receive $page, we increment it by one to get the next page, which I call $nextpage.

```
$nextpage=$page+1;

// A batch request that retrieves two pages at once
$request='http://webservices.amazon.com/onca/xml?Service=AWSECommerceService&
AssociateTag='.ASSOCIATES_ID.'&SubscriptionId='.SUBID.'&Operation=ItemSearch&
ItemSearch.Shared.SearchIndex=Music&ItemSearch.Shared.Artist=Lou%20Donaldson&
ItemSearch.1.ItemPage='.$page.'&ItemSearch.2.ItemPage='.$nextpage.'&
ItemSearch.Shared.ResponseGroup=Small,Images&ItemSearch.Shared.Version='.VERSION;
```

The next step is to change the output loop. I now have two sets of responses to cycle through, so I have to change the foreach statement to loop through the responses and then add a second foreach statement that cycles through the items as before.

```
foreach ($Result['ItemSearchResponse']['Items'] as $Items) {
        foreach ($Items['Item'] as $item) {
```

Finally, in the list of pages that the user can click on, I display two numbers together and increment the loop by 2 now.

```
 for ($i=1; $i <= $Result['ItemSearchResponse']['Items'][0]['TotalPages']; $i=$i+2)
    {
        $nextpage=$i+1;
        $p = ($i == $page) ? $page.'-'.$nextpage : '<a href="lou.php?page='.$i.'">'.
$i.'-'.$nextpage.'</a>';
        echo $p.' ';
    }
```

The modified program outputs 20 CDs at a time.

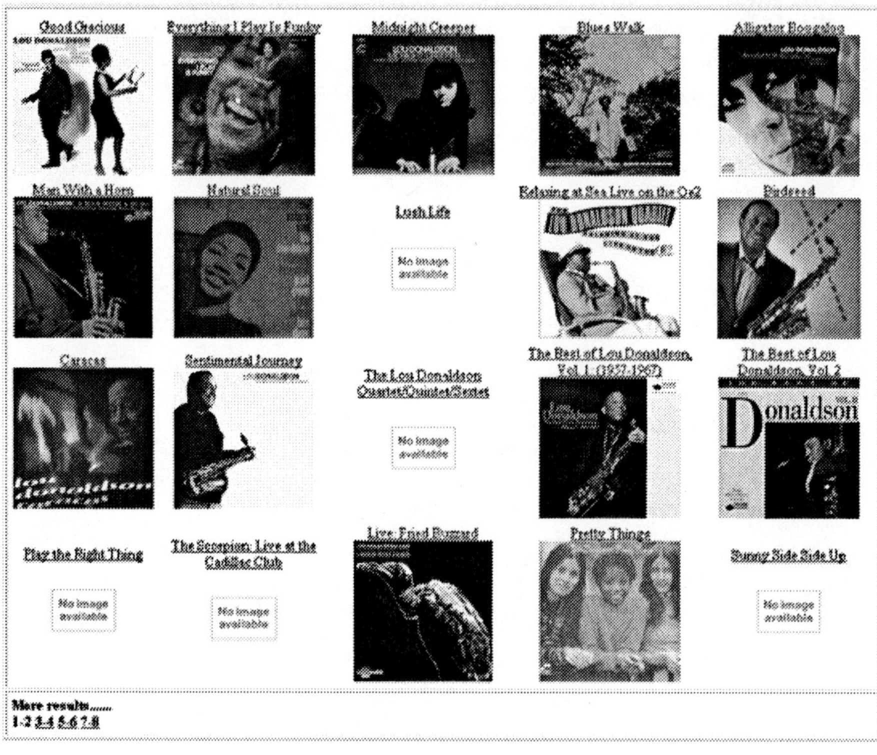

Figure 4-3 A batch request lets developers display up to 20 items per request

Sorting

So far in this book, we've only used the ItemSearch operation without specifying that the results be returned in any particular order, but ItemSearch has a parameter called Sort that returns the items in a specific order. The available sort values depend on which Search Index we are searching (Appendix G lists the available sorting parameters for each Search Index).

> The sort order also varies by locale. For a discussion of the sorting on the International Amazon sites, see Chapter 7.

The sort values for the Music Search Index are listed in table 4-2.

Sort value	Description
psrank	"Featured" items
salesrank	Bestselling items as determined by the Amazon "Sales Rank"
price	Price: lowest to highest price

Sort value	Description
-price	Price: highest to lowest price
titlerank	Alphabetical: Z to A determined by the <Title> element
-titlerank	Alphabetical: A to Z determined by the <Title> element
artistrank	Artist name: A to Z determined by the <Artist> element
orig-rel-date	Release date: newer to older

Table 4-2 Sort values for the Music Search Index

By default (no sort order specified), most Search Indexes return items sorted by "Featured" status. The definition of "Featured" (the order "psrank" in the table above) on Amazon is determined by some internal proprietary mechanisms at Amazon. All I know is that the Featured sort order will usually return items in the same order as if the person was doing the same search on the Amazon web site. So if you want your results to mimic the order of results returned when you search directly on amazon.com, you can use the Featured sort order.

operation	Pagination parameter	Sort order
ItemSearch	`ItemPage`	`Determined by Sort parameter (default is "Featured")`
SellerListingSearch	`ListingPage`	`Determined by Sort parameter (default is "Featured")`
ItemLookup	`VariationPage`	`Fixed`
ItemLookup	`ReviewPage`	`Fixed`
ItemLookup	`OfferPage`	`Lowest to highest price.`
CustomerContent Search	`CustomerPage`	`Fixed`
ListLookup	`ProductPage`	`Determined by Sort parameter (default is "Featured")`
ListSearch	`ListPage`	`Fixed`
CustomerContentLookup	`ReviewPage`	`Fixed`
SellerLookup	`FeedbackPage`	`Newest to oldest date/time of feedback.`

Table 4-3 Default sorting order for paginated objects

Sorting gives us yet another way to filter results. If we're searching for audio CDs by the Beatles, and we want to get the latest releases returned first, we can use the search from the previous section and specify the "orig-rel-date" sort value.

```
http://webservices.amazon.com/onca/xml?Service=AWSECommerceService&
AssociateTag=ws&SubscriptionId=1A7XKHR5BYD0WPJVQEG2&
Operation=ItemSearch&Artist=Beatles&SearchIndex=Music&Version=2005-02-23&
Sort=orig-rel-date
```

The Sort parameter only applies to lists of items returned by the ItemSearch, Seller-ListingSearch, and ListLookup operations -- it does not apply to customer reviews or other lists of elements returned by Amazon. Those other objects, listed in Table 4-1, are always returned in a fixed sorting -- usually by the date created for reviews and feedback.

Sorting Example

In the previous section on pagination, we listed the Lou Donaldson albums using the default item sorting. In this example, we'll let the user choose which sorting they want to use on the returned results. By adding the sort parameter to our ItemSearch request, we'll be able to offer the user a number of different ways of viewing the CDs.

We only need to make a few changes to example 4-1 in order to add sorting. We'll use six different sorts.

```
define ('SORT_RELDATE', 'orig-rel-date');
define ('SORT_BESTSELLING', 'salesrank');
define ('SORT_CHEAPEST', 'price');
define ('SORTAZ', 'titlerank');
define ('SORTZA', '-titlerank');
define ('DEFAULT_SORT', 'psrank');
```

"Featured Items," which is the default sorting for the Music Search Index, is our default sort. We'll also be retrieving the selected sorting via HTTP GET:

```
$sort=(isset($_GET['sort'])) ? $_GET['sort'] : DEFAULT_SORT;
```

and then using that sort parameter in the ItemSearch request:

```
$request='http://webservices.amazon.com/onca/xml?Service=AWSECommerceService&
AssociateTag='.ASSOCIATES_ID.'&SubscriptionId='.SUBID.'&Operation=ItemSearch&
SearchIndex=Music&Artist=Lou%20Donaldson&ItemPage='.$page.'&
ResponseGroup=Small,Images&Version='.VERSION.'&Sort='.$sort;
```

A left side menu is added to the display so that the user can select their desired sorting method:

```
function theLeftMenu() {
    echo '<div><h3><a href="lou.php?sort=salesrank">Best Sellers</a></h3></div>
    <div><h3><a href="lou.php?sort=orig-rel-date">Latest Releases</a></h3></div>
    <div><h3><a href="lou.php?sort=price">Least Expensive</a></h3></div>
    <div><h3><a href="lou.php?sort=titlerank">All CDs, A-Z</a></h3></div>
    <div><h3><a href="lou.php?sort=-titlerank">All CDs, Z-A</a></h3></div>';
}
```

For each page request, we need to add the sort parameter to the URL:

```
$p = ($i == $page) ? $page : '<a href="lou.php?page='.$i.'&sort='.$sort.'">'.$i.'</a>
';
```

And then add an extra display area for the left side menu:

```
<td width="25%" height="250">
    <?php theLeftMenu(); ?>
</td>
```

The revised lou.php offers different sorting methods:

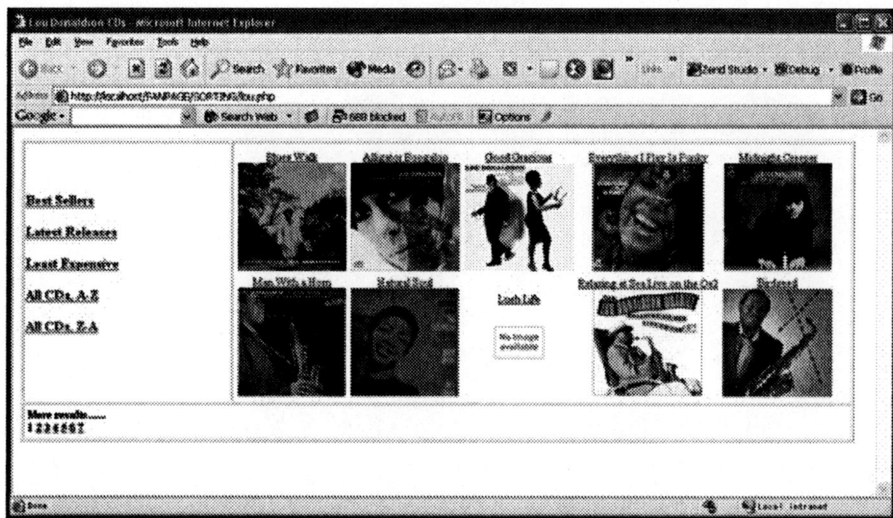

Figure 4-4 Using the sort parameter to provide users with display options

The user clicks on the type of sorting they want (e.g. "Latest Releases") and then then can page through the results by clicking on the result page numbers in the lower left-hand corner.

Getting At Product Details

Amazon offers up varying degrees of information about different products. Besides things like the title, price, and availability, which are returned for all products, there are many other data points available which depend on the Search Index and on how much information Amazon, or a third party, has decided to enter into the Amazon product database for a given item.

In this section, we're focusing on the product details that are returned inside of the <ItemAttributes> element in responses from Amazon E-Commerce Service. These product details include things like the material a wrist watch band is made out of, the computer platforms a video game runs on, whether a camera has red eye reduction, the number of issues per year that a magazine publishes, or the director(s) of a movie on DVD. We can use these details to add richness to our product descriptions and to give users a basis on which to do things like comparison shop.

To find the latest list of item attributes, we can use the Help operation and ask for help with the ItemAttributes Response Group.

```
http://webservices.amazon.com/onca/xml?Service=AWSECommerceService&
SubscriptionId=1A7XKHR5BYD0WPJVQEG2&AssociateTag=ws&Operation=Help&
HelpType=ResponseGroup&About=ItemAttributes&Version=2005-02-23
```

A partial listing of the output shows part of the huge list of attributes that Amazon may return.

```
<Elements>
  <Element>ItemAttributes/IsLabCreated</Element>
  <Element>ItemAttributes/TotalVGAOutPorts</Element>
  <Element>ItemAttributes/HardDiskCount</Element>
  <Element>ItemAttributes/HoursOfOperation/Hours</Element>
  <Element>ItemAttributes/IssuesPerYear</Element>
  <Element>ItemAttributes/StoneColor</Element>
  <Element>ItemAttributes/RunningTime</Element>
  <Element>ItemAttributes/IsFragile</Element>
  ..........
  ..........
```

Around 200 item attributes are available as this book goes to press and Amazon is adding more on a regular basis. Although the list is somewhat daunting, we can make best use of it by choosing one or two product types and focusing on the item details for those products.

> Amazon does not yet provide a guide that tells what attributes are returned for which types of products. You have to figure this out yourself by using the ItemAttributes Response Group while retrieving specific items. Yes, this sucks.

For the Star Wars Trilogy (Widescreen Edition) DVD, a simple request that returns the item details utilizes the ItemAttributes Response Group on an ItemLookup operation (we could also use the Medium or Large Response Groups since they both include the ItemAttributes Response Group):

```
http://webservices.amazon.com/onca/xml?Service=AWSECommerceService&
SubscriptionId=1A7XKHR5BYD0WPJVQEG2&AssociateTag=ws&Operation=ItemLookup&
ItemId=B00003CXCT&ResponseGroup=ItemAttributes&Version=2005-02-23
```

The call yields a plethora of details about the DVD in the ItemAttributes element:

```
<ItemAttributes>
      <Actor>Harrison Ford</Actor>
      <AspectRatio>2.35:1</AspectRatio>
      <AudienceRating>PG (Parental Guidance Suggested)</AudienceRating>
      <Creator Role="Primary Contributor">Harrison Ford</Creator>
      <Director>George Lucas</Director>
      <Director>Irvin Kershner</Director>
      <Director>Richard Marquand</Director>
      <Format>Color</Format>
      <Format>Widescreen</Format>
      <Format>Dolby</Format>
```

```
        <Languages>
          <Language>
            <Name>French</Name>
            <Type>Dubbed</Type>
          </Language>
          <Language>
            <Name>English</Name>
            <Type>Subtitled</Type>
          </Language>
          <Language>
            <Name>English</Name>
            <Type>Original Language</Type>
            <AudioFormat>Dolby Digital 5.1 EX</AudioFormat>
          </Language>
          <Language>
            <Name>Spanish</Name>
            <Type>Original Language</Type>
            <AudioFormat>Dolby Digital 5.1 EX</AudioFormat>
          </Language>
        </Languages>
        <ListPrice>
          <Amount>6998</Amount>
          <CurrencyCode>USD</CurrencyCode>
          <FormattedPrice>$69.98</FormattedPrice>
        </ListPrice>
        <NumberOfItems>4</NumberOfItems>
        <PictureFormat>Anamorphic Widescreen</PictureFormat>
        <ProductGroup>DVD</ProductGroup>
        <RegionCode>1</RegionCode>
        <ReleaseDate>2004-09-21</ReleaseDate>
        <RunningTime Units="minutes">387</RunningTime>
        <Studio>Twentieth Century Fox Home Video</Studio>
        <Title>Star Wars Trilogy (Widescreen Edition)</Title>
        <UPC>024543123415</UPC>
    </ItemAttributes>
```

Item Attributes For Variations

This DVD is a regular ASIN. Parent ASINs return most of the Item Attributes minus the attributes that are specific to their Child ASINs -- typically attributes like size and color are missing. For example, we can do an ItemLookup on the Parent ASIN for this Edwardian women's jacket in order to retrieve the ItemAttributes, and the list of Child ASINs:

```
http://webservices.amazon.com/onca/xml?Service=AWSECommerceService&
AssociateTag=ws&SubscriptionId=1A7XKHR5BYD0WPJVQEG2&Operation=ItemLookup&
ItemId=B0000B0KL9&MerchantId=All&ResponseGroup=ItemAttributes,VariationMinimum&
Version=2005-02-23
```

> Note that we must use the MerchantId=All parameter in order to get the list of Child ASINs returned. That's because Amazon (the merchant) doesn't sell any items with Variations, so we must search among all merchants in order to find Child ASINs.

The call yields the following XML structure containing the Item Attributes for the Parent ASIN, and the list of Child ASINs:


```
<Item>
  <ASIN>B0000B0KL9</ASIN>
  <ItemAttributes>
  <Brand>Newport News Brands</Brand>
  <Department>womens</Department>
  <Feature>Edwardian jacket in soft, luxurious velvet. Cutaway front, princess seams.
Cotton, fully lined. Dry clean. Imported.</Feature>
  <ProductGroup>Apparel</ProductGroup>
  <Title>Edwardian jacket</Title>
  </ItemAttributes>
  <Variations>
  <Item>
  <ASIN>B0000B0MBJ</ASIN>
  </Item>
  <Item>
  <ASIN>B0000B0MBL</ASIN>
  </Item>
  <Item>
  <ASIN>B0000B0MBN</ASIN>
  </Item>
  <Item>
  <ASIN>B0000B0MBQ</ASIN>
  </Item>
  <Item>
  <ASIN>B0000B0MBS</ASIN>
  </Item>
  <Item>
  <ASIN>B0000B0MBV</ASIN>
  </Item>
  <Item>
  <ASIN>B0000B0MBY</ASIN>
  </Item>
  <Item>
  <ASIN>B0000B0MC0</ASIN>
  </Item>
  <Item>
  <ASIN>B0000B0MC4</ASIN>
  </Item>
  <Item>
  <ASIN>B0002TF4YG</ASIN>
  </Item>
  </Variations>
  </Item>
  </Items>
  </ItemLookupResponse>
```


Choosing a Child ASIN from the list above, we can then get the Item Attributes for it using this request:

```
http://webservices.amazon.com/onca/xml?Service=AWSECommerceService&
```

```
AssociateTag=ws&SubscriptionId=1A7XKHR5BYDOWPJVQEG2&Operation=ItemLookup&
ItemId=B0002TF4YG&ResponseGroup=ItemAttributes&Version=2005-02-23
```

This Child ASIN, which corresponds to a specific size and color of coat, yields the same Item Attributes with the size and color added:

```
<Item>
  <ASIN>B0002TF4YG</ASIN>
  <ItemAttributes>
  <Brand>Newport News Brands</Brand>
  <ClothingSize>14W</ClothingSize>
  <Color>Black</Color>
  <Department>womens</Department>
  <Feature>Edwardian jacket in soft, luxurious velvet. Cutaway front, princess seams.
Cotton, fully lined. Dry clean. Imported.</Feature>
  <ProductGroup>Apparel</ProductGroup>
  <Title>Edwardian jacket (14W Black)</Title>
  </ItemAttributes>
  </Item>
```

Code Sample: WatchCompare

The rich detail available for some classes of Amazon products makes for good comparison shopping. In this sample application, WatchCompare, customers can search for watches using various criteria, and then compare selected watches to find the one that best fits their needs.

To find out what kinds of criteria I might be able to offer customers, I looked around on Amazon's Jewelry and Watches store, and I noticed what kinds of parameters are available with the ItemSearch operation.

A typical search for Men's watches made by Seiko that are between $50 and $100 looks like this:

```
http://webservices.amazon.com/onca/xml?Service=AWSECommerceService&
AssociateTag=ws&SubscriptionId=1A7XKHR5BYDOWPJVQEG2&
Operation=ItemSearch&SearchIndex=Jewelry&Sort=launch-date&BrowseNode=3889331&
Brand=Seiko&MinimumPrice=5000&MaximumPrice=10000&ResponseGroup=Medium&
Version=2005-02-23
```

Browse node 3889331 is Men's Watches, the Brand=Seiko, the MinimumPrice and MaximumPrice are set accordingly, and Sort=launch-date which orders the results by newest models first.

Since there are so many possible search combinations, I chose not to implement a cache for this example. Instead, if a search fails, I simply wait two seconds and try again:

```
$xml = GetData($url, 10);
if (!$xml) {
    sleep(2);
    $xml = GetData($url, 10);
```

```
}
```

Table 4-4 My search criteria for comparing watches

Search Criteria	ItemSearch Parameter	Choices	Explanation
Gender/Type	BrowseNode	Mens, Womens, Childrens, All	Amazon has specific Browse Nodes for each watch Gender/Type category. I found these by manually browsing the Watches store on Amazon.com
Brand	Brand	Seiko, Timex, Skagen, etc....., All	Amazon carries a huge number of watch brands. Also, the ItemSearch operation has a Brand search parameter. These brands are listed on the main Watches store page on Amazon.com
Price Range	MinimumPrice MaximumPrice	Various price ranges, All	These ItemSearch parameters make it easy to search by price range
Material	Keywords	gold, resin, glass, rubber, diamond, etc..., All	The Keywords parameter can be used to look for various watch materials. It's not a very reliable search, but makes enough hits to be useful.
Sort	Sort	Sort values for Jewelry	Results are returned in the desired sort order

The search is simplified by the fact that we're only looking for items in New condition and that the Watches store contains few (if any) variations, so we don't have to deal with Parent/Child ASINs. The customer search interface is shown in Figure 4-5.

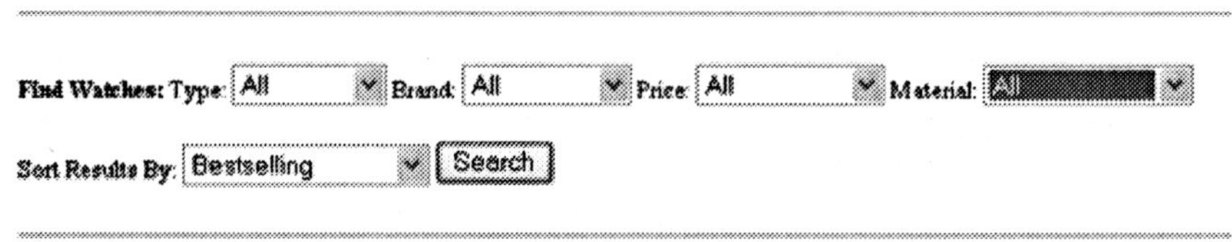

Figure 4-5 The main GUI for the Watch Compare application

After hitting the Search button, up to ten watches are displayed with checkboxes and a Compare button. The first three results are shown in Figure 4-6.

The customer can select any of the watches and click on the compare button to see a side-by-side comparison. The comparison data is generated by an ItemLookup operation which can take up to ten ASINs as a parameter. So, in this case, to compare two of the above watches, the call looks like this:

```
http://webservices.amazon.com/onca/xml?Service=AWSECommerceService&
AssociateTag=ws&SubscriptionId=1A7XKHR5BYD0WPJVQEG2&Operation=ItemLookup&
ItemId=B000371DVU,B0001QNJ42&ResponseGroup=Medium&Version=2005-02-23
```

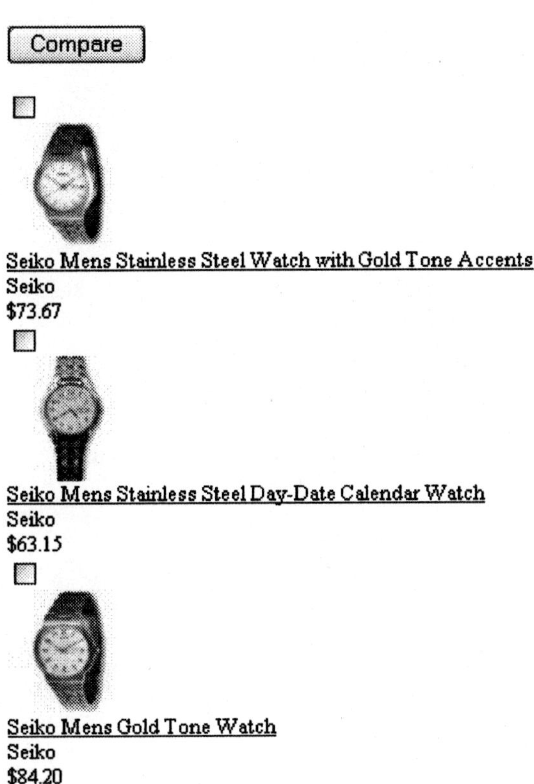

Figure 4-6 The first three results of a watch search

The Medium Response Group returns all of the ItemAttribute data as well as the DetailPageURL and OfferSummary pricing information.

The customer can then click on the name of the watch which is linked to the corresponding product page on Amazon for purchase.

The WatchCompare sample consists of two files: layout.php and watches.php; layout.php contains most of the HTML code for the layout; watches.php contains the of the program logic.

The code for layout.php includes function calls embedded in the search form in order to make the customer choices "sticky" -- once the user hits the "Submit" button, their choices are still displayed in the form when the results are returned.

Name:	Seiko Mens Gold Tone Watch	Seiko Mens Stainless Steel Day-Date Calendar Wat
Brand:	Seiko	Seiko
Your Price:	$84.20	$63.15
Model:	-	-
Wrist Band:	Gold Tone	Stainless Steel
Clasp Type:	-	-
Bezel:	-	-
Dial Color:	White	Ivory
Calendar Type:	-	-
Casing:	Gold Tone	Stainless Steel
Metal Type:	-	-
Watch Movement:	Japan	Japan
Water Resistance Depth:	30.00 meters	30.00 meters
Weight:	-	-

Figure 4-7 Watch comparison output for two watches

The first part of layout.php merely outputs the search form shown in figure 4-5 above. The actual results are output by the function theContent() which is called at the bottom of layout.php:

```
<!DOCTYPE HTML PUBLIC "-//W3C//DTD HTML 4.01 Transitional//EN"
"http://www.w3.org/TR/html4/loose.dtd">
<html>
<head>
<meta http-equiv="Content-Type" content="text/html; charset=iso-8859-1">
<title>Watch Compare</title>
</head>
<body>
<form action="" method="post" name="watch_search" target="_self" id="watch_search">
  <hr />
  <p><b>Find Watches:</b> Type:
    <select name="type" id="type">
      <option value="all" <?php select_type('all')?> >All</option>
      <option value="mens" <?php select_type('mens')?> >Mens</option>
      <option value="womens" <?php select_type('womens')?> >Womens</option>
      <option value="childrens" <?php select_type('childrens')?> >Childrens</option>
    </select>
    Brand:
    <select name="brand" id="brand">
      <option value="all" <?php select_brand('all')?> >All</option>
      <option value="Anne%20Klein" <?php select_brand('Anne%20Klein')?> >Anne Klein</
option>
      <option value="Seiko" <?php select_brand('Seiko')?> >Seiko</option>
```

```
      <option value="Timex" <?php select_brand('Timex')?> >Timex</option>
      <option value="Skagen" <?php select_brand('Skagen')?> >Skagen</option>
      <option value="Fossil" <?php select_brand('Fossil')?> >Fossil</option>
      <option value="Guess" <?php select_brand('Guess')?> >Guess</option>
    </select>
    Price:
    <select name="price" id="price">
      <option value="all" <?php select_price('all')?> >All</option>
      <option value="0-5000" <?php select_price('0-5000')?> >$1-$50</option>
      <option value="5000-10000" <?php select_price('5000-10000')?> >$50-$100</
option>
      <option value="10000-25000" <?php select_price('10000-25000')?> >$100-$250</
option>
      <option value="25000-50000" <?php select_price('25000-50000')?> >$250-$500</
option>
      <option value="50000-100000" <?php select_price('50000-100000')?> >$500-$1000</
option>
      <option value="100000-500000" <?php select_price('100000-500000')?> >$1000-
$5000</option>
      <option value="500000-9999999" <?php select_price('500000-9999999')?> >$5000-
?</option>
    </select>
    Material:
    <select name="material" id="material">
      <option value="all" <?php select_material('all')?> >All</option>
      <option value="stainless steel" <?php select_material('stainless steel')?> >
stainless steel</option>
      <option value="glass" <?php select_material('glass')?> >glass</option>
      <option value="resin" <?php select_material('resin')?> >resin</option>
      <option value="rubber" <?php select_material('rubber')?> >rubber</option>
      <option value="diamond" <?php select_material('diamond')?> >diamond</option>
      <option value="gold" <?php select_material('gold')?> >gold</option>
      <option value="gem" <?php select_material('gem')?> >gem</option>
    </select>
  </p>
  <p>Sort Results By:
    <select name="sort" id="sort">
      <option value="salesrank" <?php select_sort('salesrank')?> >Bestselling</
option>
      <option value="launch-date" <?php select_sort('launch-date')?> >Newest
Arrivals</option>
      <option value="pmrank" <?php select_sort('pmrank')?> >Featured Items</option>
      <option value="pricerank" <?php select_sort('pricerank')?> >Price: Low to
High</option>
      <option value="inverseprice" <?php select_sort('inverseprice')?> >Price: High
to Low</option>
    </select>
    <input type="submit" name="search" value="Search">
  </p>
</form>
<hr />
<?php theContent() ?>
</body>
</html>
```

The main file, watches.php, is somewhat long, but fairly simple to follow.

```
<?php
// Bring in our XML parser
require_once("tools.inc.php");

define('SUBID', '1A7XKHR5BYD0WPJVQEG2');    // Our Subscription ID
define('VERSION', '2004-08-01');            // Version of ECS
define('ASSOCIATES_ID','tapdanceinfo-20'); // Amazon Associates ID
define('DEFAULT_SORT', 'salesrank');        // Default sorting
define('NO_BRAND', '');                     // Defaults for search parameters
define('NO_TYPE', 'all');
define('NO_PRICE', '');
define('NO_MATERIAL', '');
define('NO_IMAGE', 'http://g-images.amazon.com/images/G/01/jewelry/nav/jewelry-icon-
no-image-avail.gif');                       // Empty Image
define('SEARCHINDEX', 'Jewelry');           // The Search Index

// Browse Nodes for "Type" search parameter
$browsenodes=array(
'all' => '3888811',
'mens' => '3889331',
'womens' => '3889801',
'childrens' => '3888821'
);

// If the user hit the "Compare" button, collect the ASINS they
// want to compare, and put them in the $asins string, separated by commas
$asins='';
$count_asins=0;
if (isset($_POST['compare']) and ($_POST['compare'] == 'Compare')) {
    foreach ($_POST as $key => $value) {
        if ($value == 'asin') {
            $count_asins++;
            $asins .= $key.',';
        }
    }
    $asins=substr($asins, 0, strrpos($asins, ","));
}

// If the user requested a search, collect the search parameters or
// take the defaults
$price=(isset($_POST['price']) && $_POST['price'] != 'all') ? $_POST['price'] : NO_
PRICE ;
$brand=(isset($_POST['brand']) && $_POST['brand'] != 'all') ? $_POST['brand'] : NO_
BRAND ;
$type=isset($_POST['type']) ? $_POST['type'] : NO_TYPE ;
$material=(isset($_POST['material']) && $_POST['material'] != 'all' ) ? $_
POST['material'] : NO_MATERIAL ;
$sort=isset($_POST['sort']) ? $_POST['sort'] : DEFAULT_SORT ;
$browsenode=$browsenodes[$type];
```

```
// Functions to make the search form "sticky"
// The customer's search selections will be maintained after
// they submit the form
function select_type ($t) {
    global $type;
    if ($type == $t) { echo 'selected'; }
}

function select_brand ($t) {
    global $brand;
    if ($brand == $t) { echo 'selected'; }
}

function select_material ($t) {
    global $material;
    if ($material == $t) { echo 'selected'; }
}

function select_price ($t) {
    global $price;
    if ($price == $t) { echo 'selected'; }
}

function select_sort ($t) {
    global $sort;
    if ($sort == $t) { echo 'selected'; }
}

// The min/max price comes in as two numbers separated by a '-', so
// we split it in two here and create a suffix for the request
$parr=split('-',$price);
$Sprice= ($price == NO_PRICE) ? '' : '&MinimumPrice='.($parr[0]).'&MaximumPrice='.
($parr[1]);

// Create the Brand parameter for the request
$Sbrand= ($brand == NO_BRAND)? '' : '&Brand='.$brand;

// Create the Keywords parameter for the request
$Skeywords= ($material == NO_MATERIAL)? '' : '&Keywords='.urlencode($material);

// If the user selected items to compare, then $asins will be set. Otherwise
// We assume a search has been requested and do a search
if ($asins == '') {
    $task='ItemSearchResponse';
    $url='http://webservices.amazon.com/onca/
xml?Service=AWSECommerceService&AssociateTag='.ASSOCIATES_ID.'&SubscriptionId='.
SUBID.'&Operation=ItemSearch'.$Skeywords.'&SearchIndex='.SEARCHINDEX.'&Sort='.$sort.
'&BrowseNode='.$browsenode.$Sbrand.$Sprice.'&ResponseGroup=Medium&Version='.VERSION;
} else {
    $task='ItemLookupResponse';
    $url='http://webservices.amazon.com/onca/
xml?Service=AWSECommerceService&AssociateTag='.ASSOCIATES_ID.'&SubscriptionId='.
SUBID.'&Operation=ItemLookup&ItemId='.$asins.'&ResponseGroup=Medium&Version='.
VERSION;
```

```
}

// Because the user can do so many variations on searches, and I don't
// expect very heavy usage on this application, I opted not to use a cache.
// Instead, if the request fails, I wait two seconds and try again before
// notifying the user of the error:
$xml = GetData($url, 10);
if (!$xml) {
    sleep(2);
    $xml = GetData($url, 10);
}

$Result = xmlparser($xml);

// Bring in the layout form
require_once('layout.php');

// Here's the routine that does all the real work
function theContent() {
    global $Result;
    global $task;
    global $asins;

    // Check for errors and exit if there are any
    if (isset($Result[$task]['Items'][0]['Request']['IsValid'])) {
        // The request should never be invalid, but we check anyway
        if ($Result[$task]['Items'][0]['Request']['IsValid'] == 'False') {
            echo '<h2>Sorry, your request is invalid</h2>';
            return;
        } elseif
(isset($Result[$task]['Items'][0]['Request']['Errors']['Error'][0]['Code']))  {
            // Check for an error code
            if  ($Result[$task]['Items'][0]['Request']['Errors']['Error'][0]['Code']
== 'AWS.ECommerceService.NoExactMatches') {
                echo '<h2>Sorry, Amazon found no exact matches for your search
request</h2>';
                return;
            } else {
                echo '<h2>Sorry, Amazon found the error '.
$Result[$task]['Items'][0]['Request']['Errors']['Error'][0]['Code'].' with your
request';
                return;
            }
        }
    } else {
       // If nothing is returned, it's probably a 500 or 503 HTTP error
        echo '<h2>Sorry, We are having trouble connecting to Amazon. Try again in a
few minutes.</h2>';
        return;
    }

    // If there is nothing in the $asins string, then we display search results
    if ($asins == '') {
```

```
        echo '<form action="" method="post" name="watch_compare" target="_self"
id="watch_compare"><input type="submit" name="compare" value="Compare"><br /><br /></
<table>';

        foreach ($Result['ItemSearchResponse']['Items'][0]['Item'] as $item) {

            $image = (isset($item['SmallImage']['URL'])) ? $item['SmallImage']['URL']
: NO_IMAGE;
            $title = $item['ItemAttributes']['Title'];

            // Check for item availability
          $yourprice=(isset($item["OfferSummary"]["LowestNewPrice"]["FormattedPrice"]))?
$item["OfferSummary"]["LowestNewPrice"]["FormattedPrice"] : '';

            // If we can't find a price in new condition, skip this item
            if ($yourprice == '') continue;

            // Display the Brand, which may be under "Manufacturer" or
            // under "Brand"
            if (isset($item['Manufacturer'])) {
                $brand = $item['Manufacturer'];
            } else if (isset($item['ItemAttributes']['Brand'])) {
                $brand = $item['ItemAttributes']['Brand'];
            } else {
                $brand = '';
            }

            // The output string
            $outstring= '<tr><td><input type="checkbox" name="'.$item['ASIN'][0].'"
value="asin"/></td><td><div><img src="'.$image.'" /></div><div><a href="'.
$item['DetailPageURL'].'" class="boxname" target="_blank">'. $title .'</a></div><div
class="boxpublisher">'. $brand. '</div><div class="boxprice">'. $yourprice.'<br /></
div></td></tr>';

            echo $outstring;
        }

        echo '</table><input type="submit" name="compare" value="Compare"></form>';
    } else {
        // Here's the product detail comparision output
        echo '<table>';

        // The real name of each displayed item attribute
        $row=array(
        '<tr><td style="text-align: left; height:80px"></td>',
        '<tr><td style="text-align: left">Name:</td>',
        '<tr><td style="text-align: left">Brand:</td>',
        '<tr><td style="text-align: left">Your Price:</td>',
        '<tr><td style="text-align: left">Model:</td>',
        '<tr><td style="text-align: left">Wrist Band:</td>',
        '<tr><td style="text-align: left">Clasp Type:</td>',
        '<tr><td style="text-align: left">Bezel:</td>',
        '<tr><td style="text-align: left">Dial Color:</td>',
        '<tr><td style="text-align: left">Calendar Type:</td>',
```

```
        '<tr><td style="text-align: left">Casing:</td>',
        '<tr><td style="text-align: left">Metal Type:</td>',
        '<tr><td style="text-align: left">Watch Movement:</td>',
        '<tr><td style="text-align: left">Water Resistance Depth:</td>',
        '<tr><td style="text-align: left">Weight:</td>'
        );

        // Go through each item
        foreach ($Result['ItemLookupResponse']['Items'][0]['Item'] as $item) {

            $image = (isset($item['SmallImage']['URL'])) ? $item['SmallImage']['URL']
: NO_IMAGE;
            $title = (isset($item['ItemAttributes']['Title'])) ?
$item['ItemAttributes']['Title'] : 'No Name'  ;

            // Check for item availability
 $yourprice=(isset($item["OfferSummary"]["LowestNewPrice"]["FormattedPrice"]))?
$item["OfferSummary"]["LowestNewPrice"]["FormattedPrice"] : '';

            // Skip the item if it's not available
            if ($yourprice == '') continue;

            // Display the Brand, which may be under "Manufacturer" or
            // under "Brand"
            if (isset($item['Manufacturer'])) {
                $brand = $item['Manufacturer'];
            } else if (isset($item['ItemAttributes']['Brand'])) {
                $brand = $item['ItemAttributes']['Brand'];
            } else {
                $brand = '-';
            }

            // Retrieve all the item attributes we're going to display
            // Note that they may be empty because they weren't entered
            // into Amazon's database properly.
            $bandm = (isset($item["ItemAttributes"]["BandMaterialType"])  and
(trim($item["ItemAttributes"]["BandMaterialType"]) != ''))  ?
$item["ItemAttributes"]["BandMaterialType"] : '-';
            $bezelm = (isset($item["ItemAttributes"]["BezelMaterialType"])  and
(trim($item["ItemAttributes"]["BezelMaterialType"]) != ''))  ?
$item["ItemAttributes"]["BezelMaterialType"] : '-';
            $casem = (isset($item["ItemAttributes"]["CaseMaterialType"])  and
(trim($item["ItemAttributes"]["CaseMaterialType"]) != ''))  ?
$item["ItemAttributes"]["CaseMaterialType"] : '-';
            $calt = (isset($item["ItemAttributes"]["CalendarType"])  and
(trim($item["ItemAttributes"]["CalendarType"]) != ''))  ?
$item["ItemAttributes"]["CalendarType"] : '-';
            $claspt = (isset($item["ItemAttributes"]["ClaspType"])  and
(trim($item["ItemAttributes"]["ClaspType"]) != ''))  ?
$item["ItemAttributes"]["ClaspType"] : '-';
            $dialc = (isset($item["ItemAttributes"]["DialColor"])  and
(trim($item["ItemAttributes"]["DialColor"]) != ''))  ?
$item["ItemAttributes"]["DialColor"] : '-';
```

```
            $metals = (isset($item["ItemAttributes"]["MetalStamp"])  and
(trim($item["ItemAttributes"]["MetalStamp"]) != ''))  ?
$item["ItemAttributes"]["MetalStamp"] : '-';
            $model = (isset($item["ItemAttributes"]["Model"])  and
(trim($item["ItemAttributes"]["Model"]) != ''))  ? $item["ItemAttributes"]["Model"] :
'-';
            $watchmt = (isset($item["ItemAttributes"]["WatchMovementType"])  and
(trim($item["ItemAttributes"]["WatchMovementType"]) != ''))  ?
$item["ItemAttributes"]["WatchMovementType"] : '-';
            $weight = (isset($item["ItemAttributes"]["Weight"]["Weight"])  and
(trim($item["ItemAttributes"]["Weight"]["Weight"]) != '')) ?
$item["ItemAttributes"]["Weight"]["Weight"] : '-';
            $weightu = (isset($item["ItemAttributes"]["Weight"]["Units"])  and
(trim($item["ItemAttributes"]["Weight"]["Units"]) != '')) ?
$item["ItemAttributes"]["Weight"]["Units"] : '';
            $waterr =
(isset($item["ItemAttributes"]["WaterResistanceDepth"]["WaterResistanceDepth"])  and
(trim($item["ItemAttributes"]["WaterResistanceDepth"]["WaterResistanceDepth"]) !=
''))  ? $item["ItemAttributes"]["WaterResistanceDepth"]["WaterResistanceDepth"] : '-
';
            $waterru =
(isset($item["ItemAttributes"]["WaterResistanceDepth"]["Units"])  and
(trim($item["ItemAttributes"]["WaterResistanceDepth"]["Units"]) != ''))  ?
$item["ItemAttributes"]["WaterResistanceDepth"]["Units"] : '';

            // Output the item attributes
            $row[0] .= '<td style="text-align: center; height:80px"><img src="'.
$image.'" alt="'.$title.'" /></td>';
            $row[1] .= '<td style="text-align: center"><a href="'.
$item['DetailPageURL'].'" class="boxname" target="_blank" title="'.$title.'">'.
$title .'</a></td>';
            $row[2] .= '<td style="text-align: center">'. $brand. '</td>';
            $row[3] .= '<td style="text-align: center">'. $yourprice.'</td>';
            $row[4] .= '<td style="text-align: center">'.$model.'</td>';
            $row[5] .= '<td style="text-align: center">'.$bandm.'</td>';
            $row[6] .= '<td style="text-align: center">'.$claspt.'</td>';
            $row[7] .= '<td style="text-align: center">'.$bezelm.'</td>';
            $row[8] .= '<td style="text-align: center">'.$dialc.'</td>';
            $row[9] .= '<td style="text-align: center">'.$calt.'</td>';
            $row[10] .= '<td style="text-align: center">'.$casem.'</td>';
            $row[11] .= '<td style="text-align: center">'.$metals.'</td>';
            $row[12] .= '<td style="text-align: center">'.$watchmt.'</td>';
            $row[13] .= '<td style="text-align: center">'.$waterr.' '.$waterru.'</td>
';
            $row[14] .= '<td style="text-align: center">'.$weight.' '.$weightu.'</td>
';
        }

        foreach ($row as $r) {
            $r .= '</tr>';
            echo $r;
        }

        echo '</table>';
```

```
        }
    }
    ?>
```

One thing to be careful of when retrieving Item Attributes is that they sometimes aren't entered into the Amazon database properly. An attribute that probably shouldn't be there at all is returned as a string comprised of just one or more spaces. I use the PHP trim() function on them to identify them as missing data points:

```
$claspt = (isset($item["ItemAttributes"]["ClaspType"]) and
(trim($item["ItemAttributes"]["ClaspType"]) != '')) ?
$item["ItemAttributes"]["ClaspType"] : '-';
```

Working With Variations

When you perform an ItemSearch request, you get back a list of items and each item has an ASIN. Those ASINs are either regular ASINs or Parent ASINs. The vast majority of products in Amazon's database are regular ASINs, but Parent ASINs do appear in some Search Indexes, notably Apparel, where all the products are represented by Parent ASINs.

From Chapter One, we know that Parent ASINs identify a product that comes in Variations, e.g. different colors and sizes. Child ASINs of that Parent identify a specific color and size. Functionally speaking, the only difference between a Parent ASIN and a Child ASIN is that a Parent ASIN cannot be purchased (it has no Offers), and a Child ASIN is never returned as the result of a search.

Up to now, we've spent most of our time looking at regular ASINs because they are, by far, the most common. But Variations require special handling to use effectively and can be easily manipulated to provide a rich user online user experience.

Variation Images

Amazon E-Commerce Service does not yet return images for Child ASINs in an ItemSearch request, it only returns the image for the Parent ASIN. That means you have to make a second request to fetch the images of the Child ASIN. This is necessary because the Child ASINs sometimes come in different colors and we'd certainly like to display them for our customers. However, the overhead of making a second request just to fetch the images is unnecessary. As noted in Chapter Three, we can manually build the image links we need.

Once we build the image links, however, we also have to test them to determine whether they actually return images. From Chapter Three, we know that any syntactically correct Amazon image URL will return a transparent 1x1 pixel GIF if there's no real image available. So, you can build the link and test to see if it's a one pixel

GIF or a real image. An easy way to test for the presence of the one pixel GIF is to use the getimagesize() function:

```
$url='http://images.amazon.com/images/P/B0001BKAEY.01._SCMZZZZZZZ_.jpg';
$size=getimagesize($url);
if ($size[0] == 1) {
    echo "It is a one pixel image";
} else {
    echo "The image is valid";
}
```

> You must have PHP's GD extension installed in order to use the getimagesize() function.

Also from Chapter Three, I pointed out that, if there are alternative views of the item available, they can be found by taking the Parent ASIN image URL and adding the string "PTnn" to it, where "nn" is a number from "01" to "99". Alternative image

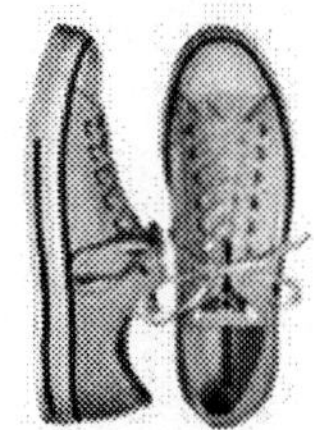

Parent ASIN Image
http://images.amazon.com/images/P/B00022AP2E.01-A3K8MJJG7C5G9B._SCTHUMBZZZ_.jpg

Alternate view #1
http://images.amazon.com/images/P/B00022AP2E.01-A3K8MJJG7C5G9B.PT01._SCTHUMBZZZ_.jpg

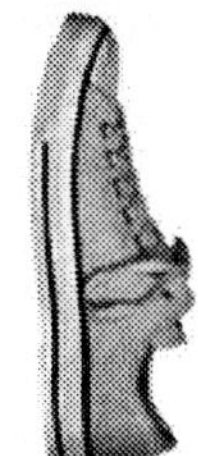

Alternate view #2
http://images.amazon.com/images/P/B00022AP2E.01-A3K8MJJG7C5G9B.PT02._SCTHUMBZZZ_.jpg

Figure 4-8 A Parent ASIN Image With Two Alternate Views

views are not currently returned by E-Commcerce Service so, if you want them, you manually build the image URLs and test them to see if they return 1x1 pixel GIF images or real images.

Code Sample: Converse All Stars Store

The goal of this sample application, the Converse All Stars Store, is to let customers browse and purchase all of the possible Converse All Star shoe variations presented. The store uses only two operations, ItemSearch and ItemLookup. The ItemSearch operation is used to retrieve all of the Parent ASINs and the ItemLookup is used to find the variations details for a given Parent ASIN.

Using the search techniques discussed in Chapter Three, I found a good search combination that yields most, if not all, of the Converse All Stars in the Apparel Search Index.

There is no specific Browse Node for Converse All Stars that I could find, so I chose the Browse Node for the brand "Converse" in the shoes category. To find only Convse All Stars shoes (and there are a lot of them), I do an ItemSearch using that Browse Node, along with Brand=Converse and Keywords=All Stars. By using Keywords=All Stars, I eliminate all the Converse shoes that are not All Stars. Using Brand=Converse is probably redundant, since the Browse Node should only return shoes made by Converse, but it doesn't seem to hurt.

I'm only interested in "New" condition shoes (who wants used Converse All Stars? Ugh!) so I just used the default Condition parameter. I set MerchantId=All to make sure I got all the possible merchants selling them. The resulting search string works well and returns almost 400 Converse All Stars Parent ASINs:

```
$request='http://webservices.amazon.com/onca/xml?Service=AWSECommerceService&
AssociateTag='.ASSOCIATES_ID.'&SubscriptionId='.SUBID.'&Operation=ItemSearch&
SearchIndex=Apparel&MerchantId=All&ItemPage='.$page.'&
ResponseGroup=VariationSummary,Images,Small&BrowseNode='.$bn.'&Brand='.$brand.'&
Keywords='.urlencode($keywords).'&Version='.VERSION;
```

I only display the Parent ASIN image, the Title of the product, and the price (or price range) of the variations (Child ASINs). I use the Images Response Group to fetch the image, the Small Response Group gets the ASIN and Title, and the VariationSummary Response Group gets the price range of available variations.

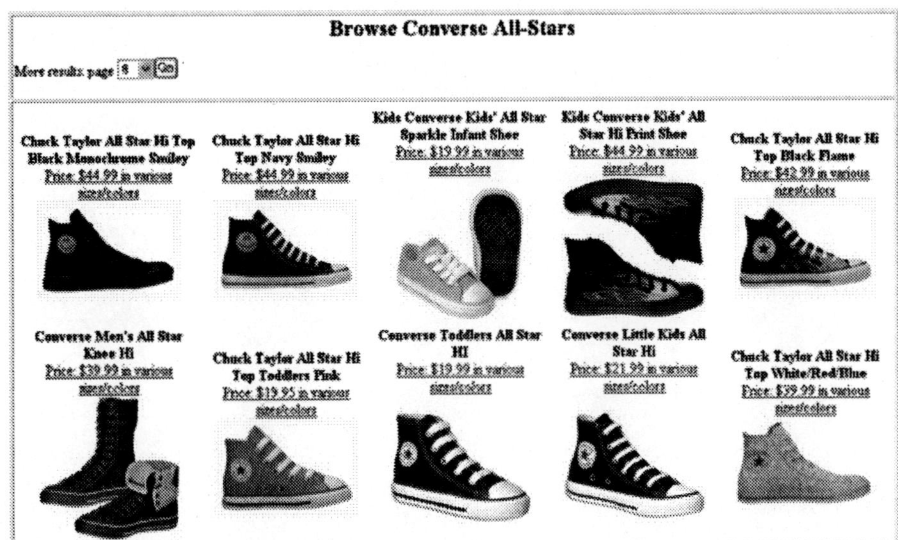

Figure 4-9 The Converse All Stars Shoe Store

If the customer wants more details about the shoe -- colors, sizes, availability and pricing -- I do an ItemLookup on the Parent ASIN in order to retrieve the Child ASINs and their details (Figure 4-9):

```
$request='http://webservices.amazon.com/onca/xml?Service=AWSECommerceService&
AssociateTag='.ASSOCIATES_ID.'&SubscriptionId='.SUBID.'&Operation=ItemLookup&
MerchantId=All&ItemId='.$asin.'&ResponseGroup=Variations,Images,Small&
VariationPage='.$page.'&Version='.VERSION;
```

I use the same Response Groups as before except that I use the Variations Response Group, instead of VariationSummary, in order to retrieve pricing and determine availability (if there's no Offer, the item is not available).

Figure 4-10 A shoe variations page in the Converse All Stars Shoe Store

To create the output shown in Figure 4-8, I cycle through the Parent ASINs, extracting the item information:

```
foreach ($Result['ItemSearchResponse']['Items'][0]['Item'] as $item)
```

The "low price" among the Child ASINs for a given Parent ASIN, is either the LowestSalePrice, if it exists, or the LowestPrice:

```
        $lowprice =
(isset($item['VariationSummary']['LowestSalePrice']['FormattedPrice'])) ?
$item['VariationSummary']['LowestSalePrice']['FormattedPrice'] :
((isset($item['VariationSummary']['LowestPrice']['FormattedPrice'])) ?
$item['VariationSummary']['LowestPrice']['FormattedPrice'] : null);
```

The High price is either the HighestSalePrice or the HighestPrice:

```
        $highprice =
(isset($item['VariationSummary']['HighestSalePrice']['FormattedPrice'])) ?
$item['VariationSummary']['HighestSalePrice']['FormattedPrice'] :
((isset($item['VariationSummary']['HighestPrice']['FormattedPrice'])) ?
$item['VariationSummary']['HighestPrice']['FormattedPrice'] : null);
```

If neither of the prices exist, then there must not be any offers for Child ASINs of this Parent ASIN, and so I don't display this product:

```
        if (is_null($lowprice) and is_null($highprice)) {
            continue;
        } elseif (!is_null($lowprice) and is_null($highprice)) {
            $price = $lowprice.' - '.$highprice;
        } else {
            $price = is_null($lowprice) ? $highprice : $lowprice;
        }
```

For the variations display in Figure 4-9, I cycle through the Child ASINs of a given Parent ASIN and display the various attributes of the Child ASIN. But before I do that, I save Parent ASIN image so that I can use it to build Child ASIN images later:

```
if
(isset($Result['ItemLookupResponse']['Items'][0]['Item'][0]['MediumImage']['URL'])) {
        $oldimage =
$Result['ItemLookupResponse']['Items'][0]['Item'][0]['MediumImage']['URL'];
    } else {
        $oldimage = NOIMAGE_MED;
    }
```

In order for the Child ASIN to be buyable, there needs to be an Offer Listing Id. If there's no Offer Listing Id, then I skip the Child ASIN.

```
        if (!isset($item['Offers']['Offer'][0]['OfferListing'][0]['OfferListingId']))
continue;
$offerlistingid=$item['Offers']['Offer'][0]['OfferListing'][0]['OfferListingId'];
```

The price is either the SalePrice or the Price element. If there is an OfferListingId present, then there must be a price element (this is still a bit of hubris on my part as stranger elements have been known to be missing).

```
$price=
(isset($item['Offers']['Offer'][0]['OfferListing'][0]['SalePrice']['FormattedPrice'])
) ? $item['Offers']['Offer'][0]['OfferListing'][0]['SalePrice']['FormattedPrice'] :
$item['Offers']['Offer'][0]['OfferListing'][0]['Price']['FormattedPrice'] ;
```

I also grab the Availability element. Note that even if this element doesn't exist, the item is still buyable because there's an Offer Listing Id. The Availability element will only indicate the delay in shipping.

```
$availability =
(isset($item['Offers']['Offer'][0]['OfferListing'][0]['Availability'])) ?
$item['Offers']['Offer'][0]['OfferListing'][0]['Availability'] : '' ;
```

PurchaseURLs are not very convenient when using variations because the user still has to choose the color and/or size before they can add the item to their cart. A quicker approach is to use an immediate "buy box," which I'll explain in more detail in Chapter Six. The HTML form code will place the item pointed to by the Offer Listing Id into their Amazon cart.

```
$buybutton='<form method="POST" action="http://www.amazon.com/gp/aws/cart/add.html">
<input type="hidden" name="SubscriptionId" value="'.SUBID.'" />
<input type="hidden" name="AssociateTag" value="'.ASSOCIATES_ID.'" />
<input type="hidden" name="OfferListingId.1" value="'.$offerlistingid.'" />
<input type="hidden" name="Quantity.1" value="1" />
<input type="submit" name="add" value="Buy Now" />
</form>';
```

As in previous examples, the layout is controlled by a rudimentary PHP file, layout.php:

```
<html>
<head>
<title><?php global $asin; if (is_null($asin)) echo 'Browse Converse All-Stars';
else echo 'Browse Specific Shoe Variations'; ?></title>
</head>
<body>
<table width="1000" border="1" cellpadding="2" cellspacing="2">
  <tr>
    <td colspan="2"><?php theHeader(); ?></td>
  </tr>
  <tr>
    <td height="250"><?php global $asin; if (is_null($asin)) theProductWindow();
else theVariationWindow(); ?>
    </td>
  </tr>
  </table>
</body>
</html>
```

Example 4-2 layout.php, controls the layout of the Converse All Stars Shoe Store

The complete listing follows:

```
?php

error_reporting(E_ALL);

require_once('tools.inc.php');

define('SUBID', '1A7XKHR5BYDOWPJVQEG2');
define('ASSOCIATES_ID','ws');
define('VERSION','2004-11-10');
define ('NOIMAGE_MED', 'http://g-images.amazon.com/images/G/01/x-site/icons/no-img-
lg.gif');
define('DEFAULT_PAGE', '1');

// The page number (for either Parent or Child ASINs)
```

```
$page=(isset($_GET['page'])) ? $_GET['page'] : DEFAULT_PAGE;

// The Parent ASIN to find details about
$asin=(isset($_GET['asin'])) ? $_GET['asin'] : null;

// The browse node, brand, and keywords search parameters
$bn='1040668';
$brand='Converse';
$keywords='All Star';

// Find Parent ASINs
if (is_null($asin)) {
    $request='http://webservices.amazon.com/onca/
xml?Service=AWSECommerceService&AssociateTag='.ASSOCIATES_ID.'&SubscriptionId='.
SUBID.'&Operation=ItemSearch&SearchIndex=Apparel&MerchantId=All&ItemPage='.$page.
'&ResponseGroup=VariationSummary,Images,Small&BrowseNode='.$bn.'&Brand='.$brand.
'&Keywords='.urlencode($keywords).'&Version='.VERSION;

    // Find Child ASINS for the given Parent ASIN
} else {

    $request='http://webservices.amazon.com/onca/
xml?Service=AWSECommerceService&AssociateTag='.ASSOCIATES_ID.'&SubscriptionId='.
SUBID.'&Operation=ItemLookup&MerchantId=All&ItemId='.$asin.
'&ResponseGroup=Variations,Images,Small&VariationPage='.$page.'&Version='.VERSION;

}

// Make the request
$xml = GetData($request, 60);

// Parse the results
$Result = xmlparser($xml);

// Generate the output
require_once("layout.php");

// Generate the main display
function theProductWindow() {
    global $Result;

    echo '<table cellspacing="2" cellpadding="2"><tr>';
    $rowcount=0;

    // Go through all the Parent ASINs
    foreach ($Result['ItemSearchResponse']['Items'][0]['Item'] as $item) {

        // Fetch the image
        if (isset($item['MediumImage']['URL'])) {
            $image = $item['MediumImage']['URL'];
        } else {
            $image = NOIMAGE_MED;
        }
```

```
        // Get the lowest price
        $lowprice =
(isset($item['VariationSummary']['LowestSalePrice']['FormattedPrice'])) ?
$item['VariationSummary']['LowestSalePrice']['FormattedPrice'] :
((isset($item['VariationSummary']['LowestPrice']['FormattedPrice'])) ?
$item['VariationSummary']['LowestPrice']['FormattedPrice'] : null);

        // Get the highest price
        $highprice =
(isset($item['VariationSummary']['HighestSalePrice']['FormattedPrice'])) ?
$item['VariationSummary']['HighestSalePrice']['FormattedPrice'] :
((isset($item['VariationSummary']['HighestPrice']['FormattedPrice'])) ?
$item['VariationSummary']['HighestPrice']['FormattedPrice'] : null);

        // Ignore this entry if neither price exists
        if (is_null($lowprice) and is_null($highprice)) {
            continue;
        } elseif (!is_null($lowprice) and is_null($highprice)) {
            $price = $lowprice.' - '.$highprice;
        } else {
            $price = is_null($lowprice) ? $highprice : $lowprice;
        }

        // Build an output string with the title
        $title = '<b>'.$item["ItemAttributes"]["Title"].'</b><br /><a href="'.$_
SERVER["PHP_SELF"].'?asin='.$item["ASIN"][0].'" target="_blank">Price: '.$price.' in
various sizes/colors</a>';

        // Only display five items per row
        if (is_int($rowcount/5)) echo '</tr><tr>';

        // Output an item
        echo '<td><div style="text-align: center;">'.$title.'</div><div style="text-
align: center;"><img src="'.$image.'" </img></div></td>';
        $rowcount++;
    }
    echo '</tr></table>';
}

// Display the variations window
function theVariationWindow() {
    global $Result;
    global $asin;

    echo '<table cellspacing="2" cellpadding="2"><tr>';

    // Store the Parent ASIN image for later use
    if
(isset($Result['ItemLookupResponse']['Items'][0]['Item'][0]['MediumImage']['URL'])) {
        $oldimage =
$Result['ItemLookupResponse']['Items'][0]['Item'][0]['MediumImage']['URL'];
    } else {
        $oldimage = NOIMAGE_MED;
    }
```

```
    $rowcount=0;

    // Go through the items
    foreach
($Result['ItemLookupResponse']['Items'][0]['Item'][0]['Variations']['Item'] as $item)
{

        // Save the title
        $title = $item['ItemAttributes']['Title'];

        // Ignore this item if there's no Offer Listing Id
        if (!isset($item['Offers']['Offer'][0]['OfferListing'][0]['OfferListingId']))
continue;

$offerlistingid=$item['Offers']['Offer'][0]['OfferListing'][0]['OfferListingId'];

        // Get the price
        $price=
(isset($item['Offers']['Offer'][0]['OfferListing'][0]['SalePrice']['FormattedPrice'])
) ? $item['Offers']['Offer'][0]['OfferListing'][0]['SalePrice']['FormattedPrice'] :
$item['Offers']['Offer'][0]['OfferListing'][0]['Price']['FormattedPrice'] ;

        // Get the availability
        $availability =
(isset($item['Offers']['Offer'][0]['OfferListing'][0]['Availability'])) ?
$item['Offers']['Offer'][0]['OfferListing'][0]['Availability'] : '' ;

        // Create an immediate buy button using the Offer Listing Id
        $buybutton='<form method="POST" action="http://www.amazon.com/gp/aws/cart/
add.html">
<input type="hidden" name="SubscriptionId" value="'.SUBID.'" />
<input type="hidden" name="AssociateTag" value="'.ASSOCIATES_ID.'" />
<input type="hidden" name="OfferListingId.1" value="'.$offerlistingid.'" />
<input type="hidden" name="Quantity.1" value="1" />
<input type="submit" name="add" value="Buy Now" />
</form>';

        // Save the size and color
        $size = '<b>Size:</b> '.$item['ItemAttributes']['ClothingSize'];
        $color = '<b>Color:</b> '.$item['ItemAttributes']['Color'];

        // Replace the Parent ASIN with the Child ASIN and test to see if the image
exists
        $image = str_replace($asin, $item['ASIN'][0] , $oldimage);
        $imagesize = getimagesize($image);
        if ($imagesize[0] == 1) {
            $image = NOIMAGE_MED;
        }

        // Only display five items per row
        if (is_int($rowcount/5)) echo '</tr><tr>';

        // Output the item
```

```
        echo '<td><div style="text-align: center;">'.$title.'</div><div style="text-
align: center;">'.$size.'</div><div style="text-align: center;">'.$color.'</div><div
style="text-align: center;"><img src="'.$image.'" </img></div><div style="text-align:
center;">'.$availability.'</div><div style="text-align: center;">'.$price.'</div><div
style="text-align: center;">'.$buybutton.'</div></td>';

        $rowcount++;
    }
    echo '</tr></table>';
}

// Display the list of available pages
function theHeader() {
    global $page;
    global $Result;
    global $asin;

    // Display the Parent ASIN pages
    if (is_null($asin)) {
        $totalpages =
(isset($Result['ItemSearchResponse']['Items'][0]['TotalPages'])) ?
$Result['ItemSearchResponse']['Items'][0]['TotalPages'] : null;
    } else {
        // Display the Child ASIN pages
        $totalpages =
(isset($Result['ItemLookupResponse']['Items'][0]['Item'][0]['Variations']['TotalVaria
tionPages'])) ?
$Result['ItemLookupResponse']['Items'][0]['Item'][0]['Variations']['TotalVariationPag
es'] : null;
    }

    $title = (is_null($asin)) ? "Browse Converse All-Stars" : "Browse Specific Shoe
Variations";
    echo '<div style="text-align: center;"><h2>'.$title.'</h2></div>';

    // Create a list of pages that the user can choose from
    if (!is_null($totalpages)) {
        echo '<div style="text-align: left;">';
        echo '<form action="'.$_SERVER["PHP_SELF"].'" method="get">More results: page
<select name="page">';
        for ($i=1; $i <= $totalpages; $i++)
        {
            $sel= ($i == $page) ? 'selected' : '';
            echo '<option value="'.$i.'"'.$sel.'>'.$i.'</option>';
        }
        echo '</select>';
        if (!is_null($asin)) echo '<input type="hidden" name="asin" value="'.$asin.'"
/>';
        echo '<input type="submit" value="Go" /></form></div>';
    } else {
        '<div style="text-align: left;"><b>All results are displayed</b></div>';
    }
}
```

```
?>
```

Example 4-3 allstars.php, an example of handling product variations

Adding Caching To The Converse All Stars Store

The Converse All Stars Store is a good candidate for caching. The Child ASIN requests tend to be quite large and the same sets of data are retrieved frequently. For this caching example, I'm going to use the Cache Lite library which is part of PEAR (PHP Extension and Application Repository).

> Cache Lite can be found at http://pear.php.net/package/Cache_Lite. I used version 1.31 for this example.

Cache Lite is simple and fast caching system that using both file locking and hashes to ensure cache integrity. Adding Cache Lite to Example 4-3 requires on a few lines of code.

First we need to include the library, Set the Cache options, and then fetch an instance of the cache:

```
require_once('Cache/Lite.php');
require_once('tools.inc.php');

// Cache Lite options
$cache_options = array(
'cacheDir' => '/cachelite/',   // Directory to place cache files
'lifeTime' => 3600             // Update every hour since we display the pricing
);

/ Fetch a Cache instance
$CL = new Cache_Lite($cache_options);
```

I store and retrieve the cache based on the HTTP GET parameters. The main windows are stored by page number with the prefix "main". The variations windows are stored by the page number with a prefix of the Child ASIN. If I find a stored page, I output it and then exit. Otherwise, I proceed and generate a new page to cache.

```
// The page number (for either Parent or Child ASINs)
$page=(isset($_GET['page'])) ? $_GET['page'] : DEFAULT_PAGE;

// The Parent ASIN to find details about
$asin=(isset($_GET['asin'])) ? $_GET['asin'] : null;

// Check for cached page.  Either ASIN+PAGE# or "main"+PAGE#
// If we have a hit, display it and exit
$cache_id = (!is_null($asin)) ? $asin.$page : 'main'.$page;
if ($layout = $CL->get($cache_id)) {
    echo $layout;
    exit(0);
}
```

To cache a page, I need to capture the output of layout.php. The easiest way to do that is to buffer the output. I start the buffering, generate the output, save the buffer using Cache Lite and the output it.

```
// Buffer the output
ob_start();
require_once("layout.php");

// Fetch the buffered output
$buffer = ob_get_contents();
ob_end_clean();

// Save the buffered output to the cache
$CL->save($buffer);

// Display the buffer
echo $buffer;
```

Exercises For The Reader

Modify the WatchCompare code to use batch requests that fetch up to twenty watches at once and allow comparisons.

Modify WatchCompare so that editorial reviews are displayed in the comparison output

Modify WatchCompare and add caching.

CHAPTER 5

Customers And Sellers

It's always good business to know about new customers before they walk in your door

—Ferengi Rule Of Acquisition #194

There are real people behind all the buying and selling on Amazon.com. Millions of them. Every Amazon user who has a login and password is automatically part of what Amazon calls the "Amazon Community." The Amazon Community is an effort by Amazon to get people involved in the sharing, recommendation, and feedback aspects of Amazon.com. You may have added content to the Amazon Community by creating a list or writing a review of a product on Amazon.com. You can see the contributions that you've made to the Amazon Community by logging in to your Amazon customer account and visiting your "About You" area at this URL:

```
http://www.amazon.com/exec/obidos/subst/community/community-home.html
```

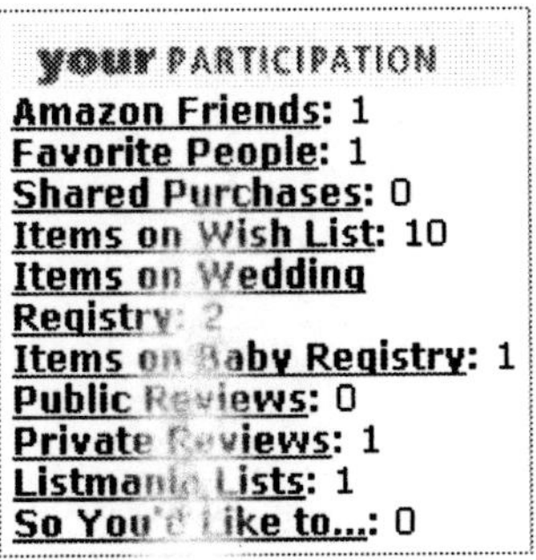

Figure 5-1 The "Your Participation" box indicates your level of Amazon Community participation

If you've made any contributions to the Amazon Community, you'll see a box like Figure 5-1 on the right-hand side of the page. The box shows the number of contributions you've made to the Amazon Community.

> If you've made no contributions to the Amazon Community, you'll see a box labeled "Things To Do" containing some suggestions for contributing to the Community.

Every Amazon user has an Amazon Customer ID. If you know a user's Customer ID, you can access their Community page information using a URL like this:

```
http://www.amazon.com/exec/obidos/tg/cm/member-glance/-/XXXXXXXXXX
```

Where, "XXXXXXXXXX" is the users' Customer ID (See Appendix A for tips on finding Amazon Customer IDs).

There are also lots of third-party businesses selling goods on Amazon, although there are no community features for sellers like there are for users. Still, most sellers have a page that Amazon calls a Glance Page. The Glance Page summarizes their customer feedback and other information. You can access a seller's Glance Page by using a URL like this:

```
http://www.amazon.com/gp/help/seller/home.html?seller=XXXXXXXXXXXXX
```

Where, "XXXXXXXXXXXXX" is the seller's Seller ID or Merchant ID (See Appendix A for tips on finding Amazon Seller and Merchant IDs).

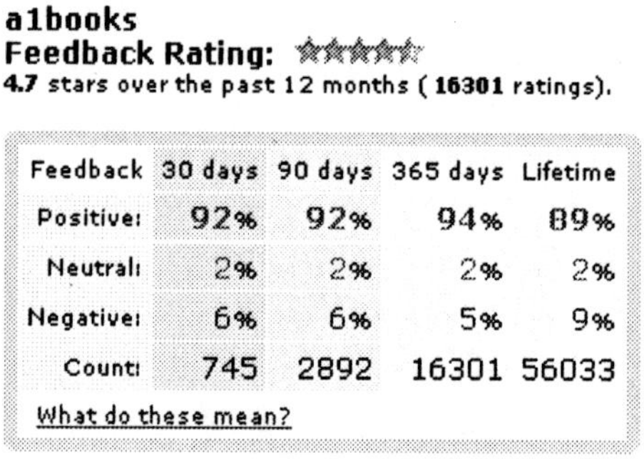

a1books
Feedback Rating: ★★★★☆
4.7 stars over the past 12 months (**16301** ratings).

Feedback	30 days	90 days	365 days	Lifetime
Positive:	92%	92%	94%	89%
Neutral:	2%	2%	2%	2%
Negative:	6%	6%	5%	9%
Count:	745	2892	16301	56033

What do these mean?

Figure 5-2 Feedback summary for Amazon sellers

Among other information, you'll see a summary of the seller's customer feedback, if any exists. The feedback summary for seller **a1books** is in Figure 5-2.

In this chapter, I'll show how to use Amazon E-commerce Service to access these bits of customer and seller information. You'll be able to find out some things about most of the sellers and some of the customers that use Amazon.

> You can only find out so much, though, before privacy restrictions kick in. For security reasons, only certain bits of Amazon customer information are available, and only if a customer chooses to make it public (their buying habits are never made public). Amazon seller information, on the other hand, is usually easy to access.

In particular, you may want to know the reputation of the sellers by looking at their Amazon Feedback rating (similar to Ebay's Feedback Score) that tells you what people thought about their buying experience with that seller. You might also be interested in where a seller is located so that you can minimize shipping time for a product or purchase it from a state that won't charge you sales tax.

Similarly, you may be interested in the "reputation" of Amazon customers. If they've written a lot of interesting reviews you may trust their opinion more than someone who has little to say. You may also be able to discover that someone you know has an Amazon Wishlist.

Finding Information About Sellers

As we learned in Chapter One, there are three basic classes of sellers at Amazon.com (in addition to Amazon itself):

- Individuals
- Pro Merchants
- Merchants@ Sellers

The Pro Merchants class is further subdivided into Marketplace Pro Merchants and Merchants@ Pro Merchants.

There are two types of identifiers that Amazon uses to identify sellers: a Merchant ID and a Seller ID. Merchant IDs only identify Merchants@ (pronounced Merchants At) Sellers. Seller IDs identify Individual, Pro, and (almost) all Merchants@ Sellers. In general, you should always use the Seller ID, not the Merchant ID. Fortunately, Merchant IDs and Seller IDs can be used interchangeably in all ECS operations that have a SellerId parameter.

> At some point (far in the future, perhaps), the Merchant Id will be deprecated in favor of the Seller Id.

The SellerLookup Operation

The Amazon operation for finding detailed information about sellers is the SellerLookup operation. It takes as its required parameter a Seller ID (but you can use a

Merchant ID instead). A request to find information about the merchant "Wholesale Audio/Video" takes their Seller ID, AXEKE1OSF85BK, as its input parameter.

```
http://webservices.amazon.com/onca/xml?Service=AWSECommerceService&
SubscriptionId=1A7XKHR5BYD0WPJVQEG2&AssociateTag=ws&Operation=SellerLookup&
ResponseGroup=Seller&SellerId=AXEKE1OSF85BK&Version=2005-02-23
```

Placing this request in a web browser yields a description of the merchant:


```
........
        <Seller>
            <SellerId>AXEKE1OSF85BK</SellerId>
            <SellerName>WholeSaleAudioVisual</SellerName>
            <Nickname>wholesaleaudiovideo</Nickname>
             <GlancePage>http://www.amazon.com/gp/help/seller/at-a-glance.
html?seller=AXEKE1OSF85BK&marketplaceSeller=1</GlancePage>
            <Location>
                <City>W. Seneca</City>
                <State>NY</State>
            </Location>
            <AverageFeedbackRating>4.08</AverageFeedbackRating>
            <TotalFeedback>1223</TotalFeedback>
            <TotalFeedbackPages>245</TotalFeedbackPages>
            <SellerFeedback>
                <Feedback>
                    <Rating>5</Rating><Comment>Quick service</Comment>
                    <Date>2004-11-06T20:12+0000</Date>
                    <RatedBy>A33UW2EIP6E6TI</RatedBy>
                </Feedback>
                <Feedback>
                    <Rating>5</Rating><Comment>Item arrived quickly and was in good
shape.  Would buy from again.</Comment>
                    <Date>2004-11-06T18:49+0000</Date>
                    <RatedBy>AAPK9DNAHHLGV</RatedBy>
                </Feedback>
                <Feedback>
                    <Rating>5</Rating>
                    <Comment>Excellent seller, Great New Radar Delivery was fast
and reliable.</Comment>
                    <Date>2004-11-06T16:36+0000</Date>
                    <RatedBy>A1M8JMHW6ORX4W</RatedBy>
                </Feedback>
                <Feedback>
                    <Rating>5</Rating>
                    <Comment>Very fast shipment and informative correspondence -
will buy from again</Comment><Date>2004-11-06T04:51+0000</Date>
                    <RatedBy>A286QXCYBHCD03</RatedBy>
                </Feedback>
                <Feedback>
                    <Rating>1</Rating>
                    <Comment>I did not receive  Apple iPod Dock Kit (M9602G/A).
The seller shipped iPod FireWire + USB 2.0 Cable (M9688G/A).  I contacted them on 10/
29/04 but have not received a response.</Comment>
                    <Date>2004-11-06T02:33+0000</Date>
```

```
                <RatedBy>A2MNZMSLZH3L3W</RatedBy>
            </Feedback>
        </SellerFeedback>
    </Seller>
```

The Rating is a 1 to 5 "star" rating, where 1 is the worst rating and 5 is the best, and the Date is in a particular ISO format (see Chapter Two, "Some Common Amazon Units" for more information on Amazon's star ratings and date format). The RatedBy element is actually the Customer ID of the person who gave the seller feedback.

Table 5-1 summarizes all of the elements that may be returned by the SellerLookup operation. Unlike customer information, none of these seller information elements are considered private information. However, for reasons known only to Amazon, some of this information is not returned for their higher tier Merchants@ partner sellers. For example, there are no customer reviews available for the merchant Target though certainly there have been varying degrees of customer satisfaction with them.

Element	Description
SellerId	The Seller ID of this seller
SellerName	The Name of this seller -- typically a business name
Nickname	A short string that uniquely identifies the seller
GlancePage	The URL of a page on Amazon.com that summarizes feedback ratings and other information about this seller
About	A paragraph or so of text about the seller (written by the seller)
MoreAbout	More detailed text about the seller (written by the seller)
Location (City, State, Country)	The location of the seller's business
AverageFeedbackRating	The average of all the feedback ratings given to this seller by their customers
TotalFeedback	The total number of feedback ratings given to this seller by their customers
TotalFeedbackPages	The total number of pages of feedback ratings (10 feedbacks per page)
SellerFeedback (Rating, Comment, Date, RatedBy)	An array of customer reviews which include an up to 5 star rating, a short comment, the date the seller was rated, and the Customer ID of the person who rated the seller.

Table 5-1 Seller information returned by Amazon E-Commerce Service

Still, for the vast majority of sellers, most of the elements in Table 5-1 are returned.

> As this book goes to press, some ECS operations will return somewhat different (though still correct) data points if you use a seller's Merchant ID instead of their Seller ID.

Finding Information About Customers

There are two E-Commerce Service operations for finding information about Amazon customers, CustomerContentLookup and CustomerContentSearch. These operations are not particularly useful because, by default, all information about Amazon customers is private. As an Amazon customer starts to contribute to the Amazon community, they may choose to make some bits of their private information public, such as their Wishlist, the reviews they've made of various products, or the Country that they live in. These bits of information are then available via ECS.

The CustomerContentLookup Operation

The CustomerContentLookup Operation takes a Customer ID as input and returns information about an Amazon customer that the customer has made publicly available.

Table 5-2 Customer information returned by Amazon E-Commerce Service

Element	Description
CustomerId	The Amazon Customer ID
Nickname	The Amazon nickname
Birthday	Their birthday (as entered by the user -- can you trust them?)
WishListId	Their Amazon Wishlist ID
Location (City, State, Country)	The City, State, and Country where the user is located
AverageRating	The average of all ratings the user have made (this is probably a bogus data point and never seems to be returned)
TotalReviews	The total number of product reviews this person has done
TotalReviewPages	The total number of pages of reviews (10 reviews per page)
Review (ASIN, Rating, HelpfulVotes, CustomerId, TotalVotes, Date, Summary, Content)	An array of reviews this person has done which include the ASIN of the product reviewed, up to a 5 star rating, the number of helpful votes, the customer's ID (if different than the CustomerId element above), the total votes (both helpful and not helpful), the date the review was made, a summary of the review, and the review itself.

Table 5-2 summarizes all the data points that may be returned by the CustomerContentLookup operation.

A customer's email address, shipping address, billing address, and phone number, as well as their purchasing history, is never returned.

Each Review element represents a review of some Amazon product that the user has made. These reviews are listed on Amazon product pages:

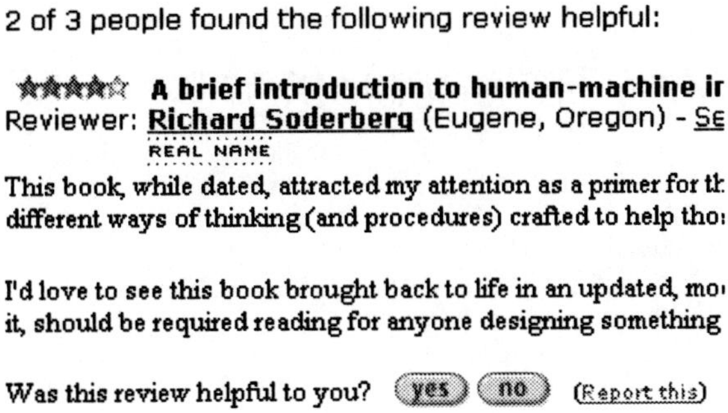

2 of 3 people found the following review helpful:

★★★★☆ **A brief introduction to human-machine ir**
Reviewer: **Richard Soderberg** (Eugene, Oregon) - Se
REAL NAME

This book, while dated, attracted my attention as a primer for th
different ways of thinking (and procedures) crafted to help tho

I'd love to see this book brought back to life in an updated, mo
it, should be required reading for anyone designing something

Was this review helpful to you? yes no (Report this)

Figure 5-3 A product review on Amazon.com

For each Review, the ASIN of the product is included, as well as a 0 to 5 start rating (0 is worst, 5 is best). HelpfulVotes are the number of people who clicked on the "yes" button in Figure 5-3 while TotalVotes is the total number who voted (TotalVotes minus HelpfulVotes is the "no" count). The Summary is the first 128 characters of the review.

To see all of the accessible contributions that an Amazon customer has made, use the CustomerFull Response Group in your request.

```
http://webservices.amazon.com/onca/xml?Service=AWSECommerceService&
SubscriptionId=1A7XKHR5BYD0WPJVQEG2&AssociateTag=ws&Operation=CustomerContentLookup&
CustomerId=A2KEKKJ9CAC2KC&ResponseGroup=CustomerFull&Version=2005-02-23
```

This particular Amazon.com customer has an Amazon Wish List and eight product reviews that are returned.

> Due to an unresolved bug in E-Commerce Service as this book goes to press, the Date element returned by the CustomerContentLookup operation is in Unix time() format instead of the ISO 8601 format used by other E-Commerce Service operations.

```
.....
.....
.....
<Customer>
      <Nickname>jeff</Nickname>
      <WishListId>BUWBWH9K2H77</WishListId>
      <CustomerReviews>
        <TotalReviews>8</TotalReviews>
        <TotalReviewPages>1</TotalReviewPages>
        <Review>
          <ASIN>6305692688</ASIN>
          <Rating>1</Rating>
          <HelpfulVotes>20</HelpfulVotes>
          <TotalVotes>33</TotalVotes>
          <Date>951796692</Date>
```

```
            <Summary>one star is indeed one too many</Summary>
            <Content>Let's face facts.  This is a terrible, terrible movie.  We have to
guess that all involved in this project are hiding.  Really, I'm generally quite easy
on movies, but this endless stream of uninteresting battle scenes with  pointless
dialogue and no discernable plot is perhaps one of the worst  movies ever made.
Sorry if this seems harsh, but I just don't want anyone  to buy it unknowingly.</
Content>
        </Review>
        <Review>
            <ASIN>B00001U0DP</ASIN>
            <Rating>5</Rating>
            <HelpfulVotes>11</HelpfulVotes>
            <TotalVotes>12</TotalVotes>
            <Date>953327781</Date>
            <Summary>Wow.  A masterpiece.</Summary>
            <Content>This movie is absolutely all it's cracked up to be. Hysterically
funny and simultaneously a tear jerker -- it's ultimately very uplifting.  The
cinematography is also fantastic -- amazing use of color. &lt;p&gt; The DVD has
dubbed english as an option, but I strongly recommend going with the  subtitles
instead so you can hear Benigni's amazing acting and passion. &lt;p&gt;  Too bad the
DVD doesn't include any deleted scenes.  With Benigni, I think  it would be
particularly fun to see out-takes. &lt;p&gt;&lt;p&gt;Absolutely a great  movie!</
Content>
        </Review>
              .....
              .....
              .....
              .....
    </CustomerReviews>
</Customer>
```

Note that in the Content element, characters such as the less than '<' and greater than '>' signs have been replaced with the HTML entities ';<' and ';>' to ensure that the XML is well-formed.

The CustomerContentSearch Operation

The CustomerContentSearch operation lets you search for Amazon customers by either email address or name (but not both at the same time). Only the Customer ID, name, nickname, and location (city and state) are returned (if available) for each customer.

> The WSDL implies that much more customer information might be returned by CustomerContentSearch requests. This is currently not the case, however.

A search by email address typically only returns one customer or none. That's because you must enter a valid email address in order to get any useful results. Entering a partial email address, or just a string, for the email parameter will just return an empty result. A search for the Amazon customer with email address jeff@amazon.com (note that I use the urlencoded value of %40 in place of the "@" symbol):

```
http://webservices.amazon.com/onca/xml?Service=AWSECommerceService&
SubscriptionId=1A7XKHR5BYD0WPJVQEG2&AssociateTag=ws&Operation=CustomerContentSearch&
Email=jeff%40amazon.com&Version=2005-02-23
```

yields a brief summary:

```
<Customer>
    <CustomerId>A2KEKKJ9CAC2KC</CustomerId>
    <Nickname>jeff</Nickname>
    <Location>
      <City>Seattle</City>
      <State>WA</State>
      <Country>United States</Country>
      </Location>
 </Customer>
```

When searching by name, on the other hand, you can use any full or partial names you wish. A search for Amazon CEO "Jeff Bezos":

```
http://webservices.amazon.com/onca/xml?Service=AWSECommerceService&
SubscriptionId=1A7XKHR5BYD0WPJVQEG2&AssociateTag=ws&Operation=CustomerContentSearch&
Name=Jeff%20Bezos&Version=2005-02-23
```

yields four somewhat mysterious results:

```
<TotalResults>4</TotalResults>
<TotalPages>1</TotalPages>
<Customer>
  <CustomerId>AIXBOXQ4HOD3S</CustomerId>
</Customer>
<Customer>
  <CustomerId>A3L8233II0XX53</CustomerId>
  <Nickname>michaelmaurer2</Nickname>
  <Location>
    <City>Wien</City>
    <Country>Österreich</Country>
  </Location>
</Customer>
<Customer>
  <CustomerId>A39BL3V214CS4T</CustomerId>
  <Nickname>sizzlingbacon</Nickname>
  <Location>
    <City>seattle</City>
    <State>wa</State>
    <Country>United States</Country>
  </Location>
</Customer>
<Customer>
  <CustomerId>A2KEKKJ9CAC2KC</CustomerId>
  <Nickname>jeff</Nickname>
  <Location>
    <City>Bellevue</City>
    <State>WA</State>
```

```
      <Country>USA</Country>
    </Location>
  </Customer>
```

As mentioned earlier, information will only be returned if the Amazon customer has explicitly made their information public by changing the default privacy settings in their Amazon account. So, it's quite possible that none of these results are Amazon CEO Jeff Bezos.

Code Sample: findseller

Findseller lets you do research to find the right seller with the right price. It takes as input an ASIN, and optionally, the desired condition of the item, and the state(s) where the sellers are located. It then uses ItemLookup to find all the sellers (or as many as are available via ECS) selling that item on Amazon.com in that condition and in the desired states. Each seller can also be clicked on, and I use SellerLookup to find all the details, and all the customer feedback, for that seller.

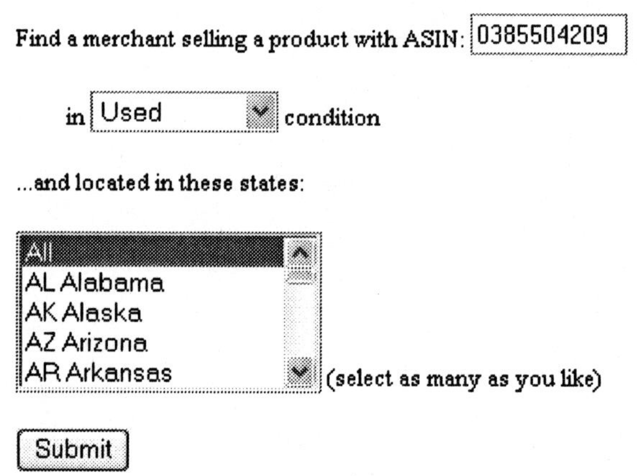

Figure 5-4 The GUI for the findseller application

Finally, the user can click on the Customer ID in each review to find out details (if any are available) about the user who gave a certain favorable (or unfavorable) review. Allowing filtering of results by condition gives you some leverage to find less expensive (e.g. used) items. You may also be interested in filtering by the location of the seller -- some states may be closer, and thus shipping could be cheaper, and some states require no sales tax. Customer feedback is useful for getting an impression of trust. If the seller has a lot of negative feedback, you may be willing to pay a bit more money to buy from a seller with mostly positive feedback.

ITEM: Hanes 5170 Adult/Youth Heavyweight 50/50 T-Shirt
PRODUCT GROUP: Apparel

Lowest New Price: $2.91
Highest New Price: $8.83
Lowest Sale Price: n/a
Highest Sale Price: n/a

Total Variations: 220

Variations pages (Up to 10 variations per page).......1-2 3-4 5-6 7-8 9-10 11-12 13-14 15-16 17-18 19-20 21-22

Product: Hanes 5170 Adult/Youth Heavyweight 50/50 T-Shirt in Red in size XL
Product: Hanes 5170 Adult/Youth Heavyweight 50/50 T-Shirt in Pebble in size XL
Product: Hanes 5170 Adult/Youth Heavyweight 50/50 T-Shirt in Pale Pink in size XL
Product: Hanes 5170 Adult/Youth Heavyweight 50/50 T-Shirt in Orange in size XL
Product: Hanes 5170 Adult/Youth Heavyweight 50/50 T-Shirt in White in size XL
Product: Hanes 5170 Adult/Youth Heavyweight 50/50 T-Shirt in Teal in size XL
Product: Hanes 5170 Adult/Youth Heavyweight 50/50 T-Shirt in Sand in size XL
Product: Hanes 5170 Adult/Youth Heavyweight 50/50 T-Shirt in Stonewashed Blue in size XL
Product: Hanes 5170 Adult/Youth Heavyweight 50/50 T-Shirt in Gold in size XL
Product: Hanes 5170 Adult/Youth Heavyweight 50/50 T-Shirt in Maroon in size XL
Product: Hanes 5170 Adult/Youth Heavyweight 50/50 T-Shirt in Light Blue in size XL
Product: Hanes 5170 Adult/Youth Heavyweight 50/50 T-Shirt in Light Steel in size XL
Product: Hanes 5170 Adult/Youth Heavyweight 50/50 T-Shirt in Ash in size XL
Product: Hanes 5170 Adult/Youth Heavyweight 50/50 T-Shirt in Black in size XL
Product: Hanes 5170 Adult/Youth Heavyweight 50/50 T-Shirt in Charcoal Heather in size XL
Product: Hanes 5170 Adult/Youth Heavyweight 50/50 T-Shirt in Cardinal in size XL
Product: Hanes 5170 Adult/Youth Heavyweight 50/50 T-Shirt in Red in size LG
Product: Hanes 5170 Adult/Youth Heavyweight 50/50 T-Shirt in Pebble in size LG
Product: Hanes 5170 Adult/Youth Heavyweight 50/50 T-Shirt in Pale Pink in size LG
Product: Hanes 5170 Adult/Youth Heavyweight 50/50 T-Shirt in Orange in size LG

Figure 5-5 Parent ASIN output for findseller

The main user interface consists of a simple form (Figure 5-4). The user enters an ASIN, selects the desired condition of the item, and then selects as many states as they want to filter by merchant location.

After hitting the submit button, there are two possible displays which depend on whether the ASIN entered was a Parent ASIN or a regular ASIN. If it was a regular ASIN, a description of the item is displayed, along with a summary of the offers, and a list of the first twenty merchants selling the item. If it's a Parent ASIN, then a description of the item is displayed, along with a summary of the variation pricing, and the first twenty variations of the product are listed.

Since I don't know beforehand whether the user will enter a Parent ASIN or a Child ASIN, I craft a batch ItemLookup request that will return all the information I need:

```
http://webservices.amazon.com/onca/xml?Service=AWSECommerceService&
AssociateTag=ws&SubscriptionId=1A7XKHR5BYDOWPJVQEG2&Operation=ItemLookup&
ItemLookup.Shared.ItemId=0385504209&ItemLookup.Shared.Condition=All&
ItemLookup.Shared.MerchantId=All&ItemLookup.Shared&
ResponseGroup=OfferFull,Variations,Small&ItemLookup.1.VariationPage=1&
ItemLookup.2.VariationPage=2&ItemLookup.1.OfferPage=1&ItemLookup.2.OfferPage=2&
Version=2005-02-23
```

This batch request shares all of the same parameters. But what I ask for are both the OfferPage, which will only be returned if it's a Regular ASIN, and the VariationPage, which will only be returned if it's a Parent ASIN. After making this request, I can check to see if it's a Parent ASIN by checking for the presence of the VariationSummary element:

```
if (isset($Result['ItemLookupResponse']['Items'][0]['Item'][0]['VariationSummary'])) {
    process_parent_asin($variationpage);
} else {
    process_regular_asin($offerpage);
}
```

If it's a Parent ASIN, I output the list of variations returned with pagination.

```
function process_parent_asin($variationpage) {
    global $Result;
    global $getagain;

// Output the Title and product category
    echo '<br />ITEM: '.
$Result['ItemLookupResponse']['Items'][0]['Item'][0]['ItemAttributes']['Title'].'<br
/>';
    echo 'PRODUCT GROUP: '.
$Result['ItemLookupResponse']['Items'][0]['Item'][0]['ItemAttributes']['ProductGroup'
].'<br /><br />';

// Retrieve the VariationSummary values
$lowestn=(isset($Result['ItemLookupResponse']['Items'][0]['Item'][0]['VariationSummar
y']['LowestPrice']['FormattedPrice'])) ?
$Result['ItemLookupResponse']['Items'][0]['Item'][0]['VariationSummary']['LowestPrice
']['FormattedPrice']  : 'n/a';
    $highestn=
(isset($Result['ItemLookupResponse']['Items'][0]['Item'][0]['VariationSummary']['High
estPrice']['FormattedPrice'])) ?
$Result['ItemLookupResponse']['Items'][0]['Item'][0]['VariationSummary']['HighestPric
e']['FormattedPrice']  : 'n/a';
    $lowestsale=
(isset($Result['ItemLookupResponse']['Items'][0]['Item'][0]['VariationSummary']['Lowe
stSalePrice']['FormattedPrice'])) ?
$Result['ItemLookupResponse']['Items'][0]['Item'][0]['VariationSummary']['LowestSaleP
rice']['FormattedPrice']  : 'n/a';
```

```
    $highestsale=
(isset($Result['ItemLookupResponse']['Items'][0]['Item'][0]['VariationSummary']['High
estSalePrice']['FormattedPrice'])) ?
$Result['ItemLookupResponse']['Items'][0]['Item'][0]['VariationSummary']['HighestSale
Price']['FormattedPrice']  : 'n/a';
    $totalvariations=
(isset($Result['ItemLookupResponse']['Items'][0]['Item'][0]['Variations']['TotalVaria
tions'])) ?
$Result['ItemLookupResponse']['Items'][0]['Item'][0]['Variations']['TotalVariations']
: 'n/a';

    echo 'Lowest New Price: '.$lowestn.'<br />';
    echo 'Highest New Price: '.$highestn.'<br />';
    echo 'Lowest Sale Price: '.$lowestsale.'<br />';
    echo 'Highest Sale Price: '.$highestsale.'<br />';

    echo '<br />Total Variations: '.$totalvariations.'<br />';

    // Display the list of variations with pagination
    $display='';
    echo '<br /><br />Variations pages (Up to 10 variations per page).......';
    for ($i=1; $i <=
$Result['ItemLookupResponse']['Items'][0]['Item'][0]['Variations']['TotalVariationPag
es']; $i=$i+2)
    {
        $nextpage=$i+1;
        $page = ($i == $variationpage) ? $variationpage.'-'.$nextpage : '<a
href="findseller.php?variationpage='.$i.$getagain.'">'.$i.'-'.$nextpage.'</a>';
        $display  .= $page.' ';
    }
    echo $display.'<br /><br />';

    foreach ($Result['ItemLookupResponse']['Items'] as $items) {
        if (!isset($items['Item'][0]['Variations']['Item'])) continue;
        foreach ($items['Item'][0]['Variations']['Item'] as $offers) {

            $childasin=$offers['ASIN'][0];
            $title=$offers['ItemAttributes']['Title'];
            echo 'Product: <a href="findseller.php?asin='.$childasin.'">'.$title.'</
a><br />';
         }
    }
    return;
}
```

The output for a Parent ASIN (a Hane's T-Shirt) is shown in Figure 5-5. Clicking on a variation re-submits the form with the Child ASIN for that variation. You then get the same display as you'd get if it was a Regular ASIN (for all practical purposes, a Child ASIN and a Regular ASIN have the same attributes) -- a list of merchants selling that particular variation.

```
function process_regular_asin($offerpage) {
```

```
    global $Result;
    global $states;
    global $condition;
    global $getagain;

    // Output Title and product category
    echo '<br />ITEM: '.
$Result['ItemLookupResponse']['Items'][0]['Item'][0]['ItemAttributes']['Title'].'<br
/>';
    echo 'PRODUCT GROUP: '.
$Result['ItemLookupResponse']['Items'][0]['Item'][0]['ItemAttributes']['ProductGroup'
].'<br />';

    // Display the information in the OfferSummary element
    $totaloffers=
(isset($Result['ItemLookupResponse']['Items'][0]['Item'][0]['Offers']['TotalOffers'])
) ? $Result['ItemLookupResponse']['Items'][0]['Item'][0]['Offers']['TotalOffers'] :
'none';
    echo '<br />TOTAL OFFERS IN <b>'.$condition.'</b> CONDITION(s): <b>'.
$totaloffers .'</b><br />';
    echo 'New: '.
$Result['ItemLookupResponse']['Items'][0]['Item'][0]['OfferSummary']['TotalNew'].'<br
/>';
    echo 'Used: '.
$Result['ItemLookupResponse']['Items'][0]['Item'][0]['OfferSummary']['TotalUsed'].
'<br />';
    echo 'Refurbished: '.
$Result['ItemLookupResponse']['Items'][0]['Item'][0]['OfferSummary']['TotalRefurbishe
d'].'<br />';
    echo 'Collectible: '.
$Result['ItemLookupResponse']['Items'][0]['Item'][0]['OfferSummary']['TotalCollectibl
e'].'<br />';

    // Display the pagination links
    $display='';
    echo '<br /><br />Offer pages (Up to 10 offers per page).......';
    if
(isset($Result['ItemLookupResponse']['Items'][0]['Item'][0]['Offers']['TotalOfferPage
s'])) {
        for ($i=1; $i <=
$Result['ItemLookupResponse']['Items'][0]['Item'][0]['Offers']['TotalOfferPages'];
$i=$i+2)
        {
            $nextpage=$i+1;
            $page = ($i == $offerpage) ? $offerpage.'-'.$nextpage : '<a
href="findseller.php?offerpage='.$i.$getagain.'">'.$i.'-'.$nextpage.'</a>';
            $display  .= $page.' ';
        }
    }
    echo $display.'<br /><br />';
    echo 'Filters: <br />';
    echo 'Only sellers in these states are shown: '.implode(', ',$states).'<br />';
    echo 'Only items in this condition are shown: '.$condition.'<br />';
```

```
    // Loop through the array of items and display the pricing and details
    foreach ($Result['ItemLookupResponse']['Items'] as $items) {
        if (!isset($items['Item'][0]['Offers']['Offer'])) continue;
        foreach ($items['Item'][0]['Offers']['Offer'] as $offer) {

            $state = (isset($offer['Seller'][0]['Location']['State'])) ?
strtoupper($offer['Seller'][0]['Location']['State']) : 'NO_STATE';

            // Only show sellers in selected states
            if ($states[0] != DEFAULT_STATE) {
                if (!in_array($state, $states)) continue;
            }

            $price = (isset($offer['OfferListing'][0]['Price']['FormattedPrice'])) ?
'<b>Price:</b> '.$offer['OfferListing'][0]['Price']['FormattedPrice'] : '<b>Price:</
b> n/a';

            $condition = (isset($offer['OfferAttributes']['Condition']))? '  <b>
Condition:</b> '.$offer['OfferAttributes']['Condition'] : '<b>Condition:</b> n/a';

            $name = (isset($offer['Seller'][0]['SellerName'])) ? '  <b>Seller Name:</
b> '.$offer['Seller'][0]['SellerName'] : ' <b>Seller name:</b> n/a';

            $sellerid = (isset($offer['Seller'][0]['SellerId'])) ?
$offer['Seller'][0]['SellerId'] : '';
            $nickname = (isset($offer['Seller'][0]['Nickname'])) ?
$offer['Seller'][0]['Nickname'] : '';

            if ($nickname != '' and $sellerid != '') {
                $nickname = '  <b>Nickname:</b> <a href="findseller.php?sellerid='.
$sellerid.' ">'.$nickname.'</a>';
            } elseif ($nickname != '') {
                $nickname='  <b>Nickname:</b> '.$nickname;
            } else {
                $nickname =  '  <b>Nickname:</b> n/a';
            }

            $merchantname = (isset($offer['Merchant']['Name'])) ?
$offer['Merchant']['Name'] : '';
            $merchantid = (isset($offer['Merchant']['MerchantId'])) ?
$offer['Merchant']['MerchantId'] : '';

            if ($merchantname != '' and $merchantid != '') {
                $merchantname = '  <b>Merchant Name:</b> <a href="findseller.
php?sellerid='.$merchantid.'">'.$merchantname.'</a>';
            } elseif ($merchantname != '') {
                $merchantname='  <b>Merchant Name:</b> '.$merchantname;
            } else {
                $merchantname =  '  <b>Merchant Name:</b> n/a';
            }

            if ((isset($offer['Seller'][0]['AverageFeedbackRating'])) and
$offer['Seller'][0]['AverageFeedbackRating'] == '0.0') {
                $avgfeedb='<b>No feedback for this seller</b>';
```

```
                $totalfeedb='';
            } else {
                $avgfeedb = (isset($offer['Seller'][0]['AverageFeedbackRating'])) ? '
<b>Average Rating:</b> '.$offer['Seller'][0]['AverageFeedbackRating'].' out of 5.0' :
'<b>Average rating:</b> n/a';
                $totalfeedb = (isset($offer['Seller'][0]['TotalFeedback'])) ? '  <b>
Total Feedback:</b> '.$offer['Seller'][0]['TotalFeedback'] : '<b>Total Feedback:</b>
n/a';
            }

            $conditionnote = (isset($offer['OfferAttributes']['ConditionNote'])) ?
'<br /><b>Condition notes:</b> '.$offer['OfferAttributes']['ConditionNote'] : '<b>
Condition notes:</b> n/a';

            $avail =  (isset($offer['OfferListing'][0]['Availability'])) ? '<br /><b>
Availability:</b> '.$offer['OfferListing'][0]['Availability'] : '<b>Availability:</b>
n/a';

            echo '<br />';
            echo $price.$condition.$name.$merchantname.$nickname.$avgfeedb.
$totalfeedb;
            echo $conditionnote;
            echo $avail;
        }
    }
    return;
}
```

For a Regular ASIN (the book "The DaVinci Code"), the display lists the merchants immediately (to save space, only the first four, of the first twenty merchants returned, are displayed in Figure 5-6):

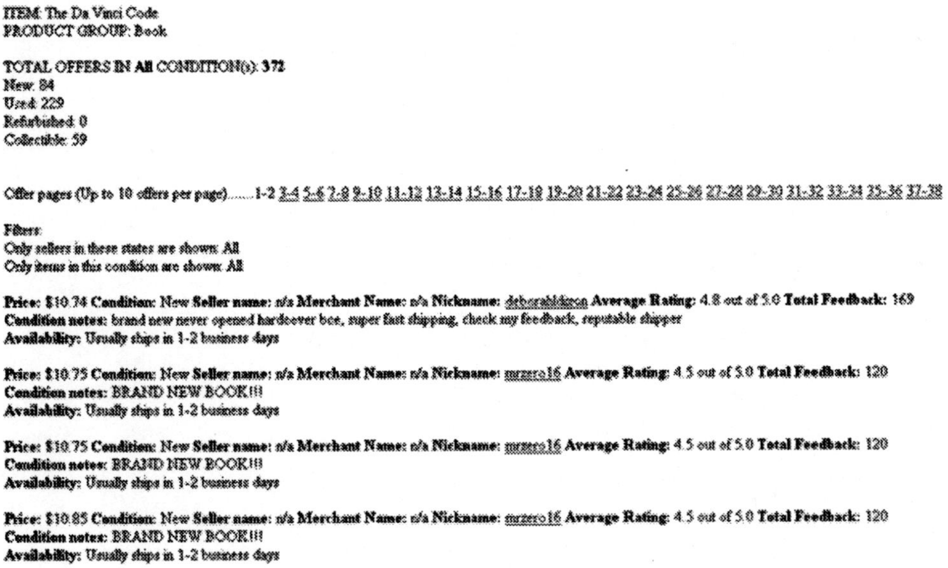

ITEM: The Da Vinci Code
PRODUCT GROUP: Book

TOTAL OFFERS IN All CONDITION(s): **372**
New: 84
Used: 229
Refurbished: 0
Collectible: 59

Offer pages (Up to 10 offers per page).......1-2 3-4 5-6 7-8 9-10 11-12 13-14 15-16 17-18 19-20 21-22 23-24 25-26 27-28 29-30 31-32 33-34 35-36 37-38

Filters:
Only sellers in these states are shown: All
Only items in this condition are shown: All

Price: $10.74 **Condition:** New **Seller name:** n/a **Merchant Name:** n/a **Nickname:** deborahldixon **Average Rating:** 4.8 out of 5.0 **Total Feedback:** 169
Condition notes: brand new never opened hardcover bee, super fast shipping, check my feedback, reputable shipper
Availability: Usually ships in 1-2 business days

Price: $10.75 **Condition:** New **Seller name:** n/a **Merchant Name:** n/a **Nickname:** mrzero16 **Average Rating:** 4.5 out of 5.0 **Total Feedback:** 120
Condition notes: BRAND NEW BOOK!!!
Availability: Usually ships in 1-2 business days

Price: $10.75 **Condition:** New **Seller name:** n/a **Merchant Name:** n/a **Nickname:** mrzero16 **Average Rating:** 4.5 out of 5.0 **Total Feedback:** 120
Condition notes: BRAND NEW BOOK!!!
Availability: Usually ships in 1-2 business days

Price: $10.85 **Condition:** New **Seller name:** n/a **Merchant Name:** n/a **Nickname:** mrzero16 **Average Rating:** 4.5 out of 5.0 **Total Feedback:** 120
Condition notes: BRAND NEW BOOK!!!
Availability: Usually ships in 1-2 business days

Figure 5-6 Regular ASIN output for findseller

Amazon always returns the items with the lowest prices first (there is no way to get Amazon to change that ordering).

Clicking on a merchant's nickname does a SellerLookup on that merchant and returns information about them. I use a batch request to fetch two pages of seller feedback at a time:

```
http://webservices.amazon.com/onca/xml?Service=AWSECommerceService&
AssociateTag=ws&SubscriptionId=1A7XKHR5BYD0WPJVQEG2&Operation=SellerLookup&
SellerLookup.Shared.SellerId=A28FWD287AIZO&SellerLookup.1.FeedbackPage=1&
SellerLookup.2.FeedbackPage=2&Version=2005-02-23
```

The process_seller() function simply cycles through the seller information and feedback reviews and displays them.

```
function process_seller($reviewpage) {
    global $Result;
    global $sellerid;

// Get the seller details
    $sellername=
(isset($Result['SellerLookupResponse']['Sellers'][0]['Seller'][0]['SellerName'])) ?
$Result['SellerLookupResponse']['Sellers'][0]['Seller'][0]['SellerName'] : 'n/a';

$nickname=(isset($Result['SellerLookupResponse']['Sellers'][0]['Seller'][0]['Nickname
'])) ? $Result['SellerLookupResponse']['Sellers'][0]['Seller'][0]['Nickname'] : 'n/
a';
```

```
$city=(isset($Result['SellerLookupResponse']['Sellers'][0]['Seller'][0]['Location']['
City'])) ?
$Result['SellerLookupResponse']['Sellers'][0]['Seller'][0]['Location']['City'] : 'n/
a';

$state=(isset($Result['SellerLookupResponse']['Sellers'][0]['Seller'][0]['Location'][
'State'])) ?
$Result['SellerLookupResponse']['Sellers'][0]['Seller'][0]['Location']['State'] : 'n/
a';

$about=(isset($Result['SellerLookupResponse']['Sellers'][0]['Seller'][0]['About'])) ?
$Result['SellerLookupResponse']['Sellers'][0]['Seller'][0]['About'] : 'n/a';

$totalpages=(isset($Result['SellerLookupResponse']['Sellers'][0]['Seller'][0]['TotalF
eedbackPages'])) ?
$Result['SellerLookupResponse']['Sellers'][0]['Seller'][0]['TotalFeedbackPages'] :
'n/a';

$averagefeed=(isset($Result['SellerLookupResponse']['Sellers'][0]['Seller'][0]['Avera
geFeedbackRating'])) ?
$Result['SellerLookupResponse']['Sellers'][0]['Seller'][0]['AverageFeedbackRating'] :
'n/a';

    echo "<br /><b>Seller Name: </b>".$sellername."<br />";
    echo "<b>Seller Nickname: </b>".$nickname." <br />";
    echo "<b>Seller Location: </b>".$city.",".$state." <br />";
    echo "<b>Seller Feedback Rating (average): </b>".$averagefeed." <br />";
    echo "<b>Total Feedback: </b>".$totalpages."<br />";
    echo "<b>About this seller: </b>".$about;

    // Display the pagination links
    $display='';
    echo '<br /><br />Seller feedback pages (Up to 5 reviews per page, two pages at a
time).......';
    if
(isset($Result['SellerLookupResponse']['Sellers'][0]['Seller'][0]['TotalFeedbackPages
'])) {
        for ($i=1; $i <=
$Result['SellerLookupResponse']['Sellers'][0]['Seller'][0]['TotalFeedbackPages'];
$i=$i+2)
        {
            $nextpage=$i+1;
            $page = ($i == $reviewpage) ? $reviewpage.'-'.$nextpage : '<a
href="findseller.php?sellerid='.$sellerid.'&reviewpage='.$i.'">'.$i.'-'.$nextpage.'</
a>';
            $display  .= $page.' ';
            if ($i == 9) break;
        }
    }
    echo $display.'<br />';

// Cycle through the seller feedback reviews on Amazon
    foreach ($Result['SellerLookupResponse']['Sellers'] as $seller)  {
```

```
        if (!isset($seller['Seller'][0]['SellerFeedback']['Feedback'])) continue;
        foreach ($seller['Seller'][0]['SellerFeedback']['Feedback'] as $review) {

            $rating = (isset($review['Rating'])) ? '<b>Rating:</b> '.
$review['Rating'] : '<b>Rating:</b> n/a';

            $comment = (isset($review['Comment']))? '  <b>Comment:</b> '.
$review['Comment'] : '<b>Comment:</b> n/a';

            $date = (isset($review['Date'])) ? '  <b>Rating Date:</b> '.date('l, F j,
Y, g:ia T', strtotime(str_replace('T', ' ', $review['Date']))) : ' <b>Rating Date:</
b> n/a';

            $ratedby = (isset($review['RatedBy'])) ? '  <b>Customer:</b> <a
href="findseller.php?customerid='.$review['RatedBy'].' ">'.$review['RatedBy'].'</a>'
: '  <b>Customer:</b>  n/a';

            echo '<br /><br />'.$rating.$ratedby.$date.'<br />'.$comment;
        }
    }
    return;
}
```

To save space in this book, only the first 5, of the 10 reviews returned, are displayed in Figure 5-7).

Seller Name: n/a
Seller Nickname: mrzero16
Seller Location: SAN ANTONIO,TX
Seller Feedback Rating (average): 4.5
Total Feedback: 24
About this seller: n/a

Seller feedback pages (Up to 5 reviews per page, two pages at a time).......1-2 3-4 5-6 7-8 9-10

Rating: 5 **Customer:** A15ZR8RGPIA3MB **Rating Date:** Sunday, February 13, 2005, 5:36am Central Standard Time
Comment: fast shipping / just what I ordered!! thanks

Rating: 5 **Customer:** A2YBUX7PF8ZPXM **Rating Date:** Saturday, February 12, 2005, 12:51am Central Standard Time
Comment: great service

Rating: 4 **Customer:** A3K0PGVQAOW4GN **Rating Date:** Wednesday, February 9, 2005, 9:32am Central Standard Time
Comment: thanks

Rating: 5 **Customer:** A2QZZZJ8QXXQEO **Rating Date:** Friday, February 4, 2005, 1:15am Central Standard Time
Comment: thank you

Rating: 5 **Customer:** A2QZZZJ8QXXQEO **Rating Date:** Friday, February 4, 2005, 1:15am Central Standard Time
Comment: Thank you

Figure 5-7 Seller display in findseller

Finally, clicking on the customer's Customer ID does a CustomerContentLookup and returns details about the customer. If the customer gives a particularly favorable (or negative) review, you might be reassured (or dissuaded) in believing in them after you check on their details. Again, I use a batch request in order to get two pages of customer reviews at a time.

```
http://webservices.amazon.com/onca/xml?Service=AWSECommerceService&
AssociateTag=ws&SubscriptionId=1A7XKHR5BYDOWPJVQEG2&
Operation=CustomerContentLookup&
CustomerContentLookup.Shared.CustomerId=A3LSMOFUYS5QY5&
CustomerContentLookup.1.ReviewPage=1&CustomerContentLookup.2.ReviewPage=2&
ResponseGroup=CustomerFull,Request&Version=2005-02-23
```

The process_customer() function displays the given page of reviews, as well as the other available customer information.

```
function process_customer($rpage) {
    global $Result;

// Fetch the customer information
$nickname=(isset($Result['CustomerContentLookupResponse']['Customers'][0]['Customer']
[0]['Nickname'])) ?
$Result['CustomerContentLookupResponse']['Customers'][0]['Customer'][0]['Nickname'] :
'n/a';

$wishlist=(isset($Result['CustomerContentLookupResponse']['Customers'][0]['Customer']
[0]['WishListId'])) ?
$Result['CustomerContentLookupResponse']['Customers'][0]['Customer'][0]['WishListId']
: 'n/a';

$birthday=(isset($Result['CustomerContentLookupResponse']['Customers'][0]['Customer']
[0]['Birthday'])) ?
$Result['CustomerContentLookupResponse']['Customers'][0]['Customer'][0]['Birthday'] :
'n/a';

$city=(isset($Result['CustomerContentLookupResponse']['Customers'][0]['Customer'][0][
'Location']['City'])) ?
$Result['CustomerContentLookupResponse']['Customers'][0]['Customer'][0]['Location']['
City'] : 'n/a';

$state=(isset($Result['CustomerContentLookupResponse']['Customers'][0]['Customer'][0]
['Location']['State'])) ?
$Result['CustomerContentLookupResponse']['Customers'][0]['Customer'][0]['Location']['
State'] : 'n/a';

$country=(isset($Result['CustomerContentLookupResponse']['Customers'][0]['Customer'][
0]['Location']['Country'])) ?
$Result['CustomerContentLookupResponse']['Customers'][0]['Customer'][0]['Location']['
Country'] : 'n/a';

    echo "<b>Customer Nickname: </b>".$nickname." <br />";
    echo "<b>Customer Wishlist: </b>".$wishlist." <br />";
    echo "<b>Customer Birthday: </b>".$birthday." <br />";
```

```
    echo "<b>Customer City: </b>".$city." <br />";
    echo "<b>Customer State: </b>".$state." <br />";
    echo "<b>Customer Country: </b>".$country." <br />";

    // Display the review pagination links
    $display='';
    echo '<br /><br />Seller feedback pages (Up to 5 reviews per page, two pages at a
time).......';

    if
(isset($Result['CustomerContentLookupResponse']['Customers'][0]['Customer'][0]['Revie
ws']['TotalReviewPages']) and
($Result['CustomerContentLookupResponse']['Customers'][0]['Customer'][0]['Reviews']['
TotalReviewPages'] != '0')) {

        for ($i=1; $i <=
$Result['CustomerContentLookupResponse']['Customers'][0]['Customer'][0]['Reviews']['T
otalReviewPages']; $i=$i+2)
        {
            $nextpage=$i+1;
            $page = ($i == $rpage) ? $rpage.'-'.$nextpage : '<a href="findseller.
php?&rpage='.$i.'">'.$i.'-'.$nextpage.'</a>';
            $display  .= $page.' ';
            if ($i == 9) break;
        }
    }

    // Cycle through the customer reviews and display them
    echo $display.'<br />';

    foreach( $Result['CustomerContentLookupResponse']['Customers'] as $customer) {
        if (isset($customer['Customer'][0]['Reviews'])) {
            foreach ($customer['Customer'][0]['Reviews']['Review'] as $review)  {

                $asin = (isset($review['ASIN'][0])) ? '<b>ASIN:</b> '.
$review['ASIN'][0] : '<b>ASIN:</b> n/a';

                $rating = (isset($review['Rating']))? '  <b>Rating:</b> '.
$review['Rating'] : '<b>Rating:</b> n/a';

                $helpfulvotes = (isset($review['HelpfulVotes'])) ? '  <b>Helpful
Votes:</b> '.$review['HelpfulVotes'] : ' <b>Helpful Votes:</b> n/a';

                $totalvotes = (isset($review['TotalVotes'])) ? '  <b>Total Votes:</b>
'.$review['TotalVotes'] : ' <b>Total Votes:</b> n/a';

                // BUG: date is still in Unix time format
                $date = (isset($review['Date'])) ? '  <b>Rating Date:</b> '.
$review['Date'] : ' <b>Rating Date:</b> n/a';
                $summary = (isset($review['Summary'])) ? '  <b>Summary:</b> '.
$review['Summary'] : ' <b>Summary:</b> n/a';
                $content = (isset($review['Content'])) ? '  <b>Content:</b> '.
$review['Content'] : ' <b>Content:</b> n/a';
```

```
                echo '<br /><br />'.$asin.$rating.$helpfulvotes.$totalvotes.$date.
$summary.'<br />'.$content;
            }
        }
    }
    return;
}
```

Most Amazon users have little public information which is reflected in the sample output (Figure 5-8). Also, various outstanding bugs in the CustomerContentLookup functions have prevented customer reviews from showing up.

Customer Nickname: imkndru
Customer Wishlist: XKWDMDV6R3J9
Customer Birthday: n/a
Customer City: n/a
Customer State: n/a
Customer Country: n/a

Seller feedback pages (Up to 5 reviews per page, two pages at a time).......

Figure 5-8 customer information display in findseller

SellerListingSearch And SellerListingLookup

SellerListingSearch and SellerListingLookup let you search for specific items, and lookup specific offers, in the Amazon Marketplace and zShops. Up to this point, we've used only the ItemSearch and ItemLookup operations to search for items on Amazon.com. Though they are powerful operations, there are few things you can do with SellerListingSearch and SellerListingLookup that you can't do with ItemSearch and ItemLookup:

- Search for items and offers in the Amazon zShops
- Retrieve very detailed information about a specific offer in the Amazon Marketplace or zShops
- Search by Seller Id
- Filter results by Seller Id

While ItemSearch will find items in the Amazon Marketplace and Stores, it does not let you search the Amazon zShops. This is usually not a problem as sellers can cross-list most common items in both the zShops and Marketplace, but for more esoteric items, such as unique collectibles without an ASIN, the item can only reside in a zShop.

> If an item in the zShops does not have an ASIN, it will still have a Listing ID (this is shown as a "zShops ID" in the Amazon zShops).

Another use of SellerListingSearch and SellerListingLookup is to get detailed information about a particular offer in the zShops and Marketplace. Only SellerListingSearch lets you search by seller zip code, or by which countries an Amazon seller will ship to. Only SellerListingLookup and SellerListingSearch will give you the start and end date of a particular offer and the quantity of the item the seller has allocated. These details can be critical if you want to determine actual availability of an item from a particular seller.

SellerListingSearch is the only way to search by Seller Id (ItemSearch only lets you search by MerchantId). This is particularly useful if you want to retrieve a specific Marketplace or zShops seller's complete Marketplace and zShops listings.

Both SellerListingSearch and SellerListingLookup return the same data structure (Table 5-3). The difference is that SellerListingSearch may return offers from many different sellers based on search criteria while SellerListingLookup is typically used to lookup specific offers.

Element	Description
TotalResults	`The total number of item listings`
TotalPages	`The total number of pages of item listings (10 listings per page)`
ExchangeId	`Identifies an offer in the Marketplace or zShops`
ListingId	`Identifies an item in the zShops`
ASIN	`The ASIN of the item (only returned for Marketplace items)`
Title	`The name of the item`
Price	`The price of the item`
StartDate	`The date the seller started selling the item`
EndDate	`The date the seller will no longer sell the item`
Status	`Either "open" or "closed"`
Quantity	`The quantity of the item in stock`
QuantityAllocated	`The quantity sold or unavailable`
Condition	`The condition of the item(s)`
SubCondition	`More condition information`
ConditionNote	`Any special condition remarks`
Availability	`The availability string`
FeaturedCategory	`The zShops category ID (a Browse Node ID within zShops)`

Element	Description
Seller (SellerId, Nickname)	[Only the SellerId and Nickname are returned for the seller]

Table 5-3 Elements returned by the SellerListingLookup and SellerListingSearch operations

An item is available if the Status element is "Open" and the Quantity is both greater than zero and greater than QuantityAllocated. The Availability string should be checked to determine how long it will take before the customer receives the item.

The FeaturedCategory element is the Browse Node Id within zShops that the seller has placed the item.

> The list of zShops category IDs (Browse Node IDs that exist only within zShops) is listed here: http://s1.amazon.com/exec/varzea/subst/home/categories-cheatsheet.html

To find all the open listings (all of the items a particular seller has available) for a particular seller, you specify the Seller's Id in the SellerId parameter to SellerListingSearch. This batch request retrieves the first two pages (20 items) for the SellerId A3ICGCER1Q4UB7:

```
http://webservices.amazon.com/onca/xml?Service=AWSECommerceService&AssociateTag=ws&
SubscriptionId=1A7XKHR5BYD0WPJVQEG2&Operation=SellerListingSearch&|
SellerListingSearch.Shared.OfferStatus=Open&
SellerListingSearch.Shared.SearchIndex=Marketplace&
SellerListingSearch.Shared.SellerId=A3ICGCER1Q4UB7&
SellerListingSearch.1.ListingPage=1&SellerLookup.2.ListingPage=2&Version=2005-02-23
```

The output gives the complete status of every open (purchasable) listing from that particular seller.

```
<TotalResults>4</TotalResults>
    <TotalPages>1</TotalPages>
    <SellerListing>
      <ExchangeId>Y03Y3713606Y5188627</ExchangeId>
      <ListingId>0309B684994</ListingId>
      <ASIN>B00007KDVI</ASIN>
      <Title>Linksys WRT54G Wireless-G Router [Electronics]</Title>
      <Price>
        <Amount>8999</Amount>
        <CurrencyCode>USD</CurrencyCode>
        <FormattedPrice>$89.99</FormattedPrice>
      </Price>
      <StartDate>2004-03-09</StartDate>
      <EndDate>2007-02-22</EndDate>
      <Status>Open</Status>
      <Quantity>1</Quantity>
      <QuantityAllocated>0</QuantityAllocated>
      <Condition>used</Condition>
      <SubCondition>acceptable</SubCondition>
```

```
        <ConditionNote>Slightly discolored. Worn around the edges. Scratches on top.</
    ConditionNote>
        <Availability>Usually ships within 1-2 business days</Availability>
        <FeaturedCategory>170161</FeaturedCategory>
        <Seller>
          <SellerId>A3ICGCER1Q4UB7</SellerId>
          <Nickname>sashimikid</Nickname>
        </Seller>
      </SellerListing>
      <SellerListing>
        <ExchangeId>Y03Y2767847Y3791049</ExchangeId>
        <ListingId>0304A801436</ListingId>
        <ASIN>0465067093</ASIN>
        <Title>The Psychology of Everyday Things [Hardcover]  by Norman, Donald A.</
    Title>
        <Price>
          <Amount>20000</Amount>
          <CurrencyCode>USD</CurrencyCode>
          <FormattedPrice>$200.00</FormattedPrice>
        </Price>
        <StartDate>2004-03-04</StartDate>
        <EndDate>2007-02-17</EndDate>
        <Status>Open</Status>
        <Quantity>1</Quantity>
        <QuantityAllocated>0</QuantityAllocated>
        <Condition>collectible</Condition>
        <SubCondition>acceptable</SubCondition>
        <Availability>Usually ships within 1-2 business days</Availability>
        <FeaturedCategory>68297</FeaturedCategory>
        <Seller>
          <SellerId>A3ICGCER1Q4UB7</SellerId>
          <Nickname>sashimikid</Nickname>
        </Seller>
      </SellerListing>
       .......
       .......
       .......
```

The Merchants Search Index

Of all the Search Indexes listed in Appendix H, only two do not represent a specific product category: Merchants and Blended. The Blended Search Index represents a cross-section of all Search Indexes. When used with the ItemSearch operation, Blended uses all Search Indexes to formulate the response.

The Merchants Search Index does the same thing as Blended, but for a specific Amazon Merchant's products. This is quite useful if you're interested in finding items sold by a specific seller, and you know that the seller has items in many different Search Indexes.

The Merchants Search Index only returns results when you specify a Merchant ID.

> Some Amazon merchants do not allow their products to be searched using E-Commerce Service.

Using the Merchant ID for Target (see Appendix A for strategies for finding Merchant IDs), we can have E-Commerce Service search all Search Indexes using the keyword "lamp" for items sold by Target.

```
http://webservices.amazon.com/onca/xml?Service=AWSECommerceService&
Version=2005-02-23&SubscriptionId=001VHHVC74XFD88KCY82&Operation=ItemSearch&
SearchIndex=Merchants&ResponseGroup=Small&MerchantId=A1VC38T7YXB528&Keywords=lamp
```

The first page of results has items from several Search Indexes.

> As this book goes to press, only the Product Group is returned for each item, not the Search Index. The Product Group is an older product category identifier used on Amazon. It does not map directly to Search Indexes and is of little value to Amazon developers.

```
  ...
  ...
  <Item>
      <ASIN>B00022HNHE</ASIN>
      <DetailPageURL>http://www.amazon.com/exec/obidos/redirect?tag=ws%26link_
code=xm2%26camp=2025%26creative=165953%26path=http://www.amazon.com/gp/redirect.
html%253fASIN=B00022HNHE%2526location=/o/ASIN/
B00022HNHE%25253FSubscriptionId=001VHHVC74XFD88KCY82</DetailPageURL>
      <ItemAttributes>
        <Manufacturer>Zelco</Manufacturer>
        <ProductGroup>Kitchen</ProductGroup>
        <Title>Zelco BookMate Book Stand</Title>
      </ItemAttributes>
    </Item>
    <Item>
      <ASIN>B0000A1EH2</ASIN>
      <DetailPageURL>http://www.amazon.com/exec/obidos/redirect?tag=ws%26link_
code=xm2%26camp=2025%26creative=165953%26path=http://www.amazon.com/gp/redirect.
html%253fASIN=B0000A1EH2%2526location=/o/ASIN/
B0000A1EH2%25253FSubscriptionId=001VHHVC74XFD88KCY82</DetailPageURL>
      <ItemAttributes>
        <Manufacturer>Yamaha</Manufacturer>
        <ProductGroup>CE</ProductGroup>
        <Title>Yamaha EZ-150AD 61-Note Portable Keyboard with Guide Lamps and AC
Adapter</Title>
      </ItemAttributes>
    </Item>
<Item>
     <ASIN>B00005OU11</ASIN>
     <DetailPageURL>http://www.amazon.com/exec/obidos/redirect?tag=ws%26link_
code=xm2%26camp=2025%26creative=165953%26path=http://www.amazon.com/gp/redirect.
html%253fASIN=B00005OU11%2526location=/o/ASIN/
B00005OU11%25253FSubscriptionId=001VHHVC74XFD88KCY82</DetailPageURL>
```

```
      <ItemAttributes>
        <Manufacturer>Style</Manufacturer>
        <ProductGroup>Home</ProductGroup>
        <Title>Textured Bronze-Finish Floor Lamp</Title>
      </ItemAttributes>
    </Item>
  ...
  ...
```

Wishlists And Other Lists

One of the most popular Amazon Community features is lists. Amazon lets customers create various kinds of lists to share their opinions or interests, or to celebrate weddings and baby births.

List	Accessible Via E-Commerce Service?	Description
Baby Registry	Yes (search only)	A list of Amazon items for a baby registry
Listmania	Yes (no search)	A (usually) helpful list of Amazon items associated with a particular topic or idea
Purchase Sharing	No	A private list of your Amazon purchases that you choose to share with other, specified, Amazon customers
So You'd Like To...	No	A "how to" guide that includes a tutorial and list of associated Amazon items
Wedding Registry	Yes (search only)	A list of Amazon items for a wedding registry
Wishlist	Yes	A list of Amazon items you desire

Table 5-4 Lists you can create on Amazon.com

Amazon E-Commerce Service 4.0 lets developers lookup and search for various lists using the ListLookup and ListSearch operations.

Each list has a unique ID that identifies that list. If you know an ID for a particular list (see Appendix A for instructions on how to find list IDs), you can go directly to that list using the URLs in Table 5-5. This can particularly helpful when you're checking E-Commerce service output for errors or omissions. For each list in Table 5-5, replace the "XXXXXXXXXX" with the relevant list ID.

List	Direct Link To List
Baby Registry	http://www.amazon.com/exec/obidos/registry/XXXXXXXXXX
Listmania	http://www.amazon.com/exec/obidos/tg/listmania/list-browse/-/XXXXXXXXXX
Purchase Sharing	Links are only accessible to your invited Amazon "Friends"

List	Direct Link To List
So You'd Like To...	http://www.amazon.com/exec/obidos/tg/guides/guide-display/-/XXXXXXXXXX
Wedding Registry	http://www.amazon.com/exec/obidos/registry/XXXXXXXXXX
Wishlist	http://www.amazon.com/gp/registry/XXXXXXXXXX

Table 5-5 Direct links to Amazon lists

ListLookup And ListSearch

ListLookup and ListSearch let developers retrieve Wishlists, Listmania and Wedding Registry lists, and search for Wishlists, Wedding Registry, and Baby Registry lists. You can search for existing lists using a name, email address, city, or state, and ListSearch will return basic information about the list, including the list ID. ListSearch does not, however, return the items in the list. You can only get the items in a list by using the ListLookup function and specifying the list ID.

There is also currently no way to search for, or access, Purchase Sharing or So You'd Like To... lists, and there is no way to retrieve the items in Baby Registries.

> Future versions of E-Commerce Service will let you retrieve Baby Registries.

Using ListSearch

The ListSearch operation lets you search for WishLists, Wedding Registries, and Baby Registries using a number of criteria: full name, first name, last name, and email address.

> When Amazon customers create their lists, the lists are searchable by default. However, customers may choose to make any of their lists unsearchable. If they don't make them searchable, you won't find them with the ListSearch operation.

In practice, using a full or partial name will rarely result in a perfect hit unless the name is decidely unusual. Searching for my Wishlist using my full name, for example, resulted in four hits.

```
http://webservices.amazon.com/onca/xml?Service=AWSECommerceService&
AssociateTag=ws&SubscriptionId=1A7XKHR5BYDOWPJVQEG2&Operation=ListSearch&
ListType=WishList&Name=Jason%20Levitt&Version=2005-02-23
```

The first result from this request is, in fact, my Wishlist, but the only reason it came up first is because the other Jason Levitts didn't capitalize their first and last names.

```
<TotalResults>4</TotalResults>
<TotalPages>1</TotalPages>
<List>
  <ListId>1PQ2HOS74O1DU</ListId>
```

```
    <ListURL>http://www.amazon.com/gp/registry/1PQ2HOS74O1DU</ListURL>
    <ListType>WishList</ListType>
    <TotalItems>9</TotalItems>
    <TotalPages>1</TotalPages>
    <DateCreated>2003-01-30</DateCreated>
    <CustomerName>Jason Levitt</CustomerName>
  </List>
  <List>
    <ListId>3CF23HSYBX8YC</ListId>
    <ListURL>http://www.amazon.com/gp/registry/3CF23HSYBX8YC</ListURL>
    <ListType>WishList</ListType>
    <TotalItems>1</TotalItems>
    <TotalPages>1</TotalPages>
    <DateCreated>2002-03-25</DateCreated>
    <CustomerName>dr. jason levitt</CustomerName>
  </List>
  <List>
    <ListId>2LVSD2VD9YYTF</ListId>
    <ListURL>http://www.amazon.com/gp/registry/2LVSD2VD9YYTF</ListURL>
    <ListType>WishList</ListType>
    <TotalItems>17</TotalItems>
    <TotalPages>2</TotalPages>
    <DateCreated>2004-04-18</DateCreated>
    <CustomerName>Jason levitt</CustomerName>
  </List>
  <List>
    <ListId>3GDBH7Y6QV6HK</ListId>
    <ListURL>http://www.amazon.com/gp/registry/3GDBH7Y6QV6HK</ListURL>
    <ListType>WishList</ListType>
    <TotalItems>1</TotalItems>
    <TotalPages>1</TotalPages>
    <DateCreated>2004-05-07</DateCreated>
    <CustomerName>jason levitt</CustomerName>
  </List>
```

Searching by email address is a much better way to get an exact match since it is a unique identifier -- it either returns one list or no lists.

> Searching by partial email addresses, e.g. searching for "jason", doesn't work. You have to specify the entire email address.

Using ListLookup

The ListLookup operation lets you retrieve Wishlists, Listmania and Wedding Registry lists by specifying the Wishlist, Wedding Registry, or Listmania list ID. You can only look up one list at a time, though you can use a batch request to lookup two lists in one request. I can fetch my Wishlist using the list ID returned from the previous section:

```
http://webservices.amazon.com/onca/xml?Service=AWSECommerceService&
AssociateTag=ws&SubscriptionId=1A7XKHR5BYD0WPJVQEG2&Operation=ListLookup&
ListType=WishList&ListId=1PQ2HOS74O1DU&Version=2005-02-23
```

The default Response Group for ListLookup is ListFull which returns all the basic information about the list but does not return the list of items on the list:

```
<List>
  <ListURL>http://www.amazon.com/gp/registry/1PQ2HOS74O1DU</ListURL>
  <ListType>WishList</ListType>
  <TotalItems>9</TotalItems>
  <TotalPages>1</TotalPages>
  <DateCreated>2003-01-30</DateCreated>
  <CustomerName>Jason Levitt</CustomerName>
</List>
```

Like the ItemLookup operation, ListLookup returns the total number of items on the list and the total number of pages (10 items per page) which makes it easy to create paginated lists.

By adding a Response Group for items, such as Small, Medium, or Large, the items and offers can be returned in the response:

```
http://webservices.amazon.com/onca/xml?Service=AWSECommerceService&
AssociateTag=ws&SubscriptionId=1A7XKHR5BYD0WPJVQEG2&Operation=ListLookup&
ListType=WishList&ListId=1PQ2HOS74O1DU&ResponseGroup=ListFull,Small&
Version=2005-01-19
```

Code Sample: Wishlist Widget

Amazon Wishlists make a fun addition to any blog or personal website. You might even be the developer of a multi-user web site or blog and want to provide access to Amazon Wishlists for any user who registers at your site. The Wishlist Widget, as I call it, is simply a convenient way to access and display Amazon Wishlists. The Wishlist Widget is similar to the ProductSense application that I developed in Chapter Three, but with some important differences.

The Wishlist Widget displays Wishlists of any length in a scrolling box, so even if your Wishlist has a hundred items in it (and many do), people can view all the items in your list. The Widget also lets people sort the items by all three of the sorting options for Wishlists: price, date added to the list, and the most recent updated items (an item is updated on your Wishlist when you change the quantity desired or add a comment about it on Amazon.com).

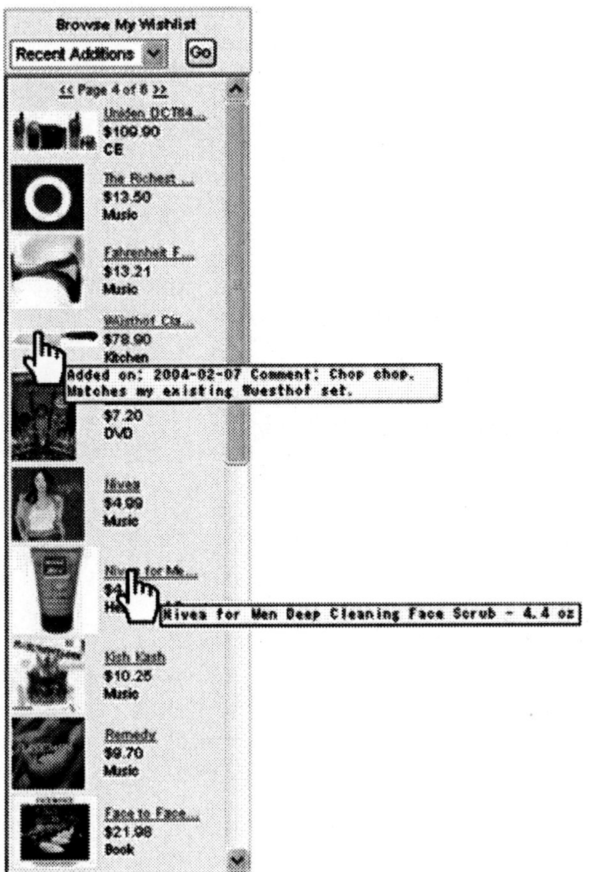

Figure 5-9 The Wishlist Widget display

For ProductSense, I used Javascript to insert the box into the web page. With the Wishlist Widget, I'm using an HTML iframe, which is an independent web page embedded in a box on a web page. Using an iframe makes it fairly easy to paginate the list since I can redisplay each page in the iframe without having to reload the main page. Figure 5-9 shows the pagination controls (the arrows next to "page 4 of 6") and tooltips effects available to users. Rolling the cursor over the truncated item name reveals the full name in a tooltip, and rolling the cursor over the product image reveals the date the item was added to the list and the comment (if any) that you've added for that item.

The box outline for the Wishlist Widget is created with a small amount of HTML that you insert on the web page where you want your Wishlist displayed.

```
<table width="170" border="0" cellspacing="0" style="background-color:#B4D0DC">
  <tr>
```

```
    <td> <table width="100%"" border="0" cellspacing="2" style="background-color:
#ECF8FF">
        <form name="AmazonSearch" method="GET" action="wishlist.php" target="inline_
frame">
          <tr>
            <td><div style="font-family: Arial, Helvetica, sans-serif; font-size:
10px; font-weight: bold; text-align:center">Browse My Wishlist</div></td>
          </tr>
          <tr>
              <td>
                <select name="sort">
                  <option value="Price" selected>Least Expensive</option>
                  <option value="DateAdded">Recent Additions</option>
                  <option value="LastUpdated">Recent Updates</option>
                </select>
                <input type="hidden" name="page" value="1" />
                <input type="hidden" name="id" value="2ED2ZE7OME6Y8" />
                <input type="submit" name="Go" value="Go" /> </td>
          </tr>
        </form>
      </table></td>
  </tr>
</table>
<iframe name="inline_frame" src="wishlist.php?id=2ED2ZE7OME6Y8" width="170"
height="550" marginwidth="0" marginheight="0" frameborder="1" scrolling="yes"> YOUR
BROWSER DOES NOT SUPPORT IFRAMES </iframe>
```

The HTML uses no Javascript or PHP. However, your Wishlist ID must be hard-coded into the form and the iframe src attribute so that so that your Wishlist ID is sent to the PHP script. Multiple Wishlists can be supported by a single PHP script by simply replacing the Wishlist ID in the HTML with a different Wishlist ID.

The PHP script used by the HTML, wishlist.php, takes three parameters: $page, the page of results you want returned; $sort, the sort order; and $id, the Wishlist ID of the Amazon Wishlist.

There are two actions that a user can take on the Wishlist Widget (Figure 5-9). They can click "Go" button, which returns the first page of the selected sort order from the drop-down menu, or they can click on the pagination arrow, which returns the next, or previous, page of results for the current sort order. I set the $page, $sort, and $id accordingly:

```
$page=isset($_GET['page']) ? $_GET['page'] : DEFAULT_PAGE ;
$sort=isset($_GET['sort']) ? $_GET['sort'] : DEFAULT_SORT ;
$id = $_GET['id'];
```

I use a batch request to fetch twenty items (two pages) from the Wishlist at a time.

```
$nextpage=$page+1;
$url='http://webservices.amazon.com/onca/xml?Service=AWSECommerceService&
AssociateTag='.ASSOCIATES_ID.'&SubscriptionId='.SUBID.
'&Operation=ListLookup&ListLookup.Shared.ListType=WishList&
ListLookup.Shared.ListId='.$id.'&ListLookup.Shared.Sort='.$sort.'&
```

```
ListLookup.Shared.ResponseGroup=ListFull,Medium,Offers&
ListLookup.1.ProductPage='.$page.'&ListLookup.2.ProductPage='.$nextpage.'&
Version='.VERSION;
```

The default sort order I use is "Price" which orders the items from least to most expensive. The price used to determine this ordering is the Amazon price, not the list price or a 3rd party price. In order to have only the Amazon price returned, I use the Offers Response Group with no MerchantId parameter specified. I also specify the ListFull Response Group to get all the basic list information, and the Medium Response Group to get the images and other basic item information.

Since the iframe is actually an entire HTML page embedded in the page, I start creating the output with the standard HTML header. Note that I specify charset as UTF-8 so that any 8-bit characters (such as an umlaut character, if this Wishlist was from Amazon.de) are properly rendered. To give the Widget a bit of style, I include a simple stylesheet, wishlist.css.

```
$data = '<html><head><link href="wishlist.css" rel="stylesheet" type="text/css"><META
HTTP-EQUIV="Content-Type" CONTENT="text/html; charset=UTF-8"> </head><body
style="background-color:ECF8FF"><table>';
```

Next, I determine the totalpages -- which I divide by two since I'm doing a batch request and retrieving twice as many pages per request -- and then the previous and next pages which I wrap around so that clicking for the previous page on page one takes you to the last page.

```
$totalpages =
(int)($Result['ListLookupResponse']['Lists'][0]['List'][0]['TotalPages']/2);
$previouspage = (($page - 2) < 0) ? $totalpages : $page - 1;
$nextpage = (($page + 1) > $totalpages) ? 1 : $page + 1;
```

If the TotalPages element is greater than two, then I would have to make more requests to display the data, so I build the pagination display.

```
if ($Result['ListLookupResponse']['Lists'][0]['List'][0]['TotalPages'] > 2) {
    $data .= '<tr><td colspan="2"><div class="pagination"><a href="wishlist.
php?page='.$previouspage.'&sort='.$sort.'&id='.$id.'" target="_self">&#60;&#60;</a>
Page '.$page.' of '.$totalpages.' <a href="wishlist.php?page='.$nextpage.'&sort='.
$sort.'&id='.$id.'" target="_self">&#62;&#62;</a></div></td></tr>';
}
```

Note that the less than and greater than symbols have to be represented by their HTML entity equivalents or else the HTML would be invalid.

Finally, I create the bulk of the output. If only one request is needed (ten items or fewer in the Wishlist), then I skip the nested foreach.

```
foreach ($Result['ListLookupResponse']['Lists'] as $L) {
    // Skip the nested foreach if less than 10 items on the list
    if (!isset($L['List'][0]['ListItem'])) continue;
```

```
    foreach ($L['List'][0]['ListItem'] as $list) {

        // Fetch the image, title, and url
        $image = (isset($list['Item'][0]['SmallImage']['URL'])) ?
$list['Item'][0]['SmallImage']['URL'] : EMPTY_IMAGE ;

        $realtitle = $list['Item'][0]['ItemAttributes']['Title'];
        $itemurl = $list['Item'][0]['DetailPageURL'];
        $title = (strlen($realtitle) > MAXNAMELEN) ? substr($realtitle, 0,
MAXNAMELEN).'...' : $realtitle;

        // If there's an offer, it should be the Amazon offer
        $price =
(isset($list['Item'][0]['Offers']['Offer'][0]['OfferListing'][0]['Price']['FormattedP
rice'])) ?
$list['Item'][0]['Offers']['Offer'][0]['OfferListing'][0]['Price']['FormattedPrice']
: '$check Amazon';

        // Fetch the Product Group, Comment, and Date Added
        $pg = (isset($list['Item'][0]['ItemAttributes']['ProductGroup'])) ?
$list['Item'][0]['ItemAttributes']['ProductGroup'] : '';
        $comment = (isset($list['Comment'])) ? ' Comment: '.$list['Comment'] : '';
        $status = 'Added on: '.$list['DateAdded'].$comment;

        // Add an entry to our list
        $data .= '<tr><td><img title="'.$status.'" src="'.$image.'" /></td><td><a
title="'.$realtitle.'" href="'.$itemurl.'" class="boxname" target="_blank">'.$title.
'</a><div class="boxprice">'.$price.'</div><div class="boxproduct">'.$pg.'</div></td>
</tr>';

    }
}
$data .= "</table></body></html>";
```

The complete listing includes a file swap cache (see the ProductSense example in Chapter Three for an explanation).

Example 5-1 The Wishlist Widget source

```
<?php
error_reporting(E_ALL);
require_once("tools.inc.php");

define('VERSION','2005-02-23');      // E-Commerce Service Version
define('SUBID', '1A7XKHR5BYDOWPJVQEG2'); // Subscription ID
define('ASSOCIATES_ID','ws');        // Associates ID
define('DEFAULT_PAGE', 1);           // Default page to fetch
define('MAXNAMELEN', 12);            // Maximum length of the product title to display
define('DEFAULT_SORT', 'Price');     // Default sorting order
define('EMPTY_IMAGE', 'http://g-images.amazon.com/images/G/01/x-site/icons/no-img-sm.
gif');                               // The generic "empty image" image
define('CACHE_PATH','/cache/');      // File swap cache location
define('CACHE_FILEPREFIX', 'wish_'); // Prefix for cached files
define('CACHE_REFRESH', '1');         // Hours before cache becomes stale
```

```
// Get the page, sort order, and Wishlist ID
$page=isset($_GET['page']) ? $_GET['page'] : DEFAULT_PAGE ;
$sort=isset($_GET['sort']) ? $_GET['sort'] : DEFAULT_SORT ;
$id = $_GET['id'];

// Check the cache. If the page is there, return it and exit
$cachefile=getcwd().CACHE_PATH.CACHE_FILEPREFIX.$id.$sort.$page.'.txt';
if (file_exists($cachefile)) {
    $modtime=filemtime($cachefile);
    if ((time() - $modtime) < CACHE_REFRESH*60*60) {
        $data=file_get_contents($cachefile);
        echo $data;
        exit;
    }
    unlink($cachefile);
}

// Fetch two pages at once using a batch request
$nextpage=$page+1;

$url='http://webservices.amazon.com/onca/
xml?Service=AWSECommerceService&AssociateTag='.ASSOCIATES_ID.'&SubscriptionId='.
SUBID.'&Operation=ListLookup&ListLookup.Shared.ListType=WishList&ListLookup.Shared.
ListId='.$id.'&ListLookup.Shared.Sort='.$sort.'&ListLookup.Shared.
ResponseGroup=ListFull,Medium,Offers&ListLookup.1.ProductPage='.$page.'&ListLookup.2.
ProductPage='.$nextpage.'&Version='.VERSION;

// Fetch the request and parse it
$xml = GetData($url, 5);
$Result = xmlparser($xml);

// If an error or no result is returned, display a message and exit
if (!$Result or
(isset($Result['ItemLookupResponse']['Items'][0]['Request']['Errors']['Error'][0]['Co
de']))) {
    echo 'Amazon is unavailable right now.<br /> Try again later.';
    exit;
}

// Build the display output
$data = '<html><head><link href="wishlist.css" rel="stylesheet" type="text/css"><META
HTTP-EQUIV="Content-Type" CONTENT="text/html; charset=UTF-8"> </head><body
style="background-color:ECF8FF"><table>';

// Build the pagination display
$totalpages =
(int)($Result['ListLookupResponse']['Lists'][0]['List'][0]['TotalPages']/2);
$previouspage = (($page - 2) < 0) ? $totalpages : $page - 1;
$nextpage = (($page + 1) > $totalpages) ? 1 : $page + 1;

// Only display the pagination output if there are more than two pages of results
if ($Result['ListLookupResponse']['Lists'][0]['List'][0]['TotalPages'] > 2) {
```

```
    $data .= '<tr><td colspan="2"><div class="pagination"><a href="wishlist.
php?page='.$previouspage.'&sort='.$sort.'&id='.$id.'" target="_self">&#60;&#60;</a>
Page '.$page.' of '.$totalpages.' <a href="wishlist.php?page='.$nextpage.'&sort='.
$sort.'&id='.$id.'" target="_self">&#62;&#62;</a></div></td></tr>';
}

// Loop through the results and build the output list
foreach ($Result['ListLookupResponse']['Lists'] as $L) {
    // If there are less than 10 items in the list, skip the nested loop
    if (!isset($L['List'][0]['ListItem'])) continue;
    foreach ($L['List'][0]['ListItem'] as $list) {

        // Get the image, title, url, and abbreviated title
        $image = (isset($list['Item'][0]['SmallImage']['URL'])) ?
$list['Item'][0]['SmallImage']['URL'] : EMPTY_IMAGE ;
        $realtitle = $list['Item'][0]['ItemAttributes']['Title'];
        $itemurl = $list['Item'][0]['DetailPageURL'];
        $title = (strlen($realtitle) > MAXNAMELEN) ? substr($realtitle, 0,
MAXNAMELEN).'...' : $realtitle;

        // If there's an offer, it should be the Amazon offer
        $price =
(isset($list['Item'][0]['Offers']['Offer'][0]['OfferListing'][0]['Price']['FormattedP
rice'])) ?
$list['Item'][0]['Offers']['Offer'][0]['OfferListing'][0]['Price']['FormattedPrice']
: '$check Amazon';

        // Get the Product Group, Comment, and Status
        $pg = (isset($list['Item'][0]['ItemAttributes']['ProductGroup'])) ?
$list['Item'][0]['ItemAttributes']['ProductGroup'] : '';
        $comment = (isset($list['Comment'])) ? ' Comment: '.$list['Comment'] : '';
        $status = 'Added on: '.$list['DateAdded'].$comment;

        // Output the item using the style sheet styles
        $data .= '<tr><td><img title="'.$status.'" src="'.$image.'" /></td><td><a
title="'.$realtitle.'" href="'.$itemurl.'" class="boxname" target="_blank">'.$title.
'</a><div class="boxprice">'.$price.'</div><div class="boxproduct">'.$pg.'</div></td>
</tr>';

    }
}
$data .= "</table></body></html>";

// Create new cache file
$cachefile_tmp=$cachefile.getmypid();
$fp=fopen($cachefile_tmp, 'w');
fwrite($fp, $data);
fclose($fp);
@rename($cachefile_tmp, $cachefile);

// Output the list
echo $data;
?>
```

Exercises For The Reader

Add a front-end to the findseller example that lets a user pick the best selling, or most recently released, item in a specific category or browse node, and let them use findseller with that ASIN.

Modify the Wishlist Widget to use DHTML, CSS, and Javascript to make a better looking paginated Wishlist display.

Modify the findseller code, adding a SellerListingLookup operation by Exchange ID for each seller listing returned, if an Exchange ID is returned in the offer. To do this, modify the SellerLookup with a Multioperation request that does the same SellerLookup, but adds a SellerListingLookup by ExchangeID. You'll then have some more information you can display about the offer in the results.

CHAPTER 6

The Remote Cart

Possession is 11/10 of the law
—Ferengi Rule of Acquisition #219

Shopping carts have become a standard part of any online store. Amazon's particular online shopping cart implementation, which is called the Remote Cart, isn't quite like your typical online shopping cart. It's a virtual shopping cart that's really just an extension of the shopping cart service on Amazon's web site. It can only be used to buy items on Amazon and it links your customers to Amazon's site for payment and fulfillment of any purchase.

That said, you can add Amazon's Remote Cart to your web application just like any other online shopping cart, and it will give your customers a way to quickly "checkout" when they're ready to pay for their items.

The Remote Cart is truly a virtual shopping cart in that it does not actually reside in your application or on your server. The cart exists on Amazon's servers. Amazon's E-Commerce Service merely provides an API -- five operations that you can use to create, modify, and delete the shopping cart. You use the operations to remotely modify the attributes of the cart.

When your customer is ready to "checkout", you redirect them to a specific URL on Amazon.com, where they login and see the actual Amazon shopping cart filled with the items they added from your site (or, if they do not have an account on Amazon, they create one and then they see their shopping cart).

Remote Cart Overview

The Amazon E-Commerce Service Remote Cart operations mimic the functionality of an actual Amazon shopping cart. When you login to Amazon.com and view your shopping cart, you can add or delete items from the cart, change the quantity of an item in your cart, and do some special functions such as move items to your "Save For Later" area (the "Saved Items -- To Buy Later" in Figure 6-1).

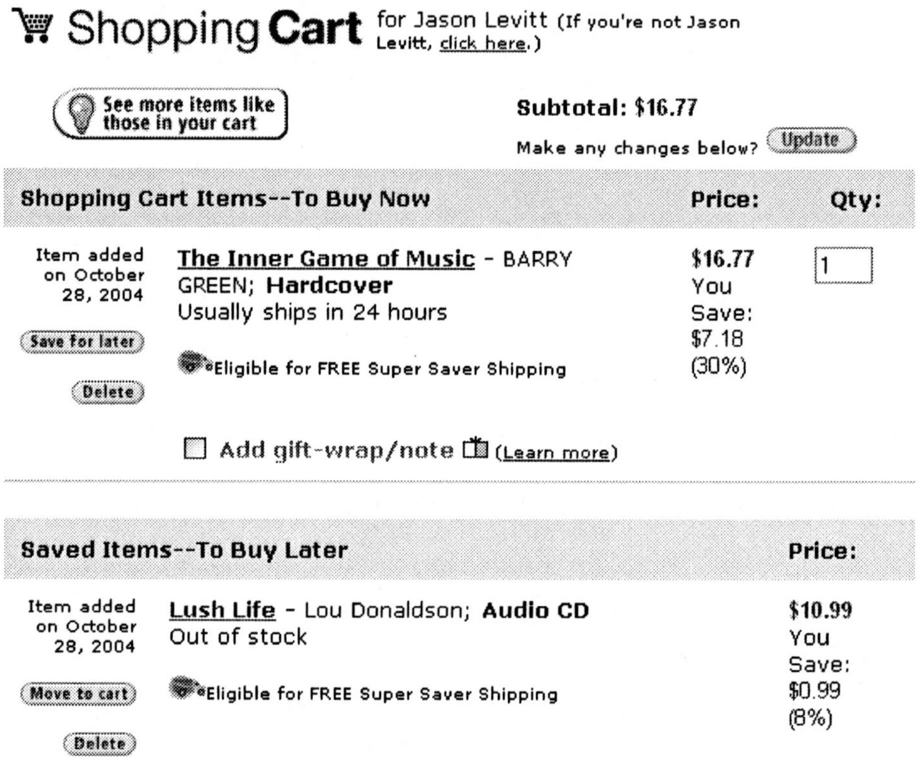

Figure 6-1 An Amazon.com shopping cart

The Saved For Later area is simply a holding area for items which are either not yet available for purchase (because they are temporarily out of stock or not yet released), or for items which you don't feel like purchasing yet.

I'm also unable to move the Lush Life CD to the shopping cart because it is temporarily "Out of Stock" -- only items that are available for purchase can be in the shopping cart.

The five Amazon E-Commerce Service operations, listed in Table 6-1, essentially let you do all of the types of shopping cart management illustrated in Figure 6-1 (except for the "Add gift-wrap/note")

Remote Cart Lifecycle

Cart Creation

Remote Carts are uniquely identified by two strings, an HMAC (Hashed Message Authentication Code) and an Amazon Cart Id. Both are returned by the successful completion of a CartCreate operation.

Remote Cart Operation	Description
CartAdd	Adds a new item to a cart (this operation can't be used to increase the quantity of an item already in the cart)
CartClear	Removes all items from a cart
CartCreate	Creates a Remote Cart
CartGet	Retrieves all of the contents of a Remote Cart
CartModify	Lets you change the quantity of an item in the Remote Cart as well as changing cart merge and "save for later" status

Table 6-1 The Remote Cart operations

The CartCreate operation is always the first operation you must use to create a new Remote Cart. The HMAC and CartId returned by the CartCreate operation must be used in all subsequent Remote Cart operations to properly identify the Remote Cart.

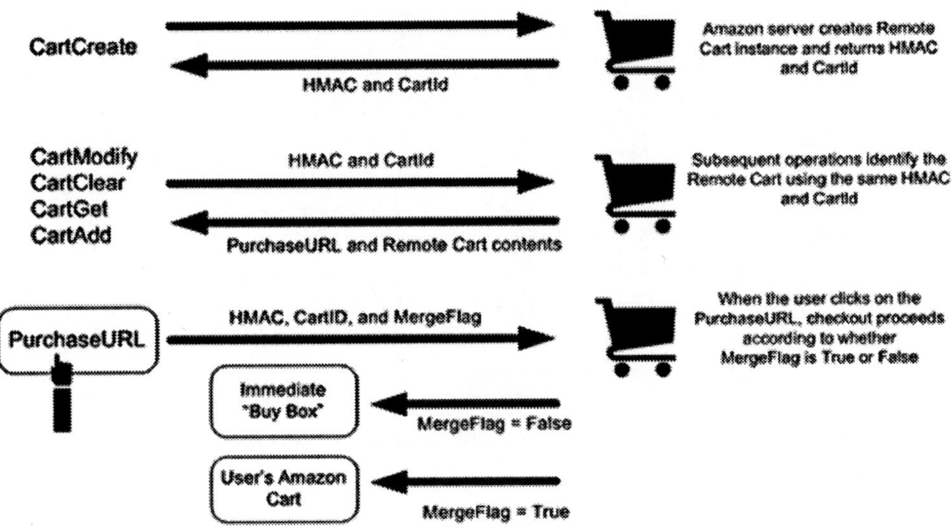

Figure 6-2 Life cycle of an Amazon Remote Cart

Cart Lifespan

Once you've created a Remote Cart, it remains registered in Amazon's Server for 90 days after which it's deleted automatically by Amazon. However, the 90 day lifespan is renewed every time a Remote Cart operation occurs. So, in practice, a Remote Cart can last much longer than 90 days. During the Remote Cart's lifespan, items that have been placed in the Remote Cart may change. They may become out of stock or otherwise unavailable. Even their price may change. When these events occur, Amazon automatically adjusts the contents of the Remote Cart accordingly. For example, if a customer puts five copies of the book "The Inner Game Of Music" in a Remote Cart and then doesn't look at the Remote Cart for several weeks, they may come back and find that three of the five copies have been magically moved to the "Save For Later" section of the cart because only two copies are now available for sale.

Death Of A Cart

There is no way for developers to delete a Remote Cart once it's created. However, once the contents of a Remote Cart are transferred to Amazon -- when the user clicks on the <PurchaseURL> -- the Remote Cart should no longer be used (it will still be accessible, but you shouldn't use it). Amazon will automatically delete the Remote Cart when it lies unused for 90 days.

CartCreate: Creating A Remote Cart

The CartCreate operation creates a remote cart. You must use CartCreate before using any of the other Remote Cart operations. In order to create a Remote Cart, you must add one or more items to the cart when you create it. You aren't allowed to create an empty cart. Here, I create a Remote Cart and add the book "Animal Farm" to it.

```
http://webservices.amazon.com/onca/xml?Service=AWSECommerceService&AssociateTag=ws&
SubscriptionId=1A7XKHR5BYD0WPJVQEG2&Operation=CartCreate&Item.1.ASIN=0451526341&
Item.1.Quantity=2&Version=2005-02-23
```

The output yields two identifiers, the HMAC (Hashed Message Authentication Code) and the CartId, that we must use to access the Remote Cart in all further operations. The response also includes a urlencoded version of the HMAC, URLEncodedHMAC, that is handle for using in REST calls. You would normally have to create a urlencoded version of the HMAC manually using PHP's urlencode function.

The total amount of all items (items x quantity) in the Remote Cart is returned as the <SubTotal> and the amount of each item (item x quantity) is returned as <ItemTotal>.

```
<CartId>104-0605622-4675113</CartId>
<HMAC>7bXJMo9MXR8ljAohCVajR1iyK4s=</HMAC>
```

```
    <URLEncodedHMAC>7bXJMo9MXR8ljAohCVajR1iyK4s=</URLEncodedHMAC>
    <PurchaseURL>https://www.amazon.com/gp/cart/aws-merge.html?cart-id=
104-0605622-4675113%26associate-id=ws%26hmac=7bXJMo9MXR8ljAohCVajR1iyK4s=
%26SubscriptionId=1A7XKHR5BYDOWPJVQEG2%26MergeCart=False</PurchaseURL>
    <SubTotal>
      <Amount>1432</Amount>
      <CurrencyCode>USD</CurrencyCode>
      <FormattedPrice>$14.32</FormattedPrice>
    </SubTotal>
    <CartItems>
      <CartItem>
        <CartItemId>U2ON8BUEHHJ6S6</CartItemId>
        <ASIN>0451526341</ASIN>
        <MerchantId>ATVPDKIKX0DER</MerchantId>
        <SellerId>A2R2RITDJNW1Q6</SellerId>
        <Quantity>2</Quantity>
        <Title>Animal Farm</Title>
        <ProductGroup>Book</ProductGroup>
        <Price>
          <Amount>716</Amount>
          <CurrencyCode>USD</CurrencyCode>
          <FormattedPrice>$7.16</FormattedPrice>
        </Price>
        <ItemTotal>
          <Amount>1432</Amount>
          <CurrencyCode>USD</CurrencyCode>
          <FormattedPrice>$14.32</FormattedPrice>
        </ItemTotal>
      </CartItem>
    </CartItems>
```

If we try to create a cart, adding an item to the cart that is temporarily out of stock, such as the Lou Donaldson CD in Figure 6-1 above, it gets put in the "Save For Later" area:

```
http://webservices.amazon.com/onca/xml?Service=AWSECommerceService&AssociateTag=ws&
SubscriptionId=1A7XKHR5BYDOWPJVQEG2&Operation=CartCreate&Item.1.ASIN=B000002URK&
Item.1.Quantity=2&Version=2005-02-23
```

The item is returned in <SaveForLaterItems> instead of <CartItems>

```
    <CartId>002-4273004-2638442</CartId>
    <HMAC>nYRX1oMLeXX+DbuHaYJGarPgFcA=</HMAC>
    <URLEncodedHMAC>nYRX1oMLeXX%2BDbuHaYJGarPgFcA=</URLEncodedHMAC>
    <PurchaseURL>https://www.amazon.com/gp/cart/aws-merge.html?cart-id=
002-4273004-2638442%26associate-id=ws%26hmac=nYRX1oMLeXX%2BDbuHaYJGarPgFcA=
%26SubscriptionId=1A7XKHR5BYDOWPJVQEG2%26MergeCart=False</PurchaseURL>
    <SubTotal>
      <Amount>2396</Amount>
      <CurrencyCode>USD</CurrencyCode>
      <FormattedPrice>$23.96</FormattedPrice>
    </SubTotal>
    <SavedForLaterItems>
      <SavedForLaterItem>
        <CartItemId>U1DSVPJFZTHJ1M</CartItemId>
```

```
            <ASIN>B000002URK</ASIN>
            <MerchantId>ATVPDKIKX0DER</MerchantId>
            <SellerId>A2R2RITDJNW1Q6</SellerId>
            <Quantity>2</Quantity>
            <Title>Lush Life</Title>
            <ProductGroup>Music</ProductGroup>
            <Price>
              <Amount>1198</Amount>
              <CurrencyCode>USD</CurrencyCode>
              <FormattedPrice>$11.98</FormattedPrice>
            </Price>
            <ItemTotal>
              <Amount>2396</Amount>
              <CurrencyCode>USD</CurrencyCode>
              <FormattedPrice>$23.96</FormattedPrice>
            </ItemTotal>
          </SavedForLaterItem>
        </SavedForLaterItems>
```

Another important element returned is the <PurchaseURL>. This is the URL that your customers should click on when they're ready to checkout and buy the items in their shopping cart. If they don't use this URL, then you won't get credit for the items they purchase. Note that your Associates ID is embedded in the link.

By analyzing the parameters in the Purchase URL, you can see what will happen when your customer clicks on it:

```
 <PurchaseURL>https://www.amazon.com/gp/cart/aws-merge.html?cart-id=
002-4273004-2638442%26associate-id=ws%26hmac=nYRX1oMLeXX%2BDbuHaYJGarPgFcA=
%26SubscriptionId=1A7XKHR5BYD0WPJVQEG2%26MergeCart=False</PurchaseURL>
```

The CartId and HMAC are embedded, so that Amazon can identify which Remote Cart to access. Your SubscriptionId identifies the developer who generated the Remote Cart, and your Associates Id (associate-id) ensures that you get paid for anything that the user purchases from the cart. Finally, the MergeCart=False means that the user will see an immediate "buy box" and can purchase only the contents of the Remote Cart. If MergeCart were set to True, then the contents of the Remote Cart would be merged with the user's existing Amazon cart (if it exists) before checkout (see "Changing Merge Cart Status" later in this Chapter for more on MergeCart).

Recall that Parent ASINs cannot be purchased -- only their corresponding Child ASINs can be purchased. If you try to add a Parent ASIN to a Remote Cart, you will receive an error:

```
          <Errors>
            <Error>
              <Code>AWS.ECommerceService.ItemNotEligibleForCart</Code>
              <Message>The item you specified, B00008TLU5, is not eligible to be added
to the cart. Check the item's availability to make sure it is available.</Message>
           </Error>
          </Errors>
      </Request>
```

```
<CartId>104-5074766-5015143</CartId>
<HMAC>arjhq4ZSQ8ZL2rVSXOORFFdvhzE=</HMAC>
```

An HMAC and CartId are still returned, but they aren't usable.

Security Note

The HMAC and Cart Id are tied to the Associates Id you use to create the Remote Cart. All Remote Cart operations must use the same HMAC, Cart Id, and Associates Id. if a villain hijacks your HMAC and CartId, and happens to know your Associates Id, they can manipulate the contents of the Remote Cart. If you don't use an Associates Id when you create your Remote Cart (the Associates Id is an optional parameter) then you should not use an Associates Id with subsequent Remote Calls.

CartAdd: Adding Items To A Remote Cart

Now that we have the HMAC and CartId of our Remote Cart, we can use CartAdd to add more items to the cart. Items can be added to a Remote Cart using either the ASIN of the item or the OfferListingId of the item. If the ASIN is used, then the item is always purchased from Amazon (the merchant). If the OfferListingId is used, then the item will be purchased from the corresponding merchant (typically a third-party merchant, but it could be Amazon).

CartAdd can be used to add more items to the cart, in any quantity from 1 to 999, but it cannot be used to increase or decrease the quantity of an item already in the cart. For that, you use CartModify.

I'll use the CartId and HMAC from the previous section:

```
<CartId>104-0605622-4675113</CartId>
<HMAC>7bXJMo9MXR8ljAohCVajR1iyK4s=</HMAC>
```

The HMAC identifier sometimes contains characters, such as a slash "/" or plus "+" sign, which we must URL encode in order to use in a URL. You can use PHP's urlencode() function, which also encodes the equals sign "=", or simply use the <URLEncodedHMAC> element returned in the response.

```
http://webservices.amazon.com/onca/xml?Service=AWSECommerceService&
SubscriptionId=1A7XKHR5BYD0WPJVQEG2&AssociateTag=ws&Operation=CartAdd&
CartId=002-4273004-2638442&HMAC=nYRX1oMLeXX%2BDbuHaYJGarPgFcA=&Item.1.
ASIN=0395177111&Item.1.Quantity=5&Version=2005-02-23
```

The request added five copies of "The Hobbit" to our Remote Cart which already had two copies of Animal Farm in it:

> If you try to add a quantity greater than the number available for sale on Amazon, or if the item is unavailable because it's out of stock, the item will be automatically moved to the "Saved For Later" area.

```
<CartId>104-0605622-4675113</CartId>
```

```
    <HMAC>7bXJMo9MXR8ljAohCVajR1iyK4s=</HMAC>
    <URLEncodedHMAC>7bXJMo9MXR8ljAohCVajR1iyK4s=</URLEncodedHMAC>
    <PurchaseURL>https://www.amazon.com/gp/cart/aws-merge.html?cart-id=104-0605622-
4675113%26associate-
id=ws%26hmac=7bXJMo9MXR8ljAohCVajR1iyK4s=%26SubscriptionId=1A7XKHR5BYD0WPJVQEG2%26Mer
geCart=False</PurchaseURL>
    <SubTotal>
      <Amount>12457</Amount>
      <CurrencyCode>USD</CurrencyCode>
      <FormattedPrice>$124.57</FormattedPrice>
    </SubTotal>
    <CartItems>
      <CartItem>
        <CartItemId>U31Q2GG8PLRJWF</CartItemId>
        <ASIN>0395177111</ASIN>
        <MerchantId>ATVPDKIKX0DER</MerchantId>
        <SellerId>A2R2RITDJNW1Q6</SellerId>
        <Quantity>5</Quantity>
        <Title>The Hobbit (Leatherette Collector's Edition)</Title>
        <ProductGroup>Book</ProductGroup>
        <Price>
          <Amount>2205</Amount>
          <CurrencyCode>USD</CurrencyCode>
          <FormattedPrice>$22.05</FormattedPrice>
        </Price>
        <ItemTotal>
          <Amount>11025</Amount>
          <CurrencyCode>USD</CurrencyCode>
          <FormattedPrice>$110.25</FormattedPrice>
        </ItemTotal>
      </CartItem>
      <CartItem>
        <CartItemId>U20N8BUEHHJ6S6</CartItemId>
        <ASIN>0451526341</ASIN>
        <MerchantId>ATVPDKIKX0DER</MerchantId>
        <SellerId>A2R2RITDJNW1Q6</SellerId>
        <Quantity>2</Quantity>
        <Title>Animal Farm</Title>
        <ProductGroup>Book</ProductGroup>
        <Price>
          <Amount>716</Amount>
          <CurrencyCode>USD</CurrencyCode>
          <FormattedPrice>$7.16</FormattedPrice>
        </Price>
        <ItemTotal>
          <Amount>1432</Amount>
          <CurrencyCode>USD</CurrencyCode>
          <FormattedPrice>$14.32</FormattedPrice>
        </ItemTotal>
      </CartItem>
    </CartItems>
```

Items You Can't Add To A Remote Cart

Some items can't be added to a Remote Cart because of contractual agreements Amazon has with partner merchants. Also, items listed only in the zShops cannot be added to a Remote Cart. When an item cannot be added to a Remote Cart, Amazon should return an AWS.ECommerceService.ItemNotEligibleForCart error. A workaround you can use to let customers purchase these items is to use a special HTML form which I cover later in this chapter.

CartModify: Changing Attributes Of A Remote Cart

The CartModify operation lets you change three different types of information about a cart and its items. First, you can change the quantity of any item already in the cart, including setting the quantity to zero, which removes the item from the cart. Second, you can move items that are in the "Save For Later" area of the cart to the cart, or vice versa. Finally, you can change the Merge Cart status of the cart, which says whether or not the Remote Cart will be merged with the customer's existing Amazon.com shopping cart (if one exists) upon checkout.

Changing Item Quantities

In order to change the quantity of an item in a Remote Cart, we must use the Cart Item Id of an item. Cart Item Ids are created by Amazon's server solely to identify items that are in Remote Carts. Cart Item Ids are returned by the CartCreate and CartAdd calls.

Our Remote Cart from the previous section has five copies of The Hobbit, and two copies of Animal Farm in it. Using CartModify, I'll reduce the quantities to one copy of each:

```
http://webservices.amazon.com/onca/xml?Service=AWSECommerceService&AssociateTag=ws&
SubscriptionId=1A7XKHR5BYD0WPJVQEG2&Operation=CartModify&
CartId=104-0605622-4675113&HMAC=7bXJMo9MXR8ljAohCVajR1iyK4s=&
Item.1.CartItemId=U31Q2GG8PLRJWF&Item.1.Quantity=1&
Item.2.CartItemId=U2ON8BUEHHJ6S6&Item.2.Quantity=1&Version=2005-02-23
```

The quantity of each item in the Remote Cart is set to exactly the number specified by the request -- the quantity is not added or subtracted from the existing quantity.

```
     <CartId>104-0605622-4675113</CartId>
    <HMAC>7bXJMo9MXR8ljAohCVajR1iyK4s=</HMAC>
    <URLEncodedHMAC>7bXJMo9MXR8ljAohCVajR1iyK4s=</URLEncodedHMAC>
    <PurchaseURL>https://www.amazon.com/gp/cart/aws-merge.html?cart-id=104-0605622-
4675113%26associate-
id=ws%26hmac=7bXJMo9MXR8ljAohCVajR1iyK4s=%26SubscriptionId=1A7XKHR5BYD0WPJVQEG2%26Mer
geCart=False</PurchaseURL>
    <SubTotal>
```

```
    <Amount>2921</Amount>
    <CurrencyCode>USD</CurrencyCode>
    <FormattedPrice>$29.21</FormattedPrice>
  </SubTotal>
  <CartItems>
    <CartItem>
      <CartItemId>U31Q2GG8PLRJWF</CartItemId>
      <ASIN>0395177111</ASIN>
      <MerchantId>ATVPDKIKXODER</MerchantId>
      <SellerId>A2R2RITDJNW1Q6</SellerId>
      <Quantity>1</Quantity>
      <Title>The Hobbit (Leatherette Collector's Edition)</Title>
      <ProductGroup>Book</ProductGroup>
      <Price>
        <Amount>2205</Amount>
        <CurrencyCode>USD</CurrencyCode>
        <FormattedPrice>$22.05</FormattedPrice>
      </Price>
      <ItemTotal>
        <Amount>2205</Amount>
        <CurrencyCode>USD</CurrencyCode>
        <FormattedPrice>$22.05</FormattedPrice>
      </ItemTotal>
    </CartItem>
    <CartItem>
      <CartItemId>U2ON8BUEHHJ6S6</CartItemId>
      <ASIN>0451526341</ASIN>
      <MerchantId>ATVPDKIKXODER</MerchantId>
      <SellerId>A2R2RITDJNW1Q6</SellerId>
      <Quantity>1</Quantity>
      <Title>Animal Farm</Title>
      <ProductGroup>Book</ProductGroup>
      <Price>
        <Amount>716</Amount>
        <CurrencyCode>USD</CurrencyCode>
        <FormattedPrice>$7.16</FormattedPrice>
      </Price>
      <ItemTotal>
        <Amount>716</Amount>
        <CurrencyCode>USD</CurrencyCode>
        <FormattedPrice>$7.16</FormattedPrice>
      </ItemTotal>
    </CartItem>
  </CartItems>
```

Moving Items To "Save For Later"

CartModify can be used to move items to and from the Save For Later area in a Remote Cart. Once a user is transferred to their Amazon.com cart by clicking on the Purchase URL you provide for them, the items in the Save For Later area of their Remote Cart are transferred to the Save For Later area in the Amazon Cart

Our Remote Cart from the previous section has one copy of the Hobbit, and one copy of Animal Farm. To move the copy of The Hobbit to our Remote Cart's Save For Later area, you change the Quantity=1 parameter to Action=SaveForLater.

```
http://webservices.amazon.com/onca/xml?Service=AWSECommerceService&AssociateTag=ws&
SubscriptionId=1A7XKHR5BYD0WPJVQEG2&Operation=CartModify&
CartId=104-0605622-4675113&HMAC=7bXJMo9MXR8ljAohCVajR1iyK4s=&
Item.1.CartItemId=U31Q2GG8PLRJWF&Item.1.Action=SaveForLater&Version=2005-02-23
```

The Hobbit is now in the Saved For Later area, and thus it's encapsulated in the <SavedForLaterItems> tag:

```
      ...
      ...
    <SavedForLaterItems>
      <SavedForLaterItem>
        <CartItemId>U31Q2GG8PLRJWF</CartItemId>
        <ASIN>0395177111</ASIN>
        <MerchantId>ATVPDKIKX0DER</MerchantId>
        <SellerId>A2R2RITDJNW1Q6</SellerId>
        <Quantity>1</Quantity>
        <Title>The Hobbit (Leatherette Collector's Edition)</Title>
        <ProductGroup>Book</ProductGroup>
        <Price>
          <Amount>2205</Amount>
          <CurrencyCode>USD</CurrencyCode>
          <FormattedPrice>$22.05</FormattedPrice>
        </Price>
        <ItemTotal>
          <Amount>2205</Amount>
          <CurrencyCode>USD</CurrencyCode>
          <FormattedPrice>$22.05</FormattedPrice>
        </ItemTotal>
      </SavedForLaterItem>
    </SavedForLaterItems>
```

To move it back, you use Action=MoveToCart. You can mix and match quantity changing with these operations if you wish, changing the quantity of an item and moving another item to the cart or Save For Later area in a single request.

```
http://webservices.amazon.com/onca/ xml?Service=AWSECommerceService&AssociateTag=ws&
SubscriptionId=1A7XKHR5BYD0WPJVQEG2&Operation=CartModify&
CartId=104-0605622-4675113&HMAC=7bXJMo9MXR8ljAohCVajR1iyK4s=&
Item.1.CartItemId=U31Q2GG8PLRJWF&Item.1.Quantity=3&
Item.2.CartItemId=U20N8BUEHHJ6S6&Item.2.Action=SaveForLater&Version=2005-02-23
```

Changing Merge Cart Status

The Merge Cart flag determines whether or not a Remote Cart is merged with a user's existing Amazon cart before checkout. If MergeCart=False, the user will see an immediate "buy box" instead of their shopping cart. If MergeCart=True, the use will see their usual Amazon shopping cart (if it exists) with the contents of the Remote Cart merged with it.

> The ability to checkout without merging is currently only available on the U.S. site, amazon.com. See Chapter Seven for more information about the International Amazon sites.

When MergeCart Is False

The Remote Cart from the previous section currently has one copy of Animal House in the cart and one copy of The Hobbit in the Save For Later area of the Remote Cart. If I click on the Purchase URL below which has MergeCart=False (the default, by the way), I'll see an immediate "buy box" that does not include the contents of the customer's current Amazon shopping cart nor any Save For Later items in their Remote Cart.

```
<PurchaseURL>https://www.amazon.com/gp/cart/aws-merge.html?cart-id=
104-0605622-4675113%26associate-id=ws%26hmac=7bXJMo9MXR8ljAohCVajR1iyK4s=
%26SubscriptionId=1A7XKHR5BYDOWPJVQEG2%26MergeCart=False</PurchaseURL>
```

Only the copy of Animal Farm shows up in the "Buy Box". The customer's existing Amazon shopping cart (if any) is unaffected by this purchase.

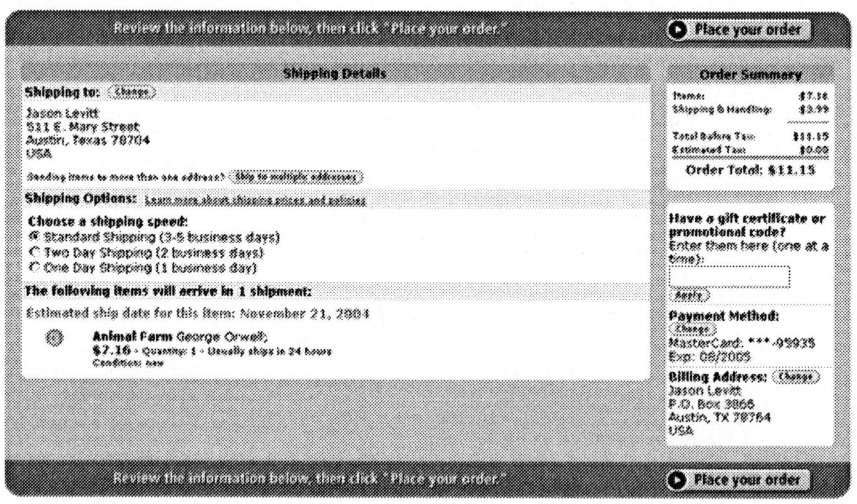

Figure 6-3 An immediate Buy Box displayed when MergeCart=False

Also, the copy of The Hobbit is still in the Remote Cart in the Saved For Later area. It can't be purchased unless you move it to the main cart for the user. For that reason, using MergeCart=False is sometimes not as convenient for users.

When MergeCart Is True

If MergeCart=True, as shown in the PurchaseURL below, the contents of the Remote Cart will be merged with the contents of the user's existing Amazon shopping cart (if any).

```
<PurchaseURL>https://www.amazon.com/gp/cart/aws-merge.html?cart-id=
104-0605622-4675113%26associate-id=ws%26hmac=7bXJMo9MXR8ljAohCVajR1iyK4s=
%26SubscriptionId=1A7XKHR5BYDOWPJVQEG2%26MergeCart=True</PurchaseURL>
```

When the user clicks on the Purchase URL, they are directed to Amazon.com where they see their existing Amazon shopping with the Remote Cart contents added to it (Figure 6-4).

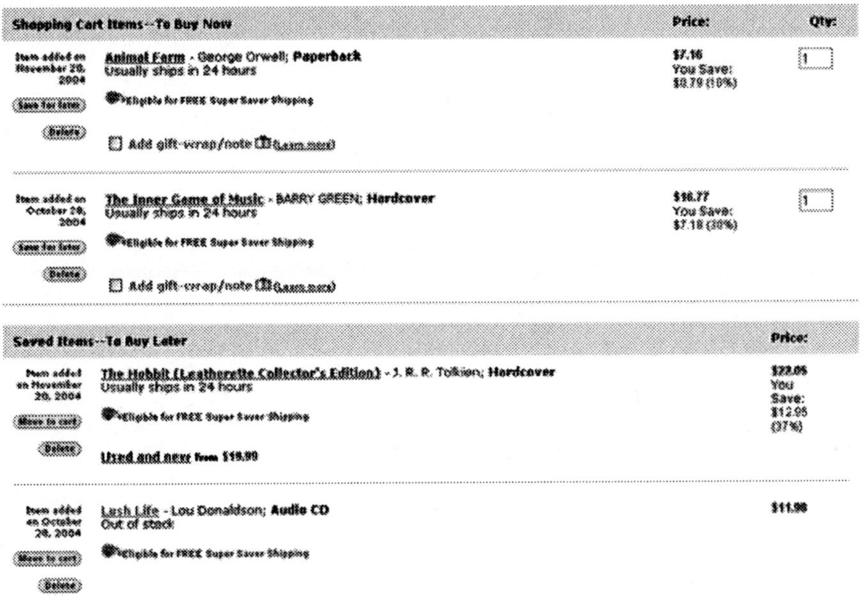

Figure 6-4 An Amazon shopping cart with merged items from a Remote Cart

CartGet: Fetching The Contents Of A Cart

CartGet fetches the current contents of a Remote Cart.

```
http://webservices.amazon.com/onca/xml?Service=AWSECommerceService&
AssociateTag=ws&SubscriptionId=1A7XKHR5BYDOWPJVQEG2&Operation=CartGet&
CartId=104-0605622-4675113&HMAC=7bXJMo9MXR8ljAohCVajR1iyK4s=&Version=2005-02-23
```

It returns a list of all items in the main Cart and in the Save For Later area:

```
<CartId>104-0605622-4675113</CartId>
<HMAC>7bXJMo9MXR8ljAohCVajR1iyK4s=</HMAC>
<URLEncodedHMAC>7bXJMo9MXR8ljAohCVajR1iyK4s=</URLEncodedHMAC>
```

```
    <PurchaseURL>https://www.amazon.com/gp/cart/aws-merge.html?cart-id=104-0605622-
4675113%26associate-
id=ws%26hmac=7bXJMo9MXR8ljAohCVajR1iyK4s=%26SubscriptionId=1A7XKHR5BYD0WPJVQEG2%26Mer
geCart=False</PurchaseURL>
    <SubTotal>
      <Amount>2921</Amount>
      <CurrencyCode>USD</CurrencyCode>
      <FormattedPrice>$29.21</FormattedPrice>
    </SubTotal>
    <CartItems>
      <CartItem>
        <CartItemId>U20N8BUEHHJ6S6</CartItemId>
        <ASIN>0451526341</ASIN>
        <MerchantId>ATVPDKIKX0DER</MerchantId>
        <SellerId>A2R2RITDJNW1Q6</SellerId>
        <Quantity>1</Quantity>
        <Title>Animal Farm</Title>
        <ProductGroup>Book</ProductGroup>
        <Price>
          <Amount>716</Amount>
          <CurrencyCode>USD</CurrencyCode>
          <FormattedPrice>$7.16</FormattedPrice>
        </Price>
        <ItemTotal>
          <Amount>716</Amount>
          <CurrencyCode>USD</CurrencyCode>
          <FormattedPrice>$7.16</FormattedPrice>
        </ItemTotal>
      </CartItem>
    </CartItems>
    <SavedForLaterItems>
      <SavedForLaterItem>
        <CartItemId>U31Q2GG8PLRJWF</CartItemId>
        <ASIN>0395177111</ASIN>
        <MerchantId>ATVPDKIKX0DER</MerchantId>
        <SellerId>A2R2RITDJNW1Q6</SellerId>
        <Quantity>1</Quantity>
        <Title>The Hobbit (Leatherette Collector's Edition)</Title>
        <ProductGroup>Book</ProductGroup>
        <Price>
          <Amount>2205</Amount>
          <CurrencyCode>USD</CurrencyCode>
          <FormattedPrice>$22.05</FormattedPrice>
        </Price>
        <ItemTotal>
          <Amount>2205</Amount>
          <CurrencyCode>USD</CurrencyCode>
          <FormattedPrice>$22.05</FormattedPrice>
        </ItemTotal>
      </SavedForLaterItem>
    </SavedForLaterItems>
```

CartClear: Emptying A Cart

The CartClear operation is simply a quick way of emptying the contents of a Remote Cart. When executed, the contents of the RemoteCart are thrown away and the cart is empty, but still usable. Carts currently last for 90 days before Amazon deletes them.

```
http://webservices.amazon.com/onca/ xml?Service=AWSECommerceService&AssociateTag=ws&
SubscriptionId=1A7XKHR5BYDOWPJVQEG2&O peration=CartClear&
CartId=104-0605622-4675113&HMAC=7bXJMo9MXR8ljAohCVajR1iyK4s=&Version=2005-02-23
```

A successful CartClear request returns just the CartId, HMAC and urlencoded HMAC:

```
<CartId>104-0605622-4675113</CartId>
<HMAC>7bXJMo9MXR8ljAohCVajR1iyK4s=</HMAC>
<URLEncodedHMAC>7bXJMo9MXR8ljAohCVajR1iyK4s=</URLEncodedHMAC>
```

A Remote Cart Class With Cookies

Remote Cart operations are different than other E-Commerce Service operations because we're actually sending some data that acts upon an object (the Remote Cart) that is stored on Amazon's server. In all other E-Commerce requests, there is no application "state" involved -- once the Amazon server responds, it "forgets" everything about the request.

To access a Remote Cart, you need to use the Remote Cart's HMAC and CartId. So, storing a Remote Cart's HMAC and Cart Id is essential. With the HMAC and CartId available to our application, we can perform Remote Cart operations whenever the customer returns to shop, possibly days or weeks later.

This is a perfect situation for using cookies. Cookies are little bits of data that can be stored in a file in your customer's web browser. By storing a user's HMAC and Cart Id in a cookie, we can retrieve their Remote Cart when they return to your web site.

Remote Cart Details

Because of the modularity of the Remote Cart operations in Amazon E-Commerce Service, I implemented a fully functional Remote Cart class in PHP4 in surprisingly few lines of code. The class I wrote, which I call AmazonCookieCart, is geared towards PHP web applications. It lets you perform four kinds of tasks:

- **Create** a Remote Cart
- **Add** an item to a Remote Cart
- **Show** the contents of a Remote Cart
- **Modify** the contents of a Remote Cart

In order to maintain application state and retrieve the customer's Remote Cart, I store an array value in a Cookie. The array, cartinfo, has three values in it:

- **cartinfo[0]**: Number of items currently in the Remote Cart
- **cartinfo[1]**: Cart Id
- **cartinfo[2]**: HMAC

Saving the number of items currently in the Remote Cart is handy for notifying the customer of the number of items currently in the Remote Cart. If that number wasn't in the Cookie, you'd have to execute a Remote Cart request to retrieve it.

AmazonCookieCart is designed to be one of the first things executed by a PHP web application. It checks to see if the user has a cookie for it, and extracts it immediately. The constructor function handles that:

```
function AmazonCookieCart($cookie = null) {
        if (!is_null($cookie)) {
            $this->cartinfo = unserialize(stripslashes(($cookie)));
            $this->cartsize = $this->cartinfo[0];
        }
    }
```

I use the PHP serialize() function to turn the cartinfo array into a string when I store it in the cookie hence I use unserialize() here to turn it back into an array. If the user has no Cookie but wants an item added to their shopping cart, a new Remote Cart is created -- the HMAC and Cart Id are stored in a Cookie and the item is added to the new Remote Cart. Since E-Commerce Service requires that you add an item to a Remote Cart when you create it, both cart creation and adding the item are handled by a single CartCreate operation. The actual request is built by the GetCreateCartRequest function:

```
function GetCreateCartRequest($offerlistid) {
        $this->Request='http://webservices.amazon.com/onca/
xml?Service=AWSECommerceService&SubscriptionId='.SUBID.'&AssociateTag='.ASSOCIATES_
ID.'&Operation=CartCreate&Item.1.OfferListingId='.urlencode($offerlistid).'&Item.1.
Quantity=1&ResponseGroup=Cart&Version='.VERSION;
        return true;
}
```

GetCreateCartRequest() would be a private class if PHP4 supported public and private class designations. In any case, it's only called by the ProcessCartRequest function which is the public function that handles all the of tasks: add, modify, show, and create. To create a cart, ProcessCartRequest() is called with the task name, "create", and an Offer Listing Id. The CartId and HMAC of the new cart are extracted by preg_match_all() and a new Cookie containing them is stored for the customer.

```
function ProcessCartRequest($task, $cartvals = null) {
        require_once('tools.inc.php');

        switch ($task) {
            case 'create':
```

```
            // Build the CartCreate request
            $this->GetCreateCartRequest($cartvals);
            // Do the CartCreate request
            $xml = GetData($this->Request, 10);
            $p='/<(CartId|HMAC)*>(.*?)<\/\1>/';
            $matches=array();
            // Extract the HMAC and CartId from the response
            preg_match_all ($p, $xml, $matches);
            $cartid=$matches[2][0];
            $hmac=$matches[2][1];
            $cart = array(1, $cartid, $hmac);
            // Store a cookie containing the HMAC and CartId for the user
            $this->SetCartCookie($cart);
            $this->Status_Message='Item saved to your shopping cart';
            $Result = true; // Initial cartsize
...
...
```

If the customer already has a Cookie and wants an item added to their cart, ProcessCartRequest is called with the $task set to "add" and $cartvals set to the Offer Listing Id of the item to add to the cart. I then check the XML response for a <Code> tag which indicates that some kind of error occurred. If the error is AWS.ECommerceService.ItemAlreadyInCart, then the item is already in the cart so I set Status_Message to indicate that result and immediately return. Otherwise, I update the counter for the number of items in the cart and return immediately.

```
      case 'add':
            // Build the CartCreate request
            $this->GetAddCartRequest($cartvals);
            // Do the CartCreate request
            $xml=GetData($this->Request, 10);
            $p='/<(Code)*>(.*?)<\/\1>/';
            $matches=array();
            // Extract the error code (if any)
            preg_match_all ($p, $xml, $matches);
            if ((isset($matches[2][0])) and ($matches[2][0] == 'AWS.ECommerceService.
ItemAlreadyInCart')) {
                  $this->Status_Message='That item is already in your shopping cart';
                  $Result = true;
                  break;
            }
            $this->cartinfo[0]++;
            $this->SetCartCookie($this->cartinfo);
            $this->Status_Message='Item saved to your shopping cart';
            $Result = true;
            break;
```

If the customer wants to see their cart, I first check to see if there's anything in the cart ($cartsize > 0). If it's greater than zero, then I do the CartGet request and return the current contents of the cart:

```
      case 'show':
            // Build the cart request
```

```
                $this->GetDisplayCartRequest($cartvals);
                // If there's no request, it must be because the cart is empty
                if (is_null($this->Request)) {
                    $Result = false;
                    break;
                }
                // Execute the cart request
                $xml = GetData($this->Request, 10);
                $Result = XmlParser($xml);
                $this->Status_Message='';
                break;
```

Cart modification is the most complicated since there are several modifications that the customer can make. The customer can choose from any of these operations:

- Change the quantity of any item in the cart (changing the quantity to zero removes the item from the cart)
- Move an item in the cart to the Save for Later area
- Move an item in the Save for Later area to the cart

The AmazonCoookieCart modification routine expects that each item is represented with a string of this format:

item_[location]_[quantity]_[id]

where:

- **location** is where the item is located, either 'c' for 'cart' or 's' for 'saved for later'
- **quantity** is the quantity of an item in that location -- a positive integer
- **id** is the offer listing id of the item

An item in the Save for Later area with Offer Listing Id U3HGSI438UIJP8 and quantity one would be encoded using this string:

item_s_1_U3HGSI438UIJP8

In the HTML form for cart modification, the input box for modifications would use this HTML FORM tag:

```
Quantity: <input type="text" name="item_s_1_U3HGSI438UIJP8" size="4" maxlength="3"
value="1" />
```

The modification routine, GetModifyCartRequest() takes the $_POST array as input and searches for any strings that start with "item" -- parsing those for requested changes.

```
function GetModifyCartRequest($postarray) {
        // Build the parameter strings
        $suffix='';
        // Keep count of any changes
        $count=0;
        // Go through the $_POST variables
        foreach ( $postarray as $name => $change ) {
```

```
            // $change is the customer's input
            $change=strtolower(trim($change));
            // Get the pieces of the encoded string
            $pieces=explode('_', $name);
            // We found one
            if ($pieces[0] == 'item') {
                // A quantity change
                if (is_numeric($change)) {
                    // change the quantity
                    if ($change != $pieces[2]) {
                        $count++;
                        // Build the parameter suffix for the Amazon request
                        $suffix .= '&Item.'.$count.'.CartItemId='.$pieces[3].'&Item.
'.$count.'.Quantity='.$change;
                    }
                // A location change
                } elseif ($change == 'c' or $change == 's') {
                    // change the location
                    if ($pieces[1] != $change) {
                        $count++;
                        // Build the parameter suffix for the Amazon request
                        $action = ($change == 'c') ? 'MoveToCart' : 'SaveForLater';
                        $suffix .= '&Item.'.$count.'.CartItemId='.$pieces[3].'&Item.
'.$count.'.Action='.$action;
                    }
                } else {
                    $this->Status_Message='I did not understand this change request:
'.$change;
                }
            }
        }
        // If there are changes to be made, build the request
        if ($suffix != '') {
            $this->Request='http://webservices.amazon.com/onca/
xml?Service=AWSECommerceService&SubscriptionId='.SUBID.'&AssociateTag='.ASSOCIATES_
ID.'&Operation=CartModify&HMAC='.urlencode($this->cartinfo[2]).'&CartId='.$this->
cartinfo[1].'&ResponseGroup=Cart'.$suffix.'&Version='.VERSION;
        } else {
        // There are no changes to be made or I didn't understand the change request
            $this->Status_Message= (empty($this->Status_Message)) ? 'You did not
request any changes to the cart' : $this->Status_Message;
            return false;
        }
        return true;
    }
```

The routine builds the parameter strings for the request and then adds them to the REST request string. If there are no changes to be made, either because the customer didn't request any or because the customer made an error entering a change request, then I just display a status notice to that effect.

ProcessCartRequest with $task set to "modify" and $cartvals to $_POST calls GetModifyCartRequest() to build the cart request and then executes it. I use a regular expression and the PHP array_sum() function to make sure that I know that quantity of items currently in the customer's cart.

```
case 'modify':
            // Build the request. If the return code is false, no request was built
            $rc=$this->GetModifyCartRequest($cartvals);
            if (!$rc) {
                $Result=false;
                break;
            }
            // Process the request
            $xml = GetData($this->Request, 10);
            $Result = XmlParser($xml);
            // Get the new cartsize by extracting and summing all the <Quantity> tags
            $p='/<(Quantity)*>(.*?)<\/\1>/';
            $matches=array();
            preg_match_all ($p, $xml, $matches);
            $cart = array(array_sum($matches[2]), $this->cartinfo[1], $this->
cartinfo[2]);
            $this->SetCartCookie($cart);
            break;
```

Using AmazonCookieCart

To illustrate use of AmazonCookieCart, I added a Remote Cart to Example 4-1 (to simplify the code a bit, I removed the pagination routine). The only differences in the

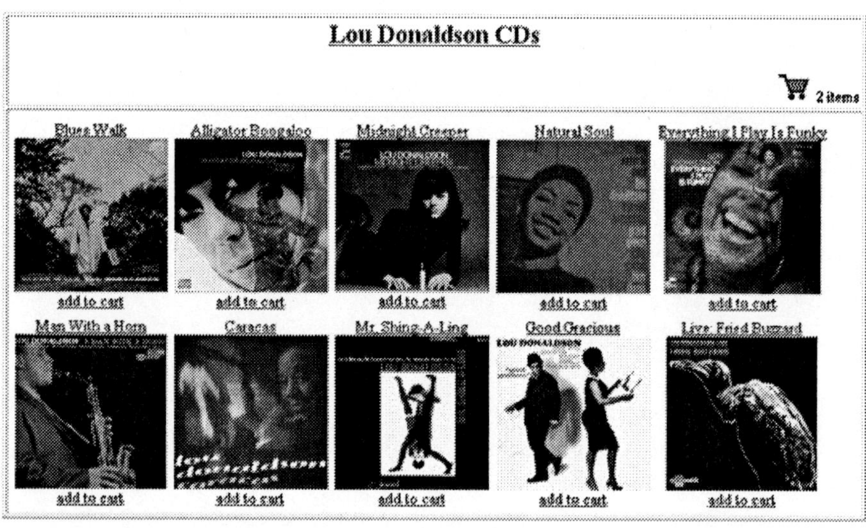

Figure 6-5 Example 4-1 with Remote Cart code added

main GUI of Example 4-1 is the addition of a shopping cart icon that displays the number of items in the cart next to it, and "Add to Cart" links for each item (Figure 6-6). Clicking on the shopping cart icon reveals the shopping cart contents and a form for changing the quantities and status of items in the cart.

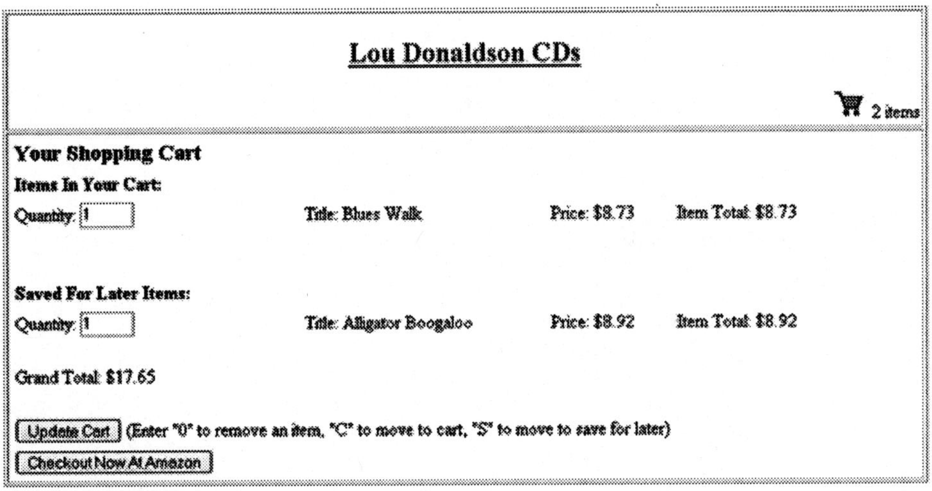

Figure 6-6 The Remote Cart GUI

The "Add to Cart" links in are constructed using the Offer Listing Id for each item.

Program Flow

Using AmazonCookieCart(), program execution always starts by going through a short series of Remote Cart checks illustrated by the flow chart in Figure 6-7. The actual code I added to Example 4-1 follows nearly the same program flow:

```
// Include the Amazon Cookie Cart class
require_once("class.amazoncart.php");
// Check to see if the user has a cookie
$cookie = (empty($_COOKIE[COOKIE_NAME])) ? null : $_COOKIE[COOKIE_NAME];
// Instantiate the Cart class
$cart = new AmazonCookieCart($cookie);

 // Is there a cookie
 (empty($_COOKIE[COOKIE_NAME])) {
    // Add item to cart?
    if (!empty($_GET['add'])) {
        $Result=$cart->ProcessCartRequest('create', $_GET['add']);
    }
    // Display a status message if they wanted to look at an empty cart
    if (isset($_GET['showcart'])) {
        $status_message='Your shopping cart is currently empty or has expired';
```

```
        }
        // Display the Lou Donaldson records
        ShowRecords();
    // Add an item?
    } elseif (isset($_GET['add'])) {
        $Result=$cart->ProcessCartRequest('add', $_GET['add']);
        // Display the Lou Donaldson records
        ShowRecords();
    // Display the Remote Cart?
    } elseif (isset($_GET['showcart']))  {
        $Result=$cart->ProcessCartRequest('show', $_GET['showcart']);
        // If we have results, then display the Remote Cart GUI
        if ($Result) {
            $showcart= true;
        } else {
            // Display the Lou Donaldson records
            ShowRecords();
        }
    // Modify the Remote Cart?
    } elseif (isset($_POST['updatecart']))  {
        $Result=$cart->ProcessCartRequest('modify', $_POST);
        if ($Result) {
            // If we have results, then display the Remote Cart GUI
            $showcart=true;
        } else {
            ShowRecords();
        }
    // Customer clicked on the Checkout button?
    } elseif (isset($_POST['checkout']) and (!empty($_POST['purchaseurl']))) {
        // Throw away the cart credentials
        $cart->killcookie();
        // Redirect the user to Amazon for checkout
        Header('Location: '.$_POST['purchaseurl']);
    } else {
        ShowRecords();
    }
```

The only other major modification I made to Example 4-1 was the addition of a routine, TheCart(), to display the Remote Cart GUI. TheCart() displays the results of either CartGet or CartModify requests. The function shows the user a form (Figure 6-6) which mimics the functionality of Amazon's own form (Figure 6-1).

```
      function TheCart() {
        global $Result;
        global $rtype;

        // Is it a CartGet or CartModify response?
        $rtype = (key($Result) == 'CartGetResponse') ? 'CartGetResponse' :
    'CartModifyResponse';
        echo '<table cellspacing="2" cellpadding="2">';
        echo '<form action="'.$_SERVER["PHP_SELF"].'" method="post" name="lou" id="lou">
    ';
        echo '<tr><td colspan="3"><h3>Your Shopping Cart</h3></td></tr>';
        echo '<tr><td colspan="3"><h4>Items In Your Cart:</h4></td></tr>';
```

```
    // Loop through the items in the main cart
    if (isset($Result[$rtype]['Cart']['CartItems']['CartItem'][0])) {
        foreach ($Result[$rtype]['Cart']['CartItems']['CartItem'] as $item) {

            // Fetch each item price, subtotal, quantity, and title
            $price = $item['Price']['FormattedPrice'];
            $itemtotal = $item['ItemTotal']['FormattedPrice'];
            $quantity = $item['Quantity'];
            $title = $item['Title'];

            echo '<tr>';
            // Output the items in the main cart
            echo '<td><div style="text-align: left;">Quantity: <input type="text"
name="item_c_'.$quantity.'_'.$item['CartItemId'].'" size="4" maxlength="3" value="'.
$quantity.'" /></div></td>';
            echo '<td><div style="text-align: left;">Title: '.$title.'</div></td>';
            echo '<td><div style="text-align: left;">Price: '.$price.'</div></td>';
            echo '<td><div style="text-align: left;">Item Total: '.$itemtotal.'</div>
</td>';
            echo '</tr>';
        }
    } else {
        echo '<tr>';
        echo '<td><div style="text-align: left;">No regular items are in your cart</
div></td>';
        echo '</tr>';
    }

    echo '<tr><td colspan="3"><br /><h4>Saved For Later Items:</h4></td></tr>';

    // Loop through the items in the Saved For Later section of the cart
    if (isset($Result[$rtype]['Cart']['SavedForLaterItems']['SavedForLaterItem'][0]))
{
        foreach ($Result[$rtype]['Cart']['SavedForLaterItems']['SavedForLaterItem']
as $item) {

            // Save the price, itemtotal, quantity, and title for each item
            $price = $item['Price']['FormattedPrice'];
            $itemtotal = $item['ItemTotal']['FormattedPrice'];
            $quantity = $item['Quantity'];
            $title = $item['Title'];

            echo '<tr>';
            // Output the items in the Save For Later section
            echo '<td><div style="text-align: left;">Quantity: <input type="text"
name="item_s_'.$quantity.'_'.$item['CartItemId'].'" size="4" maxlength="3" value="'.
$quantity.'" /></div></td>';
            echo '<td><div style="text-align: left;">Title: '.$title.'</div></td>';
            echo '<td><div style="text-align: left;">Price: '.$price.'</div></td>';
            echo '<td><div style="text-align: left;">Item Total: '.$itemtotal.'</div>
</td>';
            echo '</tr>';
        }
    } else {
```

```
        echo '<tr>';
        echo '<td><div style="text-align: left;">No Saved For Later items are in your
cart</div></td>';
        echo '</tr>';
    }

    // Fetch the total price for everything in the cart
    $totalprice= (isset($Result[$rtype]['Cart']['SubTotal']['FormattedPrice'])) ?
$Result[$rtype]['Cart']['SubTotal']['FormattedPrice'] : '$0.00' ;
    echo '<tr>';
    echo '<td><br /><div style="text-align: left;">Grand Total: '.$totalprice.'</div>
</td>';
    echo '</tr>';

    // Get the Purchase URL
    $purchaseurl= (isset($Result[$rtype]['Cart']['PurchaseURL'])) ?
$Result[$rtype]['Cart']['PurchaseURL'] : '' ;

    // Output various option buttons
    echo '<tr><td colspan="3"><br /><input type="hidden" name="modify" value="1" />
<input type="submit" value="Update Cart" name="updatecart" /> (Enter "0" to
remove an item, "C" to move to cart, "S" to move to save for later)</td></tr><tr><td>
<input type="submit" value="Checkout Now At Amazon" name="checkout"/><input
type="hidden" name="purchaseurl" value="'.$purchaseurl.'"</td></tr>';
    echo '</form>';
    echo '</table';
    return;
}
```

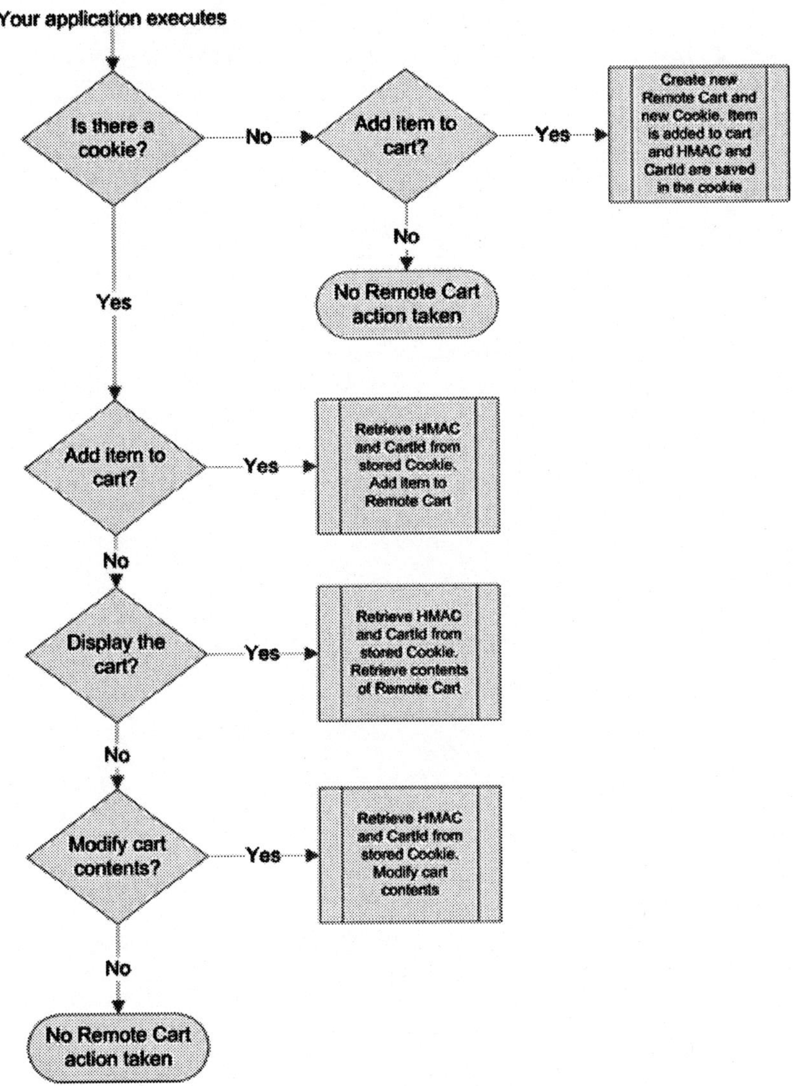

Figure 6-7 Program flow when using AmazonCookieCart class

Remote Cart Alternatives Using HTML

Amazon offers a couple of HTML forms you can use instead of the Remote Cart. For simple applications, they may be more convenient, but there is no error feedback or management API available, so they are of rather limited use to developers.

The Buy Now Box

The Buy Now Box is an alternative checkout method that lets you add your own logo to the Amazon checkout pages. It's really just a small HTML form that, when submitted by your customers, initiates an Amazon checkout procedure. Compared to the Remote Cart, the Buy Now Box is quite limited. It only allows one item, and it must be sold from a zShop. Still, for some sites, the "co-branding" opportunity may be more important than the Remote Cart's expanded functionality.

The HTML form has six form elements (listed in table 6-2).

Table 6-2 Element attributes of Amazon's Buy Now form

Form Parameter	Description
purchase-navbar	This is an image that Amazon displays at the top of the purchase pages when your customer clicks through to Amazon. Typically, this is your web site, application, or store logo, but it can be any size image displayable in a web browser, usually GIF, JPEG, or PNG format.
purchase-store-name	This is a text string that is displayed underneath the purchase-navbar image. Typically, this is the name of your web site, application, or store. Amazon will prefix this string with "Click on the image above to return to" before displaying it.
purchase-return-url	The URL that is activated if the user clicks on the purchase-navbar image for some reason. Typically, this is the URL of your web site, application, or store.
purchase-storefront-name	This text string appears on the customer's final checkout form as the name of the seller. Typically, this is the name of your web site, application, or store (probably the same value as purchase-store-name).
purchase-exchange-id	The Exchange Id of the item being sold
purchase-quantity	The quantity requested

I can easily create an HTML form, either manually or programatically that will create a branded checkout when the user clicks on my "buy" button:

```
<html>
<body>
<form action="http://s1.amazon.com/exec/varzea/dt/cbop/order-checkout/"
method="post">
<input type="hidden" name="purchase-navbar" value="http://www.jasonimg.com/amazon.
gif"/>
<input type="hidden" name="purchase-store-name" value="Sushi and Science MegaCorp"/>
<input type="hidden" name="purchase-return-url" value="http://www.amazon.com/shops/
sashimikid"/>
<input type="hidden" name="purchase-exchange-id" value="Y03Y4719404Y6459826"/>
<input type="hidden" name="purchase-quantity" value="1" size="2"/>
<input type="hidden" name="purchase-storefront-name" value="Sushi And Science
MegaCorp"/>
<input type="image" name="submit"
```

```
  src="http://images.amazon.com/images/G/04/buttons/buy-now-from-seller-with-
payments.gif"
  width="170" height="29" border="0" alt="Submit"/>
</form>
</body>
</html>
```

My logo is specified by a URL in the purchase-navbar form element. The Exchange ID of the item is required (see Appendix A for instructions on how to find Exchange IDs on Amazon.com). The submit button can be any type of button -- I just happened to choose an Amazon image.

The form will fail if the image URL is inaccessible or if the Exchange ID is invalid.

When the user clicks on the buy button displayed by this form, it takes the user to Amazon where my "Sushi And Science" logo is displayed during the checkout process (Figure 6-8)

Figure 6-8 My co-branded Amazon checkout using the Buy Now form

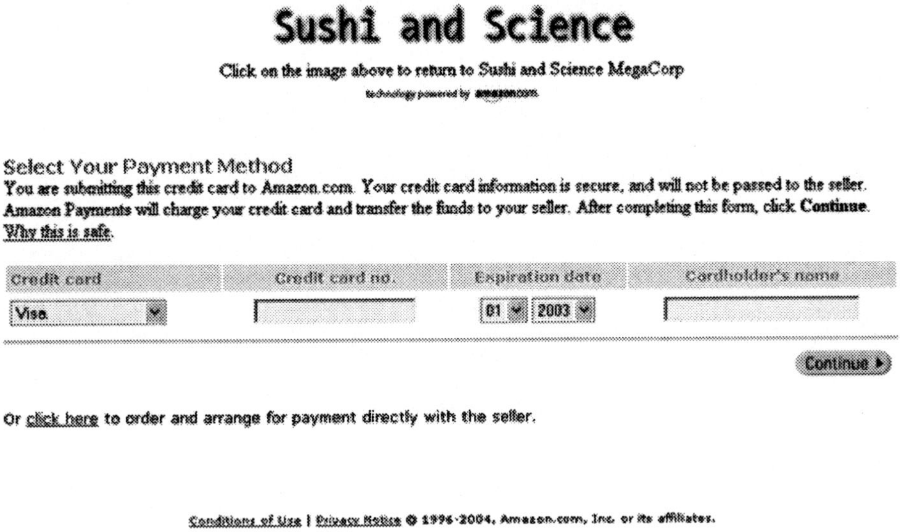

Sushi and Science

Click on the image above to return to Sushi and Science MegaCorp

Select Your Payment Method

You are submitting this credit card to Amazon.com. Your credit card information is secure, and will not be passed to the seller. Amazon Payments will charge your credit card and transfer the funds to your seller. After completing this form, click **Continue**. Why this is safe.

Credit card	Credit card no.	Expiration date	Cardholder's name
Visa		01 2003	

Continue

Or click here to order and arrange for payment directly with the seller.

Conditions of Use | Privacy Notice © 1996-2004, Amazon.com, Inc. or its affiliates.

The Add To Cart Form

When submitted by a user, the Add to Cart form takes the user to their Amazon shopping cart and attempts to add the form items to their cart. Essentially, it mimics the action of clicking of the Remote Cart's PurchaseURL with MergeCart=True. The main disadvantage of using this form compared to the Remote Cart is the inability to move items to and from the "Save For Later" area or specify the MergeCart value. Also, there is no error feedback.

You cannot use the Add To Cart form with zShops items

Table 6-3 Parameters of Amazon's Add To Cart form

Form Parameter	Description
ASIN.x	Specifies one or more product ASINs to add, where x is a unique identifier
ExchangeId.x	Specifies one or more products using the exchange ID, where x is a unique identifier. Exchange IDs are available for every item offered by a third-party seller.
OfferListingId.x	An alternative way to specify one or more product offer listings from third-party sellers
Quantity.x	Specifies the amount of a certain product to add to the cart, where x matches an ASIN, OfferListingId, or ExchangeId parameter. You must specify the quantity for each item you add to the cart.
SellerId.x	Use the SellerId parameter to ensure that the customer purchases the product from a particular seller, where x matches an ASIN parameter.
SubscriptionId	Your subscription ID. You may want to specify this as a hidden parameter.
AssociateTag	Your associate tag. You may want to specify this as a hidden parameter.

As with Amazon E-Commerce Service, using the ASIN implies that the merchant is Amazon, while using the Exchange or Offer Listing IDs targets the particular Offer (and seller) associated with that ID. A simple Add To Cart form that adds one item when the "Add" button is pressed looks like this:

```
<html>
<body>
<form method="POST" action="http://www.amazon.com/gp/aws/cart/add.html">
<input type="hidden" name="SubscriptionId" value="001VHHVC74XFD88KCY82" />
<input type="hidden" name="AssociateTag" value="ws" />
<input type="hidden" name="OfferListingId.1"
value="WJbLFp1hQaFC2vUTh%2FlDTJmFELwTISq3lp6g%2FcnqJ9KcoztCxqfyVVm2M9xiwAT%2FkOkbLU8Y
SF16h4189qYG5w%3D%3D" />
<input type="hidden" name="Quantity.1" value="1" />
<input type="submit" name="add" value="add" />
</form>
</body>
</html>
```

Exercises For The Reader

Add Amazon Remote Cart capabilities to an existing open source PHP shopping cart implementation such as Zen Cart, *http://www.sf.net/projects/zencart*

Use PHP to add sessions capability to the Remote Cart class, *http://www.php.net/session*

CHAPTER 7

International Amazon E-Commerce Service

Make your shop easy to find
—Ferengi Rule of Acquisition #46

A big part of the E-Commerce Service value proposition is taking advantage of Amazon's native language product databases in locations other than the United States. Making your applications location-savvy increases your user audience and makes your application or site more accessible and, potentially, profitable. This chapter explains how to modify your code to access the non-U.S. Amazon sites.

International Overview

As I mentioned in Chapter One, Amazon runs six other sites besides the US site, Amazon.com. There are Amazon web sites for Japan (www.amazon.co.jp), France (www.amazon.fr), Germany (www.amazon.de), Canada (www.amazon.ca), China (www.joyo.com), and England (www.amazon.co.uk).

> As this book goes to press, only the Chinese site, www.joyo.com, does not have Amazon E-Commerce Service yet. Joyo.com has also not yet been restructured to look and feel like the other Amazon sites. For that reason, I don't cover it in this chapter.

In this chapter, I'll refer to the British, Canadian, French, German, and Japanese Amazon sites as the "international" Amazon sites.

Fortunately, we can use the same code and techniques that we've already learned in previous chapters, and, with only a few modifications, access E-Commerce Service on the international Amazon sites.

Internationalization And Localization

Internationalization and localization are words used to describe the process of presenting information in multiple languages and with cultural details specific to a particular region or country.

> Internationalization is often abbreviated as i18n, and localization as l10n. The number 18 and 10 refer to the number of letters in between the first and last letters of each word.

Internationalization is concerned with creating applications that can use different languages. Localization refers to cultural specifics for whatever country or region is being dealt with. For example, if English is the language, and England is the country, then the use of the British Pound symbol for currency would be a localization detail. The combination of the language and country or region is often referred to as the locale.

In Amazon's product databases for each country, internationalization, and most localization, is already taken care of for developers. Products are described in the local language and money is represented by the local currency for each country. Date and time formats are presented in a standard format, so they can be massaged into whatever output format works for the locale (see Chapter 2, "Some Common Amazon Units," for more information about currency and date formats used by Amazon E-Commerce Service 4.0).

International SOAP And REST URLs

Amazon has made it easy to access their international sites. The only required adjustment are the access URLs -- the URL prefix for REST connections and the appropriate WSDL file for SOAP connections. You also need to have an Associate ID for each foreign site that you want to make money from.

For REST connections, each URL that you use to call E-Commerce Service needs to be prefixed with the appropriate prefix. For SOAP calls, the appropriate WSDL or SOAP service address should be referenced. Table 7-1 below lists the URL prefix and WSDL location for each Amazon site.

Country	REST Server and prefix	SOAP WSDL
Canada amazon.ca	http://webservices.amazon.ca/onca/xml?Service=AWSECommerceService	http://webservices.amazon.ca/AWSSchemas/AWSECommerceService/beta/CA.wsdl
England amazon.co.uk	http://webservices.amazon.co.uk/onca/xml?Service=AWSECommerceService	http://webservices.amazon.co.uk/AWSSchemas/AWSECommerceService/beta/UK.wsdl
France amazon.fr	http://webservices.amazon.fr/onca/xml?Service=AWSECommerceService	http://webservices.amazon.fr/AWSSchemas/AWSECommerceService/beta/FR.wsdl

Country	REST Server and prefix	SOAP WSDL
Germany amazon.de	http://webservices.amazon.de/onca/xml?Service=AWSECommerceService	http://webservices.amazon.de/AWSSchemas/AWSECommerceService/beta/DE.wsdl
Japan amazon.co.jp	http://webservices.amazon.co.jp/onca/xml?Service=AWSECommerceService	http://webservices.amazon.co.jp/AWSSchemas/AWSECommerceService/beta/JP.wsdl
United States amazon.com	http://webservices.amazon.com/onca/xml?Service=AWSECommerceService	http://webservices.amazon.com/AWSSchemas/AWSECommerceService/beta/US.wsdl

Table 7-1 REST prefixes and SOAP WSDL URLs for the Amazon sites

Note that REST prefix and SOAP WSDL URLs are all identical except for the domain name of the Amazon site.

Domain Names For XSLT Calls

If you want to use Amazon's XSLT server, then your REST requests must use a special domain name as listed in Table 7-2. Only the domain name differs from the prefix used in non-XSLT REST requests.

Country	XSLT Server and prefix
Canada amazon.ca	http://xml-ca.amznxslt.com/onca/xml?Service=AWSECommerceService
England amazon.co.uk	http://xml-uk.amznxslt.com/onca/xml?Service=AWSECommerceService
France amazon.fr	http://xml-fr.amznxslt.com/onca/xml?Service=AWSECommerceService
Germany amazon.de	http://xml-de.amznxslt.com/onca/xml?Service=AWSECommerceService
Japan amazon.co.jp	http://xml-jp.amznxslt.com/onca/xml?Service=AWSECommerceService
United States amazon.com	http://xml-us.amznxslt.com/onca/xml?Service=AWSECommerceService

Table 7-2 Prefixes when making XSLT requests

Versioning For The International Amazon Sites

When new versions of E-Commerce Service are introduced, all sites are typically updated to the new version simultaneously. In any case, the versioning system for the international Amazon sites is the same as that used for Amazon.com. Refer to the relevant sections in Chapter Two for the various SOAP and REST versioning schemes used by Amazon.

Shipping Restrictions

As a developer, the primary motivation for integrating access to the other Amazon sites into your project is to greatly expand the audience for your site. You might, for example, want to sell the US editions of Harry Potter books to browsers who visit your site from the US, and offer the German editions of Harry Potter books to browsers who visit your site from Germany.

However, Amazon will only ship products ordered from an Amazon site to certain countries (see Table 7-3). And the shipping details may vary depending on the type of product ordered. Customs restrictions sometimes prohibit shipment of certain types of items to certain countries, and your customers may not find out the shipment is prohibited until after they order the item. Local laws may also block shipments.

For example, home and garden products, as well as electronics, purchased from the British Amazon site, amazon.co.uk, are available only to people who have a shipping address in England, Scotland, or Ireland. However, books from amazon.co.uk may be shipped to any place in the world.

Unfortunately, Amazon does not provide any way for developers to know whether there are shipping restrictions on any specific product other than what is spelled out in these guidelines. Along with these guidelines, using common sense may help -- items like toys and electronics, which may differ in both safety and power standards, DVDs with region encoding, and any religious items, are more likely to be subject to restrictions than, say, audio CDs of the pop music genre.

Amazon Site	Shipment Restrictions URL
Canada **amazon.ca**	http://www.amazon.ca/exec/obidos/tg/browse/-/3486581
England **amazon.co.uk**	http://www.amazon.co.uk/exec/obidos/tg/browse/-/524836
France **amazon.fr**	http://www.amazon.fr/exec/obidos/tg/browse/-/548588
Germany **amazon.de**	http://www.amazon.de/exec/obidos/tg/browse/-/505014 http://www.amazon.de/exec/obidos/tg/stores/static/-/help/shipping-list
Japan **amazon.co.jp**	http://www.amazon.co.jp/exec/obidos/tg/browse/-/1039608
United States **amazon.com**	http://www.amazon.com/exec/obidos/tg/browse/-/468634

Table 7-3 Where to find the locations where Amazon ships products

International Associates IDs

Your users can purchase products using the links returned from any of the international Amazon sites. Amazon user logins are shared across all amazon sites except Japan, so users can actually login and purchase from any of the sites, but they may have to pay very high shipping charges. If a user purchases something from amazon.fr, but they live in California, they'll end up paying overseas shipping charges.

In the case of the Japanese site, Amazon.co.jp, the user will have to sign-up for an account on that site in order to purchase an item.

As mentioned in the previous section, Amazon may not allow users to purchase certain items from foreign Amazon sites. Users find this out when they attempt to finalize their purchase through the Amazon site. For example, the British Amazon site, amazon.co.uk, wouldn't let me purchase a particular product, and displayed this message:

```
We are sorry but this item cannot be delivered to the country you have specified.
Please select another address or change the quantity to zero.
```

Customs restrictions and other laws, such as those covering safety of electronics, vary from country to country and may prohibit the sale of certain products to certain countries.

Although Amazon shares customer logins across all of its sites except Japan, Amazon Associates logins are *not* shared across sites. Your Amazon.com Associates ID isn't usable with Amazon.de, and vice versa. So, you won't get credit for a sale unless you have both an Associates ID from the Amazon site the user purchases from, and that same Associates ID is used in any relevant links or requests.

This means that you need to go to each international Amazon site you want to sell items from and apply for an Associates Id from that site. Fortunately, Amazon Associates Ids are always free. The only problem obtaining them is a language barrier. How do you obtain an Associates ID from Amazon.co.jp if you can't read Japanese?

Amazon Site	Amazon Associates Signup Page
France **amazon.fr**	http://www.amazon.fr/exec/obidos/subst/associates/join/associates.html
Canada **amazon.ca**	http://www.amazon.ca/associates
Germany **amazon.de**	http://www.amazon.de/exec/obidos/subst/associates/join/associates.html
Japan **amazon.co.jp**	http://www.amazon.co.jp/associates
England **amazon.co.uk**	http://www.amazon.co.uk/associates

Amazon Site	Amazon Associates Signup Page
United States amazon.com	http://www.amazon.com/associates

Table 7-4 Where to sign up for Amazon Associates IDs

There are a couple of tricks you can use to make signup easier.

Getting Your Associates ID Using Babelfish

The site babelfish.altavista.com is useful for translating web pages on-the-fly. The translations are often clumsy, but they are usually good enough to get you through the sign-up process. To initiate sign-up process in a foreign language, go to http://babelfish.altavista.com and enter the URL for the associates signup page from table 7-3 into the "Translate a web page" box. Then select the appropriate language translation from the pull-down menu (Figure 7-1). Babelfish will open a browser window and guide you through the pages.

> I had trouble submitting the last sign-up page via Babelfish, but since that last page was just asking for demographic information, it didn't affect the sign-up process.

Although all the text on the pages will translate, the words that are in images, such as GIF image buttons, won't translate. For that reason, it's helpful to keep another window open with the Babelfish translator so that you can manually type in words or phrases that might need translation.

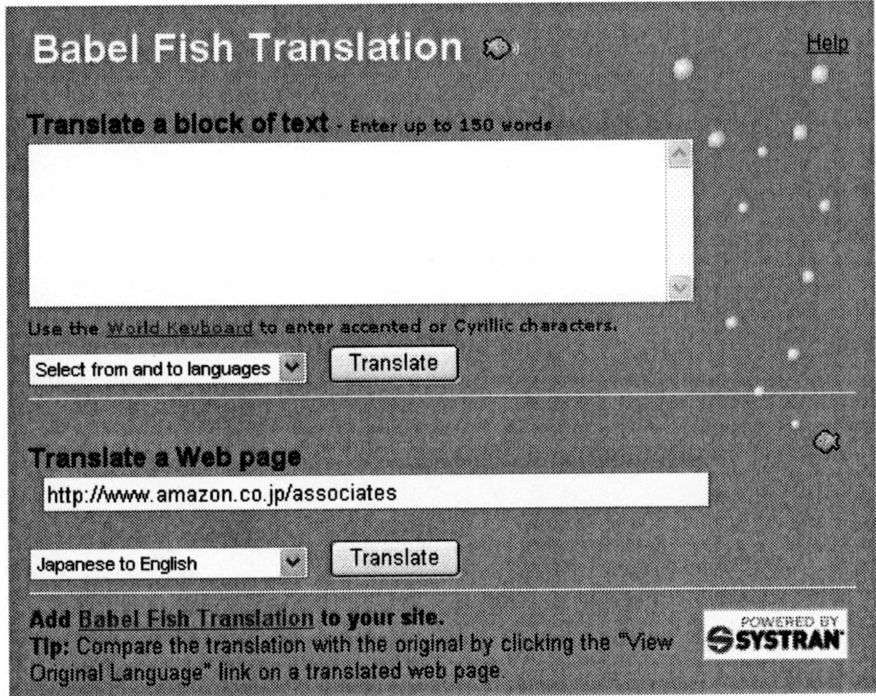

Figure 7-1 Using Babelfish to aid in Associates ID signup

If you want to use the same email address for your Associates login at the German, U.S., or British Associates sites, choose a different password for each site. If you don't, Amazon will complain with a message like:

```
The password selected by you is already used with another partner account. Please
select another password.
```

Getting Your Associates ID Using Page Comparison

It turns out that the Associates sign-up pages for each country are almost identical. So, you can refer to the English sign-up pages when registering for the Japanese site, or vice-versa. You might want to register for the British and Japanese sites at the same time so that you can follow the text. Open them in separate browser windows and follow along.

You will notice certain differences in Associates policies on each Amazon site. For example, if you are not a resident of Japan, but you generate sales on amazon.co.jp, the Japanese site will only pay you in amazon.co.jp gift certificates (yes, that does suck), while the British site will cut you a check for your sales. Limited English language help is available on Amazon.co.jp here: http://www.amazon.co.jp/exec/obidos/tg/browse/-/1039576

Amazon Character Encodings

By using the right path name for the WSDL or REST call, you can easily fetch data from any Amazon site. But in order to make sure that Amazon product data is properly displayed in a user's web browser or in an application, you have to pay attention to character encodings.

Computers work with numbers, not characters. Character encodings are algorithms that map each character in an alphabet into a unique number. When your web browser receives a web page, there is always a character encoding associated with that page that tells the web browser how to properly decode the page so that you see alphabetic characters and not a jumbled mess.

Character encodings have names like EUC_KR, Shift_JIS, UTF-8, ISO-8859-1, and Western Latin 1.

The official list of character encodings used on the Internet is maintained by the Internet Assigned Numbers Authority at http://www.iana.org/assignments/character-sets.

Because character encodings also have character sets associated with them, you see the terms "character set," "character encoding," "character set encoding," and "language encoding" used interchangeably. I'll use "character encoding" because that's the terminology used in web browser menus. However, be aware that some standards documents refer to the same thing as "character set".

All characters returned by Amazon E-Commerce Service are encoded as UTF-8. Amazon E-Commerce Service responses (in fact, responses from all of Amazon's various Web Services) are always returned as XML which specifically specifies the character encoding as UTF-8 in the first line of the response:

```
<?xml version="1.0" encoding="UTF-8" ?>
```

If the encoding isn't specified in the XML header, applications are allowed to guess the encoding using techniques described in the standard here: http://www.w3.org/TR/2004/REC-xml-20040204/#sec-guessing

UTF-8 is part of the Unicode standard which is an attempt to provide a uniform encoding system for all of the world's languages.

> Those interested in the gory details of the Unicode standard are free to browse www.unicode.org. Good luck!

UTF stands for Universal character set Transformation Format (whew!). The eight means that each character is encoded as a series of 8-bit bytes. UTF-8 encodings may use up to six bytes per character for more complex character sets such as some Chinese dialects, but only uses 1 byte per character for American English language characters.

UTF-8 Or Not UTF-8? A Minor Debate

Amazon E-Commerce Service 4.0 returns all data with UTF-8 encoding. However, Amazon's web sites display web pages in the native encoding for the target country (Table 7-5).

> I'm not covering Amazon's new Chinese site, joyo.com, but it's interesting to note that it also uses a native encoding for Chinese characters (gb2312) instead of UTF-8.

Amazon site	Language used	Native character encoding
Canada amazon.ca	British English	ISO-8859-1
England amazon.co.uk	British English	ISO-8859-1
France amazon.fr	French	ISO-8859-1
Germany amazon.de	German	ISO-8859-1
Japan amazon.co.jp	Japanese	Shift_JIS
United States amazon.com	American English	ISO-8859-1

Table 7-5 Character encodings used by Amazon web sites

Despite Amazon's choice to display their web sites with ISO-8859-1 and Shift_JIS character encodings, more and more web applications are choosing to display their web pages using UTF-8 encoding. When working with Amazon E-Commerce Service, if you display web pages using UTF-8 character encoding, then you don't have to mess with any character encoding translations.

However, There may be cases where your Amazon application is displayed on only part of an existing web page (such as my ProductSense application from Chapter Three) and that web page might use a character encoding other than UTF-8. Also, as I'll explain later, the default character encoding for text on web pages is ISO-8859-1, not UTF-8, so the vast majority of web pages are not UTF-8 encoded. For these reasons, the examples I demonstrate in this chapter assume that your web applications need to translate from UTF-8 to the encodings in Table 7-5.

> Nevertheless, the W3C recommends using UTF-8 to encode internationalized HTML forms (see http://www.w3.org/International/questions/qa-forms-utf-8.html) and there seems to be few technical reasons why UTF-8 can't be used to display your web pages for nearly any language. The move to Unicode as a standard for character encoding has been slow, but it's happening.

If you want to keep all the data in UTF-8, it's easy to simplify the PHP code and keep the data in UTF-8. This is left as an exercise for the reader.

Developing With International Character Sets

Before I discuss how to handle UTF-8 character I/O in PHP and XSLT, I need to make sure your web browser and development tools are properly configured. If you can't look at the international characters sets in your web browser, and manipulate them with our tools, then you'll be quite frustrated.

Testing Your Web Browser

A good browser test is to simply browse to Amazon's Japanese site, www.amazon.co.jp and look carefully at the page. If you see a lot of garbage characters then your browser needs some help.

If you see any garbage like the stuff in Figure 7-2 above, check your browser menu settings. If you're using. Internet Explorer 5 or 6, the menu setting (view > encoding) should point to "(Japanese) Shift-JIS". With Netscape Navigator, the menu (view > character coding) should be set to "(Japanese) Shift_JIS". If it's not, you can manually select it in IE by going to the more menu selection (view > encoding > more) or (view > character coding > more) in Navigator.

You probably noticed that UTF-8 is one of the character encoding choices on the menu, but you don't want to select that because UTF-8 isn't what you're end-users will be using to view pages in their web browsers. They'll probably be using Shift_JIS (also written as "SJIS") encoding if they're browsing from Japan, and probably ISO-

8859-1 (listed as "Western (ISO-8859-1)" or "Western European (ISO)" on the encoding menus) encoding for Germany, England, and the United States.

> The encoding "Western European (Windows)" is "Windows-1252" encoding, an encoding specific to the Windows operating system. It is superset of ISO-8859-1 and should never be used as a substitute for ISO-8859-1.

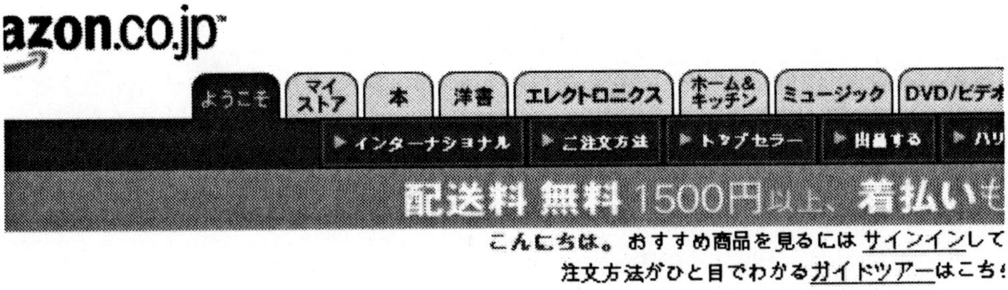

Figure 7-2 Viewing amazon.co.jp in your web browser with the correct character encoding

Figure 7-3 Viewing amazon.co.jp in your web browser with the incorrect character encoding

All modern web browsers should have fonts that can display the accents, currency symbols, and other localized language details of the German, British, and French languages. In order to display Japanese characters using the Shift_JIS encoding, fonts such as Arial Unicode MS, MS PGothic, and MS Mincho are typically used under Windows.

When you select Shift-JIS encoding from the encoding menu, your browser should automatically use those fonts to display Japanese characters. If it doesn't you may need to add additional fonts to your operating system.

For the U.S., British, German, French, and Canadian Amazon sites, you should use the "Western Latin" or simply "Western" encoding selected on your encoding menu.

To verify that it's working properly, browse www.amazon.de and check the encoding menu to make sure that "Western Latin" or "Western" is selected in the menu and that diacritical markings such as umlauts (for Germany) and pound currency symbols (for Britain) display properly.

> It's not unusual for Internet Explorer to automatically choose the UTF-8 encoding for you as you bounce around foreign web sites. While some web sites may specify UTF-8 in their META tags, none of the Amazon sites specify UTF-8.

Configuring Other Development Tools

As mentioned earlier, I'll be using Shift_JIS (for Japan) and ISO-8859-1 (for Western countries) encodings when I display Amazon data for users, but during development, I'll always maintain UTF-8 encoding so that development tools will be able to manipulate the data without turning it into garbage.

In order to make sure that your UTF-8 encoded characters maintain their encoding while you're developing with them, you need to make sure that your tools can deal with UTF-8. Most Microsoft programs like Wordpad, Notepad, Frontpage 2000, and Microsoft Word will maintain UTF-8 encoding provided you pay attention to the application's encoding settings. The W3C maintains a guide to setting the encoding on many popular applications at *http://www.w3.org/International/questions/qa-setting-encoding-in-applications*

For simple manipulation of text, it's useful to have a word processor that can handle UTF-8 with aplomb. Decent cross-platform freeware editors are available, such as AbiWord (*www.abisource.com*). Most commercial tools, such as Zend Studio and Altova's XMLSpy also maintain UTF-8 encoding provided you select it in the preferences.

Note that, even when UTF-8 encoding is used, some foreign characters may look like garbage when you're viewing them in tools such as Zend Studio because the default font can't display foreign characters. In these cases, you may want to manually change the font to one that can handle foreign characters or diacritical markings.

> Most web browsers will automatically switch to the correct font for the appropriate language. That's because they are considered "smart agents," -- they test the characters to intelligently determine which font to select. Most other applications aren't so smart.

However, the UTF-8 encoding is intact, and your output will still display correctly through a web browser.

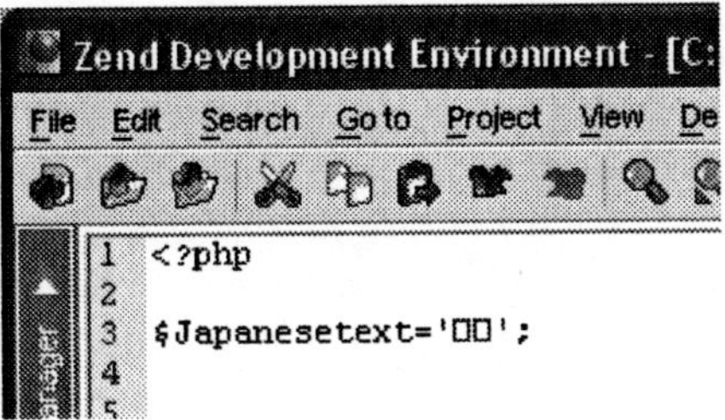

Figure 7-4 Applications that use the correct encoding but don't have the display font

In Figure 7-4, UTF-8 encoding is being enforced, but the character set used cannot display the correct Japanese characters. That's ok. Just don't forget that it's encoded text and not garbage!

UTF-8 Encoding With AWS

Once you've verified that your browser can display the proper encodings and character sets, and that your development tools are UTF-8 savvy, you need to make sure that your programs that interact with AWS also maintain UTF-8 integrity.

SOAP And UTF-8

Nusoap defaults to ISO-8859-1 encoding when sending and receiving data from its SOAP client, so you have to explicitly set the encoding to UTF-8 to make sure that Amazon's server accepts your requests. There is no constructor provided for that purpose, so we have to set the correct value manually.

```
// Set the encoding to UTF-8
$this->Client->soap_defencoding = 'UTF-8';
```

Both PEAR SOAP and PHP5 SOAP default to UTF-8 encoding so you don't need to change anything when using them.

REST And UTF-8

REST requests default to UTF-8 encoding for output so you don't need to do anything to make sure you get UTF-8 encoded output. A current bug in Amazon E-Commerce Service 4.0, which is in all of the Amazon sites except for Japan, is that input character encoding is expected to be ISO-8859-1 instead of UTF-8. The Input-ContentEncoding parameter for REST requests also doesn't work.

```
$keyword_jis=' 曲 ';
```

```
$request='http://webservices.amazon.co.jp/onca/xml?Service=AWSECommerceService&
AssociateTag=ws&SubscriptionId=1A7XKHR5BYDOWPJVQEG2&Operation=ItemSearch&
SearchIndex=Books&Keywords='.urlencode($keyword_jis).'&
InputContentEncoding=Shift_JIS&Version=2005-02-23';

$xml=file_get_contents($request);
echo $xml;
```

Here, the variable $keyword_jis contains a Japanese character encoded using Japanese Shift_JIS encoding. You can specify that your request will use this encoding by specifying InputContentEncoding=Shift_JIS in the request.

Amazon's response will be encoded as UTF-8, as always.

XSLT And UTF-8

When you create your stylesheets for use with Amazon's XSLT engine, you should specify the language encoding in the header. The encoding should always be UTF-8. To make sure HTML output from your stylesheets has the right encoding, you let the XSL process handle the encoding change by using the xsl:output statement. For all Amazon users except Japan, the XSL header should look like this.

```
<?xml version="1.0" encoding="UTF-8"?>
<xsl:stylesheet version="1.1" xmlns:xsl="http://www.w3.org/1999/XSL/Transform" xmlns:
fo="http://www.w3.org/1999/XSL/Format" xmlns:aws="http://xml.amazon.com/
AWSECommerceService/2005-02-23">
<xsl:output method="html" encoding="ISO-8859-1"
    indent="no"/>
```

The xml header says that you'll be using UTF-8 encoded data in the XSL transformation, but the xsl:output statement says to convert the data to ISO-8859-1 format for output. For Japanese users, the xsl:output encoding attribute should be set to encoding="Shift_JIS".

> As mentioned in Chapter Two, the MIME type returned by the Amazon XSLT server is not affected by the xsl:output tag. Instead, the MIME type is defined by the ContentType parameter in your REST requests e.g. ContentType=text%2Fhtml.

Of course, if you are creating an HTML page, you should make sure you generate the appropriate META tag to match the encoding type specified in the xsl:output encoding. For HTML pages destined for Japanese readers, the HTML header should look something like this:

```
<html>
<head>
      <META http-equiv="Content-Type" content="text/html; charset=Shift_JIS"/>
</head>
```

For all sites except Japan, use charset=ISO-8859-1.

Working with UTF-8 Data in PHP

PHP has several extensions, and a couple of functions, that are useful for converting between language encodings. The iconv extension is bundled with PHP5 (but can also be used with PHP4). The mbstring extension is popular with PHP4 sites, and the GNU Recode extension is also available under PHP4. I'll show examples using iconv under PHP5, and mbstring under PHP4, since they are the most common. PHP's utf8_decode and utf8_encode functions are convenient for translating to and from UTF-8 and ISO-8859-1.

There are many PHP configuration options available with the mbstring and iconv extensions. A full discussion of the possible ways to handle international character encodings is not included in this book.

By default, nearly all PHP4 and PHP5 functions assume that strings are encoded as ISO-8859-1, that means you have to be careful whenever you manipulate string data. Since Amazon returns data with UTF-8 encoding, you translate the encoding to ISO-8859-1 (for German, US, French, England, and Canada) before manipulating it. For Germany, the US, France, England, and Canada, use PHP's builtin utf8_decode() function to convert from UTF-8 to ISO-8859-1 encoding

```
$textutf8='Büchern';
$textISO8859 = utf8_decode($textutf8);
```

For Japan, you need to use functions that can handle Shift_JIS encoding. Under PHP5, use the iconv library. Under PHP4, the mbstring library.

By default, the iconv library is active in PHP5 so, out-of-the-box, PHP5 can easily handle character conversions. Under PHP4, the mbstring library is not active by default. For instructions on adding mbstring to PHP4, see the manual page at *http://www.php.net/mbstring*.

The iconv library can also be added to PHP4 but there are more iconv functions in the PHP5 version of iconv.

Using the mb_convert_encoding() function in PHP4, you can easily convert a Japanese word from UTF-8 to Shift_JIS encoding as this program illustrates.

```
<?php

$request='http://webservices.amazon.co.jp/onca/xml?Service=AWSECommerceService&
AssociateTag=ws&SubscriptionId=1A7XKHR5BYD0WPJVQEG2&Operation=ItemLookup&
ItemId=0375414576&ResponseGroup=Small&Version=2005-02-23';

$xml=file_get_contents($request);
$p='/<Creator Role="(.*?)">/';
preg_match ($p, $xml, $matches);

echo '<html><head><META HTTP-EQUIV="Content-Type" content="text/html;  charset=SHIFT-
JIS"></head><body>';
```

```
echo 'The UTF-8 encoded Japanese character for "author" is '.$matches[1]. ' <br />';
echo 'The Shift_JIS encoded Japanese character for "author" is '.mb_convert_
encoding($matches[1],"Shift_JIS","UTF-8");
echo '   </body></html>';

?>
```

Example 7-1 Using mb_convert_encoding to change character encodings

I use a regular expression to isolate the only Japanese character returned in this request. The output is:

```
The UTF-8 encoded Japanese character for "author" is 闡
The Shift_JIS encoded Japanese character for "author" is 著
```

Try switching your browser's encoding from UTF-8 to Shift_JIS and back again to see how the Japanese character changes.

For the PHP5 version using iconv, just replace the mb_convert_encoding() call with the equivalent iconv call.

```
iconv("UTF-8", "Shift_JIS", $matches[1]);
```

Multi-Language HTML Pages

There are two main ways of specifying the character encoding for a web page -- either have the web server specify the encoding, or have the web page itself specify the encoding.

> By default, if no encoding is specified by either the web server or the web page, the HTTP 1.1 specification says that the default is ISO-8859-1 encoding for text. For other MIME types, the default is usually undefined.

If the web server is specifying the page encoding, the encoding is sent in the HTTP header when the client requests the web page. The HTTP Content-Type header's charset parameter is set to indicate the encoding of the web page requested.

```
Content-Type: text/html; charset=Shift_JIS
```

PHP installations can be configured to always supply the Content-Type header by uncommenting the default charset line in the php.ini file:

```
default_charset = "Shift_JIS"
```

> This will only include the Content-Type header for files generated by PHP. You'll still need to make sure that your web server provides this header for regular HTML files. If you're using the Apache web server, you can add the line "AddDefaultCharset Shift_JIS" to your httpd.conf file.

You can also send the Content-Type header manually using PHP's header() function:

```
header("Content-type: text/html; charset=Shift_JIS");
```

In practice, these methods are a bit more cumbersome than just supplying the encoding in the http-equiv META tag of the web page. You only need specify the http-equiv META tag with the charset parameter to inform the users' web browser of the appropriate encoding to use for the page. The HTML META tag for Japanese users will look like this:

```
<html>
<head>
      <META http-equiv="Content-Type" content="text/html; charset=Shift_JIS"/>

</head>
```

> The HTML 4.01 specification says that the HTTP Content-Type header should take precedence over the HTML META tag if each indicates a character encoding for a page. Most user agents (e.g. web browser software) seems to follow this edict. So, if your web server or PHP installation is sending a conflicting encoding in the Content-Type header, you'll need to turn that off.

Multi-Language Web Pages Using A Switch Statement

A simple way to create a multi-language web page is to use a PHP switch statement to choose the desired language based on a user-defined country string. All of the language strings are isolated in define statements and are encoded before display.

```
<?php
$country='jp';

switch ($country) {
    case 'us':
    define('TO_ENCODING','ISO-8859-1');
    define('FROM_ENCODING','UTF-8');
    define('LABEL1','Search for Books');
    define('LABEL2','Submit');
    break;
    case 'de':
    define('TO_ENCODING','ISO-8859-1');
    define('FROM_ENCODING','UTF-8');
    define('LABEL1','Suche nach Büchern');
    define('LABEL2','Senden');
    break;
    case 'jp':
    define('TO_ENCODING','Shift_JIS');
    define('FROM_ENCODING','UTF-8');
    define('LABEL1','本のための調査');
    define('LABEL2','検索');
    break;
    default:
    die('Unknown Country');
}
?>
```

```
<html>
<head>
<meta http-equiv="Content-Type" content="text/html; charset=<?php echo TO_ENCODING ?>
">
</head>
<body>
<form accept-charset="<?php echo TO_ENCODING ?>" method="post" name="lang_stuff"
target="_self">
<?php echo mb_convert_encoding(LABEL1,TO_ENCODING,FROM_ENCODING) ?>
<input type="text" name="tinput" />
<input type="submit" value="<?php echo mb_convert_encoding(LABEL2,TO_ENCODING,FROM_
ENCODING) ?>" />
</form>
</body>
</html>
```

Example 7-2 Multi-language encoding using a switch statement

I pasted the LABEL1 and LABEL2 strings into Example 7-2 after encoding them using the FROM_ENCODING encoding. If your editing program does not handle UTF-8 encoding, then the Japanese text and the German umlaut character will look garbled. The program will still run correctly, however. By setting $country to either 'fr', 'ca', 'jp', 'de', or 'us', you will see the form localized to the native language of those users.

With $country='jp',

With $country='de',

If you need to use the user input in a request to Amazon such as in a keyword search, you can use it directly in REST requests by specifying the encoding in the InputContentEncoding parameter.

> As this book goes to press, the InputContentEncoding parameter is not working. The input encoding is assumed to be in ISO-8859-1 encoding for all sites except Japan, which is assumed to be UTF-8.

Multi-Language Web Pages Using Gettext

Using a switch statement is fine for small amounts of translated text, but if you are running a site that has a lot of translations, or you simply want to maintain your translations in an orderly fashion, the PHP gettext extension offers a more elegant approach.

A complete discussion of gettext is beyond the scope of this book, but I'm going to provide the basics, a sample application, and enough details to develop with.

> Gettext is offered by the Free Software Foundation. Online manuals and other information are available at http://www.gnu.org/software/gettext. PHP specific commands are at http://www.php.net/gettext.

With gettext, each language translation is maintained in its own file and translations are made on-the-fly as the application executes. Importantly, gettext not only does language translations, it also translates character encodings as well.

The loose binding between the application and the translations means that translations can be added or changed without having to edit your application.

Locales

Gettext depends on locale identifiers to properly translate from one language to another. A locale identifier is a string that defines a language and country combination (and sometimes a character encoding as well). The locale identifiers are usually expressed as pairs of language and country combinations separated by an underscore character. For example, the locale for the English language spoken in the United States might be represented by the locale identifier "en_US," where "en" stands for the English language and "US" means the "United States." For English spoken in England, "en_GB" might be the appropriate locale identifier ("GB" is one possible country code for England, "UK" is another).

> A popular list of two and three letter language abbreviations often used for locales is in this ISO 639 standards document: http://www.w3.org/WAI/ER/IG/ert/iso639.htm. It's usually (but not always) a safe bet to use the two letter country code abbreviations for the second part of the locale string.

Unfortunately, the exact format of locale identifiers varies depending on the version of operating system you are using. Some systems may accept either "de", "deu", or "German" for the German language while others may only allow "deu" (locales are case sensitive -- fr_FR is not the same as fr_fr). Further, it's not unusual for a character encoding to be specified in the locale identifier. For example, the Portuguese language spoken in Brazil, with character encoding UTF-8, might have the locale identifier pt_BR.utf-8.

The bottom line is that it takes some experimenting to find out which locale identifiers work best with your operating system.

On most flavors of FreeBSD, MacOSX, and Linux, you can find the available locale identifiers listed in the directory /usr/share/locale or you can try running the command "locale -a" from the Unix command line. The various Microsoft Windows operating systems use a specific set of language and country abbreviations.

> Windows uses languages strings listed here: http://msdn.microsoft.com/library/en-us/vclib/html/_crt_language_strings.asp, and the country strings listed here: http://msdn.microsoft.com/library/en-us/vclib/html/_crt_country_strings.asp

To specify character encodings under Windows, though, you must use Windows Code Page numbers. Under Windows XP, these can be found in the Regional and Language Options Control Panel, under the Advanced tab.

> To use ISO-8859-1 encoding, use Code Page 28591. A sample locale for English in the United States using ISO-8859-1 encoding is en_en.28591. For UTF-8 encoding, use 65001. For Shift_JIS, use 932.

PO And MO Files

Gettext uses PO (Portable Object) and MO (Machine Object) files to manage translations. PO files (.po file extension) are editable text files that contain the translation mappings. The .po files are compiled into binary MO files (.mo file extension) which are the actual files used by gettext to make translations.

In Gettext parlance, the name of the PO file is called the domain and is, by convention, the name of your application, but it can actually be any string you want. So, for my Song Search application (later in this chapter) named songsearch.php, the editable translation files are named songsearch.po, and they are compiled into binary songsearch.mo files.

Each .po and .mo file contains translations for only one target language. So, if your application is going to display text in three different languages, then you would have one .po file for each language, and thus one corresponding .mo file for each language. Each file is stored in a separate, language-specific, directory (explained in the next section).

PO files contain msgid/message pairs that tell gettext how to make a specific translation. In your PHP source file, all translations use the gettext function:

```
echo 'The word for Disc is '.gettext("Disc");
```

The PHP gettext() function takes a message id as an argument. For simplicity, I used the word "Disc", but the message id could have been any string identifier.

In the French language PO file is a line that tells gettext to get the French translation for message id "Disc":

```
msgid "Disc"
msgstr "Disque"
```

To aid in editing PO files, I recommend using the open source poedit application available at http://www.sf.net/projects/poedit

Using Gettext With PHP

If you've already written an application, the first thing you need to do is replace all of your language-specific strings with calls to gettext.

You can use poedit to create PO files, but the easiest way to make your first PO file (especially if you have a lot of translations) is to use the gettext command line utility called xgettext.

For Windows users, you can obtain the gettext command line utilities from the open source gettext project at http://www.sf.net/projects/gettext. For most Unix systems, you can get them here: http://directory.fsf.org/gettext.html.

For example, I would take Example 7-2 and remove all the LABEL1 and LABEL2 defines and instead place the English language text directly into the output:

```
<html>
<head>
<meta http-equiv="Content-Type" content="text/html; charset=<?php echo TO_ENCODING ?>
">
</head>
<body>
<form accept-charset="<?php echo TO_ENCODING ?>" method="post" name="lang_stuff"
target="_self">
<?php echo gettext("Search for Books") ?>
<input type="text" name="tinput" />
<input type="submit" value="<?php echo gettext("Submit") ?>" />
</form>
</body>
</html>
```

The English text acts as the message ids for the translations. Running xgettext on this file will produce a skeleton PO file named sample.po that I can then edit using poedit.

```
# xgettext -n sample.php
```

This creates the file sample.po containing the list of message ids, which in this case are "Search for Books" and "Submit". I can then use poedit to add the necessary translations for each language.

I'll choose the word "sample" as the domain for my translations and therefore, the translation file for each language needs to be named sample.mo.

For a given locale, gettext always looks for the translation files in the directory:

```
locale/[locale string]/LC_MESSAGES
```

So, for the locale "en_US", gettext would look for translation files in the directory:

```
locale/en_US/LC_MESSAGES
```

Typically, you will create these directories in your application's folder, but they can be located anywhere you can reference with an absolute path name.

The rest of Example 7-2 still needs a few modifications so that translations will work. Defining locales is a good start:

```
define('LOCALE_DE', 'deu_deu');
define('LOCALE_US', 'us_us');
define('LOCALE_JP', 'jpn_jpn');
```

Then I have to tell gettext where to find the locale directory hierarchy. I use the PHP bindtextdomain() function to tell gettext where to find the locale directory and what domain to use. It takes the domain and any absolute pathname as arguments.

```
bindtextdomain('example', 'C:\apache\Apache\htdocs\examples\locale');
```

Then I tell gettext explicitly what domain to use using the textdomain() function.

```
textdomain('example');
```

In the switch statement, for each locale, I need to do three things: set the LANG shell environment variable to the locale, run the PHP setlocale() function to set the locale, and use the bind_textdomain_codeset() function to set the output character encoding. Gettext will do the character encoding translation, if any, on the fly.

The new version, Example 7-3, uses gettext to make translations.

```
<?php
define('LOCALE_DE', 'deu_deu');
define('LOCALE_US', 'us_us');
define('LOCALE_JP', 'jpn_jpn');

bindtextdomain('example', 'C:\apache\Apache\htdocs\examples\locale');
textdomain('example');

$country= LOCALE_JP;

switch ($country) {
    case LOCALE_US:
    define('TO_ENCODING','ISO-8859-1');
    putenv("LANG=".LOCALE_US);
    setlocale(LC_ALL, LOCALE_US);
    bind_textdomain_codeset(MSG_DOMAIN, TO_ENCODING);
    break;
    case LOCALE_DE:
    define ('TO_ENCODING', 'ISO-8859-1');
    putenv("LANG=".LOCALE_DE);
    setlocale(LC_ALL, LOCALE_DE);
    bind_textdomain_codeset(MSG_DOMAIN, TO_ENCODING);
    break;
```

```
        case LOCALE_JP:
        define('TO_ENCODING','Shift_JIS');
        putenv("LANG=".LOCALE_JP);
        setlocale(LC_ALL, LOCALE_JP);
        bind_textdomain_codeset(MSG_DOMAIN, TO_ENCODING);
        break;
        default:
        die('Unknown Locale');
    }
    ?>
    <html>
    <head>
    <meta http-equiv="Content-Type" content="text/html; charset=<?php echo TO_ENCODING ?>
    ">
    </head>
    <body>
    <form accept-charset="<?php echo TO_ENCODING ?>" method="post" name="lang_stuff"
    target="_self">
    <?php echo gettext("Search for Books") ?>
    <input type="text" name="tinput" />
    <input type="submit" value="<?php echo gettext("Submit") ?>" />
    </form>
    </body>
    </html>
```

Example 7-3 Using gettext to make language translations

Foreign Characters Using HTML Entities

If you're only using a limited set of European languages such as German and French, you may be able to represent the 8-bit accents using 7-bit HTML entities. There is a small set of HTML entities that are widely used for such purposes (Table 7-6).

HTML Entity	Diacritical Mark	Letter Choices	Example
&Xacute;	acute	a,e,i,o,u,y,A,E,I,O,U,Y	Ý Ý
&Xcirc;	circumflex	a,e,i,o,u, A, E, I, O, U	ô ô
&Xgrave;	grave	a,e,i,o,u, A, E, I, O, U	ù ù
&Xring;	unlaut	a,A	Å Å
&Xuml;	ring	a,e,i,o,u, A, E, I, O, U	Ë Ë
&Xcedil;	cedilla	c,C	Ç Ç
&Xtilde;	tilde	a,n,o, A,N,O	Õ Õ
&Xslash;	slash	o,O	ø ø
ß	ess-zed	s	ß ß
&Xlig;	ligature	ae, AE, oe, OE	æ æ

Table 7-6 Common HTML Entities for some European languages

For example, instead of using the 8-bit umlaut in Example 7-3, you could use the HTML entity:

```
define('LABEL1','Suche nach B&uuml;chern');
```

In Table 7-6, replace the "X" with the letter of your choice to add the diacritical marking.

Code Sample: Song Title Search

To illustrate how to create an internationalized web application for Amazon E-Commerce Service, I created a web application that lets people search for song titles using keywords entered by the user. You can already search for song titles using keywords on Amazon but all you get back is a list of CDs. My application goes a step farther and displays the actual song title containing the keyword(s), and it lets you search using any of the Amazon international sites.

The application displays a localized search form for each of the sites and lets the user search for song titles using their native language. I store their country preference in a cookie so that they always see the form and results in the language they last chose.

For each song title search, I display the first ten CD results and store the matching song titles in tooltips so that they appear when the user rolls their mouse pointer over the CD cover image.

> Tooltips work well with Internet Explorer and Safari, but, due to an old bug, Mozilla-based browsers don't format them properly (see https://bugzilla.mozilla.org/show_bug.cgi?id=45375). So, the Tooltips won't work right on Firefox and other Mozilla browsers. Creating the Tooltips effect using CSS or Javascript is left as an exercise for the reader.

The application uses two input parameters: a locale and the keywords the user enters to search for song titles.

Making Translations

As discussed in the previous sections, I'll handle the locale-specific parameters and language strings using gettext. All language strings will be encoded as UTF-8 in the gettext PO files so that we maintain consistency with our development environment.

```
switch ($locale) {
     case LOCALE_DE:
     define ('TO_ENCODING', 'ISO-8859-1');
     putenv("LANG=".LOCALE_DE);
     setlocale(LC_ALL, LOCALE_DE);
     bind_textdomain_codeset(MSG_DOMAIN, TO_ENCODING);
     define ('DOMAIN', 'de');
     define ('NOIMAGE', 'http://images-eu.amazon.com/images/G/03/general/no-img-de_
90x90.gif');
```

```
        break;
        case 'jp':
        define ('TO_ENCODING', 'Shift_JIS');
    ..........
    ..........
```

The define TO_ENCODING is the target encoding for the web page that will be displayed for the user. I define two functions, lang() and langreverse(), to go back and forth between UTF-8 and the TO_ENCODING for various data elements returned by Amazon E-Commerce Service. The function lang() takes a UTF-8 encoded string and returns the string in the new encoding for the given locale.

```
function lang($string) {
    global $locale;
    switch ($locale) {
        case LOCALE_JP:
        // return iconv('UTF-8', TO_ENCODING, $string);
        return mb_convert_encoding($string, TO_ENCODING, 'UTF-8');
        break;
        default:
        return utf8_decode($string);
    }
}
```

The function langreverse() takes a string in whatever encoding is used for the current locale and returns the string with UTF-8 encoding.

```
function langreverse($string) {
    global $locale;
    switch ($locale) {
        case LOCALE_JP:
        return mb_convert_encoding($string, 'UTF-8', TO_ENCODING);
        // return iconv(TO_ENCODING, 'UTF-8', $string);
        break;
        default:
        // return utf8_encode($string); Switch to this when Amazon fixes encoding
        return $string;
    }
}
```

In order to search for strings, I created the multi-language findstring() function. I try to do a case insensitive search for each keyword the user enters. For Japan, it's easy because Japanese characters don't have case. For France and Germany, which might have some eight-bit characters, I use the mb_strtolower() function to first make the parameters lowercase and then I do the search. Only iconv under PHP5 has the iconv_strpos() function, and iconv doesn't have any strtolower function at all. My approach is to move the character encoding to ISO-8859-1 (the default for PHP) and then apply PHP's strtolower() function and then use iconv_strpos().

```
function findstring($haystack, $needle) {
    global $locale;

    switch ($locale) {
```

```
        case LOCALE_JP:
        // return iconv_strpos($haystack, $needle, 0, 'UTF-8');
        return mb_strpos($haystack, $needle, 0, 'UTF-8');
        break;
        case LOCALE_DE:
        case LOCALE_FR:
        // $haystack=strtolower(utf8_decode($haystack));
        // $needle=strtolower(utf8_decode($needle));
        // return iconv_strpos(utf8_encode($haystack), utf8_encode($needle), 0, 'UTF-
8');
        $haystack=mb_strtolower($haystack, 'UTF-8');
        $needle=mb_strtolower($needle, 'UTF-8');
        return mb_strpos($haystack, $needle, 0, 'UTF-8');
        break;
        case LOCALE_US:
        case LOCALE_UK:
        default:
        return strpos(strtolower($haystack), strtolower($needle));
    }
    return true;
}
```

I only need to make one request to Amazon to return the list of CDs that have song titles matching the keywords:

```
$request='http://webservices.amazon.'.DOMAIN.'/onca/
xml?Service=AWSECommerceService&AssociateTag='.ASSOCIATES_ID.'&SubscriptionId='.
SUBID.'&Operation=ItemSearch&SearchIndex=MusicTracks&Keywords='.$search_string.
'&ResponseGroup=Small,Tracks,Images&Version=2005-02-23';
```

Note that I use the Response Group “Tracks” to return song titles from CDs. $search_string is the keywords the user entered. DOMAIN is the domain name extension of the Amazon site that the user has chosen. The user chooses the Amazon site they want to explore by clicking on an image of a German, US, Japanese, French, or British flag.

Figure 7-5 Song title search application

The users’ choice is then stored in a cookie.

```
define('DEFAULT_LOCALE', LOCALE_US);

if (isset($_GET['locale'])) {
    //locale change requested
    $locale=$_GET['locale'];
    $oneday=time()+60*60*24*30; // Cookie lasts 30 days
```

```
        if (!setcookie('songsearch', $locale, $oneday)) {
            echo 'Your browser will not accept cookies';
        }
    } elseif (isset($_COOKIE['songsearch'])) {
        $locale = stripslashes($_COOKIE['songsearch']);
    } else {
        //No cookie. Create one
        $locale=DEFAULT_LOCALE;
        $oneday=time()+60*60*24*30;
        if (!setcookie('songsearch', $locale, $oneday)) {
            echo 'Your browser will not accept cookies';
        }
    }
```

There are three Cookie handling cases that must be handled, indicated by the if-then-else in the code above. If the user selected a new locale, then the $_GET['locale'] string will be set, and so I create and store a cookie with the new locale in it. If a new locale was not requested, then I check to see if a cookie exists. If it exists, I retrieve the stored locale inside it. If it doesn't exist, I create a cookie using the DEFAULT_LOCALE.

> The setcookie() function must executed before any script output takes place as the cookie must be sent along with the rest of the HTTP headers.

In order to separate the program logic from the HTML somewhat, the bulk of the HTML resides in a separate file, layout.php. Layout.php contains the calls to gettext.

> As mentioned previously, we are converting from UTF-8 to the native encoding -- ISO-8859-1 for US, France, Germany, and Britain, and Shift_JIS for Japan. You can choose, of course, to display everything using UTF-8 encoding. In that case, you can remove the lang and reversional references and hard code charset=UTF-8 in layout.php.

```
<html>
<head>
<META HTTP-EQUIV="Content-Type" content="text/html; charset=<?php echo TO_ENCODING ?>
" />
<title><?php echo gettext('Song Title Search') ?></title>
</head>
<body>
<table width="100%" border="1">
  <tr>
    <td width="100%" height="100"><div align="center">
        <h3><?php echo gettext('Song Title Search') ?></h3>
      </div>
      <form action="" method="post" enctype="multipart/form-data" name="musicsearch"
target="_self" id="musicsearch" accept-charset="<?php echo TO_ENCODING ?>">
        <p> <?php echo gettext('Enter Song Title Keywords') ?>: 
          <input name="songtitle" type="text" id="songtitle" value="" size="50"
maxlength="70">
  
```

```
            <input type="submit" name="submit" value="<?php echo gettext('Submit') ?>">
          </p>
        </form>
        <div style="text-align: right;">
        <?php echo gettext('Choose a site to search') ?>: 
        <a href="<?php echo $_SERVER['PHP_SELF'] ?>?locale=<?php echo LOCALE_DE ?>">
        <img src="de.png" border="0" /></a> 
        <a href="<?php echo $_SERVER['PHP_SELF'] ?>?locale=<?php echo LOCALE_US ?>">
        <img src="us.png" border="0" /></a> 
        <a href="<?php echo $_SERVER['PHP_SELF'] ?>?locale=<?php echo LOCALE_UK ?>">
        <img src="uk.png" border="0" /></a> 
        <a href="<?php echo $_SERVER['PHP_SELF'] ?>?locale=<?php echo LOCALE_JP ?>">
        <img src="jp.png" border="0"/></a> 
        <a href="<?php echo $_SERVER['PHP_SELF'] ?>?locale=<?php echo LOCALE_FR ?>">
        <img src="fr.png" border="0"/></a><b>amazon.<?php echo DOMAIN ?></b>
        </div></td>
      </tr>
      <tr><td>
     <?php theResults() ?>
  </td></tr>
</table>
</body>
</html>
```

Example 7-4 Layout.php

The function theResults(), referenced in layout.php, does all the real work of going through the Amazon response and finding the data we need.

```
function theResults() {
    global $Result;

    // If $Result is completely empty, the user didn't enter a search
    if (empty($Result)) {
        echo gettext('Please enter keywords');
    } elseif  // If there's an error message from Amazon, and no results, display it
(isset($Result['ItemSearchResponse']['Items'][0]['Request']['Errors']['Error'][0]['Me
ssage']) and ($Result['ItemSearchResponse']['Items'][0]['TotalResults'] == '0'))  {
        echo
lang($Result['ItemSearchResponse']['Items'][0]['Request']['Errors']['Error'][0]['Mess
age']);
    } else { // We have results to display
// Get all the keywords
$keywords=$Result['ItemSearchResponse']['Items'][0]['Request']['ItemSearchRequest']['
Keywords'];
         // Put each keyword into an array
        $words = explode(' ', $keywords);

        echo '<table width="100%" border="1"><tr>';
        // Main loop where we display each CD returned
        foreach ($Result['ItemSearchResponse']['Items'][0]['Item'] as $item) {
            // $trackout is the tooltips display
            $trackout='';
            if (isset($item['Tracks']['Disc'])) {
```

```
                foreach ($item['Tracks']['Disc'] as $disc) {
                    $trackout .= gettext('Disc')." ".$disc['Number']."\n";
                    foreach ($disc['Track'] as $track) {
                        foreach ($words as $word) {
                            // Use findstring to do multi-language search
                            if (findstring($track['Track'], $word) === false) {
                                $trackout .= "";
                            } else {
                                $trackout .= "   ".gettext('Track')." ".
$track['Number'].' - '.lang($track['Track'])."\n";
                            }
                        }
                    }
                }
                // Double quotes will break our HTML output, so encode them
                $trackout=str_replace('"', "&#34;", $trackout);
            } else {
                $trackout=gettext('No matching song titles were found');
            }

            // Display the item's image
            if (isset($item['SmallImage']['URL'])) {
                $image='<img src="'.$item["SmallImage"]["URL"].'" title="'.$trackout.
'" />';
            } else {
                $image='<img src="'.NOIMAGE.'" title="'.$trackout.'" />';
            }

            // If the item doesn't have a name (rare), skip it
            if (!isset($item["ItemAttributes"]["Title"])) continue;

            $title = '<a href="'.$item["DetailPageURL"].'" target="_blank">'.
lang($item["ItemAttributes"]["Title"]).'</a>';
            echo '<td><div style="text-align: center;">'.$title.'</div><div
style="text-align: center;">'.$image.'</div></td>';
        }
        echo '</tr></table>';
    }

}
```

I first search the list of track names returned for each CD for any of the requested keywords. If I find any, I save that track name for output in the Tooltips. Thus, the user will only see track names that contain one or more of the keywords.

Displaying Tooltips In Other Languages

You may be surprised to find that your tooltips have a lot of garbage characters in them, especially if you're viewing Japanese language results. That's because your web browser doesn't automatically choose the correct font for tooltips, even if the character encoding is correct. Under Internet Explorer, go to Windows Control-Panel > Display Properties > Appearance > Advanced > Item: ToolTip to set the correct font.

International Currency and Dates

Amazon E-Commerce Service 4.0 already returns internationalized pricing. For example, when you retrieve offers from amazon.de, they are in Euros and include the Euro currency identifier.

```
<Price>
  <Amount>2495</Amount>
  <CurrencyCode>EUR</CurrencyCode>
  <FormattedPrice>EUR 24,95</FormattedPrice>
</Price>
```

As I mentioned at then end of Chapter Two, E-Commerce Service returns date and time information in a particular ISO 8601 format. To output time and date information in the language of a particular locale, use PHP's setlocale() function and then use PHP's strftime() function to format the date/time.

> If you're using the gettext code from the previous section, then you've already set the locale. You can remove the setlocale() call in the code below.

Here's the example from Chapter Two with output in French

```
<?php
// Set locale to French language in France
setlocale(LC_TIME, 'fr_FR');
// Remove "T"
$date=str_replace('T', ' ', '2004-05-22T03:45-1000');
// Turn the Amazon time string into "Unix" time (seconds since January 1st, 1970)
$time = strtotime($date);
// Translate "Unix" time into desired date/time format
$strt = strftime('%A, %b %d, %Y, %I:%M%p %z', $time);
echo $strt;
?>
```

On one version of Red Hat Linux, I got this output:

```
samedi, mai 22, 2004, 09:45 -0400
```

Feature Support On International Sites

Not all E-Commerce Service features are supported across Amazon's web sites. The U.S. site, amazon.com, has more features, and a much larger product database, than any of the other five sites. When developing applications that involve the International Amazon sites you have to be careful to adjust your requests and response handling to accommodate missing product categories and features.

Product areas that aren't available on the foreign sites are noted in the Search Index table in Appendix H. The E-Commerce Service reference manual in Appendix B notes where there are differences in method requests for other sites.

Overall the primary differences that developers need to be aware of are:

- All Amazon identifiers are unique to each site.
- There are no Merchants@ sellers or Merchants@ Pro Merchants on the international sites.
- There are no Variations (e.g. Parent or Child ASINs) on the international sites.
- There is no ISPU (In Store Pick Up) on the international sites.
- The TransactionLookup, CustomerContentSearch, and CustomerContentLookup operations aren't available on the international sites
- The OfferSummary element has a minor difference on the international sites
- The MergeCart parameter works differently on the international sites

Identifier Uniqueness

All Amazon identifiers are unique to each Amazon site. For example, the ASIN for the DVD "Minority Report" (single DVD edition) is B0000SYA9Y on Amazon.de. On Amazon.com, the ASIN for the same DVD is B00009ZYC0. The only instance when ASINs may match is with import editions. For example, the ASIN for Minority Report (2 disc set) on Amazon.co.uk is B000063W29 while the UK import edition available on Amazon.de has the same ASIN.

That's a rare exception, however. All the various identifiers and text associated with reviews, lists, sellers, offers, and customers are unique to the Amazon web site they were created on.

Working With Offers

The International Amazon sites do not have stores, Merchants@ Sellers or Merchants@ Pro Merchants, so their overall product catalogs are somewhat smaller than Amazon.com's. There is also a minor difference in the way the OfferSummary

MerchantId parameter	Amazon.com	International Amazon sites
Not used	Only the Amazon offer is returned	Only the Amazon offer is returned
All	Amazon offer is included in OfferSummary	Amazon offer is not included in OfferSummary

Table 7-7 Difference between the OfferSummary element on International Amazon sites

element is returned. When doing any search that allows the MerchantId parameter, when MerchantId=All, the Amazon offer is not included in the OfferSummary results (Table 7-7). The Amazon offer is still included in the Offers section, but it's price is not included in the OfferSummary element.

International Images

Product images on the international Amazon sites can't be altered the way the images on Amazon.com can be altered. There is no way to add the "Look Inside" arrow nor add the Schmoo character (see my "Decoding Image URLs" section in Chapter Three). In fact, the only supported image enhancement is the percentage off circle.

Image URLs from each International Amazon site have an Amazon Country Code (Table 7-7) which tells Amazon's image servers which country is being served.

Amazon Site	Amazon Country Code
Canada amazon.ca	01
England amazon.co.uk	02
France amazon.fr	08
Germany amazon.de	03
Japan amazon.co.jp	09
United States amazon.com	01

Table 7-8 Amazon country codes

Most image URLs on the International Amazon sites are still served from the *images.amazon.com* domain, though image on European sites sometimes use *images-eu.amazon.com* and Japan, *images-jp.amazon.com.*

For the international Amazon sites, percentage off circles are formed the same was as with Amazon.com with the respective Country Code in the URL. For example, this Catwoman DVD from Amazon.co.uk has the Country Code for England, 02:

```
http://images.amazon.com/images/P/B000667KWO.02._PE31_SCMZZZZZZZ_.jpg
```

In practice, I found that many images retrieved through Amazon E-Commerce Service from the International Amazon sites would not accept percentage off circles. Adding it to the URL doesn't affect the image (the image is still displayed), but no percentage off circle is displayed.

Normally, all images served up the Amazon image servers will have the Amazon Country Code for the target country site. However, if the item is an import, it may have the Country Code from the import country instead.

Sorting, Search Indexes, And ItemSearch

The Sort and SearchIndex parameters are somewhat different for each Amazon site. Appendix G lists the sorting parameter choices for each Amazon site. Appendix H lists the Search Indexes. Appendix I lists the ItemSearch parameters that can be used with each Search Index on each Amazon site.

Remote Carts

On the International Amazon sites, the Remote Cart always acts as if MergeCart=True, even if MergeCart is set to False in the purchase URL. The MergeCart=False behavior isn't available on the International Amazon sites.

Exercises For The Reader

Modify the song title search and substitute the tooltips rollovers in the song title search example with Javascript rollovers.

Modify song title search to paginate the results.

Japanese users may want to mix English and Japanese words in their song searches. That presents a problem since there are no upper or lowercase Japanese words like there are in English. Modify the song search so that it can tell the difference between English and Japanese words, and have it search the results for both upper and lower case for English.

Amazon sometimes matches song title words without their accent marks, and sometimes will match the singular version of a plural song lyric e.g. matches "mots" with "mot" in French. Adjust the song title search output to recognize these words in the song title.

CHAPTER 8

Miscellaneous Operations

Everything is worth something to somebody
—Ferengi Rule Of Acquisition #49

In this chapter I discuss some of the E-Commerce Service 4.0 operations that I couldn't fit elsewhere in the book. Except for TransactionLookup, which is really only useful for Amazon merchants, the other operations in the Chapter, BrowseNodeLookup, SimilarityLookup, and Help, are quite useful

Navigation Using BrowseNodeLookup

Browse Node IDs are the foundation of Amazon's search architecture (For details, see "Amazon Search Architecture" in Chapter One). The BrowseNodeLookup operation takes a Browse Node ID as input and returns the tree-structured hierarchy of child Browse Node IDs one level below it. And along with the Browse Node ID, the corresponding category name is also returned.

Element	Description
BrowseNodeId	`A valid Browse Node ID`
Name	`The name that corresponds to the Browse Node ID`

Table 8-1 The elements returned by the BrowseNodeLookup operation

BrowseNodeLookup responses tell us one of three things depending on the response:

- The Browse Node ID is invalid. An AWS.InvalidParameterValue is returned
- The Browse Node ID is not a leaf node. One or more Children are returned
- The Browse Node ID is a leaf node. No Children are returned

So, if we start by using a Browse Node ID for a specific product category, we can follow the tree of child product categories by making successive calls to BrowseNodeLookup. The REST request using the top-level Browse Node ID for shoes is:

```
http://webservices.amazon.com/onca/xml?Service=AWSECommerceService&
AssociateTag=ws&SubscriptionId=1A7XKHR5BYDOWPJVQEG2&
Operation=BrowseNodeLookup&BrowseNodeId=1040668&Version=2005-01-19
```

I found the Browse Node ID, 1040668, by going to the Apparel store on Amazon.com and looking at the link for "Shoes" on the left side of the main page.

The request output echoes back the Browse Node ID along with the corresponding Name, and then lists the first level of child Browse Nodes below it.

```
<BrowseNode>
   <BrowseNodeId>1040668</BrowseNodeId>
   <Name>Shoes</Name>
   <Children>
     <BrowseNode>
       <BrowseNodeId>1044764</BrowseNodeId>
       <Name>Women's Shoes</Name>
     </BrowseNode>
     <BrowseNode>
       <BrowseNodeId>1045744</BrowseNodeId>
       <Name>Men's Shoes</Name>
     </BrowseNode>
     <BrowseNode>
       <BrowseNodeId>1044476</BrowseNodeId>
       <Name>Children's Shoes</Name>
     </BrowseNode>
   </Children>
 </BrowseNode>
```

If we now take one of the child Browse Node IDs, say, 1044476 which is Children's Shoes, we get the next level of child Browse Node IDs below it:

```
http://webservices.amazon.com/onca/xml?Service=AWSECommerceService&
AssociateTag=ws&SubscriptionId=1A7XKHR5BYDOWPJVQEG2&
Operation=BrowseNodeLookup&BrowseNodeId=1044476&Version=2005-02-23
```

```
<BrowseNode>
   <BrowseNodeId>1044476</BrowseNodeId>
   <Name>Children's Shoes</Name>
   <Children>
     <BrowseNode>
       <BrowseNodeId>1044478</BrowseNodeId>
       <Name>Boys</Name>
     </BrowseNode>
     <BrowseNode>
       <BrowseNodeId>1045346</BrowseNodeId>
       <Name>Girls</Name>
```

```
        </BrowseNode>
        <BrowseNode>
          <BrowseNodeId>1044504</BrowseNodeId>
          <Name>Infants &amp; Toddlers</Name>
        </BrowseNode>
      </Children>
    </BrowseNode>
```

The category navigation using Browse Node IDs is easy to demonstrate using a short PHP script:

```
<?php

error_reporting(E_ALL);
require_once("tools.inc.php");

define('SUBID', '1A7XKHR5BYDOWPJVQEG2'); // Subscription ID
define('ASSOCIATES_ID','ws');           // Associates ID
define('VERSION','2005-02-23');         // ECS Version
define('DEFAULT_BROWSENODE', '1040668'); // The top-level Browse Node ID
define('DEFAULT_NAME', 'Shoes');        // The top-level Browse Category
define('FIRST_TIME', 'FIRST');          // A flag to indicate first time through

// Fetch the Browse Node ID
$bn=(isset($_GET['bn'])) ? $_GET['bn'] : FIRST_TIME;

// If it isn't the first time through, make a request
if ($bn != FIRST_TIME) {
    $request='http://webservices.amazon.com/onca/
xml?Service=AWSECommerceService&AssociateTag='.ASSOCIATES_ID.'&SubscriptionId='.
SUBID.'&Operation=BrowseNodeLookup&BrowseNodeId='.$bn.'&Version='.VERSION;
    $xml = GetData($request, 10);
    $Result = xmlparser($xml);
}
?>
<html>
<head>
<title>Node Browser</title>
</head>
<body>
<?php
// If first time through, just display the top level Browse Node and Name
if ($bn == FIRST_TIME) {
    echo '<div><a href="navigatebn.php?bn='.DEFAULT_BROWSENODE.'">'.DEFAULT_NAME.'</
a></div>';
} else {
    // If there are any children, display them
    if
(isset($Result['BrowseNodeLookupResponse']['BrowseNodes'][0]['BrowseNode'][0]['Childr
en']['BrowseNode'])) {
        foreach
($Result['BrowseNodeLookupResponse']['BrowseNodes'][0]['BrowseNode'][0]['Children']['
BrowseNode'] as $browsenode) {
```

```
            echo '<div><a href="navigatebn.php?bn='.$browsenode['BrowseNodeId'].'">'.
$browsenode['Name'].'</a></div>';
        }
    } else {
        // Otherwise it's a leaf node
        echo '<div>No more child browse nodes</div>';
    }
}
?>
</body>
</html>
```

Example 8-1 navigatebn.php, simple Browse Node navigation

The first time through, just the word "Shoes", the name of the top-level Browse Node ID, is displayed as a link with the Browse Node ID a parameter in the link. Clicking "Shoes" takes you to the next level of child Browse Nodes which are "Womens," "Mens," and "Childrens". Clicking on "Womens" takes you to the child Browse Nodes for Womens shoes, and so on (Figure 8-1).

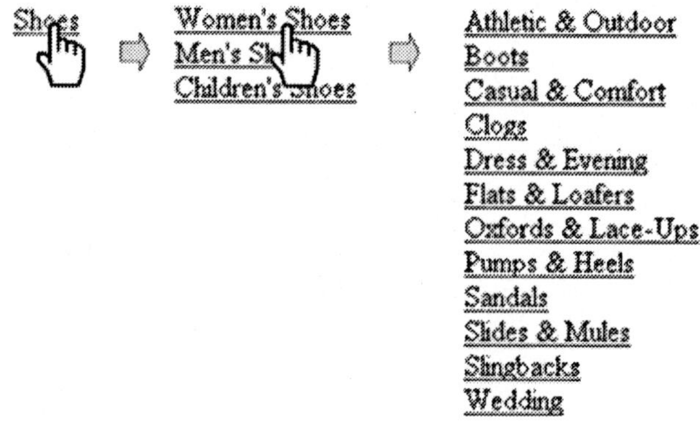

Figure 8-1 Three successive outputs of Example 8-1

Code Sample: Navigation And Items

Now that we have the code for category navigation (Example 8-1), I'll add a bit more code to fetch items so that users can see some items from the category they clicked on. To do this, we use a Multioperation request (See Chapter Two). We combine the BrowseNodeLookup operation from Example 8-1 with an ItemSearch operation that searches in the same Browse Node. Thus, we get the first page of items from the

Browse Node category from the ItemSearch request, and the list of child Browse Node (if any) from the BrowseNodeLookup request.

> We could retrieve two pages of items by using a combined Batch and Multioperation request. This is left as an exercise for the reader.

```
$request='http://webservices.amazon.com/onca/xml?Service=AWSECommerceService&
AssociateTag='.ASSOCIATES_ID.'&SubscriptionId='.SUBID.'&
Operation=ItemSearch,BrowseNodeLookup&ItemSearch.1.SearchIndex=Apparel&
ItemSearch.1.MerchantId=All&ItemSearch.1.ResponseGroup=Images,Small&
ItemSearch.1.BrowseNode='.$bn.'&BrowseNodeLookup.1.BrowseNodeId='.$bn.'&
Version='.VERSION;
```

The BrowseNodeLookup response is used to create a navigation menu on the left while the items for current Browse Node ID are displayed on the right (Figure 8-2). For this navigation menu, I start with a list of Browse Node categories instead of just one (Shoes).

```
$bnarray['1040660']='Women';
$bnarray['1040658']='Men';
$bnarray['1040662']='Kids and Baby';
$bnarray['1084666']='Teens';
$bnarray['1040668']='Shoes';
$bnarray['1036700']='Accessories';
```

The user can choose any of these paths to descend and find more relevant items in the product category.

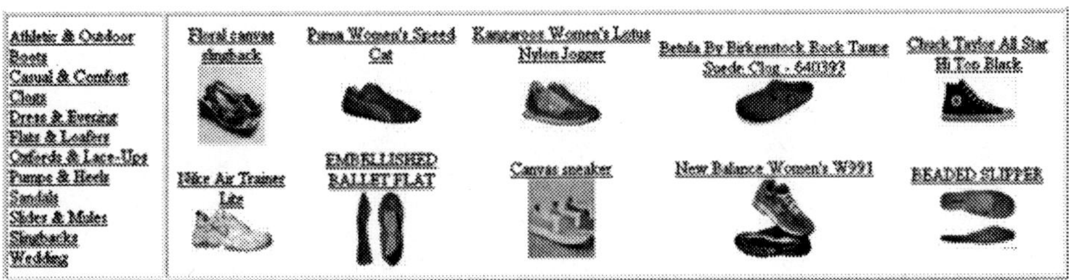

Figure 8-2 Output showing navigation (left) with items (right)

The output in Figure 8-2 corresponds to the third navigation menu from Figure 8-1. The items on the right side are the first ten items from the "Womens Shoes" Browse Node with the default sort order.

```
<?php
error_reporting(E_ALL);

require_once("tools.inc.php");
define('SUBID', '1A7XKHR5BYDOWPJVQEG2');
define('ASSOCIATES_ID','ws');
define('VERSION','2005-01-19');
```

```
define ('NOIMAGE_MED', 'http://g-images.amazon.com/images/G/01/x-site/icons/no-img-
lg.gif');
define('FIRST_TIME', 'FIRST');

$bn=(isset($_GET['bn'])) ? $_GET['bn'] : FIRST_TIME;

$bnarray['1040660']='Women';
$bnarray['1040658']='Men';
$bnarray['1040662']='Kids and Baby';
$bnarray['1084666']='Teens';
$bnarray['1040668']='Shoes';
$bnarray['1036700']='Accessories';

if ($bn != FIRST_TIME) {

    $request='http://webservices.amazon.com/onca/
xml?Service=AWSECommerceService&AssociateTag='.ASSOCIATES_ID.'&SubscriptionId='.
SUBID.'&Operation=ItemSearch,BrowseNodeLookup&ItemSearch.1.
SearchIndex=Apparel&ItemSearch.1.MerchantId=All&ItemSearch.1.
ResponseGroup=Images,Small&ItemSearch.1.BrowseNode='.$bn.'&BrowseNodeLookup.1.
BrowseNodeId='.$bn.'&Version='.VERSION;

    $xml = GetData($request, 10);
    $Result = xmlparser($xml);

}

function theItemWindow() {
    global $Result;
    global $bn;

    echo '<table cellspacing="2" cellpadding="2"><tr>';
    $rowcount=0;
    if ($bn != FIRST_TIME) {
        foreach
($Result['MultiOperationResponse']['ItemSearchResponse']['Items'][0]['Item'] as
$item) {
            if (isset($item['SmallImage']['URL'])) {
                $image='<img src="'.$item["SmallImage"]["URL"].'" />';
            } else {
                $image='<img src="'.NOIMAGE_MED.'" />';
            }
            $title = '<a href="'.$item["DetailPageURL"].'" target="_blank">'.
$item["ItemAttributes"]["Title"].'</a>';
            if (is_int($rowcount/5)) echo '</tr><tr>';

            echo '<td><div style="text-align: center;">'.$title.'</div><div
style="text-align: center;">'.$image.'</div></td>';
            $rowcount++;
        }
    } else {
        echo '<td><div style="text-align: center;">Choose a category on the left</
div></td>';
    }
```

```
    echo '</tr></table>';

}

function theLeftSide() {
    global $bnarray;
    global $bn;
    global $Result;

    if ($bn == FIRST_TIME) {
        foreach ($bnarray as $bnkey => $bnval) {
            echo '<div><a href="apparel.php?bn='.$bnkey.'">'.$bnval.'</a></div>';
        }
    }  else {
        if
(isset($Result['MultiOperationResponse']['BrowseNodeLookupResponse']['BrowseNodes'][0
]['BrowseNode'][0]['Children']['BrowseNode'])) {
            foreach
($Result['MultiOperationResponse']['BrowseNodeLookupResponse']['BrowseNodes'][0]['Bro
wseNode'][0]['Children']['BrowseNode'] as $browsenode) {
                echo '<div><a href="apparel.php?bn='.$browsenode['BrowseNodeId'].'">
'.$browsenode['Name'].'</a></div>';
            }
        } else {
            echo '<div>No more child browse nodes</div>';
        }
    }
}

?>

<html>
<head>
<title>Apparel Browser</title>
</head>
<body>
<table width="1000" border="1" cellpadding="2" cellspacing="2">
    <tr>
    <td width="15%" height="250"><?php theLeftSide(); ?>
    </td>
    <td width="85%" height="250"><?php theItemWindow(); ?>
    </td>
  </tr>
  </table>
</body>
</html>
```

Example 8-2 Code for apparel.php

More Choices With SimilarityLookup

SimilarityLookup is the operation that gives developers access to some of the internal statistics that Amazon maintains about customer buying habits. On Amazon.com, you will occasionally see links that say "See similar items." Clicking on that link will return a list of items (almost always in the same product category) that were purchased by people who also bought the original item (Figure 8-3)

> Not all items have similarities. This is especially true of items that sell at very low volume.

The SimilarityLookup operation uses exactly the same logic to arrive at similar items. We can easily see this by using the ASIN for the Reuben Wilson CD in Figure 8-3 and using it as a parameter in a SimilarityLookup request:

```
http://webservices.amazon.com/onca/xml?Service=AWSECommerceService&
SubscriptionId=1A7XKHR5BYDOWPJVQEG2&AssociateTag=ws&Operation=SimilarityLookup&
ItemId=B000005GXZ&ResponseGroup=Small&Version=2005-02-23
```

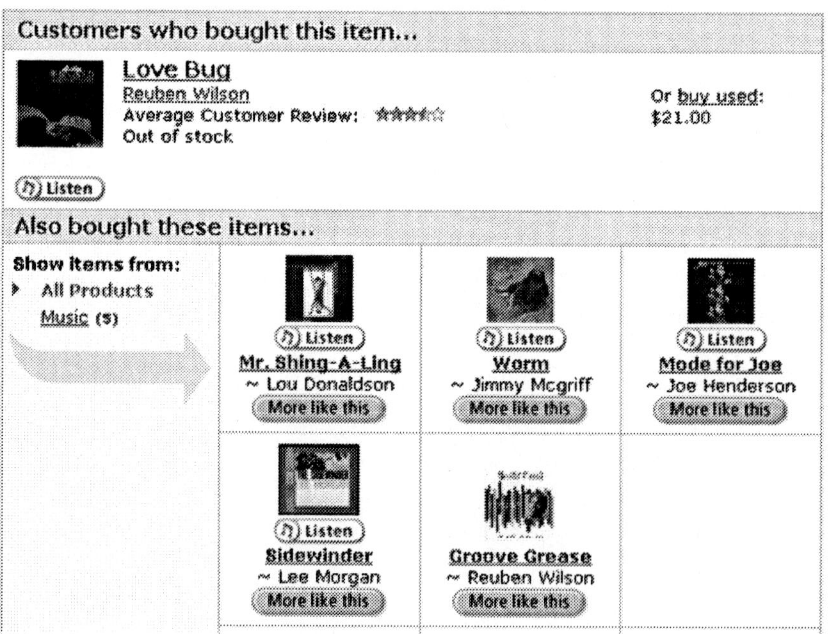

Figure 8-3 A similarity response on Amazon.com

The result is exactly the items displayed in Figure 8-3:

```
 <Item>
      <ASIN>B000005HD9</ASIN>
      <DetailPageURL>http://www.amazon.com/exec/obidos/redirect?tag=webservices-
20%26link_code=xm2%26camp=2025%26creative=165953%26path=http://www.amazon.com/gp/
redirect.html%253fASIN=B000005HD9%2526location=/o/ASIN/
B000005HD9%25253FSubscriptionId=1A7XKHR5BYD0WPJVQEG2</DetailPageURL>
      <ItemAttributes>
        <Artist>Lou Donaldson</Artist>
        <ProductGroup>Music</ProductGroup>
        <Title>Mr. Shing-A-Ling</Title>
      </ItemAttributes>
    </Item>
    <Item>
      <ASIN>B000065TS4</ASIN>
      <DetailPageURL>http://www.amazon.com/exec/obidos/redirect?tag=webservices-
20%26link_code=xm2%26camp=2025%26creative=165953%26path=http://www.amazon.com/gp/
redirect.html%253fASIN=B000065TS4%2526location=/o/ASIN/
B000065TS4%25253FSubscriptionId=1A7XKHR5BYD0WPJVQEG2</DetailPageURL>
      <ItemAttributes>
        <Artist>Jimmy Mcgriff</Artist>
        <ProductGroup>Music</ProductGroup>
        <Title>Worm</Title>
      </ItemAttributes>
    </Item>
    <Item>
      <ASIN>B0000BV20U</ASIN>
      <DetailPageURL>http://www.amazon.com/exec/obidos/redirect?tag=webservices-
20%26link_code=xm2%26camp=2025%26creative=165953%26path=http://www.amazon.com/gp/
redirect.html%253fASIN=B0000BV20U%2526location=/o/ASIN/
B0000BV20U%25253FSubscriptionId=1A7XKHR5BYD0WPJVQEG2</DetailPageURL>
      <ItemAttributes>
        <Artist>Joe Henderson</Artist>
        <ProductGroup>Music</ProductGroup>
        <Title>Mode for Joe</Title>
      </ItemAttributes>
    </Item>
    <Item>
      <ASIN>B00000IL26</ASIN>
      <DetailPageURL>http://www.amazon.com/exec/obidos/redirect?tag=webservices-
20%26link_code=xm2%26camp=2025%26creative=165953%26path=http://www.amazon.com/gp/
redirect.html%253fASIN=B00000IL26%2526location=/o/ASIN/
B00000IL26%25253FSubscriptionId=1A7XKHR5BYD0WPJVQEG2</DetailPageURL>
      <ItemAttributes>
        <Artist>Lee Morgan</Artist>
        <ProductGroup>Music</ProductGroup>
        <Title>Sidewinder</Title>
      </ItemAttributes>
    </Item>
    <Item>
      <ASIN>B00004UD4Z</ASIN>
      <DetailPageURL>http://www.amazon.com/exec/obidos/redirect?tag=webservices-
20%26link_code=xm2%26camp=2025%26creative=165953%26path=http://www.amazon.com/gp/
redirect.html%253fASIN=B00004UD4Z%2526location=/o/ASIN/
B00004UD4Z%25253FSubscriptionId=1A7XKHR5BYD0WPJVQEG2</DetailPageURL>
```

```
        <ItemAttributes>
          <Artist>Reuben Wilson</Artist>
          <ProductGroup>Music</ProductGroup>
          <Title>Groove Grease</Title>
        </ItemAttributes>
      </Item>
```

The SimilarityLookup operation gives developers more flexibility than users get on Amazon.com. It can take a list of up to ten ASINs and return similarities that are the intersection of all the sets of similarities from each ASIN in the request. However, it can be a bit tricky to find sets of ASINs that have similarities in common.

If we take two very unrelated ASINs from two different Search Indexes, such as a train toy and a plasma TV, the intersection will almost certainly be empty:

```
http://webservices.amazon.com/onca/xml?Service=AWSECommerceService&
SubscriptionId=1A7XKHR5BYD0WPJVQEG2&AssociateTag=ws&Operation=SimilarityLookup&
ItemId=B000065CML,B000233YDK&ResponseGroup=Small&SimilarityType=Intersection&
Version=2005-02-23
```

Indeed, the result is the AWS.ECommerceService.NoSimilarities error:

```
<Errors>
 <Error>
  <Code>AWS.ECommerceService.NoSimilarities</Code>
  <Message>There are no similar items for these ASINs: B000065CML, B000233YDK.</
Message>
 </Error>
</Errors>
```

But even if the items are in the same Search Index, it can hard to find items that have similarities in common.

> One tactic for finding items that will return an intersection of similar items on a SimilarityLookup is to do an ItemSearch operation and specify the Similarities Response Group. A list of similar items is returned for each item in the response. If any two or more items have the same similar items in the request, those ASINs will yield an intersection if used in a SimilarityLookup.

SimilarityLookup also lets you return a random list of similarities belonging to each ASIN in your request by specifying SimilarityType=Random.

Code Sample: Adding Similarities To Apparel.php

A natural place to offer similarities is when people are shopping for clothing. It's straightforward to add a similarities link to example 8-2 which will give customers the opportunity to find items similar to one they find while browsing.

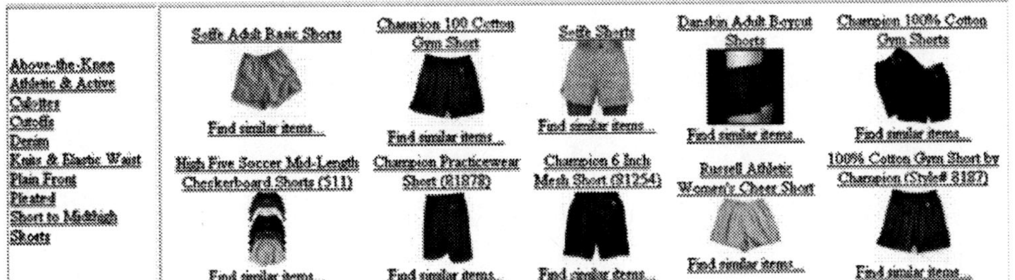

Figure 8-4 The "Find similar items" link added to example 8-2

In the new version of example 8-2, we add a "Find similar items" link underneath each item (Figure 8-4). The link contains the ASIN of the item. When the user clicks on the link to find similarities for a specific item, a new window appears with the target item in the left window and any similarities in the right window (Figure 8-5). The user can explore further similarities by clicking on the similarities link under those items as well.

Only a few additions were required to add similarities to example 8-2. The major addition was a Multioperation request that does an ItemLookup to retrieve the details of the target ASIN and a SimilarityLookup to retrieve any similarities.

```
$request='http://webservices.amazon.com/onca/xml?Service=AWSECommerceService&
AssociateTag='.ASSOCIATES_ID.'&SubscriptionId='.SUBID.'&
Operation=ItemLookup,SimilarityLookup&ItemLookup.1.ResponseGroup=Small,Images&
ItemLookup.1.ItemId='.$sim.'&SimilarityLookup.1.ItemId='.$sim.'&
SimilarityLookup.1.ResponseGroup=Small,Images&Version='.VERSION;
```

The ItemLookup response goes in the left window, and the SimilarityLookup

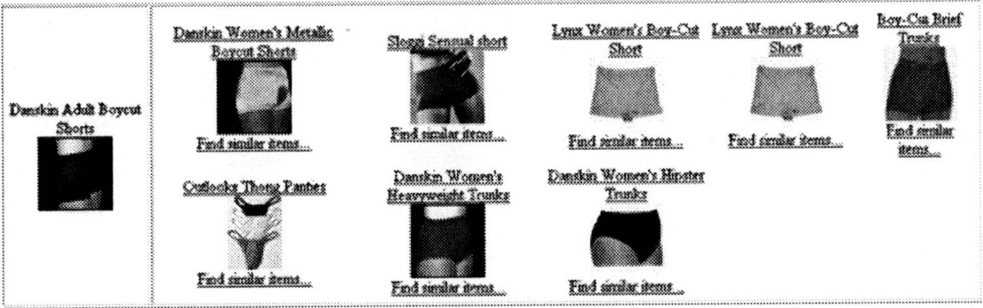

Figure 8-5 The similarities window for a pair of women's shorts

response in the right window (Figure 8-5).

The added routine to display the ItemLookup response in the left window is called theLeftSim() and does nothing more than display the contents of the ItemLookup request on the target ASIN.

```
function theLeftSim() {
    global $Result;

    // Use the image placeholder if there's no image
    if
(isset($Result['MultiOperationResponse']['ItemLookupResponse']['Items'][0]['Item'][0]
['SmallImage']['URL']))
    {
        $image='<img src="'.
$Result["MultiOperationResponse"]["ItemLookupResponse"]["Items"][0]["Item"][0]["Small
Image"]["URL"].'" />';
    } else {
        $image='<img src="'.NOIMAGE_MED.'" />';
    }

    $title =
$Result["MultiOperationResponse"]["ItemLookupResponse"]["Items"][0]["Item"][0]["ItemA
ttributes"]["Title"];

    // Display the contents of the ItemLookup response
    echo '<div style="text-align: center;">'.$title.'</div><div style="text-align:
center;">'.$image.'</div>';

}
```

The SimilarityLookup operation returns almost the exact same XML structure as the ItemSearch operation, so all I had to do was add a couple of lines to the existing theItemWindow() function so that it could handle the SimilarityLookup response.

One line lets us use the existing theItemWindow() display code:

```
$lookup = (empty($sim)) ? 'ItemSearchResponse' : 'SimilarityLookupResponse';
```

Another additional line checks to see if no similarities are found. When that happens, the AWS.ECommerceService.NoSimilarities error code is returned).

```
if
(isset($Result['MultiOperationResponse']['SimilarityLookupResponse']['Items'][0]['Req
uest']['Errors']['Error'][0]['Code']) and
($Result['MultiOperationResponse']['SimilarityLookupResponse']['Items'][0]['Request']
['Errors']['Error'][0]['Code'] == 'AWS.ECommerceService.NoSimilarities') )
        {
        echo '<td><div style="text-align: center;">There are no similar products to
display</div></td>';
        }
```

The revised theItemWindow() function uses the $lookup variable to switch between displaying the ItemSearch response and the SimilarityLookup response.

```
function theItemWindow() {
    global $Result;
```

```
    global $bn;
    global $sim;

    $lookup = (empty($sim)) ? 'ItemSearchResponse' : 'SimilarityLookupResponse';

    echo '<table cellspacing="2" cellpadding="2"><tr>';

    if
(isset($Result['MultiOperationResponse']['SimilarityLookupResponse']['Items'][0]['Req
uest']['Errors']['Error'][0]['Code']) and
($Result['MultiOperationResponse']['SimilarityLookupResponse']['Items'][0]['Request']
['Errors']['Error'][0]['Code'] == 'AWS.ECommerceService.NoSimilarities') ) {
        echo '<td><div style="text-align: center;">There are no similar products to
display</div></td>';
    } else {
        $rowcount=0;
        if ($bn != FIRST_TIME or (!empty($sim))) {
            foreach ($Result['MultiOperationResponse'][$lookup]['Items'][0]['Item']
as $item) {
                if (isset($item['SmallImage']['URL'])) {
                    $image='<img src="'.$item["SmallImage"]["URL"].'" />';
                } else {
                    $image='<img src="'.NOIMAGE_MED.'" />';
                }
                $title = '<a href="'.$item["DetailPageURL"].'" target="_blank">'.
$item["ItemAttributes"]["Title"].'</a>';
                $simlink = '<a href="apparel.php?sim='.$item["ASIN"][0].'" target="_
blank">Find similar items...</a>';
                if (is_int($rowcount/5)) echo '</tr><tr>';

                echo '<td><div style="text-align: center;">'.$title.'</div><div
style="text-align: center;">'.$image.'</div><div style="text-align: center;">'.
$simlink.'</td>';
                $rowcount++;
            }
        } else {
            echo '<td><div style="text-align: center;">Choose a category on the
left</div></td>';
        }
    }

    echo '</tr></table>';

}
```

Getting Help With The Help Operation

The Help operation returns basic parameter information for any E-Commerce Service 4.0 operation or Response Group. It is designed primarily for use by developers who are designing integrated development environment (IDE) toolkits or similar types of developer tools. Unlike the other E-Commerce Service operations, the Help operation does not offer any way to setup a purchase from Amazon, nor does it return any item, customer, or seller information, so it really is just a documentation tool.

Element	Description
HelpType	The type of help you want. Value is either "Operation" or "ResponseGroup"
About	The name of the operation or Response Group you want help for

Table 8-2 The Help operation parameters

For Response Groups, the Help operation returns a list of E-Commerce Service operations that it is allowed to be used with, and a list of all possible data elements returned the Response Group.

Suppose we want to find out what is returned by the SalesRank Response Group and which operations it can be used with.

```
http://webservices.amazon.com/onca/xml?Service=AWSECommerceService&
SubscriptionId=1A7XKHR5BYD0WPJVQEG2&Operation=Help&HelpType=ResponseGroup&
About=SalesRank&Version=2005-02-23
```

The Help operation uses only the Help Response Group and has no optional parameters. The result is the list of operations that are allowed to use the SalesRank Response Group, and a list of all the possible elements that might be included if the SalesRank Response Group is used in an operation request.

```
<ValidOperations>
        <Operation>SimilarityLookup</Operation>
        <Operation>ItemLookup</Operation>
        <Operation>ItemSearch</Operation>
        <Operation>ListLookup</Operation>
      </ValidOperations>
      <Elements>
        <Element>Errors/Error/Message</Element>
        <Element>Item/SalesRank</Element>
        <Element>Items/TotalResults</Element>
        <Element>Arguments/Argument/Value</Element>
        <Element>Errors/Error/Code</Element>
        <Element>OperationRequest/UserAgent</Element>
        <Element>Items/TotalPages</Element>
        <Element>Request/IsValid</Element>
        <Element>OperationRequest/RequestId</Element>
        <Element>Arguments/Argument/Name</Element>
      </Elements>
```

Note that the list of data elements are returned with XPath-style pathnames so that developers can more easily use them to link directly to the elements in an XML response.

For operations, the Help operation returns the list of required parameters, the list of optional parameters, and the list of default and optional Response Groups that are usable with the operation.

```
http://webservices.amazon.com/onca/
xml?Service=AWSECommerceService&SubscriptionId=1A7XKHR5BYDOWPJVQEG2&Operation=Help&He
lpType=Operation&About=SellerLookup&Version=2005-02-23
```

The response includes all available parameters, including parameters like Validate and Style which can be used with any operation.

```
<OperationInformation>
  <Name>SellerLookup</Name>
  <RequiredParameters>
    <Parameter>SellerId</Parameter>
    <Parameter>SubscriptionId</Parameter>
  </RequiredParameters>
  <AvailableParameters>
    <Parameter>AssociateTag</Parameter>
    <Parameter>ContentType</Parameter>
    <Parameter>FeedbackPage</Parameter>
    <Parameter>Marketplace</Parameter>
    <Parameter>Style</Parameter>
    <Parameter>Validate</Parameter>
    <Parameter>Version</Parameter>
    <Parameter>XMLEscaping</Parameter>
  </AvailableParameters>
  <DefaultResponseGroups>
    <ResponseGroup>Request</ResponseGroup>
    <ResponseGroup>Seller</ResponseGroup>
  </DefaultResponseGroups>
  <AvailableResponseGroups>
    <ResponseGroup>Request</ResponseGroup>
    <ResponseGroup>Seller</ResponseGroup>
  </AvailableResponseGroups>
</OperationInformation>
```

TransactionLookup

As you'll soon learn in the next Chapter (see Chapter 9, "Managing Inventory Using AIMS"), Transaction IDs are created whenever a customer buys one of your Amazon listings.

The TransactionLookup operation takes a list of up to ten Transaction IDs as input and returns the details of the sale minus any customer information.

```
http://xml.amazon.com/onca/xml?Service=AWSECommerceService&
Operation=TransactionLookup&SubscriptionId=1A7XKHR5BYDOWPJVQEG2&
TransactionId=058-1987944-0858153&Version=2005-02-23
```

The response includes the pricing details, the date of the sale, and shipping charges.

```
<Transaction>
```

```
<TransactionId>058-1987944-0858153</TransactionId>
<SellerId>A3ICGCER1Q4UB7</SellerId>
<Condition>Complete</Condition>
<TransactionDate>2005-03-06T17:10:10</TransactionDate>
<TransactionDateEpoch>1110129010</TransactionDateEpoch>
<SellerName>sashimikid</SellerName>
<Totals>
  <Total>
    <Amount>1149</Amount>
    <CurrencyCode>USD</CurrencyCode>
    <FormattedPrice>$11.49</FormattedPrice>
  </Total>
  <Subtotal>
    <Amount>900</Amount>
    <CurrencyCode>USD</CurrencyCode>
    <FormattedPrice>$9.00</FormattedPrice>
  </Subtotal>
  <Tax>
    <Amount>0</Amount>
    <CurrencyCode>USD</CurrencyCode>
    <FormattedPrice>$0.00</FormattedPrice>
  </Tax>
  <ShippingCharge>
    <Amount>249</Amount>
    <CurrencyCode>USD</CurrencyCode>
    <FormattedPrice>$2.49</FormattedPrice>
  </ShippingCharge>
  <Promotion>
    <Amount>0</Amount>
    <CurrencyCode>USD</CurrencyCode>
    <FormattedPrice>$0.00</FormattedPrice>
  </Promotion>
</Totals>
<TransactionItems>
  <TransactionItem>
    <TransactionItemId>mokptrntsqu</TransactionItemId>
    <Quantity>1</Quantity>
    <UnitPrice>
      <Amount>900</Amount>
      <CurrencyCode>USD</CurrencyCode>
      <FormattedPrice>$9.00</FormattedPrice>
    </UnitPrice>
    <TotalPrice>
      <Amount>900</Amount>
      <CurrencyCode>USD</CurrencyCode>
      <FormattedPrice>$9.00</FormattedPrice>
    </TotalPrice>
  </TransactionItem>
</TransactionItems>
<Shipments>
  <Shipment>
    <Condition>Shipped</Condition>
    <DeliveryMethod>Mail</DeliveryMethod>
    <ShipmentItems>
```

```
        <TransactionItemId>mokptrntsqu</TransactionItemId>
      </ShipmentItems>
    </Shipment>
  </Shipments>
</Transaction>
```

Exercises For The Reader

Modify the ProductSense code in Chapter Three and add a similarities button to each product that is displayed.

Create a PHP (or Javascript) application that uses the Help operation to return the complete set of parameter choices for any operation. Have it return clickable sample requests for SOAP, REST, and XSLT as well.

CHAPTER 9

Amazon Seller Services

If it gets you profit, sell your own mother
—Ferengi Rule Of Acquisition #73

As I've shown in previous chapters, the Amazon Associates program is an easy way to indirectly sell goods using Amazon E-Commerce Service. While you don't have to ship products to anyone, nor deal with the hassles of returns, payments, or other retail logistics, you also have to move a lot of Amazon product to see any appreciable income.

Amazon's Seller programs offer a potentially more profitable route. Why not sell your own products on Amazon.com? The advantage of selling products on Amazon's web sites is that you get the eyeballs of Amazon's 20 million+ registered users and your products are searchable via Amazon's search engine, one of the most heavily used retail search engines.

In the Amazon seller model, you post your new and used products on Amazon's site and get to keep the money from the sale minus commissions. It's a good deal for certain types of retailers, especially businesses specializing in small, high-volume, items such as BMVD.

> The acronym for "books, music, video and DVD" items is BMVD. Who knew?

Amazon's Seller programs have attracted major retail partners as well as numerous small and medium-sized retailers who display and sell their inventory on Amazon.

The Amazon Seller APIs

Amazon offers two different APIs for sellers, the Merchants@ API and the Amazon Inventory Management System (AIMS) API.

For Merchants@ Pro Merchants and Merchants@ Sellers, the Merchants@ version 2.0 API, a full SOAP API, was launched in September, 2004. The previous version 1. 0 API, which was a SOAP-like API (no WSDL support was provided), is still in use, but deprecated (I don't cover the 1.0 API in this book). The Merchants@ API is only available to sellers on Amazon.com -- none of the international Amazon sites have it.

The Amazon Inventory Management System (AIMS), despite the lofty-sounding name, was Amazon's first seller API and is only available to Marketplace Pro Merchant sellers. The API is rather antiquated, using HTTPS POST calls to specific URLs on Amazon.com. AIMS is available for sellers on all the international Amazon sites (except China), as well as Amazon.com

Seller Services API	Launched	API Technology
Amazon Inventory Management System (AIMS) API	Fall 2000	HTTPS POST
Merchants@ API 1.0	Fall 2002	SOAP (no WSDL support)
Merchants@ API 2.0	Summer 2004	SOAP

Table 9-1 Amazon Seller Services APIs

Types of Amazon sellers

As discussed in Chapter One, there are three basic types of third-party sellers on Amazon: individual sellers, Pro Merchant sellers, and Merchants@ Sellers (a fourth seller is Amazon itself). Pro Merchants are further divided into Marketplace Pro Merchants and Merchants@ Pro Merchants.

> There are individual and Marketplace Pro Merchants on the five international Amazon sites (Amazon.de, Amazon.co.uk, Amazon.fr, Amazon.ca, and Amazon.co.jp) but Merchants@ Pro Merchants and Merchants@ Sellers are only on Amazon.com

Each type of third-party seller is charged certain commissions and fees in order to sell their products on Amazon.com, and is subject to certain limitations in how and where they can sell products on Amazon.

Individual Sellers

Anyone with a checking account can sell items on Amazon. Individuals who choose to list items for sale on Amazon.com have no up front cost and pay Amazon only a small commission if they successfully sell a listed item.

> Individual selling is available on all the international Amazon sites as well as Amazon.com.

Individuals can only list items for sale in the Amazon Marketplace. Only items in certain product categories (Search Indexes) can be listed, and items must have an existing Amazon ASIN in order to be listed. There are also limits on the number of items individuals may have for sale at one time. You can quickly access the Marketplace listings for a particular item on Amazon.com by finding the item and clicking on the "used & new" link (see Figure 9-1).

Spider-Man 2 (Superbit Collection) (2004)
List Price: $29.96
Price: $22.47 & eligible for FREE Super Saver Shipping on orders over $25. See details.
You Save: $7.49 (25%)
Availability: Usually ships within 24 hours
Want it delivered Wednesday, January 12? Order it in the next 18 hours and 59 minutes, and choose One-Day Shipping at checkout. See details.
see larger picture
64 used & new from $21.46
Edition: DVD
Clicking on the "used & new" link brings up Marketplace listings for that item

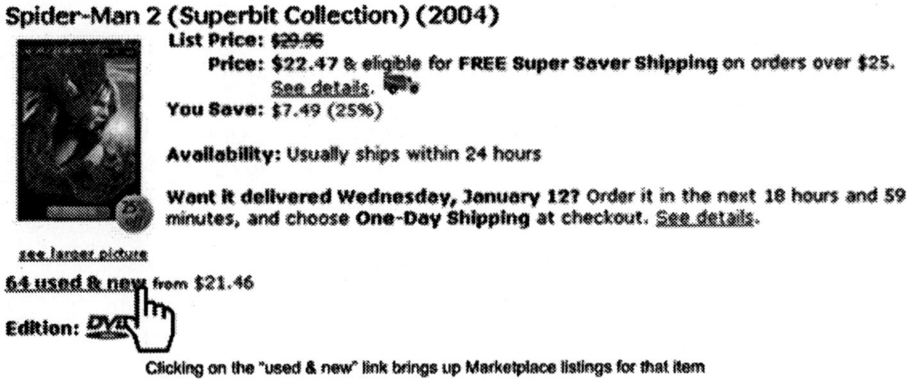

Figure 9-1 Accessing Marketplace listings for an item on Amazon.com

If an individual successfully sells an item, they are charged $0.99 plus a commission of 6 to 15 percent of the sales price (depending of type of product sold). The commission is charged to their Amazon account. All of these financial transactions are handled through Amazon Payment Services.

Amazon Payment Services

All Sellers on Amazon.com have to setup an account with Amazon's Payment Services. Amazon's Payment Services is a credit-card based service, similar in concept to Paypal. In order to use Amazon's Payment service, you must provide a checking account number (a U.S. checking account for amazon.com, a UK checking account for amazon.co.uk, etc.).

When a customer comes to Amazon.com and purchases your product using their credit card, Amazon charges their credit card and then uses ACH (Automated Clearing House) to deposit the money in your seller account. For Pro Merchants, there is a commission charged to use Amazon Payment Services.

Sellers don't have to use Amazon Payment Services for their transactions but they still must setup their Amazon Payment Services account.

After an individual seller ships an item to a buyer, Amazon forwards a shipping credit to the seller which depends on the type and weight of the item sold.

> Refer to this page for the latest shipping credits table: http://www.amazon.com/exec/obidos/tg/browse/-/1161252

Officially, there is no programmatic interface for individual sellers. Individual sellers must go to Amazon.com and use the web forms provided to manage their inventory.

> On Amazon.com, Amazon customers may access their seller web forms at this URL: http://s1.amazon.com/exec/varzea/subst/your-account/manage-your-seller-account.html

Unofficially, it's possible to inspect the HTML used in those web forms and create an application to automate the listings. This is left as an exercise for the reader.

Marketplace Pro Merchants

Anyone with a checking account can also become a Marketplace Pro Merchant. However, the commissions and fees are designed so that typically only volume sellers will find it profitable. Marketplace Pro Merchants may sell their items in the Amazon Marketplace, Amazon Auctions, the Amazon zShops, and in some Amazon Stores by creating, or adding to, product pages. This is called "Creating a Product Detail Page."

> There is currently no programmatic API for Pro Merchant Sellers to create product pages, but they can do it through their account's web interface. If you have a Pro Merchant account, you can access the product page creation interface at this URL: http://selection.amazon.com/gp/seller/validate-pro-merchant.html

zShops are a listing area on Amazon.com that is designed specifically for third-party sellers to display their listings. zShops offer third-party sellers a place to list items that Amazon does not sell (though they may list items Amazon sells as well).

Once you start listing items for sale in zShops, you'll also find that you have your own Zshops "storefront", which is a customizable page with your Amazon nickname on it.

> Your Amazon nickname is set in your Amazon account preferences.

zShops storefronts are located at www.amazon.com/shops/[your Amazon nickname]:

```
http://www.amazon.com/shops/sashimikid
```

The cost to become a Pro Merchant Seller is $39 a month plus a 6%-15% commission for every item you sell. The commission depends on the product category of the item. Sellers may have an unlimited number of Marketplace and zShops listings.

Amazon provides a set of web pages on Amazon.com where Marketplace Pro Merchants can manage their inventory, and they also may use the Amazon Inventory Management System API. When you sign-up to become a Pro Merchant, you'll be able to use your username and password to access the AIMS.

Merchants@ Pro Merchants

You cannot sign up to become a Merchants@ Pro Merchant. Merchants@ Pro Merchants are personally invited by Amazon to sell. Amazon recruits Merchants@ Pro Merchants to fill out particular product categories on Amazon.com.

Merchants@ Pro Merchants may sell in the Marketplace as well as in any Amazon Store by creating, or adding to, custom product pages. They are also allowed to sell in Amazon Auctions. Merchants@ Pro Merchants have storefront pages that are typically within a specific Amazon store (See Figure 1-6 in Chapter One for an image of a Merchants@ storefront).

Once Amazon selects a merchant to become a Merchants@ Pro Merchant, the cost is the same as for Marketplace Pro Merchants: $39 a month plus a 6%-15% commission for every item you sell. The commission depends on the product category of the item.

Inventory management for Merchants@ Pro Merchants is done at a special web site called Seller Central located at *sellercentral.amazon.com*. Merchants@ Pro Merchants can choose to use the web-based inventory management interfaces in Seller Central, or they can use the Merchants@ API to automate inventory management (or they can use both). The Merchants@ API includes a sandbox for testing called the Merchant Integration Platform (MIP).

Merchants@ Sellers

At the highest tier are Merchants@ Sellers. This status is available only through special contractual agreements with Amazon and is typically only offered to larger retailers. Companies such as Nordstrom and Peet's Coffee & Tea are typical examples of these Amazon partners though there are smaller companies in the program as well.

Merchants@ Sellers can create their own web pages on Amazon.com and typically hire third-party system integrators to tie their backend inventory management systems into Amazon.

Like Merchants@ Pro Merchants, Merchants@ Sellers also may manage their inventory using the web-based interfaces at Seller Central (*sellercentral.amazon.com*) or use the SOAP API. They may also test their Merchants@ Seller applications using the Amazon Merchant Integration Platform (MIP) sandbox.

Amazon Advantage

The Advantage program lets you sell your own CDs, videos, or books on Amazon.com but have Amazon manage the distribution for you. Advantage is designed primarily for self-publishers who can afford the steep commission costs associated with this program. Amazon charges 55% of the list price as a commission on each sale. There is no API for Amazon Advantage.

The Amazon Inventory Management System API

When Marketplace Pro Merchants post items for sale on Amazon, their inventory is managed by Amazon's backend systems. Amazon provides a web interface to this system so that sellers can view and manage their listings at *www.amazon.com/seller-account* (Figure 9-2).

For Marketplace Pro Sellers, Amazon's Inventory Management System (AIMS) API exposes these inventory management facilities. So, it's possible to automate the management of your inventory without having to use the web interface. This is useful if you want to integrate your existing inventory systems with Amazon's management system, if you want to create your own richer interface for inventory management, or if you just like the convenience of maintaining your own inventory system.

AIMS lets Marketplace Pro Sellers post inventory for sale in the Amazon Marketplace or zShops, and offers the following types of operations:

- Upload items to list for sale on Amazon.
- Modify or delete inventory items you've already listed for sale on Amazon
- Report on the status of requests you've made to list, modify, or delete items
- Retrieve reports of items ordered
- Retrieve reports of items sold
- Send refunds to customers
- Retrieve reports on the status of refunds

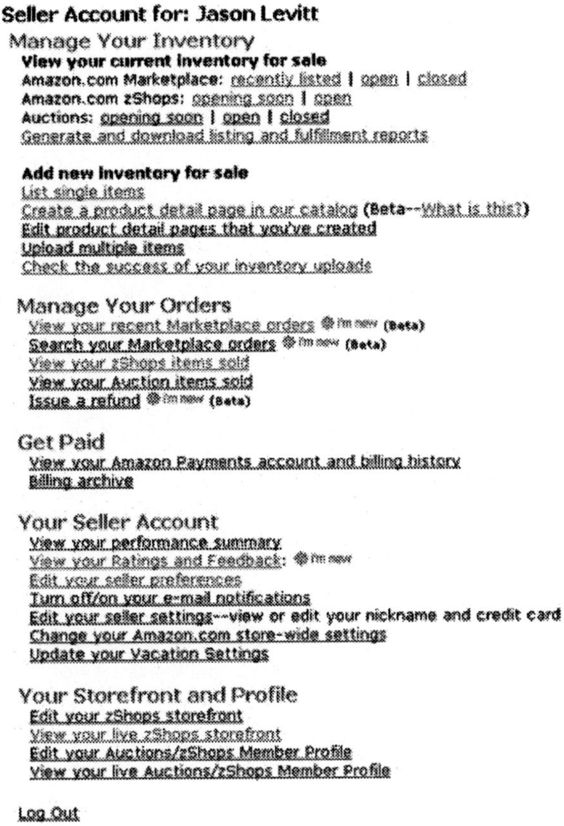

Seller Account for: Jason Levitt

Manage Your Inventory

View your current inventory for sale
Amazon.com Marketplace: recently listed | open | closed
Amazon.com zShops: opening soon | open
Auctions: opening soon | open | closed
Generate and download listing and fulfillment reports

Add new inventory for sale
List single items
Create a product detail page in our catalog (Beta--What is this?)
Edit product detail pages that you've created
Upload multiple items
Check the success of your inventory uploads

Manage Your Orders
View your recent Marketplace orders I'm new (Beta)
Search your Marketplace orders I'm new (Beta)
View your zShops items sold
View your Auction items sold
Issue a refund I'm new (Beta)

Get Paid
View your Amazon Payments account and billing history
Billing archive

Your Seller Account
View your performance summary
View your Ratings and Feedback: I'm new
Edit your seller preferences
Turn off/on your e-mail notifications
Edit your seller settings--view or edit your nickname and credit card
Change your Amazon.com store-wide settings
Update your Vacation Settings

Your Storefront and Profile
Edit your zShops storefront
View your live zShops storefront
Edit your Auctions/zShops Member Profile
View your live Auctions/zShops Member Profile

Log Out

Figure 9-2 The Marketplace Pro Merchant web interface

Accessing The Amazon Inventory Management System

Amazon's Inventory Management System API was the first API for Sellers and is still the only API available to Marketplace Pro Merchants. Introduced in 2000, it's already showing its age. The API mimics the action of a user managing inventory via web pages by using HTTPS POST calls. Developers put various parameter arguments into HTTP headers and the inventory details (if any) in the body of the POST.

Authentication is always required. You encode your Pro Merchant login credentials in a format known as HTTP Basic Authentication which is a base 64 encoded string sent as an HTTP header.

HTTP Basic Authentication is defined in RFC 2617, available at http://www.faqs.org/rfcs/rfc2617.html

Besides the Basic Authentication header, two other parameters are always required, the Content Type header and the Cookie header (see the AIMS reference manual in Appendix J for details).

Operation URL	Purpose
INVENTORY OPERATIONS	
https://secure.amazon.com/exec/panama/seller-admin/catalog-upload/add-modify-delete	Should be used when a seller has large amount of inventory add, modify, or delete in their Amazon Marketplace or zShops listings.
https://secure.amazon.com/exec/panama/seller-admin/catalog-upload/modify-only	Should be used when a seller wants to modify or delete inventory but don't want to supply all the information required by the add-modify-delete URL above.
https://secure.amazon.com/exec/panama/seller-admin/catalog-upload/purge-replace	Should be used when a seller wants to delete all of their current inventory and replace it, all in one request.
INVENTORY STATUS REPORT OPERATIONS	
https://secure.amazon.com/exec/panama/seller-admin/catalog-upload/get-batches	Should be used when a seller wants to check the status of inventory upload requests.
https://secure.amazon.com/exec/panama/seller-admin/download/errorlog	Should be used when a seller wants to download an error log of problems that occurred with an inventory upload
https://secure.amazon.com/exec/panama/seller-admin/download/quickfix	Should be used when a seller wants to download a subset of the errorlog operation above containing just the listings of inventory that were not successfully uploaded.
ORDER STATUS REPORT OPERATIONS	
https://secure.amazon.com/exec/panama/seller-admin/manual-reports/get-report-status	Should be used when a seller wants to retrieve a list of available order or refund reports.
https://secure.amazon.com/exec/panama/seller-admin/download/report	Should be used when a seller wants to download specific order or refund reports
https://secure.amazon.com/exec/panama/seller-admin/manual-reports/generate-report-now'	Should be used when a seller wants to generate a report of their orders or open listings
REFUNDS	
https://secure.amazon.com/exec/panama/seller-admin/catalog-upload/batch-refund	Should be used when a seller needs to issue a large number of customer refunds at one time.

Table 9-2 Operation URLs for Amazon Inventory Management System

The various API function operations are defined by specific URLs. For example, to request a specific order report, you would use the report operation by sending a request to this URL:

```
https://secure.amazon.com/exec/panama/seller-admin/download/report
```

There are ten operations, and thus ten corresponding URLs

Inventory Spreadsheets

You send your inventory additions, changes, and modifications to Amazon using spreadsheets that are sent in your requests. Amazon accepts a pre-defined format of

Email Address	Type of Spreadsheet Returned
bookloader-template-request@amazon.com	Spreadsheet designed specifically for book sellers.
uploader-template-request@amazon.com	A general-purpose spreadsheet that can be used with all types of products, including books.
bulk-template-request@amazon.com	Spreadsheet for Amazon Auctions selling.

Table 9-3 Where to find spreadsheet templates for Amazon Inventory Management System

either tab-delimited, or UIEE format, spreadsheets.

```
Amazon uses its own subset of UIEE format that is known in the industry as "Amazon
UIEE" format. UIEE, Universal Information Exchange Environment, is a data encoding
standard developed in 1989 to exchange information about used books. It's scope has
since broadened to include other types of products but is still mainly used by book
dealers. More information is available at the UIEE web site, www.uiee.com.
```

Amazon will email you samples of their spreadsheets by sending a blank email message to any of the email addresses in Table 9-3. Amazon doesn't return samples of UIEE format spreadsheets.

Accessing AIMS On International Amazon Sites

The AIMS API is available on all of the international Amazon sites (except China). However, in order to use it, you must purchase a Marketplace Pro Merchant subscription on each site that you intend to sell products on.

> For tips on signing up on non-English language Amazon sites, see the "International Associates IDs" section in Chapter 7.

Once you have your Marketplace Pro Merchant username and login, you can access the AIMS API using the same URLs that are in Table 9-2. Simply replace the domain name, secure.amazon.com, with the appropriate international Amazon site name, for example, secure.amazon.de. The only exception is Japan, where the domain name should be vendornet.amazon.co.jp instead of secure.amazon.co.jp.

Similarly, Amazon will email you spreadsheet templates by sending blank email messages to the addresses in Table 9-3. Simply replace the domain name amazon.com with the domain name of the international Amazon site. For example, sending a blank email address to uploader-template-request@amazon.co.jp will email you back a spreadsheet template for use with AIMS on Amazon.co.jp.

AIMS Choreography

Unlike Amazon E-Commerce Service, AIMS is a batch processing system. That means that the various tasks you request actually get done some significant amount of time after you make the initial request. Tasks such as open listings generation requests, refunds, and inventory upload and modification requests are queued along with thousands of others received by Amazon and are processed at some point in the future.

Thus, the choreography for using AIMS -- the steps you take to get a task done -- involve a series of requests. You make the request, then check the status of your request, and finally, download the results (if any).

Figure 9-3 AIMS choreography

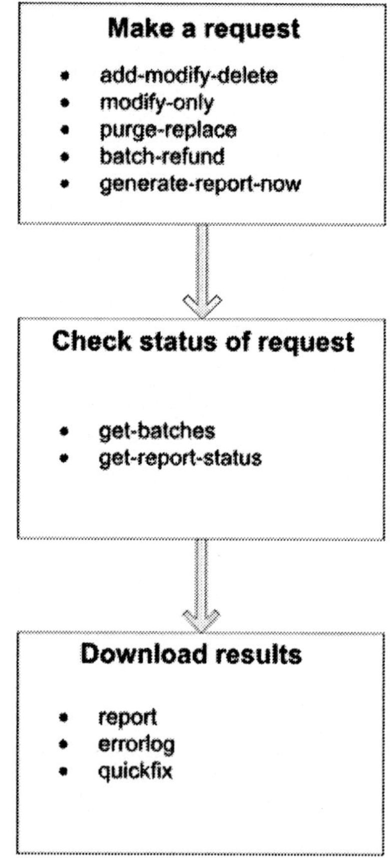

An AIMS API PHP Class

Requests to AIMS are made by making HTTPS POST requests to the URLs in Table 9-2. The request parameters are placed in HTTP headers, and inventory data (if any) is placed in the body of the POST.

Deriving a useful PHP class to use to send requests and receive responses to AIMS is straightforward. The reference manual in Appendix J outlines the inventory operations along with their various parameters. I call the class MarketplaceProMerchant. Methods for the class are listed in Table 9-4.

Method	Public/ Private	Purpose
BatchRefund	Public	Send a batch refund request
GenerateReport	Public	Request report generation
GetPendingUploadsCount	Public	Retrieve the number of inventory uploads currently pending processing
GetReport	Public	Retrieve the specified report
GetReportIds	Public	Retrieve a list of available report ids
GetUploadStatus	Public	Fetch the processing status of an upload
InventoryError	Public	Fetch quickfix or errorlog errors
InventoryUpload	Public	Upload inventory spreadsheets
AmazonPost	Private	Send a request via HTTPS POST to Amazon
parse	Private	Parse the response sent back by Amazon

Table 9-4 Methods of the AIMS API class

The constructor function for the MarketplaceProMerchant class sets up the common HTTP headers required by all AIMS requests, the Basic Authentication, Content Type and Cookie headers. It takes your Marketplace Pro Merchant username and password as parameters.

```
function MarketplaceProMerchant($username, $password)
    {
        $this->CommonHeaders[] = "Authorization: Basic " . base64_encode($username.':
'.$password);
        $this->CommonHeaders[] = "Content-Type: text/xml";
        $this->CommonHeaders[] = "Cookie: x-
main=YvjPkwfntqDKunOQEmVRPcTTZDMe?Tn?;ubid-main=002-8989859-9917520;ubid-tacbus=019-
5423258-4241018;x-tacbus=vtm4d53DvX\@Sc9LxTnAnxsFL3DorwxJa; ubid-tcmacb=087-8055947-
0795529;ubid-ty2kacbus=161-5477122-2773524; session-id=087-178254-5924832; session-
id-time=950660664";
    }
```

The bizarre looking cookie value is required by Amazon's servers in order to identify the request as an AIMS request. The meaning of the cookie's contents is proprietary.

Sending and Receiving With AmazonPost

The most problematic method is AmazonPost since it does the actual sending and receiving via HTTPS. AmazonPost mimics the interaction of your web browser with a web site when you do an HTTP POST of a web form.

In PHP, the common ways to send and receive via HTTPS are either with the Curl library or with fsockopen(). Either way requires the addition of explicit support for SSL to your PHP installation. (see Chapter Two for details on PHP installation requirements).

The AmazonPost function takes three arguments: $url, the Amazon URL (from Table 9-2); $Headers, the request parameters encoded in an array of HTTP headers; And $Data, the spreadsheet (if any) to upload. The function returns the Amazon response or false on failure.

```
function AmazonPost($url, $Headers, $Data = null)
    {
        // Add the operation-specific HTTP headers to the array of common headers
        $Headers = (is_null($Headers)) ? $this->CommonHeaders : array_merge($this->
CommonHeaders, $Headers);

        // If this fails, then either Curl or SSL has not been enabled in PHP
        if (!$session = curl_init($url))
        {
            return false;
        }

        // Set various Curl parameters
        curl_setopt($session, CURLOPT_HTTPHEADER, $Headers);
        curl_setopt($session, CURLOPT_RETURNTRANSFER, true);
        curl_setopt($session, CURLOPT_SSL_VERIFYPEER, false);
        curl_setopt($session, CURLOPT_SSLVERSION, 3);
        curl_setopt($session, CURLOPT_POST, true);
        curl_setopt($session, CURLOPT_FOLLOWLOCATION, true);
        curl_setopt($session, CURLOPT_TIMEOUT, TIMEOUT);

        // Add spreadsheet data
        if (!is_null($Data))
        {
            curl_setopt($session, CURLOPT_POSTFIELDS, $Data);
        }

        if (!($data = curl_exec($session)))
        {
            curl_close($session);
            return false;
        }
        else
        {
            curl_close($session);
            return $data;
        }
```

```
    }
```

The various Curl setopt() calls handle all the HTTPS POST logic for us allowing for a fairly simple and elegant call.

InventoryUpload

Uploading, deleting, or modifying inventory on Amazon requires that we send our spreadsheet to Amazon along with some request parameters. The InventoryUpload method makes this easy by calling AmazonPost with the appropriate parameters. InventoryUpload takes a task name (one of the three inventory upload functions), a pointer to a file or string with our data in it, and a boolean that says whether the data is a string or the name of a file that must be retrieved.

```
// Convenient defines
define('INVENTORY_ADD_MODIFY_DELETE', 1);
define('INVENTORY_MODIFY_ONLY', 2);
define('INVENTORY_PURGE_REPLACE', 3);

function InventoryUpload($Task, $Data, $Isfile)
    {
        // Parameters for inventory uploads
        $headers = array();
        $headers[] = "UploadFor: " . $this->UploadFor;
        $headers[] = "FileFormat: " . $this->FileFormat;

        // Data can be in either a file or string
        if ($Isfile) {
            if (!$contents = file_get_contents($Data)) {
                die('FATAL ERROR: Can not open inventory file');
            }
        } else {
            $contents=$Data;
        }

        switch ($Task)
        {
            case INVENTORY_ADD_MODIFY_DELETE:
            $headers[] = "Content-Length: " . strlen($contents);
            $url = ADDMODIFYDELETE_URL;
            break;
            case INVENTORY_MODIFY_ONLY:
            $headers[] = "Content-Length: " . strlen($contents);
            $url = MODIFYONLY_URL;
            break;
            case INVENTORY_PURGE_REPLACE:
            $headers[] = "Content-Length: " . strlen($contents);
            $url = PURGEREPLACE_URL;
            break;
            default:
            die('ERROR: Unknown task type in AmazonInventory. Task = '.$Task);
```

```
        }
        $this->rawxml = $this->AmazonPost($url, $headers, $contents);

        $this->parse();
        return ($this->records);
    }
```

The parameters to InventoryUpload are the variables UploadFor and FileFormat which have the default values of "MarketPlace" and "TabDelimited". Since they should rarely change, they are set as Public variables in the class.

Once uploaded, you use the GetUploadStatus method to find out if there were any errors in the upload. If there are errors, use the InventoryError method to retrieve the details of the errors.

```
    function GetUploadStatus($Num) {
        // Parameter for get upload status request
        $headers = array();
        $headers[] = "NumberOfBatches: " . $Num;
        // The URL of the function
        $url = GETBATCHES_URL;
        // Make the request on Amazon, parse the result
        $this->rawxml = $this->AmazonPost($url, $headers, null);
        $this->parse();
        return ($this->records);
    }

  define('GET_ERRORLOG', 1);
  define('GET_QUICKFIX', 2);

   function InventoryError($Task, $BatchId) {
        // Parameter for inventory error function
        $headers = array();
        $headers[] = "BatchId: " . $BatchId;

        // Fetch either the Error Log or Quick Fix document
        switch ($Task)
        {
            case GET_ERRORLOG:
            $url = ERRORLOG_URL;
            break;
            case GET_QUICKFIX:
            $url = QUICKFIX_URL;
            break;
        }

        // Make the request on Amazon, parse the result
        $this->rawxml = $this->AmazonPost($url, $headers, null);
        $this->parse();
        return ($this->records);
    }
```

AIMS Reports

AIMS has a number of different report types that can be requested (Table 9-5). Order reports are automatically created by Amazon as a result of customer orders. However, you can also use the GenerateReport method to have Amazon generate an order report containing all the orders customers have made during the specified number of days. Once generated, you use GetReportIds method to fetch the IDs of any available reports, and then download the report by using the GetReport method.

Batch Refund reports are automatically created as the result or your Batch Refund requests, so you cannot request generation of Batch Refund reports.

Report Name	Generated?	Purpose
Order	Yes	When customers purchase your products, this report lists their order information
BatchRefund	No	Customer refund details are returned in this report
Openlistings	Yes	A detailed list of your open listings
OpenListingsLite	Yes	A less detailed list of your open listings by SKU, Price, ASIN, and Quantity
OpenListingsLiter	Yes	A brief list of your open listings by SKU and Quantity

Table 9-5 Types of reports available in the AIMS

```
// All report types
$Reports = array('Order', 'BatchRefund', 'OpenListings', 'OpenListingsLite',
'OpenListingsLiter');

// Report types that can be generated
$ReportsGen = array('Order', 'OpenListings', 'OpenListingsLite',
'OpenListingsLiter');

 function GenerateReport ($ReportName, $NumDays) {
        global $ReportsGen;

        // Parameters for report generation
        $headers = array();
        $headers[] = "ReportName: " . $ReportName;
        $headers[] = "NumberOfDays: " . $NumDays;

        // Make sure that the report name is valid
        if (!in_array($ReportName, $ReportsGen)) {
            die('ERROR: The report name '.$ReportName.' is not valid.');
        }

        // The URL for report generation
        $url = GENERATEREPORTNOW_URL;

        // Send the request to Amazon, parse the result
```

```
        $this->rawxml = $this->AmazonPost($url, $headers, null);
        $this->parse();

        // Return the result
        return ($this->records);
    }

function GetReport($ReportId) {
        // Parameter for fetching reports
        $headers = array();
        $headers[] = "ReportID: " . $ReportId;

        // The report URL
        $url = REPORT_URL;

        // Send the request to Amazon, parse the result
        $this->rawxml = $this->AmazonPost($url, $headers, null);
        $this->parse();

        // Return the result
        return ($this->records);
    }

function GetReportIds ($ReportName, $Num) {
        global $Reports;

        // Parameter for fetching report IDs
        $headers = array();
        $headers[] = "ReportName: " . $ReportName;
        $headers[] = "NumberOfReports: " . $Num;

        // Make sure the report name is valid
        if (!in_array($ReportName, $Reports)) {
            die('ERROR: The report name '.$ReportName.' is not valid.');
        }

        // The URL for getting report IDs
        $url = GETREPORTSTATUS_URL;

        // Send the request to Amazon, parse the result
        $this->rawxml = $this->AmazonPost($url, $headers, null);
        $this->parse();
        return ($this->records);
    }
```

Batch Refunds

The BatchRefund method lets you issue refunds to your customers. In order to initiate a refund request, you must create a tab-delimited spreadsheet with the following headings:

```
order-id    payments-transaction-id    refund-amount    reason    message
```

Each line in the spreadsheet is a separate refund request. The meaning of each field is explained later in this chapter.

The BatchRefund method merely takes the spreadsheet and sends it to Amazon for processing.

```
function BatchRefund($Data, $IsFile)
  {
      $headers = array();
      // The batch refund URL
      $url = BATCHREFUND_URL;

      // The spreadsheet may be in a string or a file
      if ($IsFile) {
          if (!$contents = file_get_contents($Data)) {
              die('FATAL ERROR: Can not open the bulk refund file');
          }
      } else {
          $contents=$Data;
      }

      // The length of the spreadsheet is sent as a HTTP header
      $headers[] = "Content-Length: " . strlen($contents);

      // Make the request, parse the result
      $this->rawxml = $this->AmazonPost($url, $headers, $contents);
      $this->parse();
      return ($this->records);
  }
```

Parsing Responses

AIMS returns well-formed XML in response to requests. The response is missing the standard XML preamble, such as <?xml version="1.0"?>.

For example, here's the response for a recent list of upload status reports:

```
<Batches>
   <Batch>batchid=23655531 status=Done dateandtime=05/22/2004 14:55:13 PDT
activateditems=0 numberofwarnings=1 itemsnotacivated=1 </Batch>
   <Batch>batchid=23130731 status=Done dateandtime=05/11/2004 19:58:33 PDT
activateditems=0 numberofwarnings=1 itemsnotacivated=0 </Batch>
   <Batch>batchid=22464001 status=Done dateandtime=04/27/2004 17:26:44 PDT
activateditems=1 numberofwarnings=0 itemsnotacivated=0 </Batch>
</Batches>
```

XML purists will note that the XML is well-formed but not valid since there is no corresponding Document Type Declaration.

The range error responses is unusual, owing to the fact that AIMS is simulating a web browser's interaction with the Amazon server (see Appendix D for a list of possible error responses). The AIMS error response to invalid authentication returns an entire web page asking you to login again. Typical error responses are simplistic, generally consisting of just one tag with a text data element. This is the AIMS response when you request an invalid batch id:

```
<SecurityError>ACCESS_DENIED</SecurityError>
```

Since AIM returns relatively simple repeated data elements, it makes a good use case for regular expression parsing. This parser returns a human-readable string in the case of success or error, or an array with each array element containing one line of a report.

```
    function parse()
    {

        // Amazon sometimes returns a value of 1 when things fail
        if ($this->rawxml == '1') {
            $this->records[0]='The attempt to communicate with Amazon failed or
returned no results';
            return;
        }

        //remove extra spaces between tags (will create array elements otherwise)
        $this->rawxml = eregi_replace(">"."[[:space:]]+"."<", "><", $this->rawxml);
        //get rid of superfluous line terminators
        $this->rawxml=str_replace ("\n", " ", $this->rawxml);
        $this->rawxml=str_replace ("\r\n", " ", $this->rawxml);
        //trim anything hanging on the beginning or end
        $this->rawxml=trim($this->rawxml);

        $rarr=array();
        //removes all tags and leaves data in array elements
        $rarr=preg_split('/<[^>]+>/ix',$this->rawxml, -1, PREG_SPLIT_NO_EMPTY );

        // Interpretation
        if (isset($rarr[0])) {

            //Check for invalid user/password
            if (stristr($rarr[0], 'login')) {
                $this->records[0]='Amazon says that the username and/or password you
supplied is invalid';
            } else {

                switch ($rarr[0]) {
                    case 'FILE_NOT_FOUND':
                    $this->records[0]='Amazon returned '. $rarr[0] . ': the requested
file was not found';
                    break;
                    case 'ACCESS_DENIED':
                    $this->records[0]='Amazon returned '. $rarr[0] . ': you are
denied access to this report';
                    break;
                    case 'INVALID_BATCH':
```

```
                    $this->records[0]='Amazon returned '. $rarr[0] . ': the batch you
requested was invalid';
                    break;
                    case 'SUCCESS':
                    $this->records[0]='Amazon returned '. $rarr[0] . ': your request
succeeded';
                    break;
                    case 'CUSTOMER_UNAUTHORIZED':
                    $this->records[0]='Amazon returned '. $rarr[0] . ': you are not
authorized to access this resource';
                    break;
                    case 'NO_DEFAULT_PAYMENT':
                    $this->records[0]='Amazon returned '. $rarr[0] . ': a default
payment type is missing';
                    break;
                    case 'INVALID_LISTING_PROGRAM':
                    $this->records[0]='Amazon returned '. $rarr[0] . ': this listing
resource is invalid';
                    break;
                    case 'INVALID_FILE_FORMAT':
                    $this->records[0]='Amazon returned '. $rarr[0] . ': your file
format was invalid';
                    break;
                    default:
                    $this->records=$rarr;
                }
            }
        } else {
            $this->records[0]='Amazon returned XML tags with no data between them
which may mean that there is nothing to return.';
        }

        return;
    }
```

Managing Inventory Using AIMS

To illustrate how you can use the MarketplaceProMerchant class to post and manage inventory, we're going to post something for sale, someone will buy it, and you'll be able to manage the whole process using MarketplaceProMerchant operations.

The first step is to fill in our spreadsheet template (obtained using the addresses in Table 9-3) with the details of the product we want to post for sale. You can use Excel, OpenOffice, or virtually any other spreadsheet or text editor to edit the spreadsheet. Your file must be saved in plain text, tab-delimited, format, which is supported by all spreadsheet editors. The item I'm selling is something I call the Groovy Widget. There is no existing Amazon ASIN for it so it can only be sold in my zShop or in Amazon Auctions (AIMS does not let you access Amazon Auctions, so we'll be listing it in a zShop).

> The Groovy Widget is a fictional item that a friend of mine purchased. Don't sell non-existent items -- your customers won't like it and Amazon will probably revoke your seller account.:-)

In the spreadsheet, there are 22 fields per item that can be filled in, but only five are required for each zShops item: the item name, description, category, price, and SKU.

> All of the options for filling in the spreadsheet are beyond the scope of this book. For a complete summary of Marketplace options, look in the Amazon seller pages here: http://www.amazon.com/exec/obidos/tg/browse/-/1161314. For zShops, look here: http://www.amazon.com/exec/obidos/tg/browse/-/1161458. For Auctions, here: http://www.amazon.com/exec/obidos/tg/browse/-/1161394

The SKU (Stock Keeping Unit) is whatever number we use in our inventory system to keep track of items. The SKU is rather important here because we don't have the Amazon ASIN number to keep track of our item's identity. If you don't already have a SKU system setup, it's best to design one. Amazon will automatically assign a Listing ID (a zShops ID) to your item once it's uploaded to Amazon.com.

Our item will also include a picture (actually a photo of one of Charles Babbage's calculating machines) and the condition of the item -- collectible and used.

Another important field is the category1 field which places the item in a specific product category so that it is more likely to appear when people search Amazon.com.

upload.txt

	A	B	C	D	E	F	G	H	I	J	K
1	item-is-marketpla	product-id	product-id-	item-condi	item-note	price	sku	item-name	item-descr	category1	image
2	n	195019199	1	8		5	MySKU987	Groovy Wi	The ultra-m	68290	http://
3											
4											
5											
6											
7											
8											

upload

Figure 9-4 Entering Amazon inventory into a spreadsheet

I chose category number 68290 which is "Scientific Instruments".

> The list of zShops categories on Amazon.com is available here: http://s1.amazon.com/exec/varzea/subst/home/categories-cheatsheet.html

Typically, sellers upload many items at once (one item for each line of the spreadsheet) but since I only have one item, my spreadsheet only has one entry.

After filling out the spreadsheet, I save it as a tab-delimited text file which I name upload.txt. We can now upload the inventory file, upload.txt, by using MarketplaceProMerchant.

```
// Include the class
require_once('MarketplaceProMerchant.php');
// Create a new class instance using your login credentials
$t = new MarketplaceProMerchant('myemail@whereever.com','mypassword');
// Set the upload file format and destination
$t->FileFormat='TabDelimited';
$t->UploadFor='ZShops';
// Upload the inventory
$Result=$t->InventoryUpload(INVENTORY_ADD_MODIFY_DELETE, 'upload.txt', true);
// Print the results
print_r($Result);
```

Amazon returns the SUCCESS element:

```
Array ( [0] => Amazon returned SUCCESS: your request succeeded )
```

We can then check on the status of our uploaded inventory by requesting the latest three upload status reports:

```
// Include the class
require_once('MarketplaceProMerchant.php');
// Create a new class instance using your login credentials
$t = new MarketplaceProMerchant('myemail@whereever.com','mypassword');
$Result=$t->GetUploadStatus(3);
print_r($Result);
```

yields:

```
Array
(
    [0] => batchid=25584641 status=Done dateandtime=06/29/2004 12:35:17 PDT
activateditems=1 numberofwarnings=0 itemsnotacivated=0
    [1] => batchid=25560791 status=Done dateandtime=05/24/2004 08:45:09 PDT
activateditems=2 numberofwarnings=0 itemsnotacivated=0
    [2] => batchid=23655531 status=Done dateandtime=05/22/2004 14:55:13 PDT
activateditems=0 numberofwarnings=1 itemsnotacivated=1
)
```

If you make several inventory uploads in a short period of time, you need to pay attention to the order and date/time when you make the uploads in order to correctly match the batch ID to the upload.

Since our item was activated (activateditems=1) and there are no warnings or "not activated" items, we simply have to wait for the item to appear in our zShop at *http://www.amazon.com/shops/sashimikid*. Zshop and Auctions items may take four to six hours before they appear on Amazon. Marketplace items take only 15 minutes. Had

Sushi and Science

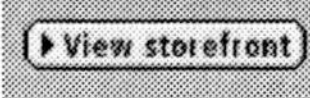

zShops / Art & Antiques / Scientific Instruments

Groovy Widget

Price: $5.00 s&h fee $2.00
(convert this currency)

Description: The ultra-modern Groovy Widget cleans, disinfects, and deodorizes without sticking. I highly recommend it for all of your domestic needs .

Merchant: Sushi and Science I'm new (0)

Figure 9-5 The Groovy Widget listing in my Amazon.com zShops

there been a warning or non-activated item, we could have queried for Error and Quickfix reports using the InventoryError operation.

To find out if anyone has bought a product from our zShop, we can request that a listing of Order reports be generated for the past five days:

```
// Include the class
require_once('MarketplaceProMerchant.php');
// Create a new class instance using your login credentials
$t = new MarketplaceProMerchant('myemail@whereever.com','mypassword');
$Result = $t->GenerateReport('Order', 5);
print_r($Result);
```

The result is:

```
Array
(
    [0] => Amazon returned SUCCESS: your request succeeded
)
```

Sometime later -- typically within 30 minutes -- a poll for Order reports should reveal a report covering the last 5 days. This request yields a list of the latest 3 Order reports that have been generated.

```
// Include the class
require_once('MarketplaceProMerchant.php');
// Create a new class instance using your login credentials
$t = new MarketplaceProMerchant('myemail@whereever.com','mypassword');
$Result = $t->GetReportIds('Order', 3);
print_r($Result);
```

Even if nothing was sold, a report is generated. We have to fetch and look at the contents of the report to determine what (if any) orders where made.

```
Array
(
    [0] => reportstarttime=06-29-2004:12-44-16 reportendtime=07-03-2004:12-44-16
reportid=101521891
    [1] => reportstarttime=06-28-2004:21-40-40 reportendtime=06-28-2004:21-40-40
reportid=101337031
    [2] => reportstarttime=06-18-2004:10-22-31 reportendtime=06-18-2004:10-22-31
reportid=98589571
 )
```

To find out if there are any orders, we fetch the report using the report ID of the latest report as listed above.

```
// Include the class
require_once('MarketplaceProMerchant.php');
// Create a new class instance using your login credentials
$t = new MarketplaceProMerchant('myemail@whereever.com','mypassword');
$Result = $t->GetReport('101521891');
print_r($Result);
```

An Order report is a tab-delimited spreadsheet report much like the inventory upload spreadsheet that we submitted earlier. This report contains a list of all orders that have been made in the past five days. Our spreadsheet response has two lines in it. One line is the spreadsheet column headers, and the other line is the order. If there were multiple orders, there would be one order per line in the spreadsheet.

```
Array
(
    [0] => payments-status    order-id    order-item-id    payments-date    payments-
transaction-id    item-name    listing-id    sku    price    shipping-fee
quantity-purchased    total-price    purchase-date    batch-id    buyer-email
buyer-name    recipient-name    ship-address-1    ship-address-2    ship-city
ship-state    ship-zip    ship-country    special-comments    upc    ship-method
paid_ship_now    700105306788          2004-06-30 14:32:55 PST    700106306788
Groovy Widget    0629L046099    MySKU9876    5    2    1    7    2004-06-30 14:33:12
PST    25584641    auserrrzz@yahoo.com    Sakeman    Sakeman    45007 Rosedale Ave
Austin    TX    78756    US    Please leave package by garage door         standard
)
```

Viewed in Excel, the response is more readable:

AIMS Buyer_order.xls

	A	B	C	D	E	F	G	H	I	J	K	L	M	
1	payments-	order-id	order-item-	payments-	payments-	item-name	listing-id	sku	price	shipping-fe	quantity-p	total-price	purchase-date	batc
2			700105306	2004-06-3	700105306	Groovy Wi	0629L046C	MySKU98	5	2	1	7	6/30/2004 14:33	
3														

Figure 9-6 An AIMS order report for an item without an ASIN

Note that there is no "order-id" returned because this item has no corresponding ASIN. The "order-id" is called a TransactionId when used with the Amazon E-Commerce Service 4.0 TransactionLookup operation (see Chapter Eight for a TransactionLookup usage example).

If we had uploaded inventory to the Amazon Marketplace that had an existing Amazon ASIN, the item would appear in the Marketplace listings, such as this used CD listing I posted via AIMS:

Acceptable

Availability: Usually ships in 1-2 business days; Ships from TX, United States.

Comments: Not much

Figure 9-7 A Marketplace listing for a used CD

When the CD is sold, AIMS returned a slightly different Order report:

```
Array
(
    [0] => payments-status  order-id  order-item-id  payments-date  payments-
transaction-id  item-name  listing-id  sku  price  shipping-fee  quantity-purchased
total-price  purchase-date  batch-id  buyer-email  buyer-name  recipient-name  ship-
address-1  ship-address-2  ship-city  ship-state  ship-zip  ship-country  special-
comments  upc  ship-method paid_ship_now  058-1987944-0858153  29602814230237  2005-
03-06 09:10:20 PST  29602814230237  Washing Machine [Audio CD] Sonic Youth
0305L333221  hg7884  9  2.49  1  11.49  2005-03-06 09:10:31 PST  43792681  f0ar@mail.
com  bill  Bill Kalepta  1107 Roselawn Ave  Austin   TX   78701-3027  US
standard
)
```

The primary difference between this order and the Groovy Widgets order is that this order has an "order-id" that can be used with the TransactionLookup operation.

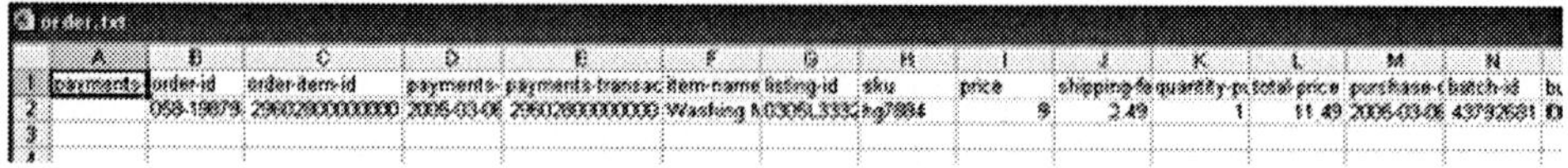

Figure 9-8 An AIMS order report for a Marketplace listing

Issuing Refunds

Using the order information we received for the Groovy Widget, we can issue a refund to our customer, since, after all, the item doesn't exist. The information we need to process a refund is in the response (Figure 9-6):

- The refund amount (not including shipping): $5.00
- The Order ID: 700105306788 (for an item without an ASIN, this is actually the Order Item ID)
- Payment Transaction ID: 700106306788

The first step is to create a tab-delimited text file with the following tab-delimited headings:

```
order-id    payments-transaction-id    refund-amount    reason    message
```

Since we are only refunding one item, only one line is necessary. If we wanted to make more than one refund, then we would put each refund on a separate line in the spreadsheet. Our refund has the following values:

```
700105306788    700106306788    5    Customer is dissastified    Thanks anyway
```

The "reason" and "message" are optional, but the headers must still be included in the spreadsheet. The "reason" is the reason for the refund. Both the "reason" and the "message" appear in the automatically generated refund message sent by Amazon to the customer via email when the refund is processed.

```
// Include the class
require_once('MarketplaceProMerchant.php');
// Create a new class instance using your login credentials
$t = new MarketplaceProMerchant('myemail@whereever.com','mypassword');
$Result = $t->BatchRefund('refund.txt', true);
print_r($Result);
```

The response is:

```
array
(
    [0] => Amazon returned SUCCESS: your request succeeded
)
```

To check on the status of the refund, we first query for any reports of type "BatchRefund"

```
// Include the class
require_once('MarketplaceProMerchant.php');
// Create a new class instance using your login credentials
$t = new MarketplaceProMerchant('myemail@whereever.com','mypassword');
$Result=$t->GetReportIds('BatchRefund', 1);
print_r($Result);
```

The response is:

```
Array
(
    [0] => reportstarttime=07-01-2004:20-37-37 reportendtime=07-01-2004:20-37-37
reportid=102198321
)
```

We then make another call to retrieve the report using the report ID from the response.

```
// Include the class
require_once('MarketplaceProMerchant.php');
// Create a new class instance using your login credentials
$t = new MarketplaceProMerchant('myemail@whereever.com','mypassword');
```

```
$Result = $t->GetReport('102198321');
print_r($Result);
```

Which yields:

```
Array ( [0] => 700105306788 order-item-id: 700106306788 SUCCESS 5 is Refunded. )
```

The Merchants@ API

All Merchants@ Pro Merchants and Merchants@ Sellers use the web interface located at Amazon's Seller Central web site, *sellercentral.amazon.com.*

Figure 9-9 Amazon's Seller Central web interface

They can choose to manage all of their inventory using the web interface (Figure 9-9) or they can automate all, or some, of their inventory management using the Merchants@ API. Amazon's Merchants@ API 2.0 is a SOAP interface for sellers that lets Merchants@ Pro Merchants and Merchant@ Sellers use a SOAP client to access their inventory and reporting functions on Amazon.com.

> Some larger Merchants@ sellers may have complex inventory needs, such as the ability to post and reconcile inventory across multiple departments and outlets. Such sellers often turn to system integrators to hook their backend systems into Amazon.

Unlike other Amazon APIs, the Merchants@ API includes a "sandbox" testing environment, called the Merchants Integration Platform (MIP), that developers can use to test their applications and feeds before they are deployed in the production environment.

Accessing The Merchants@ API

Using the Merchants@ API SOAP interface can be a bit tricky because it requires that your SOAP client supports Soap Attachments -- the ability to send and receive file attachments along with your usual SOAP messaging. SOAP attachments are still a somewhat gray area as far as SOAP standards go. There are, in fact, about five "SOAP with attachments" specifications that have come out of the World Wide Web Consortium (the SOAP standards body) in the past few years.

Amazon's Merchants@ system supports the so-called SWA (Soap With Attachments) standard for MIME (Multipurpose Internet Mail Extension) encoded file attachments. It also supports DIME (Direct Internet Message Encapsulation) encoded file attachments for use with Microsoft.NET platforms.

> The SOAP With Attachments specification is here: http://www.w3.org/TR/SOAP-attachments. Microsoft's DIME standard is here: http://msdn.microsoft.com/library/en-us/dnglobspec/html/draft-nielsen-dime-soap-01.txt.

I'm only going to discuss the use of MIME encoded attachments here. As this book goes to press, PHP5 does not yet support attachments (Table 9-6) so you have to use

SOAP Client	Status
PEAR SOAP 0.81	`Has some decoding issues`
NuSOAP 1.86	`Has some decoding issues`
PHP 5.03 SOAP	`Does not support attachments`

Table 9-6 SOAP client attachment compatibility with Merchants@ API

either NuSOAP or PEAR SOAP. Both have some difficulties with Amazon's particular implementation of SOAP With Attachments. In my examples, I use PEAR SOAP 0.81.

The difficulty PHP SOAP clients have with the way the Merchants@ API handles attachments is that the Merchants@ API does not like it when both the attachments and the SOAP Envelope are base64-encoded. The SOAP Envelope needs to be plain text.

> To get a plain text SOAP envelope when uploading attachments using PEAR SOAP version 0.81, you will need to edit the file SOAP/Base.php and change the line:
> $params['encoding'] = 'base64';
> to
> $params['encoding'] = '8bit';

The Merchants@ WSDL

There are two sets of WSDL files for the Merchants@ API, one set for the Merchants Integration Platform testing environment, and one set for the production environment. Each set consists of two WSDL files, one for SOAP clients that use MIME attachments and one for SOAP clients that use DIME attachments (Table 9-5).

The WSDLs are password-protected. To retrieve the latest WSDL, put the desired URL from Table 9-5 into your web browser and do a "save as" when the WSDL displays in your browser. When it prompts you for login credentials, use your Amazon seller login email address and password.

> Some web browsers try to interpret the XML tags in the WSDL file. You may have to do a "view source" on the page and then "save as" in order to save a usable WSDL file.

WSDL	URL
Production environment with MIME attachments	`https://merchant-api.amazon.com/gateway/merchant-interface-mime`
Production Environment with DIME attachments	`https://merchant-api.amazon.com/gateway/merchant-interface-dime`
Test (MIP) environment with MIME attachments	`https://merchant-api-qa.amazon.com/gateway/merchant-interface-mime`
Test (MIP) environment with DIME attachments	`https://merchant-api-qa.amazon.com/gateway/merchant-interface-dime`

Table 9-7 Merchants@ WSDL locations

Unlike with Amazon E-Commerce Service, there is no versioning scheme used with the Amazon Seller WSDL. Because of the high volume of inventory traffic, and the need to interface with the inventory systems of various merchants, Amazon's Merchants@ API doesn't change very often, and when it does, it supports backward compatibility for quite some time. For that reason, and also because it's password protected, I recommend saving a copy of the WSDL to your server hard disk instead of retrieving the WSDL on each request.

Secure Requests

By default, all Merchants@ SOAP requests go over the Internet unencrypted because the SOAP service port address in the WSDL files (Table 9-5) specifies HTTP protocol over port 80:

```
<soap:address location="http://merchant-api.amazon.com:80/gateway/merchant-interface-
mime"/>
```

Since each of your requests includes all of your Amazon merchant credentials, including your username and password, you should always use SSL to encrypt your requests. To make secure requests, save a copy of the WSDL file locally, and manually change the service address to use HTTPS over port 443:

```
<soap:address location="https://merchant-api.amazon.com:443/gateway/merchant-
interface-mime"/>
```

Pear SOAP uses the curl libraries with OpenSSL to negotiate this connection so you need PHP's Curl extension and the OpenSSL libraries installed on your server in order to use HTTPS.

WSDL Caching With PEAR SOAP

PEAR SOAP does not have a WSDL caching function, but you can easily use PEAR's Cache Lite function to accomplish the same thing (another example of using Cache Lite is in Chapter Four).

In PHP, the parsed WSDL file is a large PHP object structure. Since Cache Lite only knows how to cache strings, you have to use the serialize and unserialize functions in order to cache it as a string and then reconstitute it as an object when you retrieve it from the cache.

Since I don't expect the WSDL file to change very often, I use a very high lifeTime parameter for the cache.

> Your login name and password are stored in plain text as part of the WSDL cache, so you should ensure that there is no public access to the directory path you choose for Cache Lite's caching directory. You will also have to clear the cache if you want to use a different login name and password.

```
// Cache Lite options
$cache_options = array(
'cacheDir' => '/cachelite/',   // Directory to place cache files
'lifeTime' => 999999999        // Only update if the cache gets corrupted
);

// An arbitrary cache id
$cache_id = 'MerchantsAt';

// Fetch a Cache instance
$CL = new Cache_Lite($cache_options);
```

```
        // Check to see if the WSDL has been cached
        if ($temp = $CL->get($cache_id)) {

            // If yet, unserialize it into an object
            $this->client = unserialize($temp);

        } else {

            // Parse the WSDL
            $this->client = new SOAP_Client(WSDLPATH, true, false, $proxy);

            // Check for WSDL parsing error
            if (PEAR::isError($this->client)){
                $this->amazerror = "Error: " . $this->client->getMessage();
                return false;
            }

            // Cache the WSDL
            $CL->save(serialize($this->client));
        }

        return true;
    }
```

Merchants@ Operations

As this book goes to publication, eleven operations are supported by the Merchants@ WSDL (Table 9-8). Both the WSDLs used in the Merchants Integration Platform (MIP) test environment, and the WSDLs used in the production environment, have the same set of operations. The only difference is the service entry point. When you're testing in the MIP environment, your requests go to a different server where you can't hurt anything if you make a mistake. Inventory you create using the MIP environment never surfaces on Amazon.com.

Method	Purpose
getAllPendingDocumentInfo	Requests a list of all available order or payment settlement reports
getDocument	Requests a specific document using the document ID
getDocumentInfoInterfaceConformance	Used to test the getAllPendingDocumentInfo method
getDocumentInterfaceConformance	Used to test the getDocument method
getDocumentProcessingStatus	Requests the processing status for a given feed batch reference
getLastNDocumentInfo	Requests a list of a specified number of document
getLastNDocumentProcessingStatuses	Request a list of the status of the last N feeds that the Seller has sent to Amazon
getLastNPendingDocumentInfo	Requests a list of the latest N unacknowledged order or payment settlement reports
postDocument	Uploads various types of documents to Amazon

Method	Purpose
postDocumentDownloadAck	Used by the Seller to notify Amazon that a particular orders or payment report has been received (takes it out of pending status).
postDocumentInterfaceConformance	Used to test the postDocument method

Table 9-8 Merchants@ API operations

In production environments, only a handful of the API operations in Table 9-8 are typically used. The operations with the "LastN" string in them are usually only used by sellers who have a special need to retrieve a certain number of reports. The operations with the "InterfaceConformance" string in them are only used for testing and are deprecated.

Using The Merchants Integration Platform (MIP)

The Merchants Integration Platform (MIP) is a testing sandbox designed to let Merchants@ sellers test their feeds before they go live on Amazon's production server. The MIP WSDLs and the production WSDLs (see Table 9-7) are actually identical except for the service entry point. As I noted earlier, the service entry point for the production server is:

```
<soap:address location="http://merchant-api.amazon.com:80/gateway/merchant-interface-
mime"/>
```

The service entry point for the MIP server is:

```
<soap:address location="http://merchant-api-qa.amazon.com:80/gateway/merchant-
interface-mime"/>
```

Only the domain name is different. The other significant difference is that you can use the three "InterfaceConformance" functions with the MIP server. These three functions are designed to test conformance when sending and receiving. From Table 9-6, those functions are:

- getDocumentInfoInterfaceConformance
- getDocumentInterfaceConformance
- postDocumentInterfaceConformance

These three functions won't work with the production server.

The MIP offers a set of bogus inventory and users for testing purposes. For details, consult the online help at *sellercentral.amazon.com*.

Merchants@ Feeds

When you manage inventory using Seller Central's web interface (Figure 9-7), inventory additions and modifications are uploaded using spreadsheets that you create. When you manage your inventory using the Merchants@ API, however, you use

XML-encoded "feeds" that are sent as SOAP attachments. These feeds have to be crafted according to XSD files provided on Seller Central (Table 9-9).

Feed Type	Purpose	URL
Product Feed	Sets the SKU, category, description, and other basic product properties	http://sellercentral.amazon.com/help/merchant_documents/XSD/Product.xsd
Inventory Feed	Sets quantity and availability	http://sellercentral.amazon.com/help/merchant_documents/XSD/Inventory.xsd
Overrides Feed	Sets shipping restrictions	http://sellercentral.amazon.com/help/merchant_documents/XSD/Override.xsd
Pricing Feed	Sets currency amount and sale pricing	http://sellercentral.amazon.com/help/merchant_documents/XSD/Price.xsd
Product Images Feed	Sets product images	http://sellercentral.amazon.com/help/merchant_documents/XSD/ProductImage.xsd
Relationships Feed	Sets parent/child ASIN relationship	http://sellercentral.amazon.com/help/merchant_documents/XSD/Relationship.xsd

Table 9-9 The product definition feeds and their associated XSD files

In order to list an item in your inventory, you first need to craft an XML file according to the Product Feed XSD. Amazon uses the Product Feed to establish a mapping between your SKU (Stock Keeping Unit) and an item's ASIN. If your product doesn't exist on Amazon.com yet (it has no ASIN), Amazon assigns a new ASIN to your product. If an ASIN already exists for your item, Amazon's server will automatically fill-in many of the product details for you after your Product Feed is received.

Once your Product Feed has been successfully received by Amazon, and there are no errors, the item is listed in your inventory. The item surfaces in your Amazon storefront on your designated launch date (set in the Product Feed), however no "Add to Cart" button appears until you add a specific quantity of the item to your inventory using an Inventory Feed.

The Inventory Feed, and other feeds, can be sent in any order, and establish things like the quantity in your inventory, the shipping prices, your price, any special product images you want to use, and the Parent/Child ASIN relationships (for Variations items).

You can verify that your feed requests are working by going to your account on Seller Central and viewing your inventory listings.

Merchants@ Reports

The Merchants@ system automatically generates two types of reports for you, order reports and payment settlement reports. Order reports are generated for you every hour. Payment settlement reports are typically generated every seven days though that delay is configurable for every Merchants@ account.

When Amazon generates a report for you, it assigns it a unique identifier and gives it a "pending" status. You can then query for it, download it, and then acknowledge receipt of it to remove its pending status.

Merchants@ Choreography

Like AIMS, the Merchants@ system is a batch processing system -- your requests are not processed in real time. So, getting a response to your request is usually a three step process. The steps you take -- the choreography -- are slightly different depending on whether you're posting a feed or retrieving a report.

For posting feeds, you first post the feed, then check the processing status, and finally, retrieve a document containing the processing results (Figure 9-10).

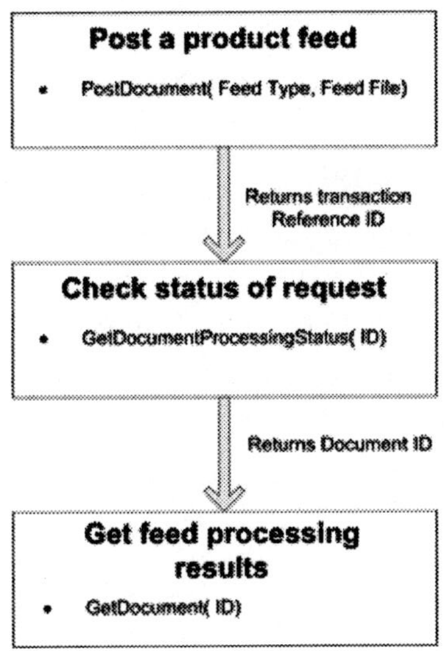

Figure 9-10 Choreography for posting a product feed using the Merchants@ API

For reports, you first check to see if there are any pending order or payment settlement reports, then you download the report, and finally, acknowledge receipt of the report. Once you acknowledge receipt of the report, Amazon removes the report from the list of pending reports (Figure 9-11).

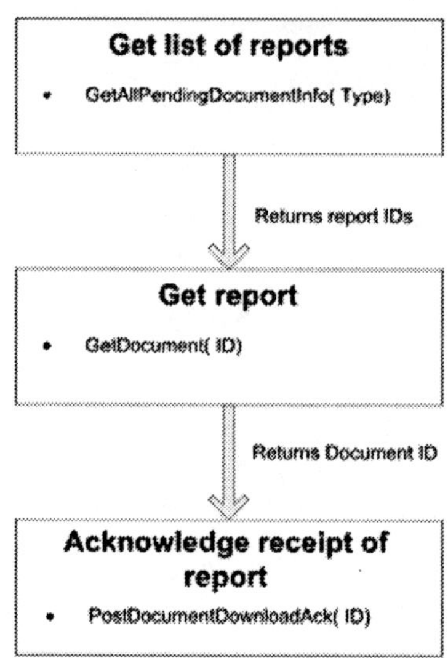

Figure 9-11 Choreography for retrieving a report using the Merchants@ API

A Merchants@ API PHP Class

I created a simple PHP class, MerchantsAtProMerchant, in order to access the Merchants@ API using SOAP. For the most part, I gave the class methods the same names as the API operations. Methods for the class are listed in Table 9-10.

The reference manual in Appendix K outlines the Merchants@ operations along with their various parameters.

Method	Public/ Private
GetAllPendingDocumentInfo	Public
GetDocument	Public
GetDocumentInfoInterfaceConformance	Public
GetDocumentInterfaceConformance	Public
GetDocumentProcessingStatus	Public
GetLastNDocumentInfo	Public
PostDocument	Public
PostDocumentDownloadAck	Public
PostDocumentInterfaceConformance	Public

Table 9-10 Methods of the Merchants@ API class

The SOAP, XML Serializer, and Cache Lite libraries from the PHP PEAR library are required to use the class. Cache Lite is used for caching the WSDL file and XML Serializer is used to parse any XML documents that are returned by the GetDocument method.

The constructor function for the MerchantsAtProMerchant class retrieves the cached WSDL file, or parses the WSDL if the cache is stale or non-existent. It takes your Merchants@ username, password, merchant ID, and merchant name as parameters and returns false on error or true if successful.

```
define('WSDLPATH', './merchant-interface-mime.wsdl');

// PHP PEAR libraries needed
require_once('SOAP/Client.php');       // PEAR SOAP client libraries
require_once('SOAP/Value.php');        // PEAR SOAP attachment libraries
require_once('XML/Unserializer.php'); // PEAR XML parser
require_once('Cache/Lite.php');        // Used for WSDL Caching

function MerchantsAtProMerchant($login, $password, $merchantid, $merchantname)
    {
        // Setup the SOAP merchant parameter used in all requests
        $this->merchant = array( 'merchantIdentifier' => $merchantid, 'merchantName'
=> $merchantname );
        $proxy=array('user'=> $login,'pass'=> $password);

        // Cache Lite options
        $cache_options = array(
        'cacheDir' => '/cachelite/',  // Directory to place cache files
        'lifeTime' => 999999999       // Only update if the cache gets corrupted
        );

        // An arbitrary cache ID string
        $cache_id = 'MerchantsAt';

        // Fetch a Cache instance
        $CL = new Cache_Lite($cache_options);

        if ($temp = $CL->get($cache_id)) {

            // Get the cached WSDL
            $this->client = unserialize($temp);

        } else {

            // Parse the WSDL and cache it
            $this->client = new SOAP_Client(WSDLPATH, true, false, $proxy);

            if (PEAR::isError($this->client)){
                $this->amazerror = "Error: " . $this->client->getMessage();
                return false;
            }
```

```
            $CL->save(serialize($this->client));
        }
        return true;
    }
```

Methods For Posting Feeds

The PostDocument method is used to post a wide range of feeds to Amazon. the feed type and the document file are sent as parameters and a Transaction Reference ID is returned.

```
// document Types for PostDocument
define('PPD', '_POST_PRODUCT_DATA_');
define('PPRD','_POST_PRODUCT_RELATIONSHIP_DATA_');
define('PPOD','_POST_PRODUCT_OVERRIDES_DATA_');
define('PPID', '_POST_PRODUCT_IMAGE_DATA_');
define('PPPD', '_POST_PRODUCT_PRICING_DATA_');
define('PIAD', '_POST_INVENTORY_AVAILABILITY_DATA_');
define('PTOD', '_POST_TEST_ORDERS_DATA_');
define('POAD', '_POST_ORDER_ACKNOWLEDGEMENT_DATA_');
define('POFD', '_POST_ORDER_FULFILLMENT_DATA_');
define('PPAD', '_POST_PAYMENT_ADJUSTMENT_DATA_');
define('PSD', '_POST_STORE_DATA_');

function PostDocument($documentType, $filename) {

        // Create a new attachment
        $att =  new SOAP_Attachment('doc', 'text/xml', $filename);

        // Don't base64 encode the attachment. Make it plain text
        $att->options['attachment']['encoding'] = '8bit';

        // Set the document/literal parameters
        $params = array('merchant' => $this->merchant, 'messageType' =>
$documentType, 'doc' => $att);

        // use MIME, not DIME, encoding
        $encoding = 'Mime';

        // Do a debug trace and set the timeout at 10 seconds
        $options=array('trace' => true, 'attachments' => $encoding, 'timeout' =>
'10');

        // Send the request to Amazon
        $Result = $this->client->call('postDocument', $params, $options);

        // Return the processing status ID
        return $Result;
    }
```

After posting a feed to Amazon, you can check on it's processing status by using the Transaction Reference ID returned from the PostDocument method as a parameter to the GetDocumentProcessingStatus method. Amazon returns a human-readable status such as "_IN_PROGRESS_" or "_DONE_".

```
function GetDocumentProcessingStatus($documentId) {

        // The document/literal parameters
        $params = array('merchant' => $this->merchant,
'documentTransactionIdentifier' => $documentId);

        // Turn on debug trace and use 10 second timeout
        $options=array('trace' => true, 'timeout' => '10');

        // Make the call to getDocumentProcessingStatus
        $Result = $this->client->call('getDocumentProcessingStatus', $params,
$options);

        // Return Document ID
        return ($Result);
    }
```

Methods For Fetching Documents

The GetDocument method is used to retrieve order and payment settlement reports from Amazon. The document ID of the document is the only parameter. The report is returned as a SOAP attachment.

```
function GetDocument($docId) {

        // Set the Merchant credentials and document ID
        $params = array('merchant' => $this->merchant, 'documentIdentifier' =>
$docId);

        // Set options to trace program and timeout after 10 seconds
        $options=array('trace' => true, 'timeout' => '10');

        // Make the API call
        $Result = $this->client->call('getDocument', $params, $options);

        // Found an attachment
        $xml=current($this->client->__attachments);

        // Parse the attachment
        $parser = & new XML_Unserializer();
        $rc = $parser->unserialize($xml);

        // Return the parsed document
        return ($parser->getUnserializedData());
    }
```

Once you've downloaded a document using the GetDocument method, you can tell Amazon to remove the remove the report from "pending" status by using the PostDocumentDownloadAck method.

```
function PostDocumentDownloadAck($idArray) {
```

```
        // An array of document IDs
        $idArray = (!is_array($idArray)) ? array($idArray) : $idArray;

        // The document/literal parameters
        $params = array('merchant' => $this->merchant, 'documentIdentifierArray' =>
$idArray);

        // Set the debug trace and 10 second timeout options
        $options = array('trace' => true, 'timeout' => '10');

        // Make the API call to Amazon
        $Result = $this->client->call('postDocumentDownloadAck', $params, $options);

        // Returns a list of the document IDs and whether the acknowledgement was
        // successful.
        return ($Result)
    }
```

A Method For Report Queries

The Merchants@ API lets you query for any "pending" order or payment settlement reports. You can easily retrieve the IDs of any available reports by using the GetAllPendingDocumentInfo method and specifying the type of report you want as the parameter.

```
// Message Types for report information
define('GOD', '_GET_ORDERS_DATA_');
define('GPSD','_GET_PAYMENT_SETTLEMENT_DATA_');

function GetAllPendingDocumentInfo($documentType) {
        $this->amazerror = null;

        $params = array('merchant' => $this->merchant, 'messageType' =>
$documentType);

        $options = array('trace' => true, 'timeout' => '10');

        $Result = $this->client->call('getAllPendingDocumentInfo', $params,
$options);

        if (PEAR::isError($Result)) {
            $this->amazerror = "Error: " . $Result->getMessage();
            if ($this->Debug) {
                echo '<h2>Request/Response</h2>';
                echo '<pre>' . htmlspecialchars($this->client->__get_wire(), ENT_
QUOTES) . '</pre>';
            }

            return false;
        }

        if ($this->Debug) {
```

```
            echo '<h2>Request/Response</h2>';
            echo '<pre>' . htmlspecialchars($this->client->__get_wire(), ENT_QUOTES)
. '</pre>';
        }

        // Return the parsed document
        return ($Result);
    }
```

Establishing Your Inventory

In order to post inventory for sale using the Merchants@ API, we have to establish the product in our inventory by uploading a Product Feed. The Product Feed is an XML file with contents described by the Product Feed XSD listed in Table 9-9.

As an example, I'll add a fictional baritone saxophone using the Product Feed I created in Example 9-1. Multiple items can be specified in a single file by adding additional <Message> elements, but for example purposes, mine has just one item:

Example 9-1 The file upload.xml, a Merchants@ Product Feed

```
<?xml version="1.0"?>
<AmazonEnvelope xmlns:xsi="http://www.w3.org/2001/XMLSchema-instance" xsi:
noNamespaceSchemaLocation="amzn-envelope.xsd">
  <Header>
    <DocumentVersion>1.01</DocumentVersion>
    <MerchantIdentifier>T_MCBEAKSR_1999</MerchantIdentifier>
  </Header>
  <MessageType>Product</MessageType>
  <Message>
    <MessageID>1</MessageID>
    <Product>
      <SKU>MySKU1234</SKU>
      <StandardProductID>
        <Type>UPC</Type>
        <Value>123456789012</Value>
      </StandardProductID>
      <ProductTaxCode>A_GEN_TAX</ProductTaxCode>
      <LaunchDate>2005-03-05T15:21:49-08:00</LaunchDate>
      <DescriptionData>
        <Title>D-9000 Baritone Saxophone</Title>
        <Description>A delightful baritone saxophone with a rich tone quality</
Description>
        <MSRP currency="USD">7000.00</MSRP>
        <LegalDisclaimer>Product does not actually exist. Buyers should not expect
product to be available for purchase.....ever.</LegalDisclaimer>
      </DescriptionData>
    </Product>
  </Message>
</AmazonEnvelope>
```

To post the Product Feed, I use the PostDocument method of my PHP class. PostDocument takes the name of the Product Feed file (in this case upload.xml) as an argument and returns the Transaction Reference ID in the response.

```
<?php
require_once('MerchantsAtProMerchant.php');

// My seller credentials
$merchantname='McBeakers';
$merchantid='T_MCBEAKSR_1999';
$login='jbeak@amazon.com';
$password='FqjxdXhvkt45E';

// Create a new instance of the API
$t = new MerchantsAtProMerchant($login, $password, $merchantid, $merchantname);
// Post the document
$rc = $t->PostDocument(PPD, './upload.xml');
// Output the result
print_r($rc);
```

Amazon returns a Transaction Reference ID (the DocumentTransactionID element) which we can then use to query for the processing status:

```
Array ( [Header] =>
      Array ( [DocumentVersion] => 1.01 [MerchantIdentifier] => T_MCBEAKSR_1999 )
               [MessageType] => ProcessingReport [Message] =>
            Array  ( [MessageID] => 1 [ProcessingReport] =>
                  Array ( [DocumentTransactionID] => 382512123 [StatusCode] =>
Complete [ProcessingSummary] =>
                       Array ( [MessagesProcessed] => 1 [MessagesSuccessful] => 1
[MessagesWithError] => 0 [MessagesWithWarning] => 0 )
                       )
                 )
           )
```

Periodically, we can query Amazon using the GetDocumentProcessingStatus method to check on the status of our feed.

```
<?php
require_once('MerchantsAtProMerchant.php');

// My seller credentials
$merchantname='McBeakers';
$merchantid='T_MCBEAKSR_1999';
$login='jbeak@amazon.com';
$password='FqjxdXhvkt45E';

// Create a new instance of the API
$t = new MerchantsAtProMerchant($login, $password, $merchantid, $merchantname);
// Post the document
$rc = $t->GetDocumentProcessingStatus('382512123');
// Output the result
print_r($rc);
```

Amazon returns the status "_IN_PROGRESS_" if it's still in the queue or processing the feed. No documentID is returned in that case:

```
Array ( [documentProcessingStatus] => _IN_PROGRESS_ [processingReport] => stdClass
Object ( [documentID] => [generatedDateTime] => 2005-03-03T23:51:21-08:00 ) )
```

When processing is finished, Amazon returns "_DONE_" as the status and also returns the documentID which contains details of the processing.

```
Array ( [documentProcessingStatus] => _DONE_ [processingReport] => stdClass Object (
[documentID] => 95639793 [generatedDateTime] => 2005-03-04T06:52:30-08:00 ) )
```

Finally, we have a Document ID that we can fetch from Amazon using the GetDocument method:

```
<?php
require_once('MerchantsAtProMerchant.php');

// My seller credentials
$merchantname='McBeakers';
$merchantid='T_MCBEAKSR_1999';
$login='jbeak@amazon.com';
$password='FqjxdXhvkt45E';

// Create a new instance of the API
$t = new MerchantsAtProMerchant($login, $password, $merchantid, $merchantname);
// Post the document
$rc = $t->GetDocument('95639793');
// Output the result
print_r($rc);
```

Amazon returns documents as plain text attachments. If there were any errors during feed processing, those are spelled out in the report. I use the XML Serializer PEAR library to parse the attachment into a PHP array:

```
Array ( [Header] =>
        Array ( [DocumentVersion] => 1.01 [MerchantIdentifier] => T_MCBEAKSR_1999 )
[MessageType] => ProcessingReport [Message] =>
             Array ( [MessageID] => 1 [ProcessingReport] => Array (
[DocumentTransactionID] => 382512123 [StatusCode] => Complete [ProcessingSummary] =>
                    Array ( [MessagesProcessed] => 1 [MessagesSuccessful] => 1
[MessagesWithError] => 0 [MessagesWithWarning] => 0 )
                      )
             )
)
```

Checking For Reports

To find out if Amazon has generated any order or payment settlement reports for you, you can periodically use the GetAllPendingDocumentInfo method which will return any pending report IDs.

```
<?php
require_once('MerchantsAtProMerchant.php');
```

```
// My seller credentials
$merchantname='McBeakers';
$merchantid='T_MCBEAKSR_1999';
$login='jbeak@amazon.com';
$password='FqjxdXhvkt45E';

// Create a new instance of the API
$t = new MerchantsAtProMerchant($login, $password, $merchantid, $merchantname);
// Post the document
$rc = $t->GetAllPendingDocumentInfo(GOD);
// Output the result
print_r($rc);
```

Any pending document IDs and the time they were generated are returned:

```
stdClass Object ( [documentID] => 97163023 [generatedDateTime] => 2005-03-11T00:14:
40-08:00 )
```

You can then retrieve them using the GetDocument method (see previous section). One additional step is needed. In order to remove the document from pending status -- so that it is no longer returned by the GetAllPendingDocumentInfo method -- you need to acknowledge receipt of the document using the PostDocumentDownloadAck method:

```
<?php
require_once('MerchantsAtProMerchant.php');

// My seller credentials
$merchantname='McBeakers';
$merchantid='T_MCBEAKSR_1999';
$login='jbeak@amazon.com';
$password='FqjxdXhvkt45E';

// Create a new instance of the API
$t = new MerchantsAtProMerchant($login, $password, $merchantid, $merchantname);
// Post the document
$rc = $t->PostDocumentDownloadAck('97163023');
// Output the result
print_r($rc);
```

The PostDocumentDownloadAck method can take an array of document IDs as input and returns the status of the acknowledgement for each document. Successful acknowledgement returns a status of "_SUCCESSFUL_".

Exercises For The Reader

Create an application that automates bulk uploading of listings for individual sellers. Look at the source of the web pages used by Amazon to determine the URLs and parameters used by Amazon as your guide. Don't forget to use HTTPS for secure connections to Amazon.

Write a client-side, browser-based inventory management application for either the AIMS or Merchants@ systems using CSS, Javascript, and the XMLHTTPRequest object. Have the GUI access results generated by a PHP script on your server so that you will not have conflicts with web browser security.

APPENDIX A

Help Resources For Amazon Developers

The Amazon portal for all of their E-Commerce Service (and other web services) support is at:

```
http://webservices.amazon.com
```

You can find links to various FAQs, as well as code samples and other support items.

Amazon employee Elena Dykhno runs the AWS Zone, a web "scratchpad" that can quickly generate PHP (as well as Java and other languages) code for your applications. It's a great way to generate REST and SOAP request parameters. It's at:

```
http://www.awszone.com
```

Amazon Forums And Blogs

An important source of technical support for Amazon developers are the forums that are managed and run by Prospero for Amazon.

For Amazon E-Commerce Service developers, the developers' forum is the primary source of bug tracking, bug fixes, and announcements related to Amazon E-Commerce Service. Check this forum often:

```
http://forums.prospero.com/am-assocdevxml
```

For Amazon Sellers, look here:

```
http://forums.prospero.com/am-sellannounce
```

Another Amazon forum that is occasionally useful for both developers and sellers is the Amazon Associates forums:

```
http://forums.prospero.com/am-associhelp
```

The Amazon Blog is another important source of announcements:

```
http://aws.typepad.com
```

Amazon's CTO, Werner Vogels, has a blog:

```
http://weblogs.cs.cornell.edu/AllThingsDistributed
```

An official blog for Amazon's Japanese site:

```
http://aws.typepad.com/aws_jp
```

How To Find Amazon IDs

There's not always a direct way to find various Amazon IDs. Often, you have to result to browsing Amazon.com and using manual search techniques. You might need to find the Seller ID of a specific merchant, or the Exchange ID of a specific item. In this section, I explain manual techniques for finding various Amazon IDs.

Finding ASINs

- ASINs can be found in the URL for nearly every product detail page. That's the page where you see the details of the product, including, price, availability, and customer reviews (if any).
- The URL will start with something like *http://www.amazon.com/exec/obidos/tg/detail/-/B000051ZZE* where B000051ZZE is the ASIN

Finding Your Wishlist, Listmania, Baby Registry, and Wedding Registry IDs

- Login to your Amazon customer account
- Click on the "WISH LIST" link at the top of the page (usually it is situated between the "View Cart" and "Your Account" links).
- Look for the breadcrumb trail "Friends & Favorites > About You > Your Wish List" on the left side and click on the "About You" link.
- Your lists will be in a box labeled "BROWSE".
- The URL for "Wish List" will look something like *http://www.amazon.com/gp/registry/1PQ2H0S74O1DU/ref=cm_aya_bb_wl/103-5547257-6251005* where 1PQ2H0S74O1DU is your Wish List ID.
- You can have multiple Listmania lists, each with its own ID, so you must click on the Listmania Lists link and look at the link for each of your Listmania lists. The URL will look something like *http://www.amazon.com/exec/obidos/tg/listmania/list-browse/-/3P9COWZU5R465/ref=cm_aya_av.lm_more/103-5547257-6251005* where 3P9COWZU5R465 is the Listmania ID
- If you have a Baby Registry, a "Baby Registry" link will be in the box and look something like *http://www.amazon.com/exec/obidos/registry/1XUKM2HJX2K93/ref=cm_aya_bb_br/103-5547257-6251005* where 1XUKM2HJX2K93 is your Baby Registry ID
- If you have a Wedding Registry, a "Wedding Registry" link will be in the box and look something like *http://www.amazon.com/gp/registry/339YHW730B1Z1/*

ref=cm_aya_bb_wl/103-5547257-6251005 where 339YHW730B1Z1 is your Wedding Registry ID

Finding Other Wishlist IDs

- Click on the "WISH LIST" link at the top of the page (usually it is situated between the "View Cart" and "Your Account" links).
- Look for the breadcrumb trail "Friends & Favorites > About You > Your Wish List" on the left side and click on the "About You" link.
- Use the "Wish List Search" box on the right side of the page to search for Wish Lists. The URL for each result will look something like *http://www.amazon.com/gp/registry/registry.html/103-5547257-6251005?%5Fencoding=UTF8&id=OGI6ZSBKTQ1J* where OGI6ZSBKTQ1J is a Wishlist ID.

Finding Amazon Customer IDs

To find your Amazon Customer ID:

- Login to your Amazon customer account
- Click on the "WISH LIST" link at the top of the page (usually it is situated between the "View Cart" and "Your Account" links).
- Look for the breadcrumb trail "Friends & Favorites > About You > Your Wish List" on the left side and click on the "About You" link.
- The "About You" link will look something like *http://www.amazon.com/exec/obidos/tg/cm/member-glance/-/A3ICGCER1Q4UB7/103-5547257-6251005* where A3ICGCER1Q4UB7 is your Amazon Customer ID.

To find other Amazon Customer IDs:

Look at Customer Reviews

- Find a Customer Review of any product
- The URL for the Reviewer will look like something like *http://www.amazon.com/exec/obidos/tg/cm/member-glance/-/A27RSV5NHZK73Y/1/ref=cm_cr_auth/103-5547257-6251005?%5Fencoding=UTF8* where A27RSV5NHZK73Y is the Customer ID of the Reviewer.

Search for people

- Login to your Amazon customer account
- Click on the "WISH LIST" link at the top of the page (usually it is situated between the "View Cart" and "Your Account" links).
- Look for the breadcrumb trail "Friends & Favorites > About You > Your Wish List" on the left side and click on the "About You" link.

- The "SEARCH" box on the left hand side lets you search for "People". Enter a name. In the results, the URL for each name will look something like *http://www.amazon.com/gp/registry/registry.html?cid=ATBR5XFXR6LSR&type=wishlist* where ATBR5XFXR6LSR is the Customer ID.

Finding Your Seller ID

- Login to your Amazon seller account at *http://s1.amazon.com/exec/varzea/subst/your-account/manage-your-seller-account.html*
- The URL for the "View Your Ratings and Feedback" link will look something like *http://s1.amazon.com/exec/varzea/tg/customer-feedback/-/A3ICGCER1Q4UB7/0/0/103-5547257-6251005* where A3ICGCER1Q4UB7 is your Seller ID. Note that your Customer ID and Seller ID may be the same.

Finding Other Seller IDs

- Go to any Amazon product detail page (See Figure 1-4)
- Click on the "Used & New" link.
- In the results, the URL for each seller name will look something like: *http://www.amazon.com/gp/help/seller/at-a-glance.html/ref=olp_offerlisting_1/103-5547257-6251005?%5Fencoding=UTF8&asin=0310205719&marketplaceSeller=1&seller=A2BLCH92VKI9YG* where A2BLCH92VKI9YG is the Seller ID.

There is no direct way to find a specific Seller ID for zShops and Marketplace sellers, but Merchants@ sellers in the Apparel Search Index are listed at Browse Node 1104880: *http://www.amazon.com/exec/obidos/tg/browse/-/*1104880. The links look like this: *http://www.amazon.com/exec/obidos/search-handle-url/index=merchants-index&dispatch=browse&results-process=default&node-subject=1036682&bc=1036682&field-merchant-id=A2IZ2ICNZ38UAZ/103-5547257-6251005* where A2IZ2ICNZ38UAZ is the Merchant ID (Merchant IDs and Seller IDs can be used interchangeably in all E-Commerce Service operations).

Finding Listing IDs

- Go to the Amazon zShops at *http://zshops.amazon.com*
- Use the "SEARCH" or "BROWSE" boxes on the left side of the page to find products in the zShops. Keep clicking on links until you're on the product detail page for a product.
- On the product detail page, scroll down to the bottom of the page and find the zShops ID for the product which will look like "zShops ID: 1217L552549". The zShops ID is a synonym for the Listing ID.

Finding Exchange IDs

- Go to the Amazon zShops at *http://zshops.amazon.com*
- Use the "SEARCH" box on the left side of the page to get a list of products that match your search.
- In the results, the URL for each product will look something like *http://s1.amazon.com/exec/varzea/ts/exchange-glance/Y01Y2688162Y8401607/103-5547257-6251005* where Y01Y2688162Y8401607 is the Exchange ID.

Finding Offer Listing IDs

- Go to any Amazon product detail page (See Figure 1-4)
- Click on the "Used & New" link.
- View the source of the resulting page using the "view > source" menu selection in your web browser. Each item on the results page has an Offer Listing ID.
- To find the Offer Listing Id for each item, search the source for the string "offering-id". The Offer Listing ID is the long string of seemingly random characters immediately following "offering-id", separated by a period. For example:

```
<input type="hidden" name="offering-id.0g720bQFk20s1wmBueDgY/
JCo2cQyB1VrklLxQ3rMeEgm15en5VQMdWt3plTRN9rVBZlp2GKv94LkljFc1UDpgKa748xzwhN" value="1"
/>
```

The Offer Listing Id is:

```
0g720bQFk20s1wmBueDgY/JCo2cQyB1VrklLxQ3rMeEgm15en5VQMdWt3plTRN9rVBZlp2GKv94Lk
ljFc1UDpgKa748xzwhN
```

Detail Pages For Small Handset Browsers

Since 1999, Amazon has served up their web site for mobile users. The initiative is called Amazon Anywhere, *www.amazon.com/anywhere*

> I couldn't think of a good place to put this information, so I decided to put it here. Maybe it should have its own appendix?

These are links that you can use to redirect users of Blackberry's, PDAs, and cell phones to an Amazon product detail page (see Figure 1-4). Amazon will return the appropriate markup format for small handsets. The France and Canadian sites are not yet enabled with this service yet and most of the functionality is only available on Amazon.com.

For cell phone browsers, Amazon will return Wireless Markup Language (WML) and a MIME type of text/vnd.wap.wml using the link formats in Table 10-1.

Amazon site	Wireless Detail Page
amazon.com	`http://www.amazon.com/exec/obidos/redirect?tag=[Your Associates ID]&creative=[Your Subscription ID]&camp=2025&link_code=xm2&path=ct/text/vnd.wap.wml/-/tg/aa/xml/glance-xml/-/[The item ASIN]`

Amazon site	Wireless Detail Page
amazon.de	http://www.amazon.de/exec/obidos/redirect?tag=[Your Associates ID]&creative=[Your Subscription ID]&camp=2025&link_code=xm2&path=ct/text/vnd.wap.wml/-/tg/aa/wml/glance/-/[The item ASIN]
amazon.co.jp	http://www.amazon.co.jp/exec/obidos/redirect?tag=[Your Associates ID]&creative=[Your Subscription ID]&camp=2025&link_code=xm2&path=ct/text/vnd.wap.wml%3B%20charset%3DSHIFT_JIS/-/tg/aa/xml/glance/-/[The item ASIN]
amazon.co.uk	http://www.amazon.co.uk/exec/obidos/redirect?tag=[Your Associates ID]&creative=[Your Subscription ID]&camp=2025&link_code=xm2&path=ct/text/vnd.wap.wml/-/tg/aa/wml/uk/glance/-/[The item ASIN]

Table 10-1 Amazon product detail pages served up as Wireless Markup Language

For PDAs capable of rendering HTML, but with small screens, a smaller version of the page is returned by the link in Table 10-2. It returns HTML with the META tags PalmComputingPlatform and HandheldFriendly included, so that PalmOS devices and devices, and devices that recognize the AvantGo HandheldFriendly tag, will load the HTML.

Amazon site	Wireless Detail Page
amazon.com	http://www.amazon.com/exec/obidos/redirect?tag=[Your Associates ID]&creative=[Your Subscription ID]&camp=2025&link_code=xm2&path=dt/upda-1.0-anywhere/tg/aa/upda/item/-/[The item ASIN]

Table 10-2 Amazon product detail pages served up for PDAs

Table 10-3 offers a link format that works with RIM Blackberry devices. It returns an XHTML subset known as XHTML Basic 1.0, *www.w3.org/TR/xhtml-basic*

Amazon site	Wireless Detail Page
amazon.com	http://www.amazon.com/exec/obidos/redirect?tag=[Your Associates ID]&creative=[Your Subscription ID]&camp=2025&link_code=xm2&path=dt/upda-1.0-i/tg/aa/upda/item/-/-/[The item ASIN]

Table 10-3 Amazon product detail pages served up for RIM Blackberry

The link format in Table 10-4 will return the Amazon product detail page in Voice XML 2.0 format, *www.w3.org/TR/voicexml20*.

Amazon site	Wireless Detail Page
amazon.com	http://www.amazon.com/exec/obidos/redirect?tag=[Your Associates ID]&creative=[Your Subscription ID]&camp=2025&link_code=xm2&path=dt/[Voice XML provider name[1]]/tg/aa/xml/glance-xml/-/[The item ASIN]

Table 10-4 Amazon product detail pages served up for Voice XML applications

[1]Valid Voice XML provider names are "vxml" for TellMe.com applications, and "vxml3" for BeVocal.com applications

APPENDIX B

Amazon E-Commerce Service 4.0 Reference Manual

Amazon E-Commerce Service 4.0 Operations

- BrowseNodeLookup
- CartAdd
- CartClear
- CartCreate
- CartGet
- CartModify
- CustomerContentLookup
- CustomerContentSearch
- Help
- ItemLookup
- ItemSearch
- ListLookup
- ListSearch
- SellerListingLookup
- SellerListingSearch
- SellerLookup
- SimilarityLookup
- TransactionLookup

Common Request Parameters

Table 11-1 Required parameters common to all requests

Parameter	Values	Description
Service	AWSECommerceService AlexaWebInfoService AWSSimpleQueueService	Specifies the Amazon Web Service to use. For E-Commerce Service 4.0, the value is AWSECommerceService.
SubscriptionId	Your Amazon-assigned Subscription Id	An identifier that Amazon assigns you. It is tied to the email address you use to sign up with.
Operation	Operation name from the list above.	An Amazon E-Commerce Service 4.0 operation

Table 11-2 Optional parameters usable by all requests

Parameter	Values	Description
AssociateTag	Amazon-assigned tag value	The AssociateTag allows product URLs returned by ECS to be tagged as originating from your Associates Web site. Be sure to specify the tag value correctly, as no error is generated for incorrect tag values. If you use those product URLs to link to Amazon, the Associate account connected to the AssociateTag you specify will be credited for traffic and items sold through your links. Since you do not need to be an Associate to use ECS, AssociateTag is not a required parameter. If you do not include AssociateTag in your requests, a default Associate tag will be embedded in the product URLs in ECS responses.
ResponseGroup	One or more Response Groups. The default values depend on the operation used.	Specifies what data is to be returned by the current operation; allows you to control the volume and content of returned data. For details about using ResponseGroup with each operation, check the operation pages.

Parameter	Values	Description
Validate	True or False. Default is False.	Use the Validate parameter to have ECS test your request without actually executing it. If this parameter is not specified, the default value is False (i.e., requests are executed normally). When present, Validate must equal True. If the request is valid, the response will contain an element called IsValid with a value of True. If the request is invalid, the response will contain 1) an element called IsValid with a value of False and 2) the errors that would be returned if the request were actually executed. Notes: Since the request is not actually executed, only a subset of the errors for the request may be returned. This is because some errors (e.g., no_exact_matches) are only generated during execution of a request. The IsValid element will always be present in any response, regardless of whether the Validate parameter was in the request.
Version	Default value is the name space identifier date from the latest WSDL file.	For REST requests, use the Version parameter to retrieve a particular version of the ECS WSDL. The value of the Version parameter is the date that is part of the WSDL's namespace. Each time changes are made to ECS (for example, changed operation parameters, response groups, or behavior), a new WSDL is created with a new date. For SOAP requests, this parameter is ignored because the version is retrieved from the WSDL namespace. If the Version parameter is omitted in a REST request, ECS uses the default namespace. The default namespace may change as new versions of ECS are released. If you use XSLT to transform ECS output, you should use the Version parameter to ensure that your stylesheets continue to work correctly when the default namespace is changed.
XMLEscaping	Default value is Single. Possible values are Single or Double.	Use the XMLEscaping parameter to specify whether responses are XML-encoded in a single pass or a double pass. By default, XMLEscaping is Single, and ECS responses are encoded only once in XML. For example, if the response data includes an ampersand character (&), the character is returned in its regular XML encoding (&). If XMLEscaping is Double, the same ampersand character is XML-encoded twice (&). The Double value for XMLEscaping is useful in some clients, such as PHP, that do not decode text within XML elements.

Table 11-3 Parameters used only with XSLT style sheet requests

Parameter	Values	Description
Style	Default Value is XML Valid Values are XML or a URL to an XSL stylesheet	The Style parameter applies to REST requests only. Use the Style parameter to control the format of the data returned by ECS in REST responses. Set this parameter to "XML" to generate a pure XML response. Set this parameter to the URL of an XSLT stylesheet to have ECS transform the XML response to another format you specify. If you omit this parameter, ECS will return a pure XML response by default.
ContentType	Default Value is text/xml. Valid values are text/xml or text/html	The ContentType parameter is valid for REST requests only. The ContentType set in your request is returned as the content type in the HTTP headers of the response that ECS returns. Generally ContentType should only be changed when it is being used in conjunction with an XSLT stylesheet specified with the Style parameter. When you use a stylesheet to transform your ECS response to HTML, set this parameter to text/html.

Reference Manual

BrowseNodeLookup

Description

All products listed on Amazon's websites are classified into groups, such as product type (books, music, tools, or apparel), brand, subject, genre, style, and so on. The hierarchy of groups is called a browse area, where each group has a particular browse node ID in the browse area. The BrowseNodeLookup operation allows you to retrieve information about a browse node, which is a specific Amazon product area. This operation returns the browse node's name and a list of browse node children. The browse node children contain a subset of the products included in the parent browse node's product area.

Locales

Amazon.com

Sample Request Using REST

```
http://webservices.amazon.com/onca/xml?Service=AWSECommerceService
&SubscriptionId=[Your Subscription ID Here]&Operation=BrowseNodeLookup&
&BrowseNodeId=1065852&Version=[Version Here]
```

Request Parameters

Parameter*	Description	Required?	Value
Operation	The Operation	Yes	BrowseNodeLookup

Parameter*	Description	Required?	Value
BrowseNodeId	Represents the desired product category	Yes	A valid Browse Node Id
ResponseGroup	A Comma-separated list of Response Groups. Indicates which data elements you want returned in Amazon's response.	Optional	Default Values • Request • BrowseNodeInfo Valid Values • Request • BrowseNodeInfo

*See "Common Request Parameters" at the beginning of this Appendix for additional parameters

CartAdd

Description

Add items to an existing remote cart.

Locales All

Sample Request Using REST

```
http://webservices.amazon.com/onca xml?Service=AWSECommerceService&
SubscriptionId=[Your Subscription ID Here]&Operation=CartAdd&
CartId=[A Cart ID]&HMAC=[An HMAC Shopping Cart Token]&
Item.1.ASIN=[An ASIN]&Item.1.Quantity=1
```

Request Parameters

Parameter*	Description	Required?	Value
Operation	The Operation	Yes	CartAdd
CartId	The CartId is a unique identifier for an Amazon remote shopping cart. CartIds are initially obtained by using the CartCreate operation.	Yes	A Cart Id
HMAC	The HMAC is a unique security token that, when used with the CartId, allows you to access and modify (add to, remove from, empty) a specific remote shopping cart that you have created from your application or Web site. HMACs are initially obtained by using the CartCreate operation.	Yes	An HMAC security token

Parameter*	Description	Required?	Value
Items	The Items parameter must be used in all SOAP requests. It cannot be used with REST requests. The Items parameter serves as a container element for the list of products that will be added to a shopping cart. An Items element would contain 1 or more Item elements in a SOAP request.	Required for SOAP	
Item	In SOAP Requests: The Item parameter serves as a container element that is a child of the Items element. As a container element, an Item holds product ID elements (like ASIN) and Quantity elements. In REST Requests: The Item parameter in a REST request serves as a means of prefixing one or more products (Item.1.ASIN) and the quantities of those products (Item.1. Quantity).	Yes	
ASIN	The ASIN parameter is a child element of the Item parameter in both SOAP and REST requests. The ASIN parameter is required in an Item element if you are not using OfferListingId to identify an item.	See Description	An ASIN
OfferListingId	The OfferListingId uniquely identifies a particular product being sold by a particular seller or merchant. The OfferListingId is required when the item being placed in the shopping cart is not being sold by Amazon. When Amazon is selling the product, you must use the ASIN parameter. The OfferListingID parameter is required in an Item element if you are not using an ASIN to identify an item.	See Description	An Offer Listing Id
Quantity	The Quantity parameter is paired with any of the product ID parameters and specifies the number to be added to the cart. It must be used as a child of an Item element in a request.	Yes	An integer between 0 and 99

Parameter*	Description	Required?	Value
ResponseGroup	A Comma-separated list of Response Groups. Indicates which data elements you want returned in Amazon's response.	Optional	Default Values: • Request • Cart Valid Values: • Request • Cart • CartSimilarities

*See "Common Request Parameters" at the beginning of this Appendix for additional parameters

CartClear

Description

Remove all contents of a remote cart.

Locales All

Sample Request Using REST

```
http://webservices.amazon.com/onca/xml?Service=AWSECommerceService&
SubscriptionId=[Your Subscription ID Here]&Operation=CartClear&
CartId=[A Cart ID]&HMAC=[An HMAC Shopping Cart Token]
```

Request Parameters

Parameter*	Description	Required?	Value
Operation	The Operation	Yes	CartAdd
CartId	The CartId is a unique identifier for an Amazon remote shopping cart. CartIds are initially obtained by using the CartCreate operation.	Yes	A Cart Id
HMAC	The HMAC is a unique security token that, when used with the CartId, allows you to access and modify (add to, remove from, empty) a specific remote shopping cart that you have created from your application or Web site. HMACs are initially obtained by using the CartCreate operation.	Yes	An HMAC security token

Parameter*	Description	Required?	Value
ResponseGroup	A Comma-separated list of Response Groups. Indicates which data elements you want returned in Amazon's response.	Optional	Default Values: • Request • Cart Valid Values: • Request • Cart • CartSimilarities

*See "Common Request Parameters" at the beginning of this Appendix for additional parameters

CartCreate

Description

The CartCreate operation allows you to create a new remote shopping cart. CartCreate returns two unique identifiers for each cart, the CartId and HMAC. These two identifiers can then be used to access and manipulate the shopping cart with the CartAdd, CartClear, CartGet, and CartModify operations.

Locales All

Sample Request Using REST

```
http://webservices.amazon.com/onca/xml?Service=AWSECommerceService&
SubscriptionId=[Your Subscription ID Here]&Operation=CartCreate&
Item.1.ASIN=[An ASIN]&Item.1.Quantity=1&Item.2.ASIN=[An ASIN]&
Item.2.Quantity=1&Item.3.ASIN=[An ASIN]&Item.3.Quantity=1&Version=[version date here]
```

Request Parameters

Parameter*	Description	Required?	Value
Operation	The Operation	Yes	CartAdd
Items	The Items parameter must be used in all SOAP requests. It cannot be used with REST requests. The Items parameter serves as a container element for the list of products that will be added to a shopping cart. An Items element would contain 1 or more Item elements in a SOAP request.	Required for SOAP	
MergeCart	Determines whether the remote cart items are merged with the customer's Amazon cart, or if the item can be immediately purchased. The default value is False, which only works with the US locale. You must set MergeCart to True for non-US locales.	Optional	True or False

Parameter*	Description	Required?	Value
Item	In SOAP Requests: The Item parameter serves as a container element that is a child of the Items element. As a container element, an Item holds product ID elements (like ASIN) and Quantity elements. In REST Requests: The Item parameter in a REST request serves as a means of prefixing one or more products (Item.1.ASIN) and the quantities of those products (Item.1.Quantity).	Yes	
ASIN	The ASIN parameter is a child element of the Item parameter in both SOAP and REST requests. The ASIN parameter is required in an Item element if you are not using OfferListingId to identify an item.	See Description	An ASIN
OfferListingId	The OfferListingId uniquely identifies a particular product being sold by a particular seller or merchant. The OfferListingId is required when the item being placed in the shopping cart is not being sold by Amazon. When Amazon is selling the product, you must use the ASIN parameter. The OfferListingID parameter is required in an Item element if you are not using an ASIN to identify an item.	See Description	An Offer Listing Id
Quantity	The Quantity parameter is paired with any of the product ID parameters and specifies the number to be added to the cart. It must be used as a child of an Item element in a request.	Yes	An integer between 0 and 99
ResponseGroup	A Comma-separated list of Response Groups. Indicates which data elements you want returned in Amazon's response.	Optional	Default Values: • Request • Cart Valid Values: • Request • Cart • CartSimilarities

*See "Common Request Parameters" at the beginning of this Appendix for additional parameters

CartGet

Description

Retrieve the contents of a remote cart.

Locales All

Sample Request Using REST

```
http://webservices.amazon.com/onca/xml?Service=AWSECommerceService&
SubscriptionId=[Your Subscription ID Here]&Operation=CartGet&
CartId=[A Cart ID]&HMAC=[An HMAC Shopping Cart Token]&Version=[version date here]
```

Request Parameters

Parameter*	Description	Required?	Value
Operation	The Operation	Yes	CartGet
CartId	The CartId is a unique identifier for an Amazon remote shopping cart. CartIds are initially obtained by using the CartCreate operation.	Yes	A Cart Id
HMAC	The HMAC is a unique security token that, when used with the CartId, allows you to access and modify (add to, remove from, empty) a specific remote shopping cart that you have created from your application or Web site. HMACs are initially obtained by using the CartCreate operation.	Yes	An HMAC security token
ResponseGroup	A Comma-separated list of Response Groups. Indicates which data elements you want returned in Amazon's response.	Optional	Default Values: • Request • Cart Valid Values: • Request • Cart • CartSimilarities

*See "Common Request Parameters" at the beginning of this Appendix for additional parameters

CartModify

Description

The CartModify operation allows you to modify the quantity of items in a remote shopping cart, as well as move items from the active area of a cart to the save for later area.

Locales All

Sample Request Using REST

```
http://webservices.amazon.com/onca/xml?Service=AWSECommerceService&
SubscriptionId=[Your Subscription ID Here]&
AssociateTag=[Your Associate ID Here]&Operation=CartModify&
CartId=[A Cart ID]&HMAC=[An HMAC Shopping Cart Token]&
Item.1.CartItemId=[A CartItemId]&Item.1.Quantity=5&
Item.2.CartItemId=[A CartItemId]&Item.2.Quantity=0&
Item.3.CartItemId=[A CartItemId]&Item.3.Action=SaveForLater
```

Request Parameters

Parameter*	Description	Required?	Value
Operation	The Operation	Yes	CartModify
CartId	The CartId is a unique identifier for an Amazon remote shopping cart. CartIds are initially obtained by using the CartCreate operation.	Yes	A Cart Id
HMAC	The HMAC is a unique security token that, when used with the CartId, allows you to access and modify (add to, remove from, empty) a specific remote shopping cart that you have created from your application or Web site. HMACs are initially obtained by using the CartCreate operation.	Yes	An HMAC security token
Items	The Items parameter must be used in all SOAP requests. It cannot be used with REST requests. The Items parameter serves as a container element for the list of products that will be added to a shopping cart. An Items element would contain 1 or more Item elements in a SOAP request.	Required for SOAP	
Item	In SOAP Requests: The Item parameter serves as a container element that is a child of the Items element. As a container element, an Item holds product ID elements (like ASIN) and Quantity elements. In REST Requests: The Item parameter in a REST request serves as a means of prefixing one or more products (Item.1.ASIN) and the quantities of those products (Item.1.Quantity).	Yes	

Parameter*	Description	Required?	Value
CartItemId	The ASIN parameter is a child element of the Item parameter in both SOAP and REST requests. The ASIN parameter is required in an Item element if you are not using OfferListingId to identify an item.	See Description	An ASIN
Quantity	The Quantity parameter is paired with any of the product ID parameters and specifies the number to be added to the cart. It must be used as a child of an Item element in a request.	Yes	An integer between 0 and 99
Action	The Action parameter is a child element of the Item parameter in both SOAP and REST requests. Use the Action parameter to change cart items to saved items (SaveForLater) or change saved items to cart items (MoveToCart).		Possible values are MoveToCart and SaveForLater
MergeCart	Determines whether the remote cart items are merged with the customer's Amazon cart, or if the item can be immediately purchased. The default value is False, which only works with the US locale. You must set MergeCart to True for non-US locales.		
ResponseGroup	A Comma-separated list of Response Groups. Indicates which data elements you want returned in Amazon's response.	Optional	Default Values: • Request • Cart Valid Values: • Request • Cart • CartSimilarities

*See "Common Request Parameters" at the beginning of this Appendix for additional parameters

CustomerContentLookup

Description

The CustomerContentLookup operation allows you to retrieve publicly available content written by specific Amazon customers. Available data are limited to information about content customers have created for any Amazon Web site, including product reviews, Listmania lists, wish lists, registries, and reviewer rank. Through this operation, you can also get any information customers have chosen to make public about themselves on the Amazon Web sites, including their nickname, their location, and their birthday. For reasons of confidentiality, CustomerContentLookup does not provide access to any customer account history or contact information (including email address, shipping address, billing address, or phone number).

Locales Amazon.com

Sample Request Using REST

```
http://webservices.amazon.com/onca/
xml?Service=AWSECommerceService&
SubscriptionId=[Your Subscription ID Here]&Operation=CustomerContentLookup&
CustomerId=[A Customer ID]&Version=[version date here]
```

Request Parameters

Parameter*	Description	Required?	Value
Operation	The Operation	Yes	CustomerContentLookup
CustomerId	Use the CustomerId parameter to specify the customer you want information about. A CustomerContentLookup request may contain only one CustomerId. If you do not know the customer ID, you can use the CustomerContentSearch operation to get it.	Yes	A valid Customer Id
ReviewPage	The ReviewPage parameter allows you to page through a specified customer's reviews, ten at a time. The value of this parameter is the page number to be returned. The ReviewPage parameter will be ignored if the CustomerReviews response group is not designated in the request. If you do not include ReviewPage in your request, the first page (with the first ten reviews, or all of the reviews if there are fewer than 10 available) are returned by default.	Optional	Default value is 1. Valid value is any integer from 1 to 10 inclusive.
ResponseGroup	A Comma-separated list of Response Groups. Indicates which data elements you want returned in Amazon's response.	Optional	Default Values: • Request • CustomerInfo Valid Values: • Request • CustomerInfo • CustomerReviews • CustomerLists • CustomerFull

*See "Common Request Parameters" at the beginning of this Appendix for additional parameters

CustomerContentSearch

Description

The CustomerContentSearch operation allows you to search for Amazon customers by name or email address.

Note: Amazon E-Commerce Service (ECS) only returns information that the customer has made public on the Amazon.com Web site. ECS never returns email addresses or mailing addresses regardless of whether or not the customer has made them public.

Locales

Amazon.com

Sample Request Using REST

```
http://webservices.amazon.com/onca/xml?Service=AWSECommerceService&
SubscriptionId=[Your Subscription ID Here]&Operation=CustomerContentSearch&
Name=Jeff+Bezos&Version=[version here]
```

Request Parameters

Parameter*	Description	Required?	Value
Operation	The Operation	Yes	CustomerContentSearch
Name	The Name parameter allows you to search for a customer by name. Search for a customer by name if you do not know their email address. You must specify either the Name or Email parameter. You cannot specify both the Email and the Name parameters in this operation.	See Description	All or part of a name. Example: Jason%20Levitt
Email	The Email parameter allows you to search for a customer by email address. Search for a customer by email address if you do not have the customer's name. You must specify either the Name or Email parameter. You cannot specify both the Email and the Name parameters in this operation.	See Description	All or part of a valid email address.

Parameter*	Description	Required?	Value
CustomerPage	The CustomerPage parameter allows you to page through the list of customers in the response, 20 at a time. This parameter specifies the number of the page that will be returned by the request. If you do not include CustomerPage in your request, the first page (containing the first 20 customers, or all customers if the search result returns less than 20 customers) is returned by default.	Optional	Default value is 1. Possible values is an integer from 1 to 20 inclusive.
ResponseGroup	A Comma-separated list of Response Groups. Indicates which data elements you want returned in Amazon's response.	Optional	Default Values: • Request • CustomerInfo Valid Values: • Request • CustomerInfo

*See "Common Request Parameters" at the beginning of this Appendix for additional parameters

Help

Description

Help lets you retrieve information about operations and Response Groups. Use it to facilitate development and documentation of your website and tools. The results returned by the Help operation are extracted from the SOAP WSDL.

Locales   All

Sample Request Using REST

```
Looking up info about the ItemLookup operation:

http://webservices.amazon.com/onca/xml?Service=AWSECommerceService&
SubscriptionId=[Your Subscription ID Here]&Operation=Help&
HelpType=Operation&About=ItemLookup&Version=[version here]

Looking up info about the Large Response Group:

http://webservices.amazon.com/onca/xml?Service=AWSECommerceService&
SubscriptionId=[Your Subscription ID Here]&Operation=Help&
HelpType=ResponseGroup&About=Large&Version=[version here]
```

Request Parameters

Parameter*	Description	Required?	Value
Operation	The Operation	Yes	Help

Parameter*	Description	Required?	Value
HelpType	Use this parameter to specify the whether you would like information about an operation or a response group.	Yes	Valid values are Operation and ResponseGroup
About	Use the About parameter to tell the Help operation what you would like help with. If you chose Operation as the HelpType, the About parameter must equal the name of a valid ECS operation. If you chose ResponseGroup as the HelpType, the About parameter must equal the name of a valid ECS response group.	Yes	Any Amazon E-Commerce Service 4.0 Operation name or Response Group name.
ResponseGroup	A Comma-separated list of Response Groups. Indicates which data elements you want returned in Amazon's response.	Optional	Default Values: • Request • Help Valid Values: • Request • Help

*See "Common Request Parameters" at the beginning of this Appendix for additional parameters

ItemLookup

Description

The ItemLookup operation allows you to retrieve catalog information for up to ten products. ItemLookup provides access to customer reviews, variations, product similarities, pricing, availability, images, product accessories, and other information.

Locales

All (however, some parameters may only be used with specific locales)

Sample Request Using REST

```
http://webservices.amazon.com/onca/xml?Service=AWSECommerceService&
SubscriptionId=[ID]&Operation=ItemLookup&ItemId=[An ASIN]&Version=[version date here]
```

Request Parameters

Parameter*	Description	Required?	Value
Operation	The Operation	Yes	ItemLookup
ItemId	Product(s) you would like information about. You may specify up to ten IDs using a comma-separated list (REST) or multiple elements (SOAP). By default the item IDs are assumed to be ASINs, unless you specify the IdType parameter.	Yes	Valid values are Operation and ResponseGroup

Parameter*	Description	Required?	Value
IdType	Type of product ID you are requesting information about. SKU requires a MerchantId (US locale only). UPC is US only. EAN is the same as JAN (Japanese article number), so you may use this parameter to look up items by JAN or EAN (DE/JP only). If you select SKU, UPC, or EAN as the IdType for your request, you also need to include the SearchIndex parameter.	Optional	Any Amazon E-Commerce Service 4.0 Operation name or Response Group name.
SearchIndex	The Amazon store to search. This parameter is ignored for ASIN searches. SearchIndex is required any time you select SKU, UPC, or EAN as the IdType for your request. The list of available SearchIndex values, segmented by locale, can be found on the search index values page. If IdType is set to EAN, the SearchIndex must be a valid Search Index for either the Amazon.de or Amazon.co.jp locales.	Only for IdType UPC, SKU or EAN	A valid (locale dependent) Search Index. Amazon.de EAN Valid Values: • Electronics • Music • Classical • DVD • VHS • Video • OutdoorLiving • HealthPersonal-Care • Kitchen • Software • SoftwareVideo-Games • VideoGames • Tools Amazon.co.jp EAN Valid Values: • Electronics • Music • Classical • DVD • Kitchen • Software • VideoGames

Parameter*	Description	Required?	Value
MerchantId	Filter the list of offerings returned by ItemLookup by the merchant offering the product. If not specified, Amazon is assumed to be the merchant for all requests. Setting MerchantId to "All" returns pricing information for Amazon and all other vendors. US only: You may also use the value "Featured," in which case Amazon ECommerce Service (ECS) returns the same merchant that is displayed when you click the "Add to Shopping Cart" button on the product detail page. US only: MerchantId must be used with the response groups Variations, VariationMinimum, and/or VariationSummary.	Only for IdType SKU	Default Value: • (Amazon's Merchant Id) Valid Values: • All • Featured (US only) • [A Merchant ID] (US only)
Condition	Returns only items in the specified condition	Optional	Default value is New Valid Values • All • New • Used • Refurbished • Collectible
DeliveryMethod	US only. Filter offers returned in the product list by delivery method. Valid values are Ship and ISPU (In-store pickup). If you use ISPU, the ISPUPostalCode parameter must be included to complete the request.	Optional	Default Value • Ship Valid Values • Ship • ISPU (US only)
ISPUPostalCode	US only. If DeliveryMethod is set to ISPU, ISPUPostalCode must specify the zip code where in store pickup is requested.	Only if Delivery Method is specified	A valid zip code
OfferPage	Returns up to 10 offer results at a time. If you do not include OfferPage in your request, the first page (the first 10 offers or all of the offers if there are less than 10 available) are returned by default. If included, this parameter specifies what page of results to include where 1 indicates the first ten results, 2 indicates the the eleventh through twentieth result, etc.	Optional	Default value is 1. Valid value is an integer 1 to 100 inclusive.

Parameter*	Description	Required?	Value
ReviewPage	ItemLookup returns up to 5 product reviews at a time. If you do not include ReviewPage in your request, the first page (the first five reviews, or all of the reviews if less than five are available) are returned by default. If included, this parameter specifies what page of results to include where 1 indicates the first five results, 2 indicates the the sixth through tenth result, etc.	Optional	Default value is 1. Valid value is an integer 1 to 20 inclusive.
VariationPage	ItemLookup returns all of the variations for a product. You can optionally include the VariationPage in your request to return 10 variations at a time where 1 indicates the first ten results, 2 indicates the the eleventh through twentieth result, etc.	Optional	Default value is 1. Valid value is an integer 1 to 150 inclusive.
ResponseGroup	A Comma-separated list of Response Groups. Indicates which data elements you want returned in Amazon's response.	Optional	Default Values • Request • Small Valid Values • Request • ItemIds • Small • Medium • Large • OfferFull • Offers • OfferSummary • Variations • VariationMinimum • VariationSummary • ItemAttributes • Tracks • Accessories • EditorialReview • SalesRank • BrowseNodes • Images • Similarities • Reviews • ListmaniaLists

*See "Common Request Parameters" at the beginning of this Appendix for additional parameters

ItemSearch

Description

Lets you to search for products by keywords, author, browse node, actor, director, etc.

Note: not all of the request parameters are compatible with all of the Search Indexes. You must make sure that your Search Index is valid in the specified locale and with the parameters used in your request.

Locales

All (however, some parameters may only be used with specific locales)

Sample Request Using REST

```
http://webservices.amazon.com/onca/xml?Service=AWSECommerceService&
SubscriptionId=[Your Subscription ID Here]&Operation=ItemSearch&
Keywords=[A Keywords String]&SearchIndex=[A Search Index String]&
Sort=[A Sort String]&Version=[version date here]
```

Request Parameters

Parameter*	Description	Required?	Value
Operation	The Operation	Yes	ItemSearch
SearchIndex	A top-level product category. The list of available SearchIndex values, listed by locale, can be found in Appendix F	Yes	A valid Search Index (varies by locale)
Keywords	Use the Keywords parameter to refine your item search based on specific words or phrases. Amazone E-Commerce Service will match the word or phrase you include in your request against various product fields, including product title, author, artist, description, manufacturer, etc. When SearchIndex equals Music-Tracks, the Keyword parameter allows you to search by song title.	Optional	A urlencoded string containing one or more words.
Title	Use the Title parameter when you want to query against product titles only. You may use all or part of a title in your query.	Optional	A urlencoded string containing one or more words.

Parameter*	Description	Required?	Value
Power	Use the Power parameter to perform book searches using a complex query string. For example the query "author:ambrose" returns a list of books that include "Ambrose" in the author name. A query of "subject:history and (spain or mexico) and not military and language:spanish" would return a list of books in the Spanish language on the subject of either Spanish or Mexican history, excluding all items with military in their subject. The Power parameter can only be used when SearchIndex equals Books. See this URL for more info on power search: http://www.amazon.com/exec/obidos/tg/browse/-/468558	Optional	A valid Power search query string
BrowseNode	Use the BrowseNode parameter to narrow your search to a specific category of products in the Amazon catalog. The BrowseNode parameter may contain the ID of any Amazon browse node. For a list of Amazon browse nodes, please see Browse Node Values. Please note that not all Amazon browse nodes have products classified under them. If you use such a browse node in your request, it will yield a no_exact_matches error.	Optional	A valid Browse Node Id
Artist	Use the Artist parameter refine your search by artist name. You may use all or part of an artist's name in your query.	Optional	A valid artist's name
Author	Use the Author parameter to refine your search by author name. You may use all or part of an author's name in your query.	Optional	A valid author's name
Actor	Use the Actor parameter to refine your search by actor name. You may use all or part of an actor's name in your query.	Optional	A valid actor's name
Director	Use the Director parameter to refine your search by Director name. You may use all or part of a director's name in your query.	Optional	A valid director's name

Parameter*	Description	Required?	Value
AudienceRating	Use the AudienceRating parameter to filter movie product search results by the expected audience maturity level. Amazon.com values are based upon MPAA (Motion Picture Association of America) ratings. Amazon.de values are based upon age. You may specify one or more values in a comma-separated list in a REST request or using multiple elements in a SOAP request.	Optional	Valid Amazon.com Values: • G • PG • PG-13 • R • NC-17 • NR • Unrated Valid Amazon.de Values • 6 • 12 • 16
Manufacturer	Use the Manufacturer parameter to refine your search by manufacturer name. You may use all or part of a manufacturer's name in your query.	Optional	A valid manufacturer's name
MusicLabel	Use the MusicLabel parameter to refine your search by the record label name. You may use all or part of a record label's name in your query.	Optional	A valid music label name
Composer	Use the Composer parameter to refine your search by music composer name. You may use all or part of a composer's name in your query.	Optional	A valid music composer's name
Publisher	Use the Publisher parameter to refine your search by publisher name. You may use all or part of a publisher's name in your query.	Optional	A valid publisher's name
Brand	Use the Brand parameter to refine your search by brand name. You may use all or part of a brand's name in your query.	Optional	A valid brand name
Conductor	Use the Conductor parameter to refine your search by conductor name. You may use all or part of a conductor's name in your query.	Optional	A valid conductor's name
Orchestra	Use the Orchestra parameter to refine your search by orchestra name. You may use all or part of an orchestra's name in your query.	Optional	A valid orchestra name

Parameter*	Description	Required?	Value
TextStream	Use the TextStream parameter to retrieve product search results based on a block of text you specify in your request. The text block could be a search term, a paragraph from a blog, an article excerpt, or any other text for which you wish to retrieve product matches. Amazon parses out recognized keywords and returns an equal number of products (ten total) for each recognized keyword. For example, if you send a request with five recognized keywords, Amazon will return two products matching each recognized keyword. The ItemPage parameter does not work when this parameter is being used--only one page can be returned.	Optional	Any urlencoded text string containing one or more words
ItemPage	The ItemPage parameter allows you to create a paginated list of search results. This parameter returns the specified page. When you use ItemPage, ItemSearch will return 10 search results at a time. The maximum ItemPage number that can be returned is 3200. If you do not include ItemPage in your request, the first page (containing the first 10 items, or all of the items if there are less than 10) will be returned by default.	Optional	Default value is 1. valid value is an integer between 1 and 3200 inclusive.
Sort	Use the Sort parameter to specify how your item search results will be ordered. Please note that valid sort values vary by search index and locale. The full list of sort options are available in Sort Values.	Optional	Varies by Search Index and locale
City	Use the City parameter to refine your restaurant search by city name. You may use all or part of a city's name in your query. At the present time, ECS return restaurants for only select cities. This parameter may be used only when SearchIndex equals Restaurant and is only applicable to US requests.	Optional	Valid Values: • Boston • Chicago • New York • San Francisco • Seattle • Washington, D.C.

Parameter*	Description	Required?	Value
Cuisine	Use the Cuisine parameter to refine your restaurant search by cuisine name (i.e., Chinese, Italian, American, etc.). You may use all or part of a cuisine's name in your query. This parameter may be used only when SearchIndex equals Restaurant and is only applicable to US requests.	Optional	A cuisine name
Neighborhood	Use the Neighborhood parameter to refine your restaurant search by neighborhood name (i.e., Capitol Hill, Arlington, North Beach, etc.). You may use all or part of a neighborhood's name in your query. This parameter may be used only when SearchIndex equals Restaurant and is only applicable to US requests.	Optional	A neighborhood name
MinimumPrice	Use the MinimumPrice parameter to set a lower price bound on products returned by ItemSearch. The MinimumPrice value must be specified in pennies (or equivalent in local currency).	Optional	A positive integer
MaximumPrice	Use the MaximumPrice parameter to set an upper price bound on products returned by ItemSearch. The MaximumPrice value must be specified in pennies (or equivalent in local currency).	Optional	A positive integer
MerchantId	Filter by the merchant offering the product. If not specified, Amazon is assumed to be the only merchant for all requests. Setting MerchantId to "All" returns pricing information for Amazon and all other vendors (US only). You may also use the value "Featured," in which case ECS returns the same merchant that is displayed when you click the "Add to Shopping Cart" button on the product detail page (US only).	Optional	Default Value • Amazon (the merchant) Valid Amazon.com Values: • All • Featured • [A Merchant ID]
Condition	Use the Condition parameter to filter the offers returned in the product list by condition type. By default, a request with the Condition parameter will return a maximum of 10 offers, with a maximum of 5 offer listings per offer.	Optional	Default Value • New Valid Values • All • New • Used • Refurbished • Collectible

Parameter*	Description	Required?	Value
DeliveryMethod	Use the DeliveryMethod parameter to filter offers returned in the product list by delivery method. Valid values are Ship and ISPU (In-store pickup). If you use ISPU, the offers returned will be ISPU offers from any postal code. To get ISPU offers from a specific postal code, you must use the ItemLookup operation. US only.	Optional	Default value is Ship. Possible values are Ship an ISPU.
ResponseGroup	A list of one or more Response Groups. Indicates which data elements you want returned in Amazon's response. You can specify as many response groups as you wish using a comma-separated list (REST) or multiple elements (SOAP).	Optional	Default Values • Request • Small Valid Values • Request • ItemIds • Small • Medium • Large • OfferFull • Offers • OfferSummary • VariationMinimum • VariationSummary • ItemAttributes • Tracks • Accessories • EditorialReview • SalesRank • BrowseNodes • Images • Similarities • Reviews • ListmaniaLists

*See "Common Request Parameters" at the beginning of this Appendix for additional parameters

ListLookup

Description

The ListLookup operation allows you to retrieve all the products in a specific Listmania list or Wishlist. In addition to returning products, ListLookup allows you to retrieve general information about the list, such as the total number of products on the list and the list's creation date...

Locales All

Sample Request Using REST

```
http://webservices.amazon.com/onca/xml?Service=AWSECommerceService&
SubscriptionId=[Your Subscription ID Here]&Operation=ListLookup&
```

```
ListType=WishList&ListId=[A Wishlist ID]&Version=[version date here]
```

Request Parameters

Parameter*	Description	Required?	Value
Operation	The Operation	Yes	ListLookup
ListType	Use the ListType parameter to specify the type of list you want to retrieve. Valid values are Listmania, WeddingRegistry, and WishList.	Yes	Valid values are Listmania, WeddingRegistry, and WishList
ListId	Use the ListId parameter to identify the list you would like to retrieve. Every Listmania List, Wish List, and Wedding Registry has a unique list ID. You may only look up one list at a time.	Yes	A Listmania, Wedding Registry, or WishList Id
ProductPage	The ProductPage parameter allows you to paginate the list of products returned by ListLookup. When you use ProductPage, ListLookup will return 10 items at a time. The maximum ProductPage number that can be returned is 30. If you do not include Product-Page in your request, the first 10 items are returned by default.	Optional	Default value is 1. Possible value is an integer from 1 to 30 inclusive.
ProductGroup	The ProductGroup parameter allows you to filter the list of products returned by ListLookup by product line. This parameter works only with WishLists.	Optional	Valid Values • Book • Music • Video • DVD • Toy • Health and Beauty • [others.....]
Sort	Use the Sort parameter to specify how the list products you retrieve will be ordered. The Sort parameter can only be used with wish lists. You may sort wish lists by DateAdded, LastUpdated, and Price.	Optional	Valid Values: • DateAdded • LastUpdated • Price

Parameter*	Description	Required?	Value
MerchantId	Filter the list of offerings returned by ListLookup by the merchant offering the product. If not specified, Amazon is assumed to be the merchant for all products. Setting MerchantId to "All" returns pricing information for Amazon and all other vendors. (US only). You may also use the value "Featured," in which case Amazon returns the same merchant that is displayed when you click the "Add to Shopping Cart" button on the product detail page.US only: MerchantId must be used with the response groups Variations, VariationMinimum, or VariationSummary.	Optional	Default value is Amazon's Merchant Id Possible values are: • Amazon??? • All • Featured • A Merchant ID
Condition	Use the Condition parameter to filter the offers returned in the product list by condition type.	Optional	Default Value • New Valid Values • All • New • Used • Refurbished • Collectible
DeliveryMethod	Use the DeliveryMethod parameter to filter offers returned in the product list by delivery method. Valid values are Ship and ISPU (In-store pickup). If you use ISPU, the offers returned will be ISPU offers from any postal code. To get ISPU offers from a specific postal code, you must use the ItemLookup operation (US only)	Optional	Default Value • Ship Valid Values • Ship • ISPU

Parameter*	Description	Required?	Value
ResponseGroup	A list of one or more Response Groups. Indicates which data elements you want returned in Amazon's response. You can specify as many response groups as you wish using a commaseparated list (REST) or multiple elements (SOAP).	Optional	Default Values: • Request • ListInfo Valid Values: • Request • ListFull • ListInfo • ListItems • ItemIds • Small • Medium • Large • Offers • OfferSummary • Variations • VariationMinimum • VariationSummary • ItemAttributes • Tracks • Accessories • EditorialReview • SalesRank • BrowseNodes • Images • Similarities • Reviews • ListmaniaLists

*See "Common Request Parameters" at the beginning of this Appendix for additional parameters

ListSearch

Description

The ListSearch operation allows you to search for an Amazon Wish List, Baby Registry, or Wedding Registry.

Locales

All

Sample Request Using REST

```
http://webservices.amazon.com/onca/xml?Service=AWSECommerceService&
SubscriptionId=[Your Subscription ID Here]&Operation=ListSearch&
ListType=WishList&Name=Jeff%20Bezos&Version=[version date here]
```

Request Parameters

Parameter*	Description	Required?	Value
Operation	The Operation	Yes	ListSearch

Parameter*	Description	Required?	Value
ListType	The ListType parameter allows you to specify the type of list you are searching for. You may only search for one type of list at a time.	Yes	Valid Values • WishList • WeddingRegistry • BabyRegistry
Name	Use the Name parameter when you want to search for lists by using the full customer name.	Optional	An Amazon customer name
FirstName	Use the FirstName parameter when you want to search for lists by using a customer's first name.	Optional	A first name
LastName	Use the LastName parameter when you want to search for lists by using a customer's last name.	Optional	A last name
Email	Use the Email parameter when you want to search for lists by using a customer's email address.	Optional	An email address
City	The City parameter allows you to search for lists created by customers living in the city you specify.	Optional	A city name
State	The State parameter allows you to search for lists created by customers living in the state you specify.	Optional	A state name
ListPage	The ListPage parameter allows you to specify which page of results will be returned by the request. The ListPage parameter allows you page through lists in the response, 10 at a time. If you do not include ListPage in your request, the first page of results will be returned, containing all items if there are less than ten or the first ten items if there are more than ten.	Optional	Default value is 1. Possible value is an integer from 1 to 20 inclusive.

Parameter*	Description	Required?	Value
ResponseGroup	A list of one or more Response Groups. Indicates which data elements you want returned in Amazon's response. You can specify as many response groups as you wish using a commaseparated list (REST) or multiple elements (SOAP).	Optional	Default Values: • Request • ListInfo Valid Values: • Request • ListInfo • ListMinimum

*See "Common Request Parameters" at the beginning of this Appendix for additional parameters

SellerListingLookup

Description

The SellerListingLookup operation allows you to request information about Amazon zShops and Marketplace products, including product descriptions, condition information, and seller information.

Locales All

Sample Request Using REST

```
http://webservices.amazon.com/onca/xml?Service=AWSECommerceService&
SubscriptionId=[Your Subscription ID Here]&Operation=SellerListingLookup&
IdType=Listing&Id=[An Offer Listing ID]&Version=[version date here]
```

Request Parameters

Parameter*	Description	Required?	Value
Operation	The Operation	Yes	SellerListingLookup
IdType	Use the IdType parameter to specify the type of seller listing you would like information about. If you are looking up an Amazon Marketplace item, you will want to use Exchange as the IdType. If you are looking up the details of a zShops item, you may use Listing as the IdType.	Yes	Valid Values • Exchange • Listing

Parameter*	Description	Required?	Value
Id	Use the Id parameter to specify either the exchange ID (for Marketplace or zShops items) or the listing ID (only for zShops items) of the product you wish to look up. You may specify comma-delimited list (REST) or multiple elements (SOAP) in the Id parameter to retrieve information for up to ten Marketplace or zShops items in a single operation.	Yes	An Offer Listing Id or and Exchange Id
SellerId	The SellerId limits the results to a single seller ID. This operation only applies to the JP, FR, and CA locales.	Yes (for JP, FR, and CA locales)	A valid Seller Id
ResponseGroup	A list of one or more Response Groups. Indicates which data elements you want returned in Amazon's response. You can specify as many response groups as you wish using a commaseparated list (REST) or multiple elements (SOAP).	Optional	Default Values • Request • SellerListing Valid Values • Request • SellerListing

*See "Common Request Parameters" at the beginning of this Appendix for additional parameters

SellerListingSearch

Description

The SellerListingSearch operation allows you to search for zShops and marketplace listings.

Locales
All

Sample Request Using REST

```
http://webservices.amazon.com/onca/xml?Service=AWSECommerceService&
SubscriptionId=[Yourv Subscription ID Here]&Operation=SellerListingSearch&
SearchIndex=Marketplace&Keywords=[A Keywords String]&Sort=+price&OfferStatus=Open&
Version=[version date here]
```

Request Parameters

Parameter*	Description	Required?	Value
Operation	The Operation	Yes	SellerListingSearch

Parameter*	Description	Required?	Value
SearchIndex	Use the SearchIndex parameter to specify the type of seller listings you would like to find, zShops listings or marketplace listings. This parameter only applies to the US, UK, and DE locales. Note that the SearchIndex parameter is not used for a Search Index here.	Yes	Valid Values: • ZShops • Marketplace
Keywords	Use the Keywords parameter to refine your seller listing search. You may not use the Keywords parameter and the Title parameter in the same request. The Keywords parameter accepts a string containing one or more words. The Keywords parameter allows SellerListingSearch to search inside listing titles and descriptions for matches. This parameter only applies to the US, UK, and DE locales.	Optional	A urlencoded string containing one or more words
Title	Use the Title parameter to refine your seller listing search to listings containing matching title words. You may not use the Title parameter and the Keywords parameter in the same request. The Title parameter accepts a string containing one or more title words.	Optional	A urlencoded string containing one or more words
ShipOption	Use the ShipOption parameter to filter your search results based on whether the seller listings matching your search request can be shipped to or from the value in the Country parameter. If the ShipOption parameter is specified, the Country parameter also must be specified. This parameter only applies to the US, UK, and DE locales.	Optional	Valid Values: • ShipTo • ShipFrom
Country	Use the Country parameter in conjunction with the ShipOption parameter to specify the country to associate with the selected shipping option (ShipTo or ShipFrom). Valid country codes can be found on the zShops country codes page. This parameter only applies to the US, UK, and DE locales.	Optional	A zShops country code

Parameter*	Description	Required?	Value
BrowseNode	Use the BrowseNode parameter to filter your seller listing search results by how they have been classified in the browse taxonomy. This parameter only applies to the US, UK, and DE locales.	Optional	A Browse Node Id
PostalCode	Use the PostalCode parameter to filter your seller listing search results by a specific postal code. This parameter only applies to the US, UK, and DE locales.	Optional	A postal code
Sort	Use the Sort parameter to specify how your seller listing search results will be ordered. The -bfp (featured listings - default), applies only to the US, UK, and DE locales.	Optional	Default Value: • -bfp Valid Values: • -bfp • -startdate • +startdate • +price • -price
ListingPage	This parameter specifies which page of listings to return with the request, where a page is up to 10 search results at a time. Specifying 1 returns the first page (items 1 through 10), specifying 2 returns the second page (items 11 through 20), etc. The maximum ListingPage number that can be specified is 500. If you do not include ListingPage in your request, all of the listings are returned if there are less than 10, the first 10 are returned if there are more than 10.	Optional	Default value is 1. Possible value is an integer between 1 and 500 inclusive.
OfferStatus	Use the OfferStatus parameter to filter your seller listing search results by whether the offer status is closed (sold or unpurchasable) or open (purchasable). This parameter only applies to the US, UK, and DE locales.	Optional	Default Value: • Open Valid Values: • Open • Closed

Parameter*	Description	Required?	Value
SellerId	Use the SellerId parameter to filter the seller listing search results by a zShops or marketplace seller ID. When SellerId is the only specified parameter (other than Operation and SearchIndex, which are required), the SellerListingSearch operation returns all of the specified seller's listings.	Optional for US, UK, and DE. Required for JP, FR, and CA.	A Seller Id
ResponseGroup	A list of one or more Response Groups. Indicates which data elements you want returned in Amazon's response. You can specify as many response groups as you wish using a commaseparated list (REST) or multiple elements (SOAP).	Optional	Default Values • Request • SellerListing Valid Values • Request • SellerListing

*See "Common Request Parameters" at the beginning of this Appendix for additional parameters

SellerLookup

Description

The SellerLookup operation allows you to retrieve information about specific sellers, including customer feedback about the sellers, their average feedback rating, their location, etc. For reasons of confidentiality, SellerLookup will not return seller email addresses or business addresses.

Note: At the present time, no customer ratings or feedback will be returned for Amazon.co.jp sellers.

Locales

All

Sample Request Using REST

```
http://webservices.amazon.com/onca/xml?Service=AWSECommerceService&
SubscriptionId=[Your Subscription ID Here]& Operation=SellerLookup&
SellerId=[A Seller ID],[A Seller ID],[A Seller ID]&Version=[version date here]
```

Request Parameters

Parameter*	Description	Required?	Value
Operation	The Operation	Yes	SellerLookup

Parameter*	Description	Required?	Value
SellerId	Use the SellerId parameter to specify IDs for Amazon sellers you want to look up. You may use SellerId to retrieve information for up to five sellers using a comma-separated list of seller IDs. In SOAP, multiple instances can be represented as multiple SellerId instances.	Yes	A Seller Id
FeedbackPage	This parameter specifies the page number, when multiple "pages" (blocks of 5 feedback items) exist. The maximum number of pages that can be returned is 10 (50 feedback items). If you do not include FeedbackPage in your request, all of the feedback items are returned if there are less than five, or if there are more than five, the first 5 are returned.	Optional	Default value is 1. Possible value is and integer from 1 to 10 inclusive.
ResponseGroup	A list of one or more Response Groups. Indicates which data elements you want returned in Amazon's response. You can specify as many response groups as you wish using a commaseparated list (REST) or multiple elements (SOAP).	Optional	Default Values • Request • Seller Valid Values • Request • Seller

*See "Common Request Parameters" at the beginning of this Appendix for additional parameters

SimilarityLookup

Description

The SimilarityLookup operation allows you to retrieve products that are similar to one or several specific Amazon products. SimilarityLookup may also be used to retrieve an intersection of similar products for up to ten specific Amazon products.

Locales All

Sample Request Using REST

```
http://webservices.amazon.com/onca/xml?Service=AWSECommerceService&
SubscriptionId=[Your Subscription ID Here]&Operation=SimilarityLookup&
ItemId=[An ASIN]&Version=[version here]
```

Request Parameters

Parameter*	Description	Required?	Value
Operation	The Operation	Yes	SellerLookup
ItemId	The products you want similarities for	Yes	Up to ten ASINs in a comma-separated list for REST requests or in multiple ItemId elements for SOAP requests.
SimilarityType	Use the SimilarityType parameter to filter the list of similar products returned by SimilarityLookup. Note that the SimilarityType parameter is ignored when when the SimilarityLookup request contains only one ItemId. Set the value of SimilarityType to Intersection if you want the list of similar products returned by SimilarityLookup to include only products that are similar to all of the items in the request. Set the value of SimilarityType to Random if you want the list of similar products returned by SimilarityLookup to include an assortment of similar products corresponding to any of the items in the request.	Optional	Default Value: • Intersection Valid Values: • Intersection • Random
MerchantId	Filter the list of offerings returned by SimilarityLookup by the merchant offering the product. If not specified, Amazon is assumed to be the merchant for all requests. Setting MerchantId to "All" returns pricing information for Amazon and all other vendors. US only: You may also use the value "Featured," in which case Amazon ECommerce Service (ECS) returns the same merchant that is displayed when you click the "Add to Shopping Cart" button on the product detail page. US only: MerchantId must be used with the response groups Variations, VariationMinimum, and VariationSummary.	Optional	Valid Values: • Amazon (the Default value) • All • Featured • A Merchant ID

Parameter*	Description	Required?	Value
Condition	Use the Condition parameter to filter the offers returned in the product list by condition type.	Optional	Default Value • New Valid Values • All • New • Used • Refurbished • Collectible
DeliveryMethod	Use the DeliveryMethod parameter to filter offers returned in the product list by delivery method. Valid values are Ship and ISPU (In-store pickup). If you use ISPU, the offers returned will be ISPU offers from any postal code. To get ISPU offers from a specific postal code, you must use the ItemLookup operation. US only.	Optional	Default Value • Ship Valid Values • Ship • ISPU
ResponseGroup	A list of one or more Response Groups. Indicates which data elements you want returned in Amazon's response. You can specify as many response groups as you wish using a commaseparated list (REST) or multiple elements (SOAP).	Optional	Default Values • Request • Small Valid Values • Request • ItemIds • Small • Medium • Large • Offers • OfferSummary • Variations • VariationMinimum • VariationSummary • ItemAttributes • Tracks • Accessories • EditorialReview • SalesRank • BrowseNodes

*See "Common Request Parameters" at the beginning of this Appendix for additional parameters

TransactionLookup

Description

The TransactionLookup operation allows you to retrieve a limited amount of information about the status of financial transactions made by Amazon customers. Specifically, it returns order total, subtotal, tax, and shipping charges. For reasons of confidentiality, it does not return customer information, shipping addresses, or a list of items in the order.

Locales US locale only

Sample Request Using REST

```
http://webservices.amazon.com/onca/xml?Service=AWSECommerceService&
SubscriptionId=[Your Subscription ID Here]&Operation=TransactionLookup&
TransactionId=[A Transaction ID]
```

Request Parameters

Parameter*	Description	Required?	Value
Operation	The Operation	Yes	TransactionLookup
TransactionId	Use the TransactionId parameter to specify transaction IDs you want information about. You may specify up to 10 transaction IDs in a single request, using a comma-separated list in a REST request or multiple elements in SOAP.	Yes	One or more Transaction Ids
ResponseGroup	A list of one or more Response Groups. Indicates which data elements you want returned in Amazon's response. You can specify as many response groups as you wish using a commaseparated list (REST) or multiple elements (SOAP).	Optional	Default Values • Request • TransactionDetails Valid Values: • Request • TransactionDetails

APPENDIX C

Using NuSOAP And PEAR SOAP With E-Commerce Service 4.0

This appendix explains how to download and use NuSOAP and PEAR SOAP with Amazon E-Commerce Service 4.0.

Using NuSOAP

Downloading and Installing the Latest version of Nusoap

NuSOAP is a set of PHP classes that lets developers create both SOAP clients and servers. It's maintained by Scott Nichols and Dietrich Ayala. To get the latest version, you should go to the NuSOAP repository on Sourceforge (http://cvs.sourceforge.net/viewcvs.py/nusoap/lib) and download the file nusoap.php. The version of NuSOAP you are using is listed near the beginning of the file nusoap.php where the variable $version is defined, but a more timely way of referring to the version is by using the CVS revision just below that.

```
class nusoap_base {

    var $title = 'NuSOAP';
    var $version = '0.6.9';
    var $revision = '$Revision: 1.86 $';
```

We'll always refer to NuSOAP by its CVS revision number, in this case, version 1.81.

Making SOAP Requests With NuSOAP

NuSOAP does all the work of fetching and parsing results from Amazon E-commerce Service for us, but we must still provide the Document/Literal format request parameters, and the URL of the Amazon WSDL file.

Example 12-1. An E-Commerce Service request using NuSOAP

```
<?php
require_once("nusoap.php");
// URL of Amazon's WSDL file
$wsdl='http://webservices.amazon.com/AWSECommerceService/2005-02-23/US/
AWSECommerceService.wsdl';

// The Document/Literal format request parameters
$params=array(
    'SubscriptionId' => '1A7XKHR5BYD0WPJVQEG2',
    'AssociateTag' => 'ws',
    'Request' => array (
                    array(
                                    'ItemId' => array('B0001BKAEY'),
                                    'IdType' => 'ASIN',
                                    'ResponseGroup' => array('Request', 'Small')
                                    )
                        )
);

// Parse the WSDL to get the method information
$client = new soapclient($wsdl, true);

// Set the character encoding to UTF-8
$client->soap_defencoding = 'UTF-8';

// Call the ItemLookup method
$Result = $client->call('ItemLookup', array('body' => $params));

// Output the results
echo '<pre>';
print_r($Result);
echo '</pre>';
?>
```

Since NuSOAP defaults to ISO-8859-1 character encoding, we have to explicitly set it to UTF-8 encoding which is required by Amazon E-commerce Service.

```
$client->soap_defencoding = 'UTF-8';
```

Using the NuSOAP call() function, we must wrap the parameters in the “body” identifier.

```
$Result = $client->call('ItemLookup', array('body' => $params));
```

That’s specified in the WSDL file where the ItemLookupRequestMsg is located.

```
<message name="ItemLookupRequestMsg">
<part name="body" element="tns:ItemLookup" />
</message>
```

It's also possible to use a direct proxy call e.g. $client->ItemLookup($params) instead of using the NuSOAP call() function. However, the call() function is more flexible since it lets us add SOAP-specific parameters.

NuSOAP's soapclient class does all the heavy lifting by parsing the Amazon E-commerce Service WSDL file and making the various AWS methods available to us. For simple XML tags, NuSOAP always returns the results in a PHP associative array where the tag names are the keys and the data are the values. For repeated XML tags, NuSOAP returns an array with numeric indexes. The current version of NuSOAP has the "No Schema Problem" (see "The No Schema Problem" section in Chapter Two for details) when dealing with array types.

Another parsing problem with NuSOAP is that it does not handle complex arrays with attributes correctly yet (note the Arguments array below), but it parses the bulk of Amazon responses well enough for most applications.

```
Array
(
    [OperationRequest] => Array
        (
            [HTTPHeaders] => Array
                (
                    [Header] => Array
                        (
                            [!Name] => UserAgent
                            [!Value] => NuSOAP/0.6.9 (1.86)
                        )
                )
            [RequestId] => 0DPCWVEH16H1EF5474XN
            [Arguments] => Array
                (
                    [Argument] => Array
                        (
                            [!Name] => Service
                            [!Value] => AWSECommerceService
                        )
                )
            [RequestProcessingTime] => 0.0115702152252197
        )
    [Items] => Array
        (
            [Request] => Array
                (
                    [IsValid] => True
                    [ItemLookupRequest] => Array
                        (
                            [IdType] => ASIN
                            [ItemId] => B0001BKAEY
                            [ResponseGroup] => Array
```

```
                                        (
                                            [0] => Request
                                            [1] => Small
                                        )
                                )
                        )
                    [Item] => Array
                        (
                            [ASIN] => B0001BKAEY
                            [DetailPageURL] => http://www.amazon.com/exec/obidos/
redirect?tag=webservices-20%26link_
code=sp1%26camp=2025%26creative=165953%26path=http://www.amazon.com/gp/redirect.
html%253fASIN=B0001BKAEY%2526location=/o/ASIN/
B0001BKAEY%25253FSubscriptionId=1A7XKHR5BYD0WPJVQEG2
                            [ItemAttributes] => Array
                                (
                                    [Actor] => Array
                                        (
                                            [0] => Lambert Wilson
                                            [1] => Carrie-Anne Moss
                                            [2] => Laurence Fishburne
                                        )

                                    [Director] => Array
                                        (
                                            [0] => Larry Wachowski
                                            [1] => Andy Wachowski
                                        )

                                    [ProductGroup] => DVD
                                    [Title] => The Matrix Revolutions (Widescreen Edition)
                                )
                        )
                )
)
```

Error Checking With NuSOAP

NuSOAP provides a built-in method, getError(), which we can use after constructing and making the SOAP request to check for errors.

```
$client = new soapclient($wsdl, true);
$err = $client->getError();
if ($err) {
     echo '<h2>Constructor error</h2><pre>' . $err . '</pre>';
}

$Result = $client->call('ItemLookup', array('body' => $params));
$err = $client->getError();
if ($err) {
     echo '<h2>SOAP call error</h2><pre>' . $err . '</pre>';
}
```

Outputting NuSOAP Debug Information

NuSOAP maintains internal variables that have the raw SOAP request and response, as well as a trace of the SOAP client's actions. These variables are available to your programs.

```
$client->request    // The raw SOAP request
$client->response  // The raw SOAP response
$client->debug_str  // A trace of your SOAP session
```

We can print these out after we make our SOAP call to see the full SOAP message envelopes of our SOAP request and the response from Amazon.

```
Result = $client->call('ItemLookup', array('body' => $params));

echo '<h2>Request</h2><pre>' . htmlspecialchars($client->request, ENT_QUOTES) . '</
pre>';
echo '<h2>Response</h2><pre>' . htmlspecialchars($client->response, ENT_QUOTES) . '</
pre>';
echo '<h2>Debug</h2><pre>' . htmlspecialchars($client->debug_str, ENT_QUOTES) . '</
pre>';
```

WSDL Caching

NuSOAP has a WSDL caching library that you can use to cache your WSDL. Caching the WSDL speeds up execution of NuSOAP scripts and is highly recommended. To use WSDL caching with NuSOAP, you include the class.wsdlcache.php library in your scripts.

```
require_once("nusoap.php");
require_once("class.wsdlcache.php");
```

You can specify the directory where cached files should be stored and the length of time to cache them. For E-Commerce Service, I recommend using zero as the cache time so that the cache never gets stale. If there is a WSDL update, you will want to test it offline before using it on your site.

```
<?php
require_once("nusoap.php");
require_once("class.wsdlcache.php");

define('CACHE_DIR', './storage');  // Directory to put cached files
define('CACHE_TIME', 0);         // Time to cache in seconds. 0 is unlimited

// URL of Amazon's WSDL file
$url='http://webservices.amazon.com/AWSECommerceService/2005-02-23/US/
AWSECommerceService.wsdl';

// Create a new instance of the caching class
$cache = new wsdlcache(CACHE_DIR, CACHE_TIME);

// Get the cached WSDL, if it exists
$wsdl = $cache->get($url);
```

```
// If WSDL is not cached, cache it
if (is_null($wsdl)) {
        $wsdl = new wsdl($url);
        $cache->put($wsdl);
}
....
....
```

Using PEAR SOAP

As we go to press, the latest version of PEAR SOAP, version 0.81, cannot correctly parse the Amazon E-Commerce Service 4.0 WSDL, so it cannot be used with E-Commerce Service. However, it can be used with Amazon Seller Services which uses a different WSDL file (See the Merchants@ section of Chapter Nine).

Downloading and Installing the latest version of Pear SOAP

Pear SOAP is another set of PHP classes that lets developers create either SOAP clients or servers. It's part of the PEAR (an acronym that stands for PHP Extension and Application Repository) libraries, which is a library of high-quality, reusable code for use in PHP applications.

Unlike NuSOAP, which is completely contained in a single file, Pear SOAP is comprised of a number of separate files and it also depends on files that are in other Pear libraries. As of this book, the latest version of Pear SOAP is version 0.81, and it depends on these other Pear libraries: Mail Mime, HTTP Request, Net URL, Pear BASE, and Net DIME.

If you are the administrator for your PHP installation, you can install the Pear libraries by running the file go-pear.bat under Windows (located at the top-level of your PHP installation directory), or, for non-Windows systems, by downloading the PHP script at *http://go-pear.php*. More detailed installation instructions can be found in the Pear manual, *http://pear.php.net/manual/index.php*

If you're using a shared hosting service, the version of PEAR SOAP installed may be out of your control, and you definitely want the latest version installed. The latest version of Pear SOAP is 0.81. Nevertheless, we need to run that version because it contains newer SOAP functionality (particularly WSDL support) that Amazon E-commerce Service requires. The Pear installation scripts, however, will only install the latest release version of SOAP, currently version 0.7.5. In order to install beta releases, such as SOAP 0.81, we have to go to the SOAP download page *http://pear.php.net/package/SOAP/download*, download the Pear SOAP package (named SOAP-0.81.tgz) and then manually run the pear command from our command line:

```
# pear install SOAP-0.81.tgz
```

If you don't have the requisite Pear SOAP dependencies installed, you'll be notified here and you will need to install them.

Making SOAP Requests With PEAR SOAP

Since both NuSOAP and Pear SOAP were derived from the same code base, their use it quite similar. Even the calls have roughly the same names.

```
<?php
require_once("SOAP/Client.php");

// The Amazon WSDL File
$wsdl='http://webservices.amazon.com/AWSECommerceService/2005-02-23/US/
AWSECommerceService.wsdl';

// Our Document/Literal request parameters
$params=array(
    'SubscriptionId' => '1A7XKHR5BYD0WPJVQEG2',
    'AssociateTag' => 'webservices-20',
    'Request' => array (
                        array(
                           'ItemId' => array('B0001BKAEY'),
                           'IdType' => 'ASIN',
                            'ResponseGroup' => array('Request', 'Small')
                              )
                        )
);

// Parse the WSDL file to get the methods
$client = new SOAP_Client($wsdl, true);

// Make the call to Amazon
$Result = $client->call('ItemLookup', $params);

// Output the results
echo '<pre>';
print_r($Result);
echo '</pre>';
?>
```

One notable difference from NuSOAP is that PEAR SOAP defaults to UTF-8 encoding so we don't have to set that. Like NuSOAP, PEAR SOAP always returns the results in a PHP associative array where the tag names are the keys and the data are the values. Also like NuSOAP, PEAR SOAP has the "No Schema Problem" (see "The No Schema Problem" in Chapter Two).

Error Checking With PEAR SOAP

To check for errors, we can use the standard Pear error method, isError.

```
$Result = $client->call('ItemLookup', $params);
```

```
if (PEAR::isError($Result)) {
    echo "Error: " . $Result->getMessage() . '<br />';
}
```

Outputting PEAR SOAP Debug Information

Pear SOAP has an internal method, called __get_wire(), that we can use to see the raw SOAP request and response. To enable it, we must set an option which will turn on tracing. Then, after making a method request, we can call __get_wire() to see the trace:

```
$options = array('trace'=> true);
$temp = array('body' => $params);
$Result = $client->call($method, &$temp, $options);
echo '<h2>Request/Response:</h2>';
echo '<pre>'.htmlspecialchars($client->__get_wire(), ENT_QUOTES).'</pre>';
```

WSDL Caching

PEAR SOAP 0.81 does not have a WSDL caching library, but you can use any cache code, such as PEAR's CacheLite, to cache the WSDL. For an example, see "WSDL Caching With PEAR SOAP" in Chapter Nine.

APPENDIX D

E-Commerce Service 4.0 Error Messages

Amazon E-Commerce Service errors provide you with information about syntactical errors in your requests, as well as errors that occur during the execution of your request (for example, a search for products returns no results). Errors are composed of two elements: *code* and *message*. The error code is a unique string that identifies the error; the error message is a human-readable description of the error that serves as an aid in debugging. These elements will be nested within an Error element. If a request generates more than one error, all Errors will appear in the response.

Errors may appear at different levels in your response. Their location reflects at what stage in the execution of the request the error was generated and what kind of error it is. Errors in syntax that prevent requests from being executed will appear as children of the response's root element. An error associated with a particular item in the response will be a child of the Item element.

ECS returns error messages in English for the Amazon.com (US), Amazon.co.uk (UK), Amazon.de (DE), Amazon.fr (FR), and Amazon.ca (CA) locales. Error messages are in Japanese for the Amazon.co.jp (JP) locale.

Error Code & Description	Message	Affected Operations
`AWS.ECommerceService.ExceededMaximumCartItems` You will receive this error message when you exceed the maximum quantity value allowed for items being added to a shopping cart.	You may not add more than [Maximum Item Quantity] items to the cart.	• CartAdd • CartCreate
`AWS.ECommerceService.InvalidCartId` You will receive this error message when the CartId you entered into your request is not recognized.	Your request contains an invalid value for CartId. Please check your CartId and retry your request.	• CartAdd • CartClear • CartGet • CartModify

AWS.ECommerceService.InvalidHMAC You will receive this error message when the shopping cart HMAC value you use in your request is not recognized by ECS. The HMAC value is a unique token that is used to associate a cart with an Amazon user and a particular session on the Amazon web site.	Your request contains an invalid value for HMAC. Please check your HMAC and retry your request. Remember that the HMAC must be URL-encoded if you are using REST.	• CartAdd • CartClear • CartGet • CartModify
AWS.ECommerceService.InvalidQuantity You will receive this error message when the quantity in your request is not valid for the current item.	You have exceeded the maximum quantity allowed for the fol lowing item(s): [ItemId].	• CartAdd • CartCreate • CartModify
AWS.ECommerceService.ItemAlreadyInCart You will receive this error message when you try to add an item to a shopping cart that already contains that item.	The item you specified, [ItemID], is already in your cart.	• CartAdd • CartCreate
AWS.ECommerceService.ItemNotAccessible Some products cannot be manipulated or viewed using ECS. You will receive this error message when the product ID you use in your request is not available through ECS.	This item is not accessible through ECS.	• ItemLookup • ListLookup
AWS.ECommerceService.ItemNotEligibleForCart Some products cannot be manipulated or viewed using ECS. You will receive this error message when you attempt to add such an item to a remote shopping cart.	The item you specified, [ItemID], is not eligible to be added to the cart. Check the item's availability to make sure it is available.	• CartAdd • CartCreate • CartModify
AWS.ECommerceService.NoExactMatches You will receive this error message when no products, restaurants, lists, or customers matching your search request can be found.	We did not find any matches for your request.	• ItemSearch • ListSearch •CustomerContentSearch
AWS.ECommerceService.NoSimilarities You will receive this error message when there are no products or restaurants similar to the item(s) you specify in your request.	There are no similar items for this ASIN(s): *[ItemID]*.	• SimilarityLookup

AWS.ExactParameterRequirement You will receive this message when the value of your parameter is longer than permitted by ECS.	Your request contains too much data for *[ParameterName]*. This parameter can have a maximum length of *[MaximumNumber]*.	All
AWS.ExceededMaximumParameterValues You will receive this error message when you specify too many values for one or more parameters in your request (i.e. 11 transaction IDs for the TransactionId parameter in Transaction-Lookup, instead often or fewer).	Your request contains too many values for *[ParameterName]*. This parameter can have a maximum of *[MaximumNumber]* values.	• ItemLookup • SimilarityLookup • SellerLookup •TransactionLookup •SellerListingLookup
AWS.InsufficientParameterValues You will receive this error message when your request contains an insufficient number of values for a required parameter.	Your request contains too few values for *[Parameter Name]*. This parameter must have a minimum of *[Minimum Value]* values.	All
AWS.InternalError You will receive this error if ECS is unable to complete your request due to an internal problem or outage. For SOAP, this will be presented as a SOAP fault rather than an error.	We are unable to process your request at this time. Please retry your request. If you encounter this error repeatedly, please post a message on the AWS discussion board.	All
AWS.InvalidEnumeratedParameter You will receive this error message when your request contains an invalid value for a parameter that has an explicit list of valid values, such as DeliveryMethod or SearchIndex.	The value you specified for *[ParameterName]* is invalid. Valid values include *[EnumeratedValues List]*.	• CartAdd • CartCreate • CartModify •CustomerContentLookup • Help • ItemLookup • ItemSearch • ListLookup • ListSearch •SellerListingLookup •SellerListingSearch • SellerLookup • SimilarityLookup

AWS.InvalidISO8601Time You will receive this error when your request contains a date or time value that is not formatted according to the profile of the ISO-8601 date/time standard that is described at http:// www.w3.org/TR/NOTE-date-time. For example, this error will be returned if your request contains an invalid value for the Version parameter.	*[ParameterName]*has an invalid value. It must contain a valid ISO 8601 date and time.	All
AWS.InvalidOperationForMarketplace You will receive this error message when you try to execute an operation in a locale where the operation is not supported.	This operation, [OperationName], is not available for this locale.	All
AWS.InvalidOperationParameter You will receive this error message when the operation name you entered is not available from ECS. For instance, if you tried to use AsinSearch (from AWS 3.0) as an operation name, you would get this error since	The Operation parameter is invalid. Please modify the Operation parameter and retry. Valid values for the Operation parameter include *[ListOfOperationValues]*.	All
AWS.InvalidParameterCombination You will receive this error message when two or more of the request parameters you have entered can not be used in the same request. For example, if you are using the CartAdd operation, you would receive this error if you tried to add items to the cart by both ASIN and OfferListingId.	Your request contains an invalid parameter combination. [ParameterName] and [ParameterName] cannot appear in the same request.	• ItemSearch • CartCreate • CartAdd •SellerListingSearch

AWS.InvalidParameterValue You will receive this error message when your request contains an invalid value for an ID parameter, such as ItemId or SellerId.	*[ParameterValue]* is not a valid value for *[ParameterName]*. Please change this value and retry your request.	• CartAdd • CartCreate • CartModify •CustomerContentLookup • Help • ItemLookup • ItemSearch • ListLookup • ListSearch •SellerListingLookup •SellerListingSearch • SellerLookup • SimilarityLookup
AWS.InvalidResponseGroup You will receive this error message when the response group name you entered in your request is incompatible with the operation you would like to perform.	Your ResponseGroup parameter is invalid. Valid response groups for *[Operation Name]* requests include *[Available Response Group List]*.	All
AWS.InvalidServiceParameter You will receive this error message when the service name you provide in your request is not recognized or supported by Amazon. All ECS requests should use the service name "AWSECommerceService."	The Service parameter is invalid. Please modify the Service parameter and retry. Valid values for the Service parameter include *[ValidServicesList]*.	All
AWS.InvalidSubscriptionId You will receive this error message when the subscription ID you use in your request is not recognized by AWS.	Your request contains an invalid subscription ID. Please retry your request with a valid subscription ID.	All
AWS.InvalidXSLTAddress You will receive this error if the AWS XSLT service is unable to access the XSLT file you used as the value for the Style parameter in your request	We are unable to access your XSLT file. Please verify that you have specified a valid address to your XSLT file.	All

AWS.MaximumParameterRequirement You receive this error message when your request contains the wrong number of parameters from an exclusive group.	Your request should have at most *[Maximum Number]* of the following parameters: *[Parameter Names]*.	All
AWS.MinimumParameterRequirement You receive this error message when your request contains the wrong number of parameters from an exclusive group.	Your request should have at least *[Minimum Number]* of the following parameters: *[Parameter Names]*.	All
AWS.MissingOperationParameter You will receive this error message when your request does not include the Operation parameter and the name of the operation you would like to perform.	Your request is missing the Operation parameter. Please add the Operation parameter to your request and retry. Valid values for the Operation parameter include *[ValidOperationsList]*.	All
AWS.MissingParameterCombination You will receive this error message when your request does not contain a combination of two or more parameters that must be present together in your request.	Your request is missing a required parameter combination. Required parameter combinations include [Parameter One].	• ItemLookup • ListSearch •SellerListingSearch
AWS.MissingParameterValueCombination You will receive this error message when your request requires a combination of parameters, one or more of which must have a specific value. For example, when you make an ItemLookup request for a product based on its Universal Product Code (or UPC), you are required to include the IdType and ItemId parameters. The value of the Id-Type parameter must be UPC.	Your request is missing a required parameter combination. When *[Parameter One]* equals *[Restricted Value]*, *[Parameter Two]* must be present.	• ItemLookup • ListSearch •SellerListingSearch

AWS.MissingServiceParameter You will receive this error message when the your request does not contain the required Service parameter.	Your request is missing the Service parameter. Please add the Service parameter to your request and retry. Valid values for the Service parameter include *[ValidServicesList]*.	All
AWS.ParameterOutOfRange You will receive this error message when you submit a parameter value that exceeds or is lower than the range of valid values for the parameter. For example, ItemSearch allows you to fetch search results page using the ItemPage parameter. The range of values for ItemPage is 1 to 500. If you supply a value outside that range (less than 1 or greater than 500), you will receive this error.	The value you specified for *[ParameterName]* is invalid. Valid values must be between *[LowerBound]* and *[UpperBound]*.	• ItemSearch • ItemLookup • ListSearch • ListLookup •CustomerContentSearch •CustomerContentLookup • SellerLookup •SellerListingSearch
AWS.ParameterRepeatedInRequest You receive this error message when you include the same parameter more than once in your request.	The parameter, [ParameterName], appeared more than once in your request.	All
AWS.RestrictedParameterValue Combination You will receive this error message when your request contains a combination of parameter values that are not permitted in the same request. For example, if you are using the ListSearch operation and have selected BabyRegistry as the ListType, you may not use the Name parameter.	Your request contains a restricted parameter combination. When *[Parameter One]* equals *[Restricted Value]*, *[Parameter Two]* cannot be present.	All
AWS.XSLTTransformationError You will receive this error message when the AWS XSLT service is unable to parse or apply the XSLT stylesheet you have provided in the Style parameter in your request. Make sure that your XSLT stylesheet is valid, and try again.	We were unable to apply your XSLT file. Please check your XSLT and retry your request.	All

APPENDIX E

E-Commerce Service 4.0 Availability Strings

The value of the Availability element indicates if the item can be purchased or when the product usually ships. For items sold by Amazon (the merchant), the possible strings are listed in the table below. For items sold by other merchants, the Availability string will vary.

The value returned by the Availability element may not match the Amazon product details page on Amazon.com because there are typically two versions of an availability message: short and long. ECS returns the short value of the statement. The longer, more verbose, availability message is used by most product detail pages.

The following table describes the possible Availability element values for products offered by Amazon.

Availability String	Description
In stock soon. Order now to get in line. First come, first served.	The item is available for purchase, but is not in stock.
Limited Availability	Used for items sold by third-parties if an item is out of stock, but may be available for purchase later.
Not yet published	The item is not available for purchase. The item may or may not have a projected release date. If there is a release date, it may show up in the ReleaseDate element of the item attributes.
Not yet released	The item is not available for purchase. The item may or may not have a projected release date. If there is a release date, it may show up in the ReleaseDate element of the item attributes.
Only %X left in stock--order soon (more on the way).	The item is available for purchase, but there may only be a few copies left where %X represents a variable amount of time.
Only %X left in stock--order soon.	The item is available for purchase, but there may only be a few copies left where %X represents a variable amount of time.
Out of Print--Limited Availability	Customers can choose to be notified if a copy becomes available.
Out of Stock	The item is currently not available for purchase, but may be in the future.
Special Order	Titles occasionally go out of print or publishers run out of stock. The buyer is notified if the item becomes unavailable."

This item is not stocked or has been discontinued.	The item is not available for purchase.
Usually ships in %X	A dynamic response where %X represents a variable amount of time.

APPENDIX F

E-Commerce Service 4.0 Response Groups

The data returned by various E-Commerce Service operations is configurable by selecting the appropriate Response Groups in the table below. Response Groups may only work with certain E-Commerce Service operations. A few Response Groups are aggregates (parents) of other Response Groups (children). If a Response Group is a parent Response Group, then it is composed of the child Response Groups listed in the column "Includes These Child Groups".

Response Group	Description	Includes These Child Groups	Can Be Used With These Operations
Accessories	The Accessories response group will return a list of accessory product ASINs and Titles for each product in the response that has accessories. For example, an ItemLookup for a digital camera will return information about accessories that may be purchased in addition to the camera, such as a camera bag, an extra flash, batteries, and a memory card.	none	ItemLookup, ItemSearch, ListLookup

Response Group	Description	Includes These Child Groups	Can Be Used With These Operations
BrowseNodeInfo	All products listed on Amazon's websites have been classified using a number of schemes such as product type (such as books, music, tools, apparel), brand, subject, genre, style, etc. This classification system is called browse. Each browse area (a unique classification area called a node) has been assigned an integer called a browse node ID. The BrowseNodeInfo response group provides information about a browse node in the browse area. Although the BrowseNodeInfo response group is similar to the BrowseNodes response group, the BrowseNodeInfo response group is intended for the BrowseNodeLookup operation. The BrowseNodes response group is intended for the ItemLookup and similar operations.	none	BrowseNodeLookup
BrowseNodes	All products listed on Amazon's websites have been classified using a number of schemes such as product type (such as books, music, tools, apparel), brand, subject, genre, style, etc. This classification system is called browse. Each browse area (a unique classification area called a node) has been assigned an integer called a browse node ID. The BrowseNodes response group provides a list of browse nodes to which the item belongs. For each browse node, this response group returns the browse node ID and name	none	ItemLookup, ItemSearch
Cart	The Cart response group provides the CartId, HMAC identifier (HMAC stands for Keyed-Hashing for Message Authentication Code), and PurchaseURL for a remote shopping cart. For each product in the cart (including those in the "saved for later" section of the cart), this response group returns the CartItemId, ProductName, ASIN, Quantity, ListPrice, and OurPrice elements.	none	CartAdd, CartClear, CartCreate, CartGet, CartModify
CartSimilarities	The CartSimilarities response group provides a list of products that are similar to the items in a remote shopping cart. For each similar product, this response group returns an ASIN and Title.	none	CartAdd, CartCreate, CartGet, CartModify

Response Group	Description	Includes These Child Groups	Can Be Used With These Operations
CustomerFull	The CustomerFull response group provides all of the content created by a customer. CustomerFull is a parent response group that contains the CustomerInfo, CustomerLists, and CustomerReviews response groups. Additionally, CustomerFull returns the About Me message that appears on each Amazon customer's member page on Amazon, as well as the customer's birthday, if this information is public on Amazon.	CustomerInfo CustomerLists CustomerReviews	CustomerContentLookup
CustomerInfo	The CustomerInfo response group provides the CustomerId, Name, NickName, and Location (City and State) for each customer listed in the response. This response group will only return information that customers have chosen to make public on Amazon.com.	none	CustomerContentLookup, CustomerContentSearch
CustomerLists	The CustomerLists response group provides the WishListId for each customer listed in the response.	none	CustomerContentLookup
CustomerReviews	The CustomerReviews response group provides the ReviewerRank, TotalHelpfulVotes, and Reviews for each customer listed in the response. Each review in the response is described by the elements for the ASIN reviewed, the product rating, the number of HelpfulVotes, the number of TotalVotes, the review Summary, the review Comment, and DateOfReview.	none	CustomerContentLookup
EditorialReview	The EditorialReview response group provides Amazon's editorial review of the product, if it exists, for each item in the response. Amazon's editorial review is typically labeled as the Product Description on Amazon detail pages.	none	ItemLookup, ItemSearch, ListLookup

Response Group	Description	Includes These Child Groups	Can Be Used With These Operations
Help	The Help response group returns information about operations and response groups that you request information about. If you request information about an operation (HelpType=Operation), the Help response group will return OperationName, OperationDescription, RequiredParameters, AvailableParameters, DefaultResponseGroup, and AvailableResponseGroups for the operation you specified in the About parameter. If you request information about a response group (HelpType=ResponseGroup), the Help response group will return the response group name, its creation date, names of operations that employ the response group, available versions, and a list of the child elements composing the response group.	none	Help
Images	The Images response group provides paths to three sizes of Amazon product images for each item in the response. The three sizes are small, medium, and large.	none	ItemLookup , ItemSearch, ListLookup
ItemAttributes	The ItemAttributes response group provides information about each item in the response that is unique to the item's product category (Books, DVD, Electronics, Apparel, etc.) For example, if an item is in the Computer product category, Amazon Web Services (AWS) will return BatteryType, CaseType, CdRwDescription, etc. (if these values are available for the item). If a response contains products that span product categories, this response group will return a different set of elements for each product in the response.	none	ItemLookup, ItemSearch, ListLookup
ItemIds	The ItemsIds response group provides the ASIN for every item in the response to ItemLookup and SimilarityLookup operations. For ItemSearch, it also provides the total number of items and the total number of pages.	none	ItemLookup, ItemSearch, ListLookup

Response Group	Description	Includes These Child Groups	Can Be Used With These Operations
Large	The Large response group is a parent response group that returns the contents of the Medium, Tracks, BrowseNodes, Reviews, ListmaniaLists, Similarities, Offers, and Accessories data. The Large response group is ideally suited to building product detail pages similar to those found on any Amazon website.	none	ItemLookup, ItemSearch, ListLookup, ListLookup
ListFull	The ListFull response group is a parent response group that returns the contents of the ListInfo and ListItems response groups. It provides all of the data necessary to display information about an Amazon wish list or Listmania list and its contents.	Listinfo ListItems	ListLookup
ListInfo	The ListInfo response group is a parent response group that returns the contents of the ListMinimum response group plus information about the list creator, the list's creation date, the list type (WishList, BabyRegistry, etc.), the number of items in the list, the number of pages in the list, and when the list was last modified.	none	ListLookup, ListSearch
ListItems	The ListItems response group is a parent response group that returns the contents of the ListMinimum response group plus general item-level data, such as the ASIN, product title, and customer's comments associated with each item in the list.	none	ListLookup
ListmaniaLists	The ListmaniaLists response group provides the Listmania list IDs and list names for each list returned.	none	ItemLookup, ItemSearch, ListLookup
ListMinimum	The ListMinimum response group provides the list IDs and list names for each list returned.	none	ListSearch
Medium	The Medium response group is a parent response group that returns the contents of the Small, Request, ItemAttributes, OfferSummary, SalesRank, EditorialReview, and Images response groups. The Medium response group is ideal for building lightweight product detail pages.	none	ItemLookup, ItemSearch, ListLookup

Response Group	Description	Includes These Child Groups	Can Be Used With These Operations
OfferFull	The OfferFull response group is a parent response group that returns the contents of the Offers response group, plus the merchant name or seller nickname.	none	ItemLookup, ItemSearch
Offers	The Offers response group is a parent response group that returns the contents of the OfferSummary response group plus, by default, all "New" offer listings. If you do not wish to receive just the New offer listings, you may specify the offer listing condition type you want to retrieve using the Condition parameter. For each offer listing, this response groups will return the SellerId and the MerchantId, as well as the offer listing condition, subcondition, and description.	none	ItemLookup, ItemSearch , ListLookup
OfferSummary	The OfferSummary response group provides the number of offer listings and the lowest price for each of the offer listing condition classes, including New, Used, Collectible, and Refurbished. The OfferSummary response is based on the item ID and is not affected by changing the MerchantId parameter or any other parameter that changes the number of offers returned in the Offers or OfferFull response groups.	none	ItemLookup, ItemSearch, ListLookup
Request	The Request response group returns all of the arguments passed in the service call. The information returned can be used for debugging, as well as accessing any additional parameters you may have passed in with your request. Up to 10 additional parameters may be included in your request, and they will be echoed back to you in your response if you specify this response group. Please note that this response group is a default response group for every operation.	none	All
Reviews	The Reviews response group provides a list of customer reviews, an average rating (1 to 5 stars), and the total number of reviews for each item in the response. Each customer review will contain the rating, summary, date of review, and full review text.	none	ItemLookup, ItemSearch, ListLookup

Response Group	Description	Includes These Child Groups	Can Be Used With These Operations
SalesRank	The SalesRank response group provides the sales rank for each item in the response.	none	ItemLookup, ItemSearch, ListLookup
Seller	The Seller response group provides the seller ID, nickname, feedback, description, and location for each seller in the response.	none	SellerLookup
SellerListing	The SellerListing response group provides zShops and marketplace listing information for each third-party product in the response.	none	SellerListingLookup, SellerListingSearch
Similarities	The Similarities response group provides the ASIN and Title for each similar product in the response.	none	ItemLookup, ItemSearch, ListLookup
Small	The Small response group provides global, item-level data (no pricing or availability), including the ASIN, product title, creator (author, artist, composer, directory, manufacturer, etc.), product group, URL, and manufacturer. Small includes all of the data necessary to display a typical item in a search results listing.	none	ItemLookup, ItemSearch
Tracks	The Tracks response group provides track title and number for each track on each CD in the response.	none	ItemLookup, ItemSearch, ListLookup
TransactionDetails	The TransactionDetails response group provides information about Amazon transactions, including the seller ID, the condition of the transaction, the date of the transaction, and the total dollar amount of the transaction. TransactionDetails does not return information about the items that were purchased or about the customers who completed the transaction.	none	TransactionLookup

Response Group	Description	Includes These Child Groups	Can Be Used With These Operations
VariationMinimum	The VariationMinimum response group provides the child ASINs for each parent ASIN in the response. For example, if the response contains "Brand X T-Shirt" as a parent ASIN, this response group will return the ASIN for each child ASIN of "Brand X T-Shirt," including "Small, Blue, Brand X T-Shirt", "Medium, Blue, Brand X T-Shirt", "Large, Blue, Brand X T-Shirt", "Small, Red, Brand X T-Shirt", etc.	none	ItemLookup, ItemSearch, ListLookup
Variations	The Variations response group is a parent response group that returns the contents of the VariationSummary and VariationMinimum response groups plus other variation details, such as item attributes, offers, and offer listings for each variation in the response.	none	ItemLookup, ListLookup
VariationSummary	The VariationSummary response group provides the lowest price, highest price, lowest sale price, and highest sale price for all child ASINs in the response.	none	ItemLookup, ItemSearch, ListLookup

APPENDIX G

E-Commerce Service 4.0 Sort Values

This appendix contains two sections. The first section is a thesaurus that matches the sort names to their meaning. Although Amazon has only eighteen different ways to sort data, each Amazon site may use somewhat different names to identify the same types of sorts. To further complicate things, different Search Indexes on the same site may also use different names to identify the same type of sort. For example, sorting by lowest to highest price might be called "pricerank" in one Search Index, and "price" in another.

The second section is a list of Search Indexes with the sort values for each Amazon site.

The possible sort values depends both on the Search Index used and the Amazon site you are using it on. The international Amazon sites have fewer sort values than Amazon.com.

Sort Thesaurus

The values grouped together in each row have the same meaning.

Sort Values	Description
-age-min -mfg-age-min	Age: high to low
artistrank	Artist name: A to Z
-date daterank -pubdate	Publication date: newer to older
-daterank pubdate	Publication date: older to newer
importrank	Imported items first

Sort Values	Description
inverse-pricerank inverseprice -price -pricerank	Price: high to low
launch-date -launch-date orig-rel-date -release-date -video-release-date	Release date: newer to older
mfg-age-min	Age: low to high
-orig-rel-date release-date	Release date: older to newer
pmrank relevance relevancerank	Featured items
price pricerank	Price: low to high
psrank salesrank subslot-salesrank	Bestselling as determined by the Amazon Sales Rank
reviewrank	Average Customer Review, high to low
sale-flag	On sale
songtitlerank	Most popular
-titlerank	Alphabetical: Z to A
titlerank	Alphabetical: A to Z
uploaddaterank	Date added

Sort Values

Possible sort values are listed by Search Index.

Search Index: Apparel

US
inverseprice
-launch-date
pricerank
relevancerank

US
sale-flag
salesrank

Search Index: Baby

US
price
-price
psrank
salesrank
titlerank

Search Index: Beauty

US
-launch-date
pmrank
price
-price
sale-flag
salesrank

Search Index: Blended

The sort parameter is not allowed when using the Blended Search Index

Search Index: Books

Sort	US	UK	JP	FR	DE	CA
daterank	✓	✓	✓			✓
-daterank				✓		
inverse-pricerank	✓	✓	✓	✓	✓	✓
pricerank	✓	✓	✓	✓	✓	✓
pubdate						
-pubdate					✓	
relevancerank	✓					
reviewrank	✓	✓			✓	

Sort	US	UK	JP	FR	DE	CA
salesrank	✓	✓	✓	✓	✓	✓
titlerank	✓	✓	✓	✓	✓	✓
-titlerank	✓	✓	✓	✓	✓	

Search Index: Classical

Sort	US	UK	JP	FR	DE	CA
inverse-pricerank				✓		
orig-rel-date	✓		✓			✓
-orig-rel-date			✓			
price	✓	✓			✓	
-price	✓				✓	
pricerank			✓	✓		
-pricerank			✓			
psrank	✓					
pubdate					✓	
-pubdate					✓	
reviewrank		✓				
salesrank	✓	✓	✓	✓	✓	✓
titlerank	✓	✓	✓	✓	✓	✓
-titlerank	✓	✓	✓	✓	✓	

Search Index: DigitalMusic

US
songtitlerank
uploaddaterank

Search Index: DVD

Sort	US	UK	JP	FR	DE	CA
daterank		✓				
inverse-pricerank		✓				
orig-rel-date			✓			
-orig-rel-date			✓			
price	✓	✓			✓	

Sort	US	UK	JP	FR	DE	CA
-price	✓				✓	
pricerank			✓			
-pricerank			✓			
-pubdate				✓		
relevancerank	✓					
reviewrank		✓				
salesrank	✓	✓	✓	✓	✓	✓
titlerank	✓	✓	✓	✓	✓	✓
-titlerank		✓	✓	✓	✓	
-video-release-date	✓					

Search Index: Electronics

Sort	US	UK	JP	DE
daterank		✓		
inverse-pricerank		✓		
-orig-rel-date	✓			
pmrank	✓			
price	✓	✓		✓
-price	✓			✓
pricerank			✓	
-pricerank			✓	
release-date			✓	
-release-date			✓	
reviewrank	✓	✓		
salesrank	✓	✓	✓	✓
titlerank	✓	✓	✓	✓
-titlerank		✓	✓	✓

Search Index: ForeignBooks

Sort	JP	DE
daterank	✓	
inverse-pricerank	✓	✓
pricerank	✓	✓
-pubdate		✓

Sort	JP	DE
reviewrank		✓
salesrank	✓	✓
titlerank	✓	✓
-titlerank	✓	✓

Search Index: GourmetFood

US
inverseprice
launch-date
pricerank
relevancerank
sale-flag
salesrank

Search Index: HealthPersonalCare

Sort	US	UK	DE
daterank		✓	
inverseprice	✓		
launch-date	✓		
pmrank	✓		
price		✓	✓
-price		✓	✓
pricerank	✓		
reviewrank		✓	
sale-flag	✓		
salesrank	✓	✓	✓
titlerank		✓	✓
-titlerank		✓	✓

Search Index: HomeGarden

Sort	UK	DE
daterank	✓	
price	✓	✓

Sort	UK	DE
-price	✓	✓
reviewrank	✓	
salesrank	✓	✓
titlerank	✓	✓
-titlerank	✓	✓

Search Index: Jewelry

US
inverseprice
launch-date
pmrank
pricerank
salesrank

Search Index: Kitchen

Sort	US	UK	JP	DE
daterank		✓		
pmrank	✓			
price	✓	✓	✓	✓
-price	✓	✓	✓	✓
release-date	✓	✓	✓	
-release-date	✓	✓	✓	
reviewrank		✓		
salesrank	✓	✓	✓	✓
titlerank	✓	✓	✓	✓
-titlerank	✓	✓	✓	✓

Search Index: Magazines

Sort	US	DE
daterank	✓	
price	✓	
-price	✓	
reviewrank	✓	

Sort	US	DE
salesrank		✓
subslot-salesrank	✓	
titlerank	✓	✓
-titlerank	✓	✓

Search Index: Merchants

US
inverseprice
-launch-date
pricerank
relevancerank
sale-flag
salesrank

Search Index: Miscellaneous

US
pmrank
price
-price
salesrank
titlerank
-titlerank

Search Index: Music

Sort	US	UK	JP	FR	DE	CA
artistrank	✓					
-importrank					✓	
inverse-pricerank		✓		✓		
orig-rel-date	✓		✓			✓
-orig-rel-date			✓			
price	✓	✓			✓	
-price	✓				✓	
pricerank			✓	✓		

Sort	US	UK	JP	FR	DE	CA
-pricerank			✓			
psrank	✓					
pubdate					✓	
-pubdate					✓	
reviewrank		✓				
salesrank	✓	✓	✓	✓	✓	✓
titlerank	✓	✓	✓	✓	✓	✓
-titlerank	✓	✓	✓	✓	✓	

Search Index: MusicalInstruments

US
-launch-date
pmrank
price
-price
sale-flag
salesrank

Search Index: MusicTracks

Sort	US	UK	JP	FR	DE
titlerank	✓	✓	✓	✓	✓
-titlerank	✓	✓	✓	✓	✓

Search Index: OfficeProducts

US
pmrank
price
-price
reviewrank
salesrank
titlerank

Search Index: OutdoorLiving

Sort	US	UK	DE
daterank		✓	
price	✓	✓	✓
-price	✓	✓	✓
psrank	✓		
reviewrank		✓	
salesrank	✓	✓	✓
titlerank	✓	✓	✓
-titlerank	✓	✓	✓

Search Index: PCHardware

Sort	US	DE
price	✓	✓
-price	✓	✓
psrank	✓	
salesrank	✓	✓
titlerank	✓	✓
-titlerank		✓

Search Index: Photo

Sort	US	DE
pmrank	✓	
price	✓	✓
-price	✓	✓
salesrank	✓	✓
titlerank	✓	✓
-titlerank		✓

Search Index: Restaurants

US
relevance

US
titlerank

Search Index: Software

Sort	US	UK	JP	FR	DE	CA
-date					✓	
daterank		✓				
-daterank						✓
inverse-pricerank		✓				✓
pmrank	✓					
price	✓	✓	✓	✓	✓	
-price	✓		✓		✓	
pricerank						✓
-pricerank				✓		
release-date			✓			
-release-date			✓			
reviewrank		✓				
salesrank	✓	✓	✓	✓	✓	✓
titlerank	✓	✓	✓	✓	✓	✓
-titlerank		✓	✓	✓	✓	

Search Index: SoftwareVideoGames

Sort	UK	DE	CA
-date		✓	
daterank	✓		
-daterank			✓
inverse-pricerank	✓		✓
price	✓	✓	
-price		✓	
pricerank			✓
reviewrank	✓		
salesrank	✓	✓	✓
titlerank	✓	✓	✓
-titlerank	✓	✓	

Search Index: SportingGoods

US
inverseprice
launch-date
pricerank
relevancerank
sale-flag
salesrank

Search Index: Tools

Sort values are not yet supported for Amazon.de in the Tools Search Index.

US
-date
pmrank
price
-price
salesrank
titlerank
-titlerank

Search Index: Toys

Sort	US	UK	JP
-age-min	✓		
mfg-age-min		✓	
-mfg-age-min		✓	
pmrank	✓		
price	✓	✓	✓
-price	✓	✓	✓
release-date			✓
-release-date			✓
salesrank	✓	✓	✓
titlerank	✓		✓
-titlerank			✓

Search Index: VHS

Sort	US	UK	JP	FR	DE	CA
daterank		✓				
orig-rel-date			✓			
-orig-rel-date			✓			
price	✓	✓			✓	
-price	✓				✓	
pricerank			✓			
-pricerank			✓			
relevancerank	✓					
reviewrank		✓				
salesrank	✓	✓	✓	✓	✓	✓
titlerank	✓	✓	✓	✓	✓	
-titlerank		✓	✓	✓	✓	✓
-video-release-date	✓					

Search Index: Video

Sort	US	UK	JP	DE	CA
daterank		✓			
inverse-pricerank		✓			
orig-rel-date			✓		
-orig-rel-date			✓		
price	✓	✓		✓	
-price	✓			✓	
pricerank			✓		
-pricerank			✓		
relevancerank	✓				
reviewrank		✓			
salesrank	✓	✓	✓	✓	✓
titlerank	✓	✓	✓	✓	✓
-titlerank		✓	✓	✓	✓
-video-release-date	✓				

Search Index: VideoGames

Sort	US	UK	JP	FR	DE	CA
date				✓		
-date					✓	
daterank		✓				
inverse-pricerank		✓				
pmrank	✓					
price	✓	✓	✓	✓	✓	
-price	✓		✓	✓	✓	
release-date			✓			
-release-date			✓			
reviewrank		✓				
salesrank	✓	✓	✓	✓	✓	✓
titlerank	✓	✓	✓	✓	✓	✓
-titlerank		✓	✓	✓	✓	✓

Search Index: Wireless

US
psrank
salesrank
titlerank
-titlerank

Search Index: WirelessAccessories

US
psrank
salesrank
titlerank
-titlerank

APPENDIX H

E-Commerce Service 4.0 Search Indexes

Here are the Search Indexes supported by each Amazon site. Note that there are some Search Indexes that are not supported on Amazon.com, such as HomeGarden.

Search Index	US	UK	JP	FR	DE	CA
Apparel	✓					
Baby	✓					
Beauty	✓					
Blended	✓	✓	✓	✓	✓	✓
Books	✓	✓	✓	✓	✓	✓
Classical	✓	✓	✓	✓	✓	✓
DigitalMusic	✓					
DVD	✓	✓	✓	✓	✓	✓
Electronics	✓	✓	✓		✓	
ForeignBooks			✓		✓	
GourmetFood	✓					
HealthPersonalCare	✓	✓			✓	
HomeGarden		✓			✓	
Jewelry	✓					
Kitchen	✓	✓	✓		✓	
Magazines	✓				✓	
Merchants	✓					
Miscellaneous	✓					
Music	✓	✓	✓	✓	✓	✓
MusicalInstruments	✓					
MusicTracks	✓	✓	✓	✓	✓	
OfficeProducts	✓					

Search Index	US	UK	JP	FR	DE	CA
OutdoorLiving	✓	✓			✓	
PCHardware	✓				✓	
Photo	✓				✓	
Restaurants	✓					
Software	✓	✓	✓	✓	✓	✓
SoftwareVideoGames		✓			✓	✓
SportingGoods	✓					
Tools	✓				✓	
Toys	✓	✓	✓			
VHS	✓	✓	✓	✓	✓	✓
Video	✓	✓	✓		✓	✓
VideoGames	✓	✓	✓	✓	✓	✓
Wireless	✓					
WirelessAccessories	✓					

APPENDIX I

E-Commerce Service 4.0 ItemSearch Parameter Combinations

This appendix lists which ItemSearch parameters can be used with the available Search Indexes for each Amazon site.

Search Index: Apparel

US
Brand
BrowseNode
Condition
DeliveryMethod
ISPUPostalCode
ItemPage
Keywords
Manufacturer
MaximumPrice
MerchantId
MinimumPrice
Sort
TextStream
Title

Search Index: Baby

US
Brand
BrowseNode

US
Condition
DeliveryMethod
ISPUPostalCode
ItemPage
Keywords
Manufacturer
MaximumPrice
MerchantId
MinimumPrice
Sort
Title

Search Index: Beauty

US
Brand
BrowseNode
Condition
DeliveryMethod
ISPUPostalCode
ItemPage
Keywords
Manufacturer
MaximumPrice
MerchantId
MinimumPrice
Sort
Title

Search Index: Blended

Parameter	US	UK	JP	FR	DE	CA
Condition				✓		
Count				✓		
DeliveryMethod				✓		

Parameter	US	UK	JP	FR	DE	CA
ItemPage				✓		
Keywords	✓	✓	✓	✓	✓	✓

Search Index: Books

Parameter	US	UK	JP	FR	DE	CA
Author	✓	✓	✓	✓	✓	✓
Brand	✓					
BrowseNode	✓	✓	✓	✓	✓	✓
Condition	✓	✓	✓	✓	✓	✓
DeliveryMethod	✓			✓		✓
ISPUPostalCode	✓					
ItemPage	✓	✓	✓	✓	✓	✓
Keywords	✓	✓	✓	✓	✓	✓
MaximumPrice	✓	✓	✓	✓	✓	✓
MerchantId	✓	✓	✓	✓	✓	✓
MinimumPrice	✓	✓	✓	✓	✓	✓
Power	✓			✓		✓
Publisher	✓	✓	✓	✓	✓	✓
Sort	✓	✓	✓	✓	✓	✓
TextStream	✓					
Title	✓	✓	✓	✓	✓	✓

Search Index: Classical

Parameter	US	UK	JP	FR	DE	CA
Artist	✓	✓	✓	✓	✓	✓
BrowseNode	✓	✓	✓	✓	✓	✓
Composer	✓	✓	✓	✓	✓	✓
Condition	✓	✓	✓	✓	✓	✓
Conductor	✓	✓	✓	✓	✓	✓
DeliveryMethod	✓			✓		✓
ISPUPostalCode	✓					
ItemPage	✓	✓	✓	✓	✓	✓
Keywords	✓	✓	✓	✓	✓	✓
MaximumPrice	✓	✓	✓	✓	✓	✓

Parameter	US	UK	JP	FR	DE	CA
MerchantId	✓	✓	✓	✓	✓	✓
MinimumPrice	✓	✓	✓	✓	✓	✓
MusicLabel	✓	✓	✓	✓	✓	✓
Orchestra	✓	✓	✓			
Sort	✓	✓	✓	✓	✓	✓
TextStream	✓			✓		✓
Title	✓	✓	✓	✓	✓	✓

Search Index: DigitalMusic

US
Actor
BrowseNode
Condition
DeliveryMethod
Director
ISPUPostalCode
ItemPage
Keywords
MaximumPrice
MerchantId
MinimumPrice
MPAARating
Publisher
Sort
TextStream
Title

Search Index: DVD

Parameter	US	UK	JP	FR	DE	CA
Actor	✓	✓	✓	✓	✓	✓
AudienceRating				✓		✓
BrowseNode	✓	✓	✓	✓	✓	✓
Condition	✓	✓	✓	✓	✓	✓
DeliveryMethod	✓			✓		✓

Parameter	US	UK	JP	FR	DE	CA
Director	✓	✓	✓	✓	✓	✓
ISPUPostalCode	✓					
ItemPage	✓	✓	✓	✓	✓	✓
Keywords	✓	✓	✓	✓	✓	✓
MaximumPrice	✓	✓	✓	✓	✓	✓
MerchantId	✓	✓	✓	✓	✓	✓
MinimumPrice	✓	✓	✓	✓	✓	✓
MPAARating	✓	✓			✓	
Publisher	✓	✓	✓	✓	✓	✓
Sort	✓	✓	✓	✓	✓	✓
TextStream	✓					
Title	✓	✓	✓	✓	✓	✓

Search Index: Electronics

Parameter	US	UK	JP	DE
Brand	✓	✓	✓	
BrowseNode	✓	✓	✓	✓
Condition	✓	✓	✓	✓
DeliveryMethod	✓			
ISPUPostalCode	✓			
ItemPage	✓	✓	✓	✓
Keywords	✓	✓	✓	✓
Manufacturer	✓	✓		✓
MaximumPrice	✓	✓	✓	✓
MerchantId	✓	✓	✓	✓
MinimumPrice	✓	✓	✓	✓
Sort	✓	✓	✓	✓
TextStream	✓			
Title	✓	✓	✓	✓

Search Index: ForeignBooks

Parameter	JP	DE
Author	✓	✓
BrowseNode	✓	✓

Parameter	JP	DE
Condition	✓	✓
ItemPage	✓	✓
Keywords	✓	✓
MaximumPrice	✓	✓
MerchantId	✓	✓
MinimumPrice	✓	✓
Publisher	✓	✓
Sort	✓	✓
Title	✓	✓

Search Index: GourmetFood

US
Actor
BrowseNode
Condition
DeliveryMethod
Director
ISPUPostalCode
ItemPage
Keywords
MaximumPrice
MerchantId
MinimumPrice
MPAARating
Publisher
Sort
TextStream
Title

Search Index: HealthPersonalCare

Parameter	US	UK	DE
Brand	✓	✓	
BrowseNode	✓	✓	✓
Condition	✓	✓	✓

Parameter	US	UK	DE
DeliveryMethod	✓		
ISPUPostalCode	✓		
ItemPage	✓	✓	✓
Keywords	✓	✓	✓
Manufacturer	✓	✓	✓
MaximumPrice	✓	✓	✓
MerchantId	✓	✓	✓
MinimumPrice	✓	✓	✓
Sort	✓	✓	✓
Title	✓	✓	✓

Search Index: HomeGarden

Parameter	UK	DE
Brand	✓	
BrowseNode	✓	✓
Condition	✓	✓
ItemPage	✓	✓
Keywords	✓	✓
Manufacturer	✓	✓
MaximumPrice	✓	✓
MerchantId	✓	✓
MinimumPrice	✓	✓
Sort	✓	✓
Title	✓	✓

Search Index: Jewelry

US
BrowseNode
Condition
DeliveryMethod
Director
ISPUPostalCode
ItemPage
Keywords

US
MaximumPrice
MerchantId
MinimumPrice
Sort
TextStream
Title

Search Index: Kitchen

Parameter	US	UK	JP	DE
Brand	✓	✓	✓	
BrowseNode	✓	✓	✓	✓
Condition	✓	✓	✓	✓
DeliveryMethod	✓			
ISPUPostalCode	✓			
ItemPage	✓	✓	✓	✓
Keywords	✓	✓	✓	✓
Manufacturer	✓	✓	✓	✓
MaximumPrice	✓	✓	✓	✓
MerchantId	✓	✓	✓	✓
MinimumPrice	✓	✓	✓	✓
Sort	✓	✓	✓	✓
Title	✓	✓	✓	✓

Search Index: Magazines

Parameter	US	DE
BrowseNode	✓	✓
Condition	✓	✓
DeliveryMethod	✓	
ISPUPostalCode	✓	
ItemPage	✓	✓
Keywords	✓	✓
MaximumPrice	✓	✓
MerchantId	✓	✓
MinimumPrice	✓	✓

Parameter	US	DE
Publisher	✓	✓
Sort	✓	✓
Title	✓	✓

Search Index: Merchants

Parameter
Actor
Artist
AudienceRating
Author
Brand
BrowseNode
City
Condition
Conductor
Cuisine
Director
ItemPage
Keywords
Manufacturer
MusicLabel
Neighborhood
Orchestra
Power
TextStream
Title

Search Index: Miscellaneous

US
Brand
Condition
DeliveryMethod
ISPUPostalCode
ItemPage

US
Keywords
MaximumPrice
MerchantId
MinimumPrice
Sort
Title

Search Index: Music

Parameter	US	UK	JP	FR	DE	CA
Artist	✓	✓	✓	✓	✓	✓
BrowseNode	✓	✓	✓	✓	✓	✓
Condition	✓	✓	✓	✓	✓	✓
DeliveryMethod	✓			✓		✓
ISPUPostalCode	✓					
ItemPage	✓	✓	✓	✓	✓	✓
Keywords	✓	✓	✓	✓	✓	✓
MaximumPrice	✓	✓	✓	✓	✓	✓
MerchantId	✓	✓	✓	✓	✓	✓
MinimumPrice	✓	✓	✓	✓	✓	✓
MusicLabel	✓	✓	✓	✓	✓	✓
Sort	✓	✓	✓	✓	✓	✓
TextStream	✓					
Title	✓	✓	✓	✓	✓	✓

Search Index: MusicalInstruments

US
Brand
BrowseNode
Condition
DeliveryMethod
ISPUPostalCode
ItemPage
Keywords
Manufacturer

US
MaximumPrice
MerchantId
MinimumPrice
Sort
Title

Search Index: MusicTracks

Parameter	US	UK	JP	FR	DE
Condition	✓	✓	✓	✓	✓
DeliveryMethod	✓			✓	
ISPUPostalCode	✓				
ItemPage	✓	✓	✓	✓	✓
Keywords	✓	✓	✓	✓	✓
MaximumPrice	✓	✓	✓	✓	✓
MerchantId	✓	✓	✓	✓	✓
MinimumPrice	✓	✓	✓	✓	✓
Sort	✓	✓	✓	✓	✓

Search Index: OfficeProducts

US
Brand
BrowseNode
Condition
DeliveryMethod
ISPUPostalCode
ItemPage
Keywords
Manufacturer
MaximumPrice
MerchantId
MinimumPrice
Sort
Title

Search Index: OutdoorLiving

Parameter	US	UK	DE
Brand	✓	✓	
BrowseNode	✓	✓	✓
Condition	✓	✓	✓
DeliveryMethod	✓		
ISPUPostalCode	✓		
ItemPage	✓	✓	✓
Keywords	✓	✓	✓
Manufacturer	✓	✓	✓
MaximumPrice	✓	✓	✓
MerchantId	✓	✓	✓
MinimumPrice	✓	✓	✓
Sort	✓	✓	✓
Title	✓	✓	✓

Search Index: PCHardware

Parameter	US	DE
Brand	✓	
BrowseNode	✓	✓
Condition	✓	✓
DeliveryMethod	✓	
ISPUPostalCode	✓	
ItemPage	✓	✓
Keywords	✓	✓
Manufacturer	✓	✓
MaximumPrice	✓	✓
MerchantId	✓	✓
MinimumPrice	✓	✓
Sort	✓	✓
Title	✓	✓

Search Index: Photo

Parameter	US	DE
Brand	✓	
BrowseNode	✓	✓
Condition	✓	✓
DeliveryMethod	✓	
ISPUPostalCode	✓	
ItemPage	✓	✓
Keywords	✓	✓
Manufacturer	✓	✓
MaximumPrice	✓	✓
MerchantId	✓	✓
MinimumPrice	✓	✓
Sort	✓	✓
TextStream	✓	
Title	✓	✓

Search Index: Restaurants

US
BrowseNode
City
Condition
Cuisine
ItemPage
Keywords
MaximumPrice
MerchantId
MinimumPrice
Neighborhood
Sort
Title

Search Index: Software

Parameter	US	UK	JP	FR	DE	CA
Brand	✓	✓	✓			
BrowseNode	✓	✓	✓	✓	✓	✓
Condition	✓	✓	✓	✓	✓	✓
DeliveryMethod	✓			✓		✓
ISPUPostalCode	✓					
ItemPage	✓	✓	✓	✓	✓	✓
Keywords	✓	✓	✓	✓	✓	✓
Manufacturer	✓	✓		✓	✓	✓
MaximumPrice	✓	✓	✓	✓	✓	✓
MerchantId	✓	✓	✓	✓	✓	✓
MinimumPrice	✓	✓	✓	✓	✓	✓
Sort	✓	✓	✓	✓	✓	✓
Title	✓	✓	✓	✓	✓	✓

Search Index: SoftwareVideoGames

Parameter	UK	DE	CA
Author			✓
Brand	✓		
BrowseNode	✓	✓	✓
Condition	✓	✓	✓
DeliveryMethod			✓
ItemPage	✓	✓	✓
Keywords	✓	✓	✓
Manufacturer	✓	✓	✓
MaximumPrice	✓	✓	✓
MerchantId	✓	✓	✓
MinimumPrice	✓	✓	✓
Sort	✓	✓	✓
Title	✓	✓	✓

Search Index: SportingGoods

US
Brand
BrowseNode
Condition
DeliveryMethod
ISPUPostalCode
ItemPage
Keywords
Manufacturer
MaximumPrice
MerchantId
MinimumPrice
Sort
Title

Search Index: Tools

US
Brand
BrowseNode
Condition
DeliveryMethod
ISPUPostalCode
ItemPage
Keywords
Manufacturer
MaximumPrice
MerchantId
MinimumPrice
Sort
Title

Search Index: Toys

Parameter	US	UK	JP
Brand		✓	

Parameter	US	UK	JP
Browsenode	✓		
Condition	✓		✓
DeliveryMethod	✓		
ISPUPostalCode	✓		
ItemPage	✓	✓	✓
Keywords	✓	✓	✓
Manufacturer		✓	✓
MaximumPrice	✓	✓	✓
MerchantId	✓	✓	✓
MinimumPrice	✓	✓	✓
Sort	✓	✓	✓
TextStream	✓		
Title	✓	✓	✓

Search Index: VHS

Parameter	US	UK	JP	FR	DE	CA
Actor	✓	✓	✓	✓	✓	✓
AudienceRating						
BrowseNode	✓	✓	✓	✓	✓	✓
Condition	✓	✓	✓	✓	✓	✓
DeliveryMethod	✓			✓		✓
Director	✓	✓	✓	✓	✓	✓
ISPUPostalCode	✓					
ItemPage	✓	✓	✓	✓	✓	✓
Keywords	✓	✓	✓	✓	✓	✓
MaximumPrice	✓	✓	✓	✓	✓	✓
MerchantId	✓	✓	✓	✓	✓	✓
MinimumPrice	✓	✓	✓	✓	✓	✓
MPAARating	✓				✓	
Publisher	✓	✓	✓	✓	✓	✓
Sort	✓	✓	✓	✓	✓	✓
Title	✓	✓	✓	✓	✓	✓

Search Index: Video

Parameter	US	UK	JP	DE	CA
Actor	✓	✓	✓	✓	✓
AudienceRating					✓
BrowseNode	✓	✓	✓	✓	✓
Condition	✓	✓	✓	✓	✓
DeliveryMethod	✓				✓
Director	✓	✓	✓	✓	✓
ISPUPostalCode	✓				
ItemPage	✓	✓	✓	✓	✓
Keywords	✓	✓	✓	✓	✓
MaximumPrice	✓	✓	✓	✓	✓
MerchantId	✓	✓	✓	✓	✓
MinimumPrice	✓	✓	✓	✓	✓
MPAARating	✓	✓		✓	
Publisher	✓	✓	✓	✓	✓
Sort	✓	✓	✓	✓	✓
TextStream	✓				
Title	✓	✓	✓	✓	✓

Search Index: VideoGames

Parameter	US	UK	JP	DE	FR	CA
Author					✓	✓
Brand	✓	✓	✓		✓	✓
BrowseNode	✓	✓	✓	✓	✓	✓
Condition	✓	✓	✓	✓	✓	✓
DeliveryMethod	✓				✓	✓
ISPUPostalCode	✓					
ItemPage	✓	✓	✓	✓	✓	✓
Keywords	✓	✓	✓	✓	✓	✓
Manufacturer	✓	✓	✓	✓	✓	
MaximumPrice	✓	✓	✓	✓	✓	✓
MerchantId	✓	✓	✓	✓	✓	✓
MinimumPrice	✓	✓	✓	✓	✓	✓
MPAARating				✓		

Parameter	US	UK	JP	DE	FR	CA
Sort	✓	✓	✓	✓	✓	✓
TextStream	✓					
Title	✓	✓	✓	✓	✓	✓

Search Index: Wireless

US
BrowseNode
Condition
DeliveryMethod
ISPUPostalCode
ItemPage
Keywords
MaximumPrice
MerchantId
MinimumPrice
Sort
Title

Search Index: WirelessAccessories

US
BrowseNode
Condition
DeliveryMethod
ISPUPostalCode
ItemPage
Keywords
MaximumPrice
MerchantId
MinimumPrice
Sort
Title

APPENDIX J

Amazon Inventory Management System API Reference Manual

Amazon Information Management System (AIMS) API Operations

- add-modify-delete
- batch-refund
- errorlog
- generate-report-now
- get-batches
- get-pending-uploads-count
- get-report-status
- modify-only
- purge-replace
- quickfix
- report

Common Request Parameters

Several HTTP headers are required by all AIMS API requests

Basic Authentication

An HTTP Basic Authentication header is required in every request. The header contains your Marketplace Pro Merchant username and password. The header has the following format:

```
Authorization: Basic [username]:[password]
```

where the string [username]:[password] is base64-encoded. For example, if your username is "jason" and your password is "levitt", then you would base64-encode the string "jason:levitt" and your Basic Authentication header would look like this for each request:

```
Authorization: Basic amFzb246bGV2aXR0
```

Content Type

Despite the fact that AIMS API requests do not return valid XML, nor does the developer send XML in requests, you should set your HTTP Content-Type header to text/xml in each request.

```
Content-Type: text/xml
```

Cookie

A special HTTP cookie header value must be specified in each request. The meaning of this cookie value is proprietary:

```
Cookie: x-main=YvjPkwfntqDKunOQEmVRPcTTZDMe?Tn?; ubid-main=002-8989859-9917520; ubid-
tacbus=019-5423258-4241018;x-tacbus=vtm4d53DvX@Sc9LxTnAnxsFL3DorwxJa; ubid-
tcmacb=087-8055947-0795529; ubid-ty2kacbus=161-5477122-2773524; session-id=087-
178254-5924832; session-id-time=950660664
```

Reference Manual

add-modify-delete

Description

A seller should use the Add/Modify/Delete request to upload a batch of Amazon Marketplace and/or zShops listings containing additions, modifications, and/or deletions to their current inventory. Deletions must be marked as such in their template, (with a "d" in the add-delete field) and the system will update changed items to reflect the modifications

URL

```
https://secure.amazon.com/exec/panama/seller-admin/catalog-upload/add-modify-delete
```

HTTP Request Parameters

Parameter*	Description	Required?	Value
UploadFor	Indicates where the inventory should be placed, either in Marketplace or ZShop.	No	Default Value: Marketplace Possible Values: Marketplace ZShop
FileFormat	Indicates the format of your inventory files, either UIEE or TabDelimited	No	Default value: TabDelimited Possible valuess: UIEE TabDelimited.

*See "Common Request Parameters" at the beginning of this Appendix for additional parameters

Request Message Body

The body of the message an inventory text file. The format of the inventory file can be found at two pages on Amazon. For zShops only, the values are here:

```
http://s1.amazon.com/exec/varzea/subst/seller-admin/fixed-price-template-fields.html
```

When uploading to Marketplace, or to both zShops and Marketplace at once, the values are here:

```
http://s1.amazon.com/exec/varzea/subst/seller-admin/marketplace-template-fields.html
```

Possible Responses

Type	Response	Explanation
Success	<Success>SUCCESS</Success>	Upload succeeeded
Error	<BusinessLogicError>CUSTOMER_UNAUTHORIZED </BusinessLogicError>	Authentication error
Error	<BusinessLogicError>INVALID_FILE_FORMAT</BusinessLogicError>	Invalid format specified
Error	<BusinessLogicError>INVALID_LISTING_PROGRAM </BusinessLogicError>	Invalid program specified

batch-refund

Description

This operation is used to submit customer order refunds in bulk. The process is very similar to uploading inventory spreadsheets, but in this case you send a tab delimited text file that contains information on your batch refunds

URL

```
https://secure.amazon.com/exec/panama/seller-admin/catalog-upload/batch-refund
```

HTTP Request Parameters

The are no parameters for this request other than the required HTTP headers (see "Common Request Parameters"). All the refund information is in the request message body.

Request Message Body

The body of the message should contain the actual refund file. The bulk refund information should be sent as a tab delimited file with the following required headers in this exact order:

- order-id
- payments-transaction-id (put the order-item-id in this field)
- refund-amount
- reason
- message

Values for "reason" and "message" do not have to be provided.

Possible Responses

Type	Response	Explanation
Success	`<Success>SUCCESS</Success>`	Upload succeeeded
Error	`<BusinessLogicError>CUSTOMER_UNAUTHORIZED </BusinessLogicError>`	Authentication error
Error	`<BusinessLogicError>INVALID_FILE_FORMAT</BusinessLogicError>`	Invalid format specified

errorlog

Description

If something goes wrong with a specific inventory upload, the seller can retrieve the upload's Error Log to determine what caused the problem. The Error Log will contain the row number of any applicable error or warning, the SKU, and the item name. It will also contain the message type (status message, data error, template error, etc.) and the message itself. The seller can use this information to fix any errors and re-upload those rows.

URL

```
https://secure.amazon.com/exec/panama/seller-admin/download/errorlog
```

HTTP Request Parameters

Parameter*	Description	Required?	Value
BatchId	The Batch Id number returned from a previous inventory upload	Yes	A valid Batch Id

*See "Common Request Parameters" at the beginning of this Appendix for additional parameters

Request Message Body

No message body is used for this request. Only HTTP headers are sent.

Possible Responses

Type	Response	Explanation
Success	An error log file	An XML-encoded error log file is returned
Error	<BusinessLogicError>CUSTOMER_UNAUTHORIZED </BusinessLogicError>	Authentication error
Error	<BusinessLogicError>FILE_NOT_FOUND </BusinessLogicError>	The error log file was not found on the server
Error	<BusinessLogicError>INVALID_FILE_FORMAT</BusinessLogicError>	Invalid format specified

generate-report-now

Description

This API can be used to request the generation of an Order Fulfillment Report or Open Listings Report. Once this report is generated (verified by using the get-report-status function), it can be downloaded using the download API.

URL

```
https://secure.amazon.com/exec/panama/seller-admin/manual-reports/generate-report-now
```

HTTP Request Parameters

Parameter*	Description	Required?	Value
ReportName	The string "Order" requests generation of an order report	Yes	Order OpenListings OpenListingsLite OpenListingsLiter
NumberOfDays	Number of days from current date to look for open listings	Yes	A positive integer greater than zero

*See "Common Request Parameters" at the beginning of this Appendix for additional parameters

Request Message Body

No message body is used for this request. Only HTTP headers are sent.

Possible Responses

Type	Response	Explanation
Success	`<Status>SUCCESS</Status>`	Report generation has been scheduled

Error	`<Fault>`
	`<FaultCode>INTERNAL_ERROR</FaultCode>`
	`<FaultString>An internal error has occurred. Please contact the account manager.</FaultString>`
	`</Fault>`
		An error occurred in the syntax of your request

get-batches

Description

This function retrieves the Batch Ids and status of the specified number of batches where a "batch" means an inventory upload request. If the status of a particular batch shows that there were problems with the batch (e.g. "numberofwarnings" is greater than zero), the seller can use the Batch Id with functions such as errorlog to retrieve more detailed status.

URL

```
https://secure.amazon.com/exec/panama/seller-admin/catalog-upload/get-batches
```

HTTP Request Parameters

Parameter*	Description	Required?	Value
NumberOfBatches	The number of batches to retrieve status on.	No	Default value is 10

*See "Common Request Parameters" at the beginning of this Appendix for additional parameters

Request Message Body

No message body is used for this request. Only HTTP headers are sent.

Possible Responses

Type	Response	Explanation
Success	<Batches> <Batch> batchid=12345 status=Done dateandtime=10/22/2004 10:47:44 PDT activateditems=20304 numberofwarnings=1 itemsnotacivated=3280 </Batch> </Batches>	An array of batch data is returned

get-pending-uploads-count

Description

This API can be used to determine the number of uploads currently pending (since uploaded files are processed one at a time).

URL

```
https://secure.amazon.com/exec/panama/seller-admin/manual-reports/get-pending-
uploads-count
```

HTTP Request Parameters

There are no request parameters for this request. See "Common Request Parameters" section for common parameters.

Request Message Body

No message body is used for this request. Only HTTP headers are sent.

Possible Responses

Type	Response	Explanation
Success	<PendingUploadsCount> N </PendingUploadsCount>	The pending uploads count is returned.

get-report-status

Description

A seller should use the Get Report Status Request when they want to check on the status of order reports. This function returns the report IDs so that the seller can then subsequently download the reports using the reports function. The NumberOfReports header parameter can be used to limit the number of results returned.

URL

```
https://secure.amazon.com/exec/panama/seller-admin/manual-reports/get-report-status
```

HTTP Request Parameters

Parameter*	Description	Required?	Value
ReportName	Generate a list of Report Ids for a report of this type.	Yes	Default Value: Order Possible Values: BatchRefund OpenListings OpenListingsLite OpenListingsLiter Order
NumberOfReports	Maximum number of reports Ids to return	No	Default is 10

*See "Common Request Parameters" at the beginning of this Appendix for additional parameters

Request Message Body

No message body is used for this request. Only HTTP headers are sent.

Possible Responses

Type	Response	Explanation
Success	<Reports> <Report>reportstarttime=10-18-2004:10-50-56 reportendtime=10-18-2004:10-50-56 reportid=12345456 </Report> <Report>reportstarttime=10-11-2004:15-02-21 reportendtime=10-11-2004:15-02-21 reportid=23664721 </Report> </Reports>	An array of report data is returned
Error	<Reports></Reports>	An invalid ReportName parameter was used.

modify-only

Description

A seller should use the modify-only request when they want to upload modifications to their current inventory but don't want to supply all of the fields that an add-modify-delete file requires. The field "sku" is required in this upload file, as well as at least one additional field that they are choosing to modify. The allowable fields of modification in the modify-only option are price and quantity. Please note: to submit a delete, use the quantity column and enter "0" as the value

URL

```
https://secure.amazon.com/exec/panama/seller-admin/catalog-upload/modify-only
```

HTTP Request Parameters

Parameter*	Description	Required?	Value
UploadFor	Indicates where the inventory should be placed, either in Marketplace or ZShop.	No	Default Value MarketplaceOnly Possible Values: MarketplaceOnly Marketplace ZShop
FileFormat	Indicates the format of your inventory files, either UIEE or TabDelimited	No	Default value is TabDelimited. Possible values are UIEE and TabDelimited.

*See "Common Request Parameters" at the beginning of this Appendix for additional parameters

Request Message Body

The body of the message an inventory text file. The format of the inventory file can be found at two pages on Amazon. For zShops only, the values are here:

```
http://s1.amazon.com/exec/varzea/subst/seller-admin/fixed-price-template-fields.html
```

When uploading to Marketplace, or to both zShops and Marketplace at once, the values are here:

```
http://s1.amazon.com/exec/varzea/subst/seller-admin/marketplace-template-fields.html
```

Possible Responses

Type	Response	Explanation
Success	<Success>SUCCESS</Success>	Upload succeeeded
Error	<BusinessLogicError>CUSTOMER_UNAUTHORIZED </BusinessLogicError>	Authentication error

Type	Response	Explanation
Error	<BusinessLogicError>INVALID_FILE_FORMAT</BusinessLogicError>	Invalid format specified
Error	<BusinessLogicError>INVALID_LISTING_PROGRAM </BusinessLogicError>	Invalid program specified

purge-replace

Description

A seller should use the purse-replace request when they want to completely purge all of their current Amazon Marketplace and/or zShops listings and replace them with a new set of offerings contained in their template

URL

`https://secure.amazon.com/exec/panama/seller-admin/catalog-upload/purge-replace`

HTTP Request Parameters

Parameter*	Description	Required?	Value
UploadFor	Indicates where the inventory should be placed, either in Marketplace or ZShop.	No	Default Value MarketplaceOnly Possible Values: MarketplaceOnly Marketplace ZShop
FileFormat	Indicates the format of your inventory files, either UIEE or TabDelimited	No	Default value is TabDelimited. Possible values are UIEE and TabDelimited.

*See "Common Request Parameters" at the beginning of this Appendix for additional parameters

Request Message Body

The body of the message an inventory text file. The format of the inventory file can be found at two pages on Amazon. For zShops only, the values are here:

`http://s1.amazon.com/exec/varzea/subst/seller-admin/fixed-price-template-fields.html`

When uploading to Marketplace, or to both zShops and Marketplace at once, the values are here:

`http://s1.amazon.com/exec/varzea/subst/seller-admin/marketplace-template-fields.html`

Possible Responses

Type	Response	Explanation
Success	<Success>SUCCESS</Success>	Upload succeeeded
Error	<BusinessLogicError>CUSTOMER_UNAUTHORIZED </BusinessLogicError>	Authentication error
Error	<BusinessLogicError>INVALID_FILE_FORMAT</BusinessLogicError>	Invalid format specified
Error	<BusinessLogicError>INVALID_LISTING_PROGRAM </BusinessLogicError>	Invalid program specified

quickfix

Description

A seller may retrieve a Quick Fix file if something goes wrong with a particular upload. A Quick Fix file is similar to an Error Log, except that it contains only the error rows that did not get uploaded to the site due to missing required information or inappropriate information.

URL

```
https://secure.amazon.com/exec/panama/seller-admin/download/quickfix
```

HTTP Request Parameters

Parameter*	Description	Required?	Value
BatchId	The Batch Id of the upload request that had problems	Yes	A valid Batch Id

*See "Common Request Parameters" at the beginning of this Appendix for additional parameters

Request Message Body

No message body is used for this request. Only HTTP headers are sent.

Possible Responses

Type	Response	Explanation
Success	A Quick Fix file	A Quick Fix file is returned
Error	<BusinessLogicError>INVALID_BATCH</BusinessLogicError>	Batch Id not specified or invalid

Type	Response	Explanation
Error	<BusinessLogicError>FILE_NOT_FOUND</BusinessLogicError>	The Quick Fix file was not found on the server

report

Description

This API can be used to download a specific order fulfillment report by specifying the ReportID parameter.

URL

```
https://secure.amazon.com/exec/panama/seller-admin/download/report
```

HTTP Request Parameters

Parameter*	Description	Required?	Value
ReportID	A Report Id	Yes	A valid Report Id

*See "Common Request Parameters" at the beginning of this Appendix for additional parameters

Request Message Body

No message body is used for this request. Only HTTP headers are sent.

Possible Responses

Type	Response	Explanation
Success	An order report	An order report is returned
Error	<FileError>FILE_NOT_FOUND</FileError>	The report was not found on the server
Error	<SecurityError>ACCESS_DENIED</SecurityError>	You specified a Report Id that does not point to one of your reports

APPENDIX K

Merchants@ API Reference Manual

Amazon Merchants@ Operations

- getAllPendingDocumentInfo
- getDocument
- getDocumentInfoInterfaceConformance
- getDocumentInterfaceConformance
- getDocumentProcessingStatus
- getLastNDocumentInfo
- getLastNDocumentProcessingStatuses
- getLastNPendingDocumentInfo
- postDocument
- postDocumentDownloadAck
- postDocumentInterfaceConformance

Common Request Parameters

The Merchants@ API is a web service using SOAP. The parameters are sent using SOAP's Document/Literal format. Several parameters are common to every request.

Basic Authentication

An HTTP Basic Authentication header is required in every request. Since Basic Authentication is an HTTP standard and not a SOAP standard, the implementation of Basic Authentication depends on which SOAP client you are using.

Your SOAP client will send a Basic Authentication header that contains your Merchants@ Pro Merchant username and password. The header has the following format:

```
Authorization: Basic [username]:[password]
```

where the string [username]:[password] is base64-encoded. For example, if your username is "jason" and your password is "levitt", then you would base64-encode the string "jason:levitt" and your Basic Authentication header would look like this for each request:

```
Authorization: Basic amFzb246bGV2aXR0
```

Merchant Identification

Your Amazon Merchant Identifier and Merchant Name are required for each request. The Merchant Identifier and Merchant Name are sent as parameters in your SOAP request.

Table 20-1 Required parameters common to all requests

Parameter	Values	Description
merchantIdentifier	A valid Amazon Merchant Identifier	You are assigned a Merchant Identifier when you join the Amazon Merchants@ program. A sample identifier is M_SEARSROEBUCK_111753
merchantName	A valid Amazon Merchant Name	You are assigned a Merchant Name when you join the Amazon Merchants@ program. A sample name is "Sears Roebuck".

Reference Manual

getAllPendingDocumentInfo

Description

Retrieves a list of pending order or payment settlement documents

Input Parameters

Parameter*	Description	Required?	Value
messageType	The type of document you wish to retrieve	Yes	Valid message types are: _GET_ORDERS_DATA_ _GET_PAYMENT_SETTLEMENT_DATA_

*See "Common Request Parameters" at the beginning of this Appendix for additional parameters

Possible Reponses

Type	Response	Explanation	Value
Success	**DocumentInfoArray**	A list of document identifiers	An array of DocumentInfo objects

Type	Response	Explanation	Value
Error	**Fault**	An error condition occurred	Possible faults are: _INVALID_MESSAGE_TYPE_ _UNRECOGNIZED_MERCHANT_ _MISSING_OR_INVALID_DATA_ _INTERNAL_ERROR_

getDocument

Description

Retrieves a specific document, given a document Id. The document is returned as a plain text (unencoded) attachment.

Input Parameters

Parameter*	Description	Required?	Value
documentIdentifier	The document Id of the document you wish to retrieve	Yes	A valid document Id

*See "Common Request Parameters" at the beginning of this Appendix for additional parameters

Possible Reponses

Type	Response	Explanation	Value
Success	A text file is appended to the SOAP response using the SOAP with attachments standard.	The requested document	A plain text SOAP attachment
Error	**Fault**	An error condition occurred	Possible faults are: _UNRECOGNIZED_MERCHANT_ _ACCESS_TO_DOCUMENT_DENIED_ _DOCUMENT_NO_LONGER_AVAILABLE_ _MISSING_OR_INVALID_DATA_ _INTERNAL_ERROR_

getDocumentInfoInterfaceConformance

Description

Used to test the getAllPendingDocumentInfo operation

Input Parameters

Parameter*	Description	Required?	Value
messageType	The type of document you wish to retrieve	Yes	Valid message types are: _GET_ORDERS_DATA_ _GET_PAYMENT_SETTLEMENT_DATA_

*See "Common Request Parameters" at the beginning of this Appendix for additional parameters

Possible Reponses

Type	Response	Explanation	Value
Success	**DocumentInfoArray**	A list of document identifiers	An array of DocumentInfo objects
Error	**Fault**	An error condition occurred	Possible faults are: _INVALID_MESSAGE_TYPE_ _UNRECOGNIZED_MERCHANT_ _MISSING_OR_INVALID_DATA_ _INTERNAL_ERROR_

getDocumentInterfaceConformance

Description

Used to test the getDocument operation

Input Parameters

Parameter*	Description	Required?	Value
documentIdentifier	The document Id of the document you wish to retrieve	Yes	A valid document Id

*See "Common Request Parameters" at the beginning of this Appendix for additional parameters

Possible Reponses

Type	Response	Explanation	Value
Success	A text file is appended to the SOAP response using the SOAP with attachments standard.	The requested document	A plain text SOAP attachment

Type	Response	Explanation	Value
Error	Fault	An error condition occurred	Possible faults are: _UNRECOGNIZED_MERCHANT_ _ACCESS_TO_DOCUMENT_DENIED_ _DOCUMENT_NO_LONGER_AVAILABLE_ _MISSING_OR_INVALID_DATA_ _INTERNAL_ERROR_

getDocumentProcessingStatus

Description

Requests the processing status for a given feed batch reference

Input Parameters

Parameter*	Description	Required?	Value
documentTransactionIdentifier	The ID of the feed batch you wish to check the processing status on	Yes	A valid feed batch reference ID

*See "Common Request Parameters" at the beginning of this Appendix for additional parameters

Possible Reponses

Type	Response	Explanation	Value
Success	DocumentProcessingInfo	A data structure which includes the batch reference ID, date, and status	A DocumentProcessingInfo data structure
Error	Fault	An error condition occurred	Possible faults are: _INVALID_MESSAGE_TYPE_ _UNRECOGNIZED_MERCHANT_ _MISSING_OR_INVALID_DATA_ _INTERNAL_ERROR_

getLastNDocumentInfo

Description

Retrieves a list of the last N pending order or payment settlement documents

Input Parameters

Parameter*	Description	Required?	Value
messageType	The type of document you wish to retrieve	Yes	Valid message types are: _GET_ORDERS_DATA_ _GET_PAYMENT_SETTLEMENT_DATA_
howMany	The number of documents you want information about	Yes	A positive integer greater than zero

*See "Common Request Parameters" at the beginning of this Appendix for additional parameters

Possible Reponses

Type	Response	Explanation	Value
Success	**DocumentInfoArray**	A list of document identifiers	An array of DocumentInfo objects
Error	**Fault**	An error condition occurred	Possible faults are: _INVALID_MESSAGE_TYPE_ _UNRECOGNIZED_MERCHANT_ _MISSING_OR_INVALID_DATA_ _INTERNAL_ERROR_ _INVALID_INTEGER_

getLastNDocumentProcessingStatuses

Description

Request a list of the statuses of the last N feeds that the Seller has sent to Amazon

Input Parameters

Parameter*	Description	Required?	Value
numberOfStatuses	The number of feeds you wish to get the status on	Yes	A positive integer greater than zero

Parameter*	Description	Required?	Value
uploadType	The type of feed that you want to get status on	Yes	Valid feed types are: _POST_PRODUCT_DATA_ _POST_PRODUCT_RELATIONSHIP_DATA_ _POST_PRODUCT_OVERRIDES_DATA_ _POST_PRODUCT_IMAGE_DATA_ _POST_PRODUCT_PRICING_DATA_ _POST_INVENTORY_AVAILABILITY_DATA_ _POST_TEST_ORDERS_DATA_ _POST_ORDER_ACKNOWLEDGEMENT_DATA_ _POST_ORDER_FULFILLMENT_DATA_ _POST_PAYMENT_ADJUSTMENT_DATA_ _POST_STORE_DATA_

*See "Common Request Parameters" at the beginning of this Appendix for additional parameters

Possible Reponses

Type	Response	Explanation	Value
Success	**DocumentProcessingInfo**	A data structure which includes the batch reference ID, date, and status	A DocumentProcessingInfo data structure
Error	**Fault**	An error condition occurred	Possible faults are: _INVALID_MESSAGE_TYPE_ _UNRECOGNIZED_MERCHANT_ _MISSING_OR_INVALID_DATA_ _INTERNAL_ERROR_

getLastNPendingDocumentInfo

Description

Requests a list of the latest N unacknowledged order or payment settlement reports

Input Parameters

Parameter*	Description	Required?	Value
messageType	The type of document you wish to retrieve	Yes	Valid message types are: _GET_ORDERS_DATA_ _GET_PAYMENT_SETTLEMENT_DATA_
howMany	The number of documents you want information about	Yes	A positive integer greater than zero

*See "Common Request Parameters" at the beginning of this Appendix for additional parameters

Possible Reponses

Type	Response	Explanation	Value
Success	DocumentInfoArray	A list of document identifiers	An array of DocumentInfo objects
Error	Fault	An error condition occurred	Possible faults are: _INVALID_MESSAGE_TYPE_ _UNRECOGNIZED_MERCHANT_ _MISSING_OR_INVALID_DATA_ _INTERNAL_ERROR_ _INVALID_INTEGER_

postDocument

Description

Send a document to Amazon. A wide range of documents can be sent including inventory, product image data, fulfillment data, and storefront configuration data.

Input Parameters

Parameter*	Description	Required?	Value
messageType	The type of document you wish to retrieve	Yes	Valid message types are: _POST_PRODUCT_DATA_ _POST_PRODUCT_RELATIONSHIP_DATA_ _POST_PRODUCT_OVERRIDES_DATA_ _POST_PRODUCT_IMAGE_DATA_ _POST_PRODUCT_PRICING_DATA_ _POST_INVENTORY_AVAILABILITY_DATA_ _POST_TEST_ORDERS_DATA_ _POST_ORDER_ACKNOWLEDGEMENT_DATA_ _POST_ORDER_FULFILLMENT_DATA_ _POST_PAYMENT_ADJUSTMENT_DATA_ _POST_STORE_DATA_
[attached document]	A plain text (unencoded) XML document attached using the SOAP with Attachments standard	Yes	A plain text XML document

*See "Common Request Parameters" at the beginning of this Appendix for additional parameters

Possible Reponses

Type	Response	Explanation	Value
Success	**DocumentSubmissionResponse**	Acknowledgement of successful receipt of the document	_SUCCESS_
Error	**Fault**	An error condition occurred	Possible faults are: _INVALID_MESSAGE_TYPE_ _UNRECOGNIZED_MERCHANT_ _MISSING_OR_INVALID_DATA_ _INTERNAL_ERROR_

postDocumentDownloadAck

Description

Acknowledges the download of a document and removes it from the list of pending documents.

Input Parameters

Parameter*	Description	Required?	Value
documentIdentifierArray	An array of document Ids	Yes	An array of document identifiers whose successful download is being acknowledged.

*See "Common Request Parameters" at the beginning of this Appendix for additional parameters

Possible Reponses

Type	Response	Explanation	Value
Success	**DocumentDownloadAckStatusArray**	Acknowledgement of successful receipt of the document	An array of DocumentDownloadAckStatus objects. Provides ack processing status for each of the given documents. Possible values are: _SUCCESSFUL_ _ACCESS_TO_DOCUMENT_DENIED_ _INVALID_DOCUMENT_IDENTIFIER_ _INTERNAL_ERROR_
Error	**Fault**	An error condition occurred	Possible faults are:- _UNRECOGNIZED_MERCHANT_ _MISSING_OR_INVALID_DATA_ _INTERNAL_ERROR_

postDocumentInterfaceConformance

Description

Used to test the postDocument method.

Input Parameters

Parameter*	Description	Required?	Value
messageType	The type of document you wish to retrieve	Yes	Valid message types are: _POST_PRODUCT_DATA_ _POST_PRODUCT_RELATIONSHIP_DATA_ _POST_PRODUCT_OVERRIDES_DATA_ _POST_PRODUCT_IMAGE_DATA_ _POST_PRODUCT_PRICING_DATA_ _POST_INVENTORY_AVAILABILITY_DATA_ _POST_TEST_ORDERS_DATA_ _POST_ORDER_ACKNOWLEDGEMENT_DATA_ _POST_ORDER_FULFILLMENT_DATA_ _POST_PAYMENT_ADJUSTMENT_DATA_ _POST_STORE_DATA_
[attached document]	A plain text (unencoded) XML document attached using the SOAP with Attachments standard	Yes	A plain text XML document

*See "Common Request Parameters" at the beginning of this Appendix for additional parameters

Possible Reponses

Type	Response	Explanation	Value
Success	**DocumentSubmissionResponse**	Acknowledgement of successful receipt of the document	_SUCCESS_
Error	**Fault**	An error condition occurred	Possible faults are: _INVALID_MESSAGE_TYPE_ _UNRECOGNIZED_MERCHANT_ _MISSING_OR_INVALID_DATA_ _INTERNAL_ERROR_

Index

Printed in the United States
34253LVS00003B/35

9 781411 625518